THE PRESENCE
OF
THE FUTURE

GEORGE ELDON LADD

THE PRESENCE
OF
THE FUTURE

The Eschatology
of Biblical Realism

WILLIAM B. EERDMANS PUBLISHING COMPANY
Grand Rapids, Michigan

The Bible text quoted in this book, except where the author has provided his own translation, is from the *Revised Standard Version of the Bible,* copyrighted 1946 and 1952 by the Division of Christian Education, National Council of Churches, and used by permission.

Copyright © 1974 by George Eldon Ladd
All rights reserved
Printed in the United States of America
First edition published under the title *Jesus and the Kingdom* by Harper and Row, New York, copyright © 1964 by George E. Ladd.

Reprinted 1996

Library of Congress Cataloging in Publication Data

Ladd, George Eldon, 1911-
    The presence of the future.

Editions for 1964-69 published under title: Jesus and the kingdom.
    Bibliography: p. 341
    1. Kingdom of God.   I.   Title.
[BT94.L23   1973]   231'.7   73-11026
ISBN 0-8028-1531-6

TO
WINNIE
WHO
SHARES MY LIFE AND LABORS

Contents

ABBREVIATIONS USED IN FOOTNOTES

Bib	*Biblica*
BKW	*Bible Key Words from Gerhard Kittel's Theologisches Wörterbuch zum Neuen Testament* (J. R. Coates, et al., eds.). New York: Harper & Row, 1951–1960. 3 vols.
CBQ	*Catholic Biblical Quarterly*
EQ	*Evangelical Quarterly*
Eschatologie	H. D. Wendland, *Die Eschatologie des Reiches Gottes bei Jesus*. Gütersloh: Bertelsmann, 1931.
ET	*Expository Times*
HDB	*A Dictionary of the Bible* (James Hastings, ed.). New York: Scribners, 1908. 5 vols.
HTR	*Harvard Theological Review*
IB	*The Interpreter's Bible* (George Arthur Buttrick, et al., eds.). Nashville: Abingdon Press, 1952–57. 12 vols.
IDB	*The Interpreter's Dictionary of the Bible* (George Arthur Buttrick, et al., eds.). Nashville: Abingdon, 1962. 4 vols.
Int	*Interpretation*
ISBE	*The International Standard Bible Encyclopaedia* (James Orr, et al., eds.). Chicago: Howard-Severance, 1930. 5 vols.
JBL	*Journal of Biblical Literature*
JBR	*Journal of Bible and Religion*
Judaism	George Foot Moore, *Judaism in the First Centuries of the Christian Era*. Cambridge: Harvard University, 1927. 3 vols.
JR	*Journal of Religion*
Kommentar	Herman L. Strack and Paul Billerbeck, *Kommentar zum Neuen Testament aus Talmud und Midrasch*. München: Beck, 1922–28. 5 vols.

Mission	Reginald H. Fuller, *The Mission and Achievement of Jesus*. (*Studies in Biblical Theology*, XII.) Naperville: Allenson, 1954.
NTS	*New Testament Studies*
RGG	*Die Religion in Geschichte und Gegenwart* (Kurt Galling, ed.; 3rd ed.). Tübingen: Mohr, 1957–61. 5 vols.
SJTh	*Scottish Journal of Theology*
StTh	*Studia Theologica*
ThTo	*Theology Today*
TLZ	*Theologische Literaturzeitung*
TWBB	*A Theological Word Book of the Bible* (Alan Richardson, ed.). London: S.C.M.; 1950. New York: Macmillan, 1962.
TZ	*Theologische Zeitschrift*
TWNT	*Theologisches Wörterbuch zum Neuen Testament* (Gerhard Kittel, et al., eds.). Stuttgart: Kohlhammer, 1933–1964. 6 vols. to date.
ZNTW	*Zeitschrift für die neutestamentliche Wissenschaft*
ZSysTh	*Zeitschrift für systematische Theologie*
ZTK	*Zeitschrift für Theologie und Kirche*

Preface

"The bond that binds [the two Testaments] together is the dynamic concept of the rule of God." So wrote John Bright in his study of the Kingdom of God, which dealt primarily with the Old Testament hope. If this is true, it should come as a surprise that few of our critical studies on the teachings of Jesus and the Kingdom of God make use of the dynamic concept of the rule of God as the integrating center for Jesus' message and mission. This lack the present book attempts to supply.

Evangelical Christians have been so exercised with the eschatological or futuristic aspects of the Kingdom of God that it has often ceased to have immediate relevance to contemporary Christian life, except as a hope. Thus the very term, the "Kingdom of God," to many Christians means first of all the millennial reign of Christ on earth. This, however, misplaces the emphasis of the Gospels. The distinctive characteristic about Jesus' teaching is that in some real sense, the Kingdom of God has come in his person and mission (Matt. 12:28). The mystery of the Kingdom (Mark 4:11) is the secret of its unexpected irruption in history. This is not to minimize the futuristic aspect of the Kingdom. The Old Testament prophets constantly looked forward to the Day of the Lord when God would establish his reign in the earth. It is also clear in the Gospels that the Kingdom of God belongs to the age to come and is an eschatological blessing (Mark 10:23-30). It is the purpose of this book to expound how and in what sense the eschatological Kingdom has become a present reality in Jesus' mission.

The first edition of the book was entitled *Jesus and the Kingdom.* This raised critical questions which the author had not intended, particularly the degree to which the Gospels accurately embody the teachings of Jesus. The author recognizes that it is not the purpose of the Evangelists to relate the *ipsissima verba* of Jesus and that we owe the present form of the Gospels to the early church rather than to strict biographical science. Nevertheless, for reasons which cannot here be expounded, the author is convinced that the Gospels embody a substantially accurate report of the teachings of Jesus.[1] Our primary purpose is to expound the theology of the Synoptic Gospels as to the Kingdom of God.

We recognize that the Synoptic Gospels are not impartial reports from neutral observers; they are the witnesses of a believing Christian community to its faith in Jesus Christ as Messiah and Son of God. This has led many scholars to conclude that the facts of history have been so reinterpreted by Christian faith as to leave only a dim outline of the historical Jesus. The historical Jesus has been transformed into the Christ of faith, and Jesus has been nearly lost in the process. Therefore many critics have felt it to be their first task as historians to extract everything from the Gospel tradition which reflects Christian faith, to isolate the resultant trustworthy historical residuum as the only firm basis for the recovery of the historical Jesus.

We must indeed recognize that our Gospels are products of faith, and that a process of interpretation is clearly discernible in them. This does not demand the conclusion, however, that the Jesus of history has been lost, or that the Gospels do not present an essentially accurate portrait of Jesus and his message. Events of the past must be

[1] See G. E. Ladd, *The New Testament and Criticism* (1967); and "The Search for Perspective," *Int*, XXV (1971), pp. 41–62.

interpreted, or they do not constitute the real stuff of meaningful history. The Gospels are both reports of what Jesus said and did, and interpretations of the meaning of his acts and words. The author is convinced that this interpretation corresponds to the events which occurred in history, and that the interpretation goes back to Jesus himself.

Our conclusion is based upon a theological understanding of history; but this appears to be the only approach by which the Gospels can be adequately understood. The message of the entire Bible is that God has acted in redemptive history; and the Gospels represent Jesus as the place in history where God's redemptive acts reached a definitive climax.

These are admittedly theological as well as historical statements. Our modern problem arises from the prevailing view of history that denies that such theologico-historical statements are valid. History, as the term is often used in modern studies, designates the critical reconstruction of the events of the past on the basis of certain scientific, secular presuppositions, not the past events themselves. The secular historian feels bound to interpret all ancient records, sacred and secular, in terms of known observable human experience, historical causality and analogy. In history as thus defined, there is no room for the acting of God, for God belongs to the theological category, not to that of observable human experience. However, the biblical records bear witness that God has acted in history, especially in Jesus of Nazareth, that in him God has disclosed his kingly rule. If this is a true claim, the secular historian has no critical tools for recognizing it, for his very presuppositions eliminate the possibility of God acting in history. Therefore, the secular approach cannot understand the Bible. A method must be employed which allows the interpreter to understand the New Testament as the record of God's act in the Jesus of history.

The present author believes with Martin Kähler that the "historical Jesus" is a creation of modern secular scholarship and that the Jesus who actually lived in history is the biblical Christ pictured in the Gospels. If the Gospels portray a dimension about him which transcends ordinary historical experience, that is not because this dimension was added to the historical Jesus by the believing community but because it was present in the Jesus of history. The inability of criticism to find a "historical Jesus" bears this out. Therefore, while we must frequently note points where interpretation has obviously affected the form of the text, the author conceives it to be his primary task to interpret the Gospels as they stand as credible reports of Jesus and his preaching of the Kingdom.

This Second Edition features a new Preface; a revised and updated first chapter, "The Debate over Eschatology"; and an updated Bibliography. The author would express his appreciation to those reviewers, particularly in Britain and on the Continent, who have interpreted the book within the context of its own purpose and have viewed it favorably, and who also have made numerous suggestions for improvements.

PART I

INTRODUCTION

1 The Debate Over Eschatology

The Kingdom of God has received such intensive study during the last few decades that a recent survey of New Testament research can speak of "the discovery of the true meaning of the Kingdom of God."[1] There is a growing consensus in New Testament scholarship that the Kingdom of God is in some sense both present and future. However, while much progress has been achieved, the question of the role of apocalyptic concepts in our Lord's teaching, and the relationship between the present and future aspects of the Kingdom continue to be vigorously debated. To place the present study in perspective, we must survey the background of the contemporary discussion, giving particular attention to the role of apocalyptic.[2]

The prevailing interpretation of fifty years ago minimized the significance of eschatological and apocalyptic concepts. Adolf von Harnack's "old liberal" view treated the apocalyptic element in

---

[1] A. M. Hunter, *Interpreting the New Testament, 1900–1950* (1951), p. 136.
[2] For other surveys see R. N. Flew, *ET*, XLVI (1934/5), pp. 214–218; C. C. McCown, *JR*, XVI (1936), pp. 30–46; A. N. Wilder, *JR*, XXVIII (1948), pp. 177–187; *Eschatology and Ethics in the Teaching of Jesus* (1950), Chap. 2; H. Roberts, *Jesus and the Kingdom of God* (1955), pp. 9–20; G. Lundström, *The Kingdom of God in the Teaching of Jesus* (1963); N. Perrin, *The Kingdom of God in the Teaching of Jesus* (1963).

Jesus' teachings as the husk which contained the kernel of his real religious message. This consisted of a few universal truths such as the fatherhood of God, the infinite value of the individual soul, and the ethic of love.[3]

Conservative scholars like James Orr and A. B. Bruce understood the Kingdom of God to be a new principle—the reign of God—introduced into the world by our Lord and destined through the church to transform all areas of human society. They interpreted apocalyptic terminology symbolically of the divine activity in history. A similar interpretation has been recently defended by Roderick Campbell.[4]

THE ESCHATOLOGICAL INTERPRETATION

The work of Johannes Weiss and Albert Schweitzer marked a turning point in biblical criticism, for these scholars recognized that apocalyptic was fundamental in Jesus' teaching and that the prevailing noneschatological views were modernizations rather than sound historical analyses. This view of Consistent Eschatology is too well known to be outlined here. Several observations are, however, in order. Schweitzer did not achieve his interpretation by an inductive study of the Gospels, but by assuming that Jesus must be interpreted in terms of his environment, which Schweitzer understood to be that of Jewish apocalyptic.[5] The result was a historical figure who belonged only to the first century. "The historical knowledge of the personality and life of Jesus will not be a help, but perhaps even an offence to religion. . . . Jesus as a concrete historical personality re-

---

[3] *What Is Christianity?* (1901), pp. 21–83.

[4] *Israel and the New Covenant* (1954). For a survey of the older conservatives, see G. E. Ladd, *Crucial Questions about the Kingdom of God* (1952), pp. 27 f.

[5] *Paul and His Interpreters* (1912), p. ix. See the penetrating observations by H. G. Wood, *Jesus in the Twentieth Century* (1960), p. 172. See also G. Lundström, *The Kingdom of God in the Teaching of Jesus* (1963), p. 93.

mains a stranger to our time . . . ,"[6] for he was a deluded fanatic who futilely threw his life away in blind devotion to a mad apocalyptic dream which was never realized and which, in Schweitzer's view, never could be realized.

Schweitzer's interpretation involved three elements which must not be confused: (a) Apocalyptic is an essential element in Jesus' message of the Kingdom. (b) Jesus' message is exclusively eschatological. In no sense of the word could the Kingdom be interpreted as a present spiritual reality. It is the apocalyptic age to come. (c) Jesus thought that the Kingdom would come at once in his lifetime. These three points must be kept in mind as we continue our survey of criticism, for one may agree with Schweitzer in part if not altogether.

ESCHATOLOGICAL INTERPRETATIONS SINCE SCHWEITZER

The history of criticism since Schweitzer may be described as a struggle over eschatology. Consistent Eschatology has found many supporters on the Continent, although often in a modified form. Wilhelm Michaelis in *Täufer, Jesus, Urgemeinde* (1928) argued that Jesus' teachings must be interpreted consistently from a single point of view: viz., that the Kingdom of God was apocalyptic and imminent. The Kingdom did not come; in its stead came Easter and Pentecost. These acts of God make possible for the church a reinterpretation of the Kingdom as both a future and a present reality. In a later work, *Der Herr verzieht nicht die Verheissung* (1942), Michaelis reacted against Consistent Eschatology to the extent of insisting that Jesus' emphasis was not upon the futurity and imminence of the Kingdom as such, but that his emphasis upon imminence

---

[6] A. Schweitzer, *The Quest of the Historical Jesus* (1911), p. 399. See also J. Weiss, *Die Predigt Jesu vom Reiche Gottes* (1892; 2nd enlarged edition, 1900). The first edition of this book has now been translated by R. H. Hiers and D. L. Holland, *Jesus' Proclamation of the Kingdom of God* (1971). See also R. H. Hiers, *The Kingdom of God in the Synoptic Tradition* (1970), who follows Weiss' view.

had the spiritual purpose of creating a response of watchfulness in the disciples.

Maurice Goguel's *La Vie de Jesus* has been one of the most widely used texts in America for the life of Christ. Goguel is not usually classed as an adherent of Consistent Eschatology, for he attempts to distinguish between apocalyptic and eschatological elements in Jesus' teachings and holds that eschatology was merely the framework of his thought.[7] Nevertheless, Goguel attributed to Jesus an exclusively futuristic view of the Kingdom, although with changing emphasis. In his early preaching mission, Jesus thought the Kingdom was to occur at once (Matt. 10:23). Later, after the Galilean crisis, he expected it within a few years (Mark 9:1). Finally, Jesus concluded that only God knew the time of the end (Mark 13:32). Goguel sees no modification of the eschatological character of the hope even though the time of its coming receded in Jesus' thought.

However, Goguel holds that Jesus' thought was eschatological and not apocalyptic. Eschatology looks forward to a future separation of men and the coming of a new order displacing the present world. Apocalyptic attempts to picture in advance the form which the cosmic drama will take and the succession of events which will accompany the transition. Therefore, apocalyptic tries to calculate the time of the end by the study of signs. Jesus dismissed this sort of apocalyptic speculation as well as all apocalyptic representations of the future (Luke 17:21).[8] In spite of this distinction, Goguel's interpretation of Jesus makes him a teacher of a thoroughgoing futuristic eschatology, for his view of the Kingdom is exclusively futuristic and catastrophic. This raises the fundamental question of whether Goguel's distinction between eschatology and apocalyptic is valid.

A second important life of Christ by a French scholar, Charles Guignebert, also espouses Consistent Eschatology. Guignebert rejects interpretations of the Kingdom as a present reality because the Kingdom "is primarily and essentially the material transformation

---

[7] *The Life of Jesus* (1933), Eng. trans., pp. 569–572.
[8] M. Goguel, *Revue d'Histoire des Religions*, CVI (1932), pp. 382 ff.

of this present evil world," i.e., the eschatological salvation of the age to come.[9] Jesus' mission was to announce the imminent end of the age and the coming of the eschatological order.

Martin Werner has written a history of dogma which assumes Consistent Eschatology in the teachings of Jesus as its point of departure and interprets the development of early dogma in terms of the church's adjustment to the failure of the Parousia to occur.[10]

A typical statement of critical German theology is that of Martin Dibelius in his *Jesus*.[11] The Kingdom is the eschatological act of God establishing his rule in the universe. Jesus taught that this divine act was about to occur; in fact, it was already in process. The tension between the future and the present is the tension between the Kingdom in complete fulfillment and the Kingdom in process of breaking in upon the present order. Thus the signs of the Kingdom are present, though not the Kingdom itself. The powers of the Kingdom are present, although the actual coming of the Kingdom awaits the apocalyptic act of God which must shortly occur. Foregleams of its splendor are already discernible in Jesus' works.[12]

The most important contemporary support of Consistent Eschatology is found in the interpretation of Rudolf Bultmann and some of his followers. For Bultmann, Jesus was only a Jewish apocalyptic prophet announcing the imminent inbreaking of the Kingdom of God. He insists that any interpretation which sees the Kingdom as a present reality in Jesus' person and in his followers is "escape-reasoning" designed to avoid the difficulty created by the failure of the announced imminent irruption of God's reign to occur. The view of a present Kingdom "cannot be substantiated by a single saying of Jesus, and it contradicts the meaning of 'God's Reign.' "[13] Thus for

⁹ *Jesus* (1935), p. 341.
¹⁰ *The Formation of Christian Dogma* (1957), pp. 9–27.
¹¹ *Jesus* (1949).
¹² *Ibid.*, pp. 69–88. See the similar statement by Erich Dinkler in *The Idea of History in the Ancient Near East* (R. C. Dentan, ed.; 1955), pp. 173–180.
¹³ *Theology of the New Testament* (1951), I, p. 22. Bultmann has apparently wavered in this conviction, for in one place, he admits that Jesus saw the "turn of the ages" in the appearance of the Baptist and understood himself to stand in the interim "between the times." See "Man between the Times" in *Existence and Faith: Shorter Writings of Rudolf Bultmann* (Schubert M. Ogden, ed.; 1960), p. 253.

Bultmann, Jesus and his apocalyptic message are not a part of New Testament theology but belong to Judaism. The one difference between the message of Jesus and that of other Jewish apocalyptists is the certainty with which Jesus asserted the immediacy of the end. So strong is this certainty that Jesus viewed the future Kingdom as actually breaking in. The Kingdom is not present, but it is dawning.[14]

Through Bultmann's influence, a number of scholars have concluded that Jesus' main emphasis was not that of a future apocalyptic kingdom but of the *immediate* coming of this kingdom. Immediacy rather than eschatology became central. Erich Grässer assumed that this note of immediacy was the heart of Jesus' proclamation, and the failure of the Parousia to occur at once was the great theological problem with which the early church had to contend.[15] Hans Conzelmann has attempted to show how Luke historicized the purely eschatological message of Jesus.[16]

In England, Consistent Eschatology has never taken deep root. F. C. Burkitt finally assented to the position;[17] but William Sanday, who at first gave cautious approval, later withdrew it.[18] J. Warschauer attempted to write a biography of Jesus from the viewpoint of Consistent Echatology,[19] and B. T. D. Smith interpreted *The Parables of the Synoptic Gospels* (1937) from this point of view. The one difference between Jesus and Jewish apocalyptists was the former's single-minded concentration upon the religious element and the complete elimination of the purely national aspect of the hope.

[14] It will be noted below that Bultmann does not derive his interpretation from purely objective exegesis but grounds Jesus' view of the future on existential presuppositions. See below, pp. 20 ff.

[15] Grässer, *Das Problem der Parusieverzögerung in den synoptischen Evangelien und in der Apostlegeschichte* (1957).

[16] *The Theology of Saint Luke* (1960). See also Conzelmann's articles on "Reich Gottes" in *RGG*, 3rd ed., V, col. 912–18; "Jesus Christus," *ibid.*, III, col. 641–46. For the entire discussion, see O. Cullmann, in *TLZ*, I.XXXIII (1958), col. 1–12.

[17] See his essay in *A History of Christianity in the Light of Modern Knowledge* (1929), p. 234.

[18] See *The Life of Christ in Recent Research* (1907), p. 121; but see his essay, "The Apocalyptic Element in the Gospels," *Hibbert Journal*, X (1911–12), pp. 83–109.

[19] *The Historical Life of Christ* (1926).

In America, Consistent Eschatology has exercised wide influence. As early as 1911, Ernest F. Scott accepted Schweitzer's interpretation that it was Jesus' mission to prepare Israel for the imminent inbreaking of the apocalyptic Kingdom. However, contrary to Schweitzer, Scott held that Jesus already realized the law of the coming Kingdom in his own person and that the Kingdom was so imminent that its powers were already manifested in Jesus' mission. Thus Scott was able to view Jesus' ethics not as "interim" in character but as an abiding ideal.[20]

Here is an important emphasis which we have discovered in later German theology. The Kingdom is apocalyptic, future, imminent; but it is in reality not *exclusively* future. It is so near that its presence can be felt, its powers experienced. This view has become widely accepted. In fact, in 1930, B. S. Easton could write that the controversy about the interpretation of the Kingdom of God had practically reached an end. The Kingdom is the new age, the purely supernatural state of affairs when God alone will rule over men. When the Kingdom comes, history will end. The sayings about the presence of the Kingdom mean that the process of the coming of the Kingdom is already under way. God's initial act has been performed; and as soon as its consequences have been felt, the next act will follow and the Kingdom will come.[21]

This emphasis upon the nearness of the apocalyptic Kingdom has been frequently repeated. The Kingdom is present only in the sense that the coming clouds in the heavens cast their shadow on the earth.[22] Jesus taught an apocalyptic, imminent, future Kingdom, but

---

[20] *The Kingdom and the Messiah* (1911). In a later eclectic study, *The Kingdom of God in the New Testament* (1931), Scott modified his earlier position and defined the Kingdom as the will of God, which is broad enough to include all the meanings which men have found in it (p. 194). The present reign of God is a higher spiritual and moral order, a present inner life, and a social ideal. The framework of apocalyptic to us is fantastic and fanatical; but it contains the inherent religious value that it is God who acts through crisis (pp. 117 f., 188).

[21] B. S. Easton, *Christ in the Gospels* (1930), pp. 158–164.

[22] Morton Scott Enslin, *The Prophet from Nazareth* (1961), p. 72. Enslin characterizes efforts to "soften and alter" the purely futuristic eschatological character of Jesus' teaching as "frivolous."

he was actually engaged in setting up this Kingdom in proleptic fashion.[23] The Kingdom was already manifesting its signs through Jesus. The reign of God was already breaking in; its full force would be felt in the near future. The bud was visible; the full bloom would shortly be seen.[24] The Kingdom was so near that its benefits were even then being partially enjoyed. Long before the sun appears above the horizon, its light dawns on the earth. So the signs of the presence of God's rule were present.[25]

Futuristic eschatology is also defended by R. H. Fuller in *The Mission and Achievement of Jesus*. Fuller recognizes only two options: an imminent eschatological Kingdom or Realized Eschatology. He examines the texts which C. H. Dodd used to prove the presence of the Kingdom and concludes that they teach the imminence of the Kingdom, not its presence. "The Kingdom of God has not yet come, but it is near, so near that it is already operative in advance. . . . The certainty of the event is so overwhelming, the signs of its impendingness so sure, that it is said to have occurred, or to be occurring already. . . . The Reign of God is already breaking in proleptically in the proclamation and signs of Jesus"; but to say that the Kingdom has come would overstate the case.[26] The decisive events lie in the future, not in the past.[27]

This review of Consistent Eschatology discloses two interesting facts. Some interpret the Kingdom of God as the eschatological act of God, others as the eschatological order, the age to come. In both cases, it is future and apocalyptic. However, many of these scholars are compelled by the language of the Gospels to admit that some-

---

[23] S. J. Case, *Jesus* (1927), pp. 436 f.

[24] D. W. Riddle and H. H. Hutson, *New Testament Life and Literature* (1946), pp. 90 f.

[25] C. T. Craig, *The Beginning of Christianity* (1943), p. 87; *IB*, VII, p. 148.

[26] R. H. Fuller, *The Mission and Achievement of Jesus* (1954), pp. 25, 26, 32. Quoted by permission, London, S. C. M. Press. Distributed in U.S.A. by Allenson's, Naperville, Illinois.

[27] Alan Richardson considers Fuller's criticism of Realized Eschatology to be convincing. See *An Introduction to the Theology of the New Testament* (1958), p. 86, n. 1.

thing was present: the signs, the dawning, the budding, the shadow of the approaching Kingdom. Furthermore, these interpretations give to the element of imminence a new significance. It is the very imminence of the Kingdom which caused it to cast its shadow ahead. Jesus thought of it as so very near that its presence could be sensed even though it had not yet come. As the morning is preceded by the dawn, as the storm is heralded by the clouds, as the flower is anticipated by the bud, so the Kingdom was near enough that signs of its coming could be seen.

NONESCHATOLOGICAL INTERPRETATIONS

Not all scholars have been satisfied to accept Schweitzer's interpretation and to define the Kingdom either exclusively or essentially in apocalyptic terms. Studies have appeared, especially in England and America, which interpret the Kingdom along spiritual noneschatological lines.

Lewis Muirhead attempted to refute the position of Weiss in *The Eschatology of Jesus* (1904). Apocalyptic imagery is dominated by ethics, not vice versa as Weiss said. The Kingdom is the supreme spiritual reality present in the experience of believers; the futuristic aspect is not important. Ernest von Dobschütz in the *Transactions of the Third Congress for the History of Religions* argued that apocalyptic was only the form of Jesus' thought and that there was nothing eschatological about the kernel of Jesus' religion, which was the rule of God.[28] In *The Eschatology of the Gospels*, Dobschütz pictured Jesus as sharing contemporary apocalyptic notions but held that his proper view was transmuted eschatology. "What was spoken of in Jewish eschatology as to come in the last days is taken here as already at hand in the lifetime of Jesus . . . , what was expected as an external change is taken inwardly."[29] "In Jesus was fulfilled whatever was expected for the messianic time."[30] Apocalyptic is the form

[28] 1908; pp. 312–320.
[29] E. von Dobschütz, *The Eschatology of the Gospels* (1910), p. 150.
[30] *Ibid.*, p. 143.

in which he interpreted the future success of the Kingdom; the form is wrong but the truth abides. God will rule.[31]

The most influential book expounding a noneschatological view is the frequently reprinted volume on *The Teaching of Jesus* by T. W. Manson. The Kingdom in its essence is the reign of God in the experience of the individual soul. In such a personal relationship, questions about time—present or future—are quite irrelevant, for the reign of God within the lives of men is independent of temporal and spatial relations.[32] Jesus' conception of God as Father determined his conception of the Kingdom. The Kingdom is where God's will is done on earth. Jesus as Messiah realized the Kingdom by utter obedience to God's will.[33] Before Caesarea Philippi, Jesus spoke of the coming of the Kingdom; but after Caesarea Philippi, he spoke of the Kingdom as having come and of people entering it.[34] The confession of Peter at Caesarea Philippi was a recognition that the Kingdom of God had come in his person.[35] The Kingdom of God is a personal relation between God and the individual.[36] The Kingdom may be said to have come with Jesus, for with him occurred "the first manifestation of the Kingdom in the world."[37] That is, Jesus was the first to experience the full meaning of the reign of God; his mission was to lead other men into this same experience of the reign of God.

It may seem erroneous to interpret Manson's view of the Kingdom as noneschatological, for he has a chapter on "The Final Consummation" in which he says, "The ideas of a Judgment, of the elimination of evil from the world, and of a blessed immortality for those who are loyal to God in this life—these ideas are necessary corollaries to the central idea of the Kingdom. . . . If there is no final victory of good over evil, the Kingdom of God becomes an empty dream."[38] However, as Ernst Percy has pointed out,[39] these words about an eschatological

[31] *Ibid.*, p. 207.
[32] T. W. Manson, *The Teaching of Jesus* (1935), p. 135.
[33] *Ibid.*, p. 211.
[34] *Ibid.*, p. 129.
[35] *Ibid.*, p. 130.
[36] *Ibid.*, p. 133.
[37] *Ibid.*, p. 134.
[38] *Ibid.*, p. 284. Quoted by permission of Cambridge University Press.
[39] E. Percy, *Die Botschaft Jesu* (1953), p. 224.

consummation are not essentially related to Manson's central concept of the Kingdom. When Manson writes, "The Church is . . . the army of the Kingdom of God, engaged in the task of conquering every hostile power and winning the world for Christ and ultimately for God," there is no need for a realistic eschatology to accomplish the final victory of God's Kingdom. It will be accomplished not by the Parousia of Christ but by the victory of the church in the world.[40]

Another influential and even more detailed study embodying a noneschatological interpretation is The Historic Mission of Jesus by C. J. Cadoux. The Kingdom of God is man's acceptance of God's gracious sovereignty which is essentially timeless,[41] for it is the individual's compliance with God's will.[42] Cadoux rejects in strong language ideas of the Kingdom which place the initiative with God.[43] The initiative rests with men, for the Kingdom is not the victory of God's irresistible royal power, but the willing personal acceptance of his fatherly rule by men.[44] Jesus was the person through whom the Kingdom became a new reality among men.[45] As the obedient son par excellence, Jesus embodied the Kingdom in his own person. His messianic mission was to lead men into the same enjoyment of God's life which he himself possessed.[46] Jesus expected the Jews to accept his message and submit to God's rule, surrender their attitude of vengeance against Rome, and trust God to frustrate the pagan hostility and to convert Rome's hostility to friendship.[47] This message of God's Kingdom would then be extended throughout the earth with such success that the time would soon be ripe for God to bring about the great eschatological climax.[48] A new race would come into being,

---

[40] T. W. Manson, The Teaching of Jesus (1935), p. 190. In a subsequent book Manson gave far more adequate recognition to eschatology. See below, p. 28.
[41] C. J. Cadoux, The Historic Mission of Jesus (n.d. [ca. 1940]), p. 133.
[42] Ibid., p. 115.
[43] Ibid., p. 204.
[44] Ibid., p. 206.
[45] Ibid., pp. 26, 129.
[46] Ibid., p. 103.
[47] Ibid., p. 173.
[48] Ibid., p. 218.

and thus God's Kingdom would come on earth as God's will is done by all mankind. When Jesus realized his message was to be rejected by the Jews, he accepted the rejection and hoped by his death to bring about the repentance which his preaching had not accomplished. Cadoux interprets apocalyptic as the product of the imaginative Oriental mind which did not understand it literally. Therefore, he feels justified in using a spiritualizing hermeneutic to interpret Jesus' eschatology.[49] The permanent value of eschatology is found in the fact that it registers the crucial urgency of those great life-values for which Jesus stood.[50]

F. C. Grant, in The Gospel of the Kingdom, interprets the Kingdom as a message of social redemption in which the divine sovereignty will be perfectly realized on earth. Jesus expected to see the reign of God established everywhere on earth in his own lifetime. The original gospel of Jesus is the social gospel. The apocalyptic element is due to the disciples' misinterpretation. They distorted his social view of the Kingdom into an apocalyptic concept, interpreting Jesus in the light of Jewish apocalyptic symbols. Grant thinks that Jesus would indeed have been insane to suppose that he was to come to earth on the clouds to hold judgment and to inaugurate an eschatological Kingdom. Such a view was incompatible with the sanity of Jesus and therefore cannot be attributed to him.[51]

H. B. Sharman in a detailed critical study concluded that Jesus taught that the Kingdom was a spiritual reality which was present in his own ministry as God's mind was expressed through him and a new influence mediated through his personality to others. The apocalyptic element in the Gospels is due to the disciples who neglected Jesus' warnings about the messianic claimants who would arise during the Jewish war—an event which Jesus foresaw. Jesus' teachings were misunderstood by the church and misinterpreted in terms of Jewish

[49] Ibid., pp. 340 ff.
[50] Ibid., p. 348.
[51] The Gospel of the Kingdom (1940). See also "The Idea of the Kingdom of God in the New Testament," in The Sacral Kingship (1959), pp. 437–446; Ancient Judaism and the New Testament (1959), Chap. 8.

apocalyptic. This apocalyptic element must be excised and the authentic teachings of Jesus recovered by critical reconstruction.[52]

A. T. Olmstead reconstructed the true Jesus as an utterly uneschatological figure. "At long last, Jesus makes his own appearance in the full light of history."[53] Olmstead's "historical Jesus" is the antipode of Schweitzer's. To Olmstead, Jesus was a prophet of righteousness who proclaimed a Kingdom of the Spirit, a living, ever present force in the hearts of its members which at the last is destined to permeate the world. Jesus had read the apocalypses but condemned their fantasies; but the early church misinterpreted Jesus as an apocalyptic figure.

In *The Religion of Jesus* (1952), Leroy Waterman follows similar lines. Waterman builds on the assumption that apocalyptic and prophetic are two mutually exclusive types of religion. Apocalyptic by definition is nationalistic and particularistic, while prophetic religion is universalistic and ethical. Since Jesus' religious teaching was spiritual in character, he could not have shared apocalyptic views, for these two types of religion do not blend. The apocalyptic form of Jesus' teachings is due to the gross misinterpretation of the early church in which his pure religion was smothered in nonspiritual apocalyptic concepts.

Another noneschatological interpretation is the so-called "Prophetic Realism" of John Wick Bowman. Bowman has suggested that this viewpoint is shared by such scholars as T. W. Manson, William Manson, Rudolf Otto, Vincent Taylor, and others.[54] However, the views of these men are so diverse that it seems difficult to classify them under a single school of thought.

Bowman's main concern is to oppose all "apocalyptic" concepts of the Kingdom of God which, according to Bowman's understanding, are incapable of seeing the activity of the Kingdom on the plane of history. He classes as apocalyptic all views which do not conceive of

[52] H. B. Sharman, *The Teaching of Jesus about the Future* (1909), pp. 301–327. Cf. also Sharman's *Son of Man and Kingdom of God* (1943).
[53] *Jesus in the Light of History* (1942), p. xi.
[54] See *ThTo*, XI (1954), pp. 173 ff.

God as working actively within history. Thus he categorizes as "apocalyptic pessimism" the Kierkegaardian dialectic which defines God as "the wholly other," the Barthian movement with its American child, Neo-orthodoxy, the Consistent Eschatology of Weiss and Schweitzer, and the modern "fundamentalist aberration."[55] All of these views are "nonprophetic" in that God never completely reveals himself or brings his Kingdom to completion on the plane of history. Prophetic Realism defines the Kingdom as the personal relationship between man and God, the individual's experience of God's sovereignty over his life when he recognizes God's right to rule and submits his will to God. The Kingdom comes when any man acknowledges God's sole sovereignty over his life, or when a group of men do the same, or when an ethically conditioned remnant—the church —acknowledge allegiance to God's sovereignty.[56]

Bowman's position is close to the older position of T. W. Manson, whom he frequently quotes; and he admits that this view makes the coming of the Kingdom on earth dependent upon man's acceptance of God's Lordship.[57] Jesus established the Kingdom on earth; but Bowman leaves it less than clear what we are to understand by this, except that Jesus persuaded men to accept God's rule.[58] The continuing task of the church is to extend the Kingdom in the world—a task which may be described by the phrase "building the Kingdom"— which leads to the redemption of mankind.[59]

Bowman insists on an absolute contrast between the apocalyptic and prophetic types of religion. In The Religion of Maturity, he recognized that these two types are not necessarily exclusive but might be combined.[60] However, his last study in this area, Prophetic Realism and the Gospel, develops one line of thought appearing in his earlier writings and excludes altogether every vestige of apoc-

[55] J. W. Bowman, Prophetic Realism and the Gospel (1955), pp. 34–37.
[56] Ibid., pp. 200–202.
[57] Ibid., p. 207.
[58] Ibid., p. 210.
[59] Ibid., pp. 222–225.
[60] J. W. Bowman, The Religion of Maturity (1948), pp. 228, 248. See G. E. Ladd, "Why Not Prophetic-Apocalyptic?" JBL, LXXVI (1957), pp. 192–200.

alyptic from prophetic religion. Apocalyptic religion, apparently by definition, can talk to God only at long range and is incapable of a concept of the Kingdom which is active on the plane of history. It is altogether otherworldly and transcendental. In an earlier book, *The Intention of Jesus*, Bowman argued that apocalyptic concepts provided the shell which enclosed the kernel of Jesus' deepest conviction.[61] Jesus made only a formal use of these apocalyptic frames, or they were simply an accommodation on our Lord's part to the thought-forms of his hearers. Later, in *The Religion of Maturity*, he wrote that apocalyptic concepts were used as "intellectual bait."[62] These molds must not be confused with the gospel which Jesus lived and preached. The church has no need of apocalyptic, which Bowman calls "the religion of the throne," for her function is not to judge the world, but with her Lord and under his leadership to effect its salvation.[63] Apparently, the consummation of the Kingdom in Bowman's view is nothing less than a world which has been brought into submission to God's rule through the church's proclamation of the gospel.[64]

Recent biblical scholarship in Great Britain has reacted strongly against the one-sided eschatological views of Schweitzer, and in the writings of C. H. Dodd has given the concept of eschatology a new content. Eschatology has to do not with the last things, temporally conceived, but with those things which possess finality and ultimacy of meaning. The Kingdom of God does not mean the eschatological order at the end of history, but the eternally present realm of God. The coming of the Kingdom means the entrance of the eternal into time, the confrontation of the finite by the infinite, the intrusion of the transcendental into the natural. The Kingdom of God is time-

---

[61] (1943), pp. 148, 153.
[62] J. W. Bowman, *The Religion of Maturity* (1948), p. 240.
[63] *Ibid.*, p. 310.
[64] In recent articles, Bowman admits a residuum of futuristic eschatology in Jesus' teaching. See "Eschatology of the New Testament," *IDB*, II, p. 137; *Peake's Commentary on the Bible* (M. Black and H. H. Rowley, eds.; 1962), pp. 739, 745. It is difficult to know how this fits into Bowman's total interpretation.

less, eternal, transcendental, and is therefore always near and always laying its demands upon men. Apocalyptic language is merely an ancient idiom in which this timeless religious truth expressed itself.[65]

Dodd has not only interpreted the teachings of Jesus in terms of Realized Eschatology, but has also reconstructed the history of primitive eschatology from this point of departure. Dodd takes as his clue for the basic meaning of the Kingdom those characteristic and distinctive sayings about the presence of the Kingdom which are without parallel in Jewish teachings.[66] Jesus saw the Kingdom present in his own life, death, resurrection, ascension, and Parousia. These are not to be taken as several events but were in the thought of Jesus facets of a single complex event. For Jesus, there was a single day of victory, and it was occurring in his ministry. Dodd tries to prove that *eggiken* in Matthew 4:17 is synonymous with *ephthasen* in Matthew 12:28 and means "has come." Jesus' proclamation was not, "The Kingdom of God has drawn near," but "The Kingdom of God has come." The parables teach a crisis of judgment which is not future but present. The long period of growth is over, the hour of decision has arrived. All that remains is to put in the sickle and reap the harvest. The resurrection, exaltation, and second advent in Jesus' thought are three aspects of one idea. It is worthy of more than passing interest that this position, which is a crucial element in Dodd's reconstruction, is admitted to be "no more than a speculative conjecture" about which "there is nothing conclusive."[67]

When the Parousia did not occur, the early church separated it from the resurrection, thus making two days of what Jesus had seen as one. It reinterpreted the message of Jesus along the lines of Jewish apocalyptic. Paul in the Thessalonian epistles at first took over this Jewish eschatology but later reinterpreted eschatology in terms of

---

[65] C. H. Dodd, *The Parables of the Kingdom* (1936); *The Apostolic Preaching and Its Developments* (1936).

[66] *The Parables of the Kingdom* (1936), p. 49.

[67] *Ibid.*, pp. 100 f. For the debate over *eggiken* and *ephthasen*, see C. T. Craig, *JBL*, LVI (1937), pp. 17–26; J. Y. Campbell, *ET*, XLVIII (1936–37), pp. 91–94; K. Clark, *JBL*, LIX (1940), pp. 367–383. See also E. E. Wolfzorn, *Ephemerides Theologicae Lovaniensis*, XXXVIII (1962), pp. 54–55.

mysticism. The problem created by the delay of the Parousia was thus solved by Paul's renewed apprehension of Realized Eschatology. This rediscovery the Fourth Gospel carried further by completely refining away the crude eschatological elements of a futurist eschatology. Thus it happens that the Gospel furthest removed from Jesus in time contains the nearest to the true substance of his teaching. The Realized Eschatology of Paul means that "all that prophecy and apocalypse had asserted of the supernatural messianic community was fulfilled in the Church." In the Fourth Gospel, "all that the church hoped for in the second coming of Christ is already given in its present experience of Christ through the Spirit."[68]

While Dodd rejects the futuristic and apocalyptic concepts of Paul, he finds the true meaning of the Kingdom of God in Jesus' use of apocalyptic language. Apocalyptic is "a series of symbols standing for realities which the human mind cannot directly apprehend."[69] The new world of apocalyptic thought is in reality "the transcendent order beyond space and time."[70] Jesus employed the traditional symbolism of apocalypse to indicate the otherworldly or absolute character of the Kingdom of God.[71] "The thought of Jesus passed directly from the immediate situation to the eternal order lying beyond all history, of which he spoke in the language of apocalyptic symbolism."[72] Apocalyptic concepts such as judgment, bliss, the Son of Man, etc., are "eschatological" in character; that is, "they are ultimates, and are proper not to this empirical realm of time and space but to the absolute order."[73] Thus the essence of Jesus' teaching is that "the ultimate, the Kingdom of God, has come into history . . . the absolute, the 'wholly other' has entered into time and space . . . 'the day of the Son of Man' stands for the timeless fact. So far as

---

[68] C. H. Dodd, *The Apostolic Preaching and Its Developments* (1936), pp. 145, 174.
[69] *The Parables of the Kingdom* (1936), p. 106.
[70] *Ibid.*, p. 56.
[71] *Ibid.*, p. 197.
[72] *Ibid.*, p. 207.
[73] *Ibid.*, p. 107.

history can contain it, it is embodied in the historic crisis which Jesus brought about."[74]

Before we leave Dodd, we should note that it is usually said that Dodd has modified his view of a completely realized eschatology to admit that there is a residue of unrealized or futuristic eschatology. This impression is based on Dodd's acceptance of Joachim Jeremias' criticism that he is one-sided in his Realized Eschatology and insists on an unnecessary contraction of eschatology.[75] Instead of speaking of Realized Eschatology, Jeremias suggests the expression, "eschatology in process of realization."[76] While Dodd accepts the validity of this criticism,[77] a careful reading of his book, *The Coming of Christ*, leaves his position in doubt. He says, "At the last frontier-post we shall encounter God in Christ";[78] but what this seems to mean is expressed in another sentence: "When each individual person reaches the frontier post of death, he steps into the presence of the Eternal. And when in due course history ends, and the human race perishes from this planet, it will encounter God."[79] This sounds more like Greek immortality than the biblical hope of the Kingdom of God which is concerned with history.

However, in one of his most recent books, Dodd seems to allow for a real futurity of the Kingdom. In *The Founder of Christianity* (1970), he speaks of "the final victory of God's cause over all the powers in the universe . . . . Jesus . . . was pointing to the final victory of God's cause, or in other words, the consummation of his kingdom, beyond history" (p. 117). "The Kingdom of God, while it is present experience, remains also a hope, but a hope directed to a consummation beyond history" (p. 115).

We have previously described Rudolf Bultmann's interpretation

---

[74] *Ibid.*, pp. 107 f. Quoted by permission of James Nisbet Co.

[75] J. Jeremias, *The Parables of Jesus* (1954), pp. 18 f.

[76] *Ibid.*, p. 159 (*Die Gleichnisse Jesu* [1947], p. 114, "sich realisierende Eschatologie").

[77] C. H. Dodd, *The Interpretation of the Fourth Gospel* (1953), p. 447.

[78] C. H. Dodd, *The Coming of Christ* (1951), p. 38.

[79] *Ibid.*, p. 26. For a defense of Dodd, see Claude H. Thompson, *Theology of the Kerygma* (1962), pp. 10–13.

as one which agrees essentially with Consistent Eschatology. However, Bultmann does not find the real *meaning* of Jesus' teaching in an imminent apocalyptic kingdom. This apocalyptic expectation was in fact only the form in which his deepest religious conviction expressed itself. Apocalyptic ideas of a future Kingdom are mythological, but in this mythology is embodied an existential meaning. The central reality in Jesus' experience was an overpowering consciousness of the sovereignty of God, the absoluteness of his will. Before this consciousness of God, the world sinks away and seems to be at its end. Jesus' expectation of the immediate end of the world is not the core of his message but is merely the reflex of his God-consciousness. "The essential thing about the eschatological message is the idea of God that operates in it and the idea of human existence that it contains—not the belief that the end of the world is just ahead."[80] Thus Bultmann cannot finally be classed with Schweitzer and Weiss, for whom the imminent end of the world is the essence of Jesus' eschatological message. For Bultmann, Jesus' mythological eschatological expectation is really incidental. The essential thing is the demand of God embodied therein. Thus the Kingdom is "wholly other," supernatural, suprahistorical; i.e.; it is "eschatological." The real meaning of the Kingdom is independent of the mythological terms in which Jesus described it. It is rather the "transcendent event, which signifies for man the ultimate Either-Or, which constrains him to decision."[81]

This existential interpretation of the Kingdom has had wide influence. F. C. Grant, whose earlier study emphasized the social gospel, has used the word "eschatological" to describe not future but final realities. The idea of Messiah is eschatological. "It stands for the finality of God's revelation in Christ, the finality of God's act in Christ."[82] New Testament theology is from beginning to end eschatologically conditioned: i.e., it has to do with the "suprahistorical;

[80] R. Bultmann, *Theology of the New Testament* (1951), I, p. 23.
[81] R. Bultmann, *Jesus and the Word* (1934), p. 41.
[82] F. C. Grant, *An Introduction to New Testament Thought* (1950), p. 206.

not so much 'beyond history' (after the end of this present age . . .) as 'above' history, outside time and place, in the ever-present 'now' of eternity—in the Mind of God."[83] Jesus' conception of the Kingdom of God as virtually present left little room for a universal judgment. In reality, judgment essentially is "not a dramatic episode at the end of history, but the confrontation of sin and every evil with the goodness, the holiness, the mercy and love of God."[84]

John Knox recognizes in Jesus' teaching both a present and a future element, and he thinks that Dodd's view of completely realized eschatology is impossible to ascribe to Jesus. Knox believes that Jesus looked for a new order in the immediate future; the element of the temporal cannot be eliminated. But one is not distorting or modernizing Jesus' teaching "when one denies that even for him [Jesus] the whole meaning of the immediacy of the Kingdom was exhausted by the expected future crisis. The Kingdom of God could be thought of as imminent in the future only because in another sense it is continually present. It will come soon because it is near. The Kingdom, in this absolute sense, did not come soon—it did not come at all—but it is still near. . . . The Kingdom of God is always at hand, not as a future event, perhaps, but in the profounder sense of an ever present reality, both within our life and above it, both immanent and transcendent."[85]

In Jesus, the Messiah, William Manson vigorously discussed the messianic question in light of Form Criticism and interpreted the Kingdom of God in noneschatological terms, similar to Bultmann. Manson claims that the central fact in our Lord's ministry was his intense consciousness of God. This consciousness led him to reason from the present to the future. His awareness of the holiness and the power of God already at work in the world led him to make certain deductions about the coming of the Kingdom. His announcement of this coming Kingdom took the form of an imminent supernatural event. However, the concept of God as Father was prior to his escha-

---

83 Ibid., p. 50.
84 Ibid., p. 185.
85 J. Knox, Christ the Lord (1945), p. 30.

tology and produced it. His vision of the coming Kingdom is a projection of the intense inwardness of his spirit's realization of the presence of God. Thus the consciousness of the presence of God was the central reality; the apocalyptic prospect of the Kingdom was merely the form in which this consciousness expressed itself. The abiding meaning of eschatology is to be found in "a spiritual encounter of our souls with him in which Jesus of Nazareth so interprets and represents to us the meaning of the Eschaton or reign of God that henceforth there can be for us no separation of the messianic good from the revelation of God in the spirit of Jesus."[86] Eschatology is "the sign or token of the inner transformation of men and of world-history."[87]

T. W. Manson has expressed similar views in one of his later works, The Servant-Messiah. Jesus' eschatology contains the "real Eschaton" which announces not the latest development in the historical process but "the last." This last development possesses a finality "which makes time-measurement irrelevant." Furthermore, this finality has invaded the present moment. The first meaning of Realized Eschatology emerges in the fact that the distinguishing quality of the Eschaton is not postremity but finality.[88] The Kingdom of God is "the actualization in history of God's power and wisdom as the secret of all true human welfare."[89]

SYNTHESIS OF FUTURISTIC AND REALIZED ESCHATOLOGY

We have traced the course of recent criticism in eschatological views which interpret the Kingdom of God as the future apocalyptic realm and in noneschatological views which see the Kingdom of God

---

[86] W. Manson, Jesus, the Messiah (1946), p. 209. Copyright, 1946, by The Westminster Press. Used by permission.

[87] Ibid., p. 208. In an earlier book, Christ's View of the Kingdom of God (1918), W. Manson had embraced an evolutionary interpretation which he later discarded. In one of his latest statements, we read, "There is a realized eschatology. There is also an eschatology of the unrealized. There can be no such thing under any imaginable conditions as a fully realized eschatology in the strict sense." (W. Manson, et al., Eschatology [n.d.], p. 7.)

[88] T. W. Manson, The Servant-Messiah (1953), p. 63.

[89] Ibid., p. 74.

as an experience of God in the present for which eschatology is quite unnecessary. However, between these two extremes stands a group of scholars who recognize the necessity of both the present and the future, the "spiritual" and the "eschatological" aspects of the Kingdom. The first four of these studies appeared within a period of five years from 1929–1934.

In 1928, Gerhard Gloege published a slim inaugural dissertation, later enlarged into a thorough study of the Kingdom of God,[90] in which he employed a fresh approach. The Kingdom of God by definition is not the eschatological realm of salvation, the age to come, but it is an abstract concept designating the royal rule of God, his kingly activity. Gloege rejected any local or "static" interpretation of the Kingdom as a "realm" or a "renovated world." God's Kingdom is his rule, active among men for their redemption. In one sense, the Kingdom is eternal; but in another sense, it is manifested in time and in history. The Kingdom is present because the rule of God is present in the person and deeds of Jesus; but in its full manifestation, the Kingdom is future. Gloege developed the concept that the present rule of God demands a soteriology and an ecclesiology.

H. D. Wendland, following a similar line of thought, found the unity of the present and future aspects of the Kingdom in the recognition that it is God's Kingdom and is therefore both future and transcendental. Because it is transcendental, it can also be present.[91] The Kingdom is indeed eschatological and future as *Endzeitlichkeit*.[92] Wendland fully recognizes the eschatological character of Jesus' preaching.[93] But the eschatological character of the Kingdom does not exhaust its meaning; it is also transcendental and eternal (*überzeitlich, ewig*), and therefore can be near and present.[94] Wend-

---

[90] *Das Reich Gottes im Neuen Testament* (1928); *Reich Gottes und Kirche im Neuen Testament* (1929). See the review by R. N. Flew in *ET*, XLVI (1935), pp. 215 ff.

[91] H. D. Wendland, *Die Eschatologie des Reiches Gottes bei Jesus* (1931), pp. 27–53. See his essay in *The Kingdom of God and History* (H. G. Wood, ed.; 1938), pp. 145–194.

[92] H. D. Wendland, *Eschatologie*, p. 45.

[93] *Ibid.*, p. 50.

[94] *Ibid.*, p. 46.

land takes his point of departure from the futurity and eschatological character of the Kingdom (*Zukünftigkeit* and *Endzcitlichkeit*); but he also insists on "an inner polarity of the concept of the Kingdom in its futurity and transcendence (*Endzeitlichkeit* and *Überzeitlichkeit*)," in which the presence of the Kingdom is to be understood as a real and essential element and not merely as a psychological anticipation.[95] The transcendent character of the future Kingdom in Wendland's thought may be illustrated when he describes futurity as "the coming to us of God" (*Zu-uns-kommen Gottes*).[96] The future Kingdom, because it is transcendental, has broken into the present world-order, demanding decision of men and manifesting itself in Jesus' works and person. The question of the Kingdom is thus inseparable from Christology; for as the future Messiah is already present among men, in him the future rule of God is present. In Christ, the Kingdom is both present and future.

Rudolf Otto's influential *The Kingdom of God and the Son of Man* understands the Kingdom of God to be the heavenly realm where God's will is done, the suprahistorical sphere where God rules. Jesus' teaching is grounded in a dualism of earth vs. heaven. The heavenly realm is a "wholly other" existence, and Jesus announced the coming of this miraculous supernatural realm. This event is exclusively God's deed and will mean the breaking off of history and the descent of the heavenly realm to earth. The Kingdom of heaven will come down from above and effect a marvelous transformation of the world. The Lord's Prayer is a petition for the coming of this supernatural, heavenly realm.

However, Jesus believed that the Kingdom was already in process of coming. This he believed because in a vision he had seen Satan overthrown in heaven (Luke 10:18). Therefore, he knew that God had already achieved victory over Satan and that the Kingdom had already been realized in heaven.[97] A tidal wave of divine victory had been set up by virtue of which the powers of the Kingdom were

[95] *Ibid.*, pp. 51 f.
[96] *Ibid.*, p. 41.
[97] R. Otto, *The Kingdom of God and the Son of Man* (1943), p. 105.

already operative on earth. This is what Otto means by his oft-quoted statement, "It is not Jesus who brings the kingdom . . . , the kingdom brings him with it."[98] The future heavenly realm is already breaking into the world through Jesus in the form of wonderful, supernatural, coercive power operating from above.[99] The Kingdom is not only the eschatological realm; it is also victorious, coercive power.[100] The eschatological realm of salvation is already breaking into the world as a divine *dynamis*.[101] In the future age Jesus will become the heavenly Son of Man; but he is already the agent of the present inbreaking power of the Kingdom.

In 1930, Joachim Jeremias published a provokingly short but suggestive study which may be translated, *Jesus the Consummation of the World*, in which the Kingdom of God is both present and future. Jeremias states that Jesus was the Messiah, the King of the *Gottesherrshaft*. It was Jesus' mission to bring the world to its consummation in two steps: humility and glory. In his humility, Jesus appeared with the claim that with his coming, the consummation of the world has broken in.[102] The Spirit had once more become active among men, the new creation had begun (Luke 4:1 ff.; Matt. 11:4-5), the new wine—a symbol of the era of salvation—was offered. The King entered Jerusalem and the temple was cleansed. Jeremias finds messianic significance in words and acts of Jesus through which Jesus claimed that the age of salvation had come and that the heavenly Son of Man, the renewer of the world, was among men. Satan was being overthrown. Yet because the King was present in humility, his role in bringing the age of salvation (*Weltvollendung*) was apparent only to the eye of faith. He was destined to be manifested in glory. At the Parousia, Satan would finally be destroyed and the old world judged by fire, a new world emerge, and the holy community enjoy the messianic feast.

[98] *Ibid.*, p. 103.
[99] *Ibid.*, p. 55.
[100] *Ibid.*, p. 98.
[101] *Ibid.*, p. 72.
[102] J. Jeremias, *Jesus als Weltvollender* (*Beiträge zur Forderung christlicher Theologie*, XXVII, 1930).

A clearer picture of some aspects of Jeremias' views emerges in *The Parables of Jesus*. The key to the meaning of the Kingdom is Christology. Jesus not only utters the message of the Kingdom of God, he is himself the message.[103] It is this fact which enables Jeremias to see messianic meaning in so many of Jesus' acts. His deeds as well as his words are parables. Jeremias holds that Jesus expected the eschatological consummation to take place in the near future. Jesus in fact lived in the expectation of the final *peirasmos* (Mark 14:48), the last crisis of history which his death would introduce.[104] The eschatological tribulation, the last attack of Satan upon the saints of God, would begin at his passion,[105] which would be the warning of the imminent catastrophe.[106] Jesus would usher in the new age; but the way to the new creation lay through disaster and destruction.[107] Jesus' death would not only usher in the end, it would also create the redeemed community. His vicarious death was a ransom for the innumerable host of the redeemed.[108] The relationship of the Kingdom as present to its future consummation is given in the explanation that the presence of salvation is only the prelude to the future consummation,[109] and is designed to bring men to a decision in view of, and in preparation for, the imminent end.

[103] J. Jeremias, *The Parables of Jesus* (1954), p. 158.
[104] *Ibid.*, pp. 32 f.
[105] *Ibid.*, p. 44.
[106] *Ibid.*, pp. 120–126.
[107] *Ibid.*, p. 122.
[108] *Ibid.*, pp. 152 f.
[109] *Ibid.*, p. 153. In view of the fact that Jeremias asserts that it is unthinkable that there should be any retreat from the essential lines laid down by Dodd for the interpretation of the parables (p. 109) and that he criticizes Dodd only for his "contraction of the eschatology" and "one-sided nature of his conception of the Kingdom" (p. 18), it is difficult to accept Lundström's conclusion that Jeremias has a purely futuristic view of the Kingdom of God (G. Lundström, *The Kingdom of God in the Teaching of Jesus* [1963], pp. 245–249. See the treatment of Jeremias by one of his own students, N. Perrin, *The Kingdom of God in the Teaching of Jesus* [1963], pp. 81–82). However, Lundström has pointed out a real difficulty in Jeremias' view. In spite of statements about the presence of the Kingdom, his view can be interpreted as a process, initiated by Jesus' mission, which will be shortly consummated. The Kingdom itself comes only at the consummation, it is not really present in the process already initiated.

In his most recent book, *New Testament Theology*, vol. I (1971), Jeremias takes the rather astounding position that the disciples' experience of the resurrection

T. W. Manson's noneschatological interpretation of the Kingdom of God in *The Teaching of Jesus* has been outlined above (p.
12). In a later commentary on the sayings of Jesus,[110] Manson reflects
the influence of Rudolf Otto and presents an interpretation of the
Kingdom whose center is the act of God rather than the experience
of man. He is therefore able to combine the present and future aspects of the Kingdom more successfully than in his earlier work. The
Kingdom of God is still the realization of the will of God on earth;
but the will of God expresses itself in "a Divine act for men." The
ministry of Jesus is "the Kingdom at work in the world."[111] The Kingdom shows its power in the work of Jesus and his messengers by overcoming those forces of evil which degrade and destroy man.[112] This
act of God has created a new period in history which succeeds that of
the law and the prophets: the period of the Kingdom of God.[113] Thus
the Kingdom is a state of affairs into which men may enter rather
than a state of mind.[114] The Kingdom is both present and future.
Jesus set in motion supernatural forces which go on inevitably until
they reach their consummation. "The consummated Kingdom is now
present in the world as really as the harvest is present in the sown
field. How the growth takes place and when it will come to full
fruition—these are questions which the sower cannot answer. They
are God's affair. But that heavenly forces, as real as the mysterious
forces of nature, are already at work in the world, moving inevitably
to the great consummation—of that Jesus had no doubt whatever.
The Kingdom is a present reality working toward a future consum-

---

of Jesus was "the dawn of the eschaton. They saw Jesus in shining light. They
were witnesses of his entry into glory. In other words, *they experienced the
parousia*" (italics in text; p. 310). Apparently there remains no realistic or
futuristic eschatology.

[110] See H. D. Major, T. W. Manson, and C. J. Wright, *The Mission and
Message of Jesus* (1938). Manson's part of this work was republished under the
title *The Sayings of Jesus* (1949). Our references are to the latter volume, for
the preface indicates that this work represents Manson's views in 1949.

[111] T. W. Manson, *The Sayings of Jesus* (1949), p. 345.

[112] *Ibid.*, p. 134.

[113] *Ibid.*

[114] *Ibid.*, p. 304.

mation."[115] This consummation which would bring the death of the present order, Jesus expected to come "quickly, suddenly, and completely."[116]

Future and present are combined by Jean Héring in *Le Royaume de Dieu et sa Venue*; but unfortunately, the study is too brief to be very helpful. The Kingdom is the imminent apocalyptic Kingdom which is so near that it casts its shadow into the present. In fact, says Héring, one must even say that the Kingdom was actually realized, although on a moral level, in the hearts of those who accepted the announcement of the coming Kingdom with faith and repentance. Thus Jesus taught that in his prediction there was present an invisible germ of the Kingdom.[117]

One of the most important recent studies is W. G. Kümmel's *Promise and Fulfilment*. For Kümmel, the Kingdom of God by definition is the future eschatological age, the Eschaton which Jesus expected to appear in the near future. However, Kümmel takes a decisive step beyond most writers who hold this view by recognizing that the Eschaton was already present in Jesus' person. Strongly opposing recent noneschatological and existential interpretations, Kümmel first establishes that Jesus announced the imminent coming of the eschatological Kingdom. It will come within a generation, but no one knows exactly when. However, Jesus saw this future eschatological consummation to be effective in his own person.[118] The future Kingdom had already begun its activity.[119] Kümmel strictly limits this present manifestation of the Kingdom to Jesus' person. It is quite mistaken to think that the actual Kingdom of God was present in the fellowship or activity of Jesus' disciples.[120] Jesus had no thought of gathering around him a new congregation in whom the Kingdom of

[115] *Ibid.*, p. 305.
[116] *Ibid.*, p. 148.
[117] J. Héring, *Le Royaume de Dieu et sa Venue* (1937), pp. 48, 254. Lundström interprets Héring's view as being purely futuristic. See G. Lundström, *The Kingdom of God in the Teaching of Jesus* (1963), p. 92.
[118] W. G. Kümmel, *Promise and Fulfilment* (1957), p. 105.
[119] *Ibid.*, pp. 107 f.
[120] *Ibid.*, p. 126.

God would be present.[121] Jesus himself was the sole sign of the coming Kingdom.

Like Goguel, Kümmel differentiates between apocalyptic and prophetic eschatology. Jesus' preaching about the imminent future Kingdom is eschatological promise, not apocalyptic instruction;[122] a prophetic message, not an apocalyptic revelation.[123] The difference between eschatology and apocalyptic, Kümmel finds in the "complete absence of any delineation of eschatological conditions."[124] Apocalyptic desires to throw light on eschatological proceedings; eschatology is concerned with the destiny of men in view of the impending judgment. Apocalyptic reveals future events; eschatology prepares men for the future. Sayings which embody apocalyptic instruction, such as many verses in Mark 13, must be ascribed to Jewish or Jewish-Christian apocalyptic rather than to Jesus. Therefore, Jesus' *Weltanschauung* stands in complete contrast to that of apocalyptic, for the significance of his proclamation of the imminent end of the world does not lie in the apocalyptic description, but in the fact that men are now summoned to prepare for the end, for they are confronted "with the end of history as it advances toward the goal set by God."[125] The real meaning of imminence is not in temporality, but in the certainty of the future and its impact on the present.

The position of A. N. Wilder in his important study *Eschatology and Ethics in the Teaching of Jesus* is difficult to analyze. It is easy to understand why Kümmel classes Wilder among those scholars who attempt to get rid of a future eschatological consummation.[126] Wilder says that Jesus was a this-worldly prophet and not the otherworldly Son of Man of Schweitzer's interpretation. Jesus saw a great process under way which was moving toward a climax, and thought himself to be the prophet of the new order. Jesus anticipated a new and revolutionary this-worldly order, and he used apocalyptic language to

---

[121] *Ibid.*, pp. 139 f.
[122] *Ibid.*, p. 95.
[123] *Ibid.*, p. 151.
[124] *Ibid.*, p. 91.
[125] *Ibid.*, p. 152.
[126] W. G. Kümmel, *Promise and Fulfilment* (1957), pp. 145 f.

lend urgency and significance to his message.[127] However, like Jewish apocalyptists, he did not intend this apocalyptic language to be taken literally.[128] Apocalyptic is language symbolic of the historical crisis which was in process.[129] Jesus' "forecast had to do with ultimates; and it rested on ultimates. It had to do with last things, and it rested on first things. But it was directed to the present moment and to the actual scene and was lived out in the concrete process of history, and it bore on that concrete process in its future aspects."[130] Jesus' forecasts of the judgment and of the Kingdom were only representations of the "unprophesiable, unimaginable but certain, God-determined future. This future and God's action in it lend immense weight and urgency to their present moral responsibility. Yet this temporal imminence of God is but a function of his spiritual imminence, and it is this latter which really determines conduct."[131]

This seems clear enough. Apocalyptic language is merely a symbolic form by which Jesus described the expected historical crisis. This appears to be a rather complete historization of eschatology. But on the other hand, Wilder expressly denies that he wishes to rule out eschatology altogether.[132] He criticizes such scholars as C. C. McCown and F. C. Grant for denying any transcendental element in Jesus' future perspective and for interpreting Jesus' hope in altogether this-worldly terms.[133] He insists that justice must be done to the Christian view of the new age as a "corporate matter" which "takes up into itself the historical life of man and its significant gains and is, therefore, by no means unrelated to our life in this age."[134] He approves of Walter Künneth's thesis[135] "that the Kingdom of God in the age to come is a fulfillment of historical existence and not its

---

[127] A. N. Wilder, *Eschatology and Ethics in the Teaching of Jesus* (1950), p. 59.
[128] *Ibid.*, pp. 26 ff.
[129] *Ibid.*, p. 60.
[130] *Ibid.*, p. 70.
[131] *Ibid.*, p. 161.
[132] *Ibid.*, p. 141.
[133] *Ibid.*, p. 61.
[134] *Ibid.*, p. 63.
[135] *Theologie der Auferstehung* (1934).

abridgment. . . ."[136] In a recent essay, Wilder clearly states that the eschatological event must include the redemption of creation as well as the total redemption of man.[137] Wilder's thesis appears to be that Jesus foresaw a historical crisis in the near future which he described in apocalyptic language to lend it urgency; but beyond the foreseeable historical crisis lay the eschatological crisis which was ineffable[138] and therefore could be described only in the symbolic language of apocalyptic. To Wilder, eschatology by definition is myth in that it represents the unknown future but nevertheless asserts the sovereignty of God.[139] The future lay beyond Jesus' knowledge. He used apocalyptic concepts to express his confidence that the final outcome would be decided by the power of God.[140]

However, the Kingdom was present as well as future. Wilder follows Otto in suggesting that Jesus felt himself to be part of a great redemption-transaction, a world-process under way and moving toward its climax. Jesus sometimes pictured the outcome of this process in apocalyptic terms, but he also pictured this process in less dualistic fashion in terms of a historical future.[141] Therefore Jesus conceived of the period that began with John and included his own work as the time of salvation which introduced a new situation. Jesus' ethics were determined primarily by this new time of salvation. The eschatological sanction exists, but it is only formal and secondary. The determinative fact is the spiritual imminence of God.[142] Thus, while Wilder's position is at times ambiguous,[143] we conclude that he intends to recognize both present and future elements in Jesus' teachings.

[136] Cited by A. N. Wilder, *Eschatology and Ethics in the Teaching of Jesus* (1950), p. 63.
[137] A. N. Wilder in *NTS*, V (1959), pp. 229–245.
[138] A. N. Wilder, *Eschatology and Ethics in the Teaching of Jesus* (1950), p. 161.
[139] *Ibid.*, pp. 21, 26.
[140] *Ibid.*, pp. 51 f.
[141] *Ibid.*, pp. 50 f.
[142] *Ibid.*, pp. 147 ff.
[143] See *New Testament Faith for Today* (1955), pp. 75 f. where the presence of the Kingdom is interpreted as its imminence which made its powers felt.

A. M. Hunter recognizes that the Kingdom is both present and future, although one could wish that he had developed in greater detail the meaning of the future aspect.[144] The Kingdom is first dynamic—the kingly rule of God; second, it is eschatological—the consummation of the divine purpose for men. The Jews conceived of this purpose at the end of history; Jesus said that the end had projected itself into history. Hunter prefers the term "inaugurated eschatology" to Dodd's "realized eschatology." Hunter follows Dodd in interpreting *eggiken* to mean "has arrived"; "the appointed time has fully come." Like Dodd, he also sees in the parables the teaching of a present harvest, not an eschatological judgment. The Kingdom is God's reign becoming effective in human affairs. It is God visiting and redeeming his people. The miracles were the Kingdom in action. The Kingdom which is centered in Christ means a new relationship to God, implies a new Israel, involves a new pattern for living, and requires Jesus' death. The Kingdom is also an eternally existent order above history where God's rule is always present; but this Kingdom which has come into history in the person of Jesus will come at the end of the existing order and will involve the breakdown of the physical universe and the emergence of another world beyond history. Hunter insists that it is impossible to set aside the expectation of a coming of Christ beyond history and an eschatological consummation of the Kingdom of God.

A somewhat different approach to the problem has been used by Ernst Percy in *Die Botschaft Jesu* (1953). He seeks to solve the problem of presence and futurity by asking whether Jesus' mission was to prepare men for a future Kingdom or to grant them participation in a present Kingdom. Did Jesus preach primarily repentance or offer salvation? Percy feels that scholars like Bousset and Weiss started with a false premise by confusing the concept of the Kingdom of God with that of the messianic Kingdom. The latter is

---

[144] A. M. Hunter, *Introducing New Testament Theology* (1957), pp. 13–51. See also *The Work and Words of Jesus* (1950), pp. 67–79, and *Interpreting the Parables* (1960). In these two books Hunter "plays down" the eschatological element even more than in his *Theology*.

political and national whereas the former is a religious concept: the eschatological rule of God. Judaism never used "the Kingdom of God" as a term for the eschatological salvation of the age to come, as Jesus did. The basic question is whether this eschatological salvation is exclusively future or in some real sense present. Percy solves the problem by a careful study of Jesus' preaching about repentance and salvation, especially in the Sermon on the Mount, and concludes that the Sermon is not primarily a call to repentance but an illustration of the perfect piety of the Kingdom. This piety (Frömmigkeit) is the gift of salvation (Heilsgabe) which is given to the poor because the Kingdom is present.

From this indirect line of approach, Percy concludes that while the Kingdom of God is the perfect eschatological rule (Herrschaft) of God, it is actually present in the gift of salvation which brings men into a new fellowship with God. In the person of Jesus, the Kingdom has already begun, Satan has been defeated, men are being delivered from demonic power, and the good news of salvation is received by the poor.

The influence of contemporary biblical theology upon Catholic scholarship is well illustrated by Rudolf Schnackenburg's Gottes Herrschaft und Reich. Schnackenburg contrasts his "progressive-heilsgeschichtlich" interpretation, which represents the newer Catholic view, with the older Catholic "church historical" view. The Gottesherrschaft is fundamentally eschatological and redemptive, but the eschatological salvation is present in the person and mission of Jesus in a real although provisional sense, in a hidden form. The best terms to describe the biblical view, Schnackenburg thinks, are promise, fulfillment, and consummation (Verheissung, Erfüllung, Vollendung).[145] The consummation of the Kingdom remains future and eschatological; but the Kingdom of God is itself present in the time of messianic fulfillment in Christ.[146] The present Kingdom is

[145] The structure of the present book had been planned long before Schnackenburg's volume came to hand. See this threefold concept in N. Q. Hamilton, Int, XIV (1960), pp. 141 ff.

[146] R. Schnackenburg, God's Rule and Kingdom (1963), pp. 116, 128. See also his review of the first edition of the present book in Biblische Zeitschrift (Spring, 1967), pp. 141–143.

not to be identified with the church. The church is the people of the Kingdom, and the Kingdom works in and through the church as it did in and through Jesus. Schnackenburg admits the validity of what F. M. Braun called the "new consensus" among Protestant scholars as to the character of the Kingdom and its relationship to the church, differing from these Protestant theologians only as to the nature of the church, the primacy of Peter, and the question of succession.[147] Schnackenburg carries his study beyond the Gospels through the preaching of the early church, Paul, and the later New Testament writings.

One of the most important developments in German theology is Günther Bornkamm's *Jesus von Nazaret*.[148] Famed as one of the most able and influential disciples of Bultmann, Bornkamm rejects Bultmann's extreme historical skepticism and purposes in this book to portray the historical Jesus as advanced German scholarship has not dared to attempt for a generation. Bornkamm frequently follows Bultmann, but deviates at one crucial point. For Bultmann, that which created Jesus' eschatological view was the overpowering sense of the presence of God. Bornkamm takes this consciousness of "unmediated presence" *(unmittelbare Gegenwart)* to be the Kingdom of God as a present reality. Since *basileia* can be used synonymously with God himself,[149] the sense of God's presence is itself the Kingdom of God. Thus the difference between John's and Jesus' proclamations, which are verbally the same, is the difference between the eleventh and the twelfth hours. Jesus announced that the turn of the ages is already present; the Kingdom of God is already dawning,[150] in his own words and deeds. Men are now confronted with the new age and therefore must render a decision.[151] In Jesus' person the Kingdom has become event.[152]

---

147 *Ibid.*, p. 161.
148 1956; Eng. trans., *Jesus of Nazareth* (1960).
149 *Ibid.*, p. 200.
150 *Ibid.*, p. 67.
151 *Ibid.*, p. 68.
152 *Ibid.*, pp. 169 f.

However, Bornkamm like Bultmann interprets the meaning of this event in existential terms. The "end of the world" does not mean an eschatological drama; it means rather that men are confronted by an event in which God becomes unmediated presence, and the result is "the end of the world": before them stands either salvation or judgment. They sustain a new relationship to both their past and the future. In this sense, "time" has come to an end. Thus every man receives a new present; for the life, the world, and the existence of every man stand now in the unmediated illuminating light of the reality and presence of the coming God. The beginning of the Kingdom of God is an invisible event in this time and in this world, which brings time and the world to an end; for the new world of God is already at work.[153]

In 1950, Herman Ridderbos published a book on the Kingdom of God, which was translated from Dutch into English by H. de Jongste, entitled, *The Coming of the Kingdom* (1962). In it he defends the same basic outline which provides the structure of the present book. He understands the Kingdom of God to be the reign of God active in history, in fulfillment of the Old Testament hope in the historical mission of Jesus, which must come to eschatological consummation at the Parousia of Jesus.

Of great interest is the book by Norman Perrin, *Rediscovering the Teaching of Jesus* (1967), in which he deals at length with the Kingdom of God.[154] It is notable especially for its use of radical form criticism in "rediscovering" the teaching of Jesus. Perrin insists upon "the criterion of dissimilarity": i.e., "we may accept as authentic material which fits in with neither Jewish thinking nor the conceptions of the later [Christian] community."[155] This is to the present writer a highly arbitrary and hypercritical norm. It is utterly unrea-

153 *Ibid.*, p. 74.

154 He had earlier published his doctoral dissertation, *The Kingdom of God in the Teaching of Jesus* (1963)—a book which, incidentally, is wrongly titled, for it is a history of interpretation, not primarily what the title suggests. For the present writer's critique of this book see *The Pattern of New Testament Truth* (1968), pp. 58–63.

155 *Rediscovering the Teaching of Jesus*, p. 43.

sonable that Jesus' teaching would not make use of contemporary Jewish idiom and thought, and it is equally unreasonable that the early church would not often have reproduced some of his teachings. This is surely an exercise in historical implausibility. We cannot here defend the integrity of the gospel portrait of Jesus; it is an involved question which involves dogmatic as well as "scientific" matters.[156] We are here interested only in the conclusions to which Perrin's radical criticism leads him.

Amazingly, his conclusions are remarkably like those of the present author. The "Kingdom of God" is first of all God's dynamic activity and it is also the "state secured for the redeemed by this intervention" (p. 60). It is also certain that Jesus proclaimed the eschatological Kingdom of God: God's final and decisive act (p. 56). Furthermore, Perrin sees the Kingdom as a present blessing (pp. 67, 74). We agree with Perrin also that because the Kingdom is present, it is something to be experienced. "Here was a situation in which the reality of God and his love was being revealed in a new and decisive way, and in which, therefore, the joys of the salvation time were suddenly available to those who had longed for them so long and so earnestly" (p. 97). Table-fellowship, which frequently characterized Jesus' ministry, "celebrated the present joy and anticipated the future consummation" (p. 107).

At three important points, however, Perrin is in error. He is one of the few scholars who maintain that *all* of the Son of Man sayings, including the eschatological sayings, are church creations. In the present writer's judgment, if criticism cannot establish that Jesus used the title "the Son of Man" of himself, it can prove very little.[157] Secondly, Perrin misreads the presence of the Kingdom of God. While Perrin rightly recognizes the presence of the Kingdom in an "eschatological-conflict" situation (Matt. 12:28), he insists that it is present in the experience of the individual (pp. 67, 74). Kümmel has recognize this error. "The presence of the Kingdom of God is divorced

---

[156] See G. E. Ladd, "A Search for Perspective," *Int*, XXV (1971), pp. 41–62.
[157] See Chap. 11 in the author's forthcoming, *A Theology of the New Testament.*

from the person of Jesus and limited to human experience. . . . The
significance of the person of Jesus for this presence is almost completely lost in Perrin's interpretation."[158] We cannot emphasize this
too strongly. We agree with Kümmel that the Kingdom of God came
among men in the person, deeds, and words of Jesus. Only because
of its presence in him could it be a matter of experience to his
disciples.

Third, when Perrin tries to interpret the meaning of futurity for
the Kingdom, he again falls into error. Many of his words, taken out
of context, are splendidly expressed. Some of the parables involve a
present beginning and a future consummation (p. 158). "The emphasis is upon God, upon what he is doing and what he will do"
(p. 158). God was active in the ministry of Jesus, and "what God
has begun he will bring to a triumphant conclusion" (p. 159). But
Perrin says that we are not to think of this future in terms of the
"western concept of linear time" (p. 204) which moves from past
to present. Rather, "time in the teaching of Jesus" is "something
which God fills and fulfills" (p. 206). It is true that time gets its
meaning from the fact that God is able to fill a moment or an hour of
time; but this does not rob time of its linear meaning. Cullmann has
proven that New Testament theology has its setting in the Jewish
concept of linear time—this age and the age to come.[159] Again,
Kümmel is right in saying that, at this point, Perrin is unhistorical
and therefore false.[160] When Perrin says that "the present that has
become God's present guarantees that all futures will be God's
future" (p. 205), he ceases to be a biblical theologian.

A synthesis of present and future in the understanding of the Kingdom of God is found in the works of a host of other scholars dealing
with other subjects. So extensively is this synthesis to be found[161]
that we must recognize it as an emerging consensus.

[158] See W. G. Kümmel's review in *JR*, XLIX (1969), p. 62.
[159] O. Cullmann, *Christ and Time* (rev. ed. 1964).
[160] W. G. Kümmel, *op. cit.*, p. 65.
[161] See J. A. Baird, *The Justice of God in the Teaching of Jesus* (1963), pp.
122 ff. (Baird thinks that the future of the discussion lies with the position
which combines present and future); C. K. Barrett, "New Testament Escha-

Conclusions

From this critical survey, several conclusions emerge. First, the growing consensus is supported by the almost universal modification of Schweitzer's Consistent Eschatology. Many of those who continue to deny that the Kingdom itself was present admit at least that it was active among men, that its powers were operative. The question of basic definition therefore becomes all-important. If the Kingdom is the future eschatological era of salvation, it is difficult to see how it can be also present. But if Otto was correct in defining the Kingdom

tology," *SJTh*, VI (1953), p. 231; H. Bietenhard, *Die Reichgottes-Erwartung im Neuen Testament* (1945); J. Bright, *The Kingdom of God* (1953), Chap. 8; F. F. Bruce, "Eschatology," in *Baker's Dictionary of Theology* (E. F. Harrison, ed.; 1960), pp. 189–193; E. C. Colwell, *An Approach to the Teaching of Jesus* (1947), p. 121; *Jesus and the Gospel* (1963), pp. 24, 33; C. E. B. Cranfield, *The Gospel according to Saint Mark* (1959), pp. 63–68; P. E. Davies, "Jesus and the Role of Prophet," *JBL*, LXIV (1945), pp. 241–254; G. S. Duncan, *Jesus, Son of Man* (1949), Chaps. 4, 13 (Duncan is rather indecisive about the eschatological element); O. E. Evans, "Kingdom of God," *IDB*, III, pp. 20–23 (Evans sees a present fulfillment and a future consummation); F. V. Filson, *Jesus Christ: The Risen Lord* (1956), Chap. 5; R. N. Flew, *Jesus and His Church* (2nd ed., 1943), Chap. 1; F. J. Foakes-Jackson and K. Lake, *The Beginnings of Christianity* (1920), I, p. 280; S. M. Gilmour, *The Gospel Jesus Preached* (1957), Chap. 6; S. E. Johnson, *Jesus in His Own Times* (1958), p. 122; E. Käsemann, *ZTK*, LI (1954), pp. 150–151; J. Lindblom, "The Idea of the Kingdom of God," *ET*, LI (1939–40), pp. 91–96; H. K. Luce, "Kingdom of God," *HDB* (rev. ed. by F. C. Grant and H. H. Rowley, 1963), p. 554; C. F. D. Moule, *The Birth of the New Testament* (1962), p. 99; O. Piper, *God in History* (1939); Herman Ridderbos, "Kingdom of God," in *The New Bible Dictionary* (J. D. Douglas, ed.; 1962), pp. 693–697; see also Ridderbos, *The Coming of the Kingdom* (1962), an important volume which came to hand too late to be used in the present study; H. Roberts, *Jesus and the Kingdom of God* (1955), Chap. 1; J. M. Robinson, "Jesus' Understanding of History," *JBR*, XXIII (1955), pp. 17–24; "The Formal Structure of Jesus' Message" in *Current Issues in New Testament Interpretation* (W. Klassen and G. F. Snyder, eds.; 1962), pp. 97 ff.; J. D. Smart, *The Interpretation of Scripture* (1961), pp. 110 f.; V. Taylor, *The Life and Ministry of Jesus* (1954), Chap. 14; H. E. W. Turner, *Jesus Master and Lord* (1953), Chap. 9; R. McL. Wilson in *Peake's Commentary on the Bible* (M. Black and H. H. Rowley, eds.; 1962), p. 801; I. W. Batdorf, *Interpreting the Beatitudes* (1966), pp. 99 ff.; E. Linnemann, *Jesus of the Parables* (1966), pp. 38 ff., 132 ff.; I. H. Marshall, *Eschatology and the Parables* (1963); J. D. Kingsbury, *The Parables of Jesus in Matthew 13* (1969), pp. 17 ff.; R. P. Berkey, "Realized Eschatology and the Post-Bultmannians," *ET*, LXXXIV (1972–3); pp. 72–77; John Reumann, *Jesus in the Church's Gospels* (1968), pp. 154 ff.

not only as a future realm but as the power of God operative in that realm, then the activity of the power of the future Kingdom means, in reality, the presence of the Kingdom itself. The question of definition is fundamental.

Second, the question of the imminence of the Kingdom has assumed new importance; for many of these recent studies, from Ernest F. Scott to W. G. Kümmel, find the present significance of the Kingdom in its imminence. The Kingdom is so *very* near that it can already be seen and felt. This fact of the imminence of the eschatological Kingdom, Wilder considers the central point of Schweitzer's reconstruction,[162] and he points out that few modern scholars challenge this conclusion. But at this point, a serious difficulty arises which, in the judgment of the present writer, has not been adequately faced. If it were a sense of imminence which caused our Lord's feeling that the Kingdom was a present power, and if in fact the Kingdom was not imminent, then his teaching of the Kingdom as a present reality rested upon a delusion; and it is difficult to see how it can have validity either for him or for us. Some scholars have tried to solve this problem by translating his sense of imminence into an ethical or spiritual equivalent (William Manson, Rudolf Bultmann, W G. Kümmel). This stratagem tends to empty eschatology of real significance. Others, like Schweitzer, have admitted that the eschatology of Jesus is an offense to modern thought. Martin Dibelius says simply that Jesus was the victim of a monstrous illusion,[163] for the very center of his message was an event which has never come to pass. Furthermore, if it were the sense of temporal imminence which gave Jesus a conviction that the powers of the Kingdom were already at work among men because the Kingdom itself was so close, and if in fact the Kingdom was not close, then the consciousness of these powers of the allegedly imminent Kingdom must itself have been illusory. The difficulty of this problem has not been fully admitted. If

---

[162] A. N. Wilder, *Eschatology and Ethics in the Teaching of Jesus* (1950), p. 38. See above, p. 32, n. 143.
[163] *Jesus* (1949), p. 70.

Jesus were in gross error as to his central mission, it is difficult to understand how his integrity or authority as a religious teacher can be preserved. If it is a fact that Jesus unequivocally thought that the Kingdom of God meant the end of the world in his lifetime, then we must not only admit that he was in error but must recognize that his entire message rested upon a delusion. We cannot take a Bultmannian position that the redemptive act occurs only in the Kerygma and needs only the fact (Dass) of Jesus to legitimate itself.

Third, the question of the role of apocalyptic is still contested. As we have seen, efforts have been made to distinguish between eschatology and apocalyptic and to attribute the former to Jesus, but not the latter. Schweitzer's school interprets Jesus as a Jewish apocalyptist. Scholars like Goguel and Kümmel differentiate between apocalyptic speculation and eschatological instruction and make Jesus an adherent of the latter type of teaching. Others, like Bowman and Waterman, define prophetic and apocalyptic as mutually exclusive types of religion and place Jesus in the prophetic type while rejecting all apocalyptic. Still others, like Dodd and Wilder, insist that apocalyptic terminology is symbolic of eternal or ineffable realities and was not meant to be taken literally. These discussions raise the problem of the definition of prophetic and apocalyptic, and Jesus' relation to both types of teaching; and this demands an analysis of the Old Testament promise and of its later apocalyptic interpretation as a background for the discussion of our Lord's teachings.

Finally, it becomes clear that the most important factor in the entire study is the point of departure and the fundamental definition of the Kingdom. If the Kingdom of God by definition is the eschatological realm of redemption, the age to come, and if Jesus proclaimed simply the imminence of this new age, it is difficult to see how the insuperable difficulties mentioned above can be avoided. On the other hand, if the Kingdom is primarily an experience of God in the human heart, a personal relationship between the individual and God, then perhaps the eschatological and apocalyptic elements have no real place in Jesus' teaching and are to be sloughed off as views which he shared with his contemporary first-century Jewish kinsmen but which lack relevance either for his real message or for the modern man. If, however, the Kingdom is the reign of God, not merely in the human heart but dynamically active in the person of Jesus and in human history, then it becomes possible to understand how the Kingdom of God can be present and future, inward and outward, spiritual and apocalyptic. For the redemptive royal activity of God could act decisively more than once and manifest itself powerfully in more than one way in accomplishing the divine end.

With these questions in mind, we must trace the prophetic expectation of the Kingdom of God in the Old Testament, pursue the developments of this expectation through the intertestamental literature, and then against this background attempt a reconstruction of the teaching and mission of our Lord with particular reference to the Kingdom of God.

PART II

THE
PROMISE
OF THE
KINGDOM

2 The Old Testament Promise

Our earliest Gospel introduces the ministry of Jesus with the words, "Jesus came into Galilee, preaching the gospel of God, and saying, 'The time is fulfilled, and the kingdom of God is at hand'" (Mark 1:14–15). Although the burden of Jesus' message was the Kingdom of God, he nowhere defined it. It is not recorded that anyone asked him what "the Kingdom of God" meant. He assumed that this was a concept so familiar that it did not require definition. To discover what the Kingdom of God meant to Jesus' hearers, we must first survey the Old Testament promise and then the Jewish interpretations of that promise in the apocryphal literature. It is not our purpose to trace the history and development of this concept,[1] but to analyze the prophetic hope as background for the New Testament message. Our concern is with the questions: How did Judaism interpret the Old Testament hope? What are the differences between the prophetic and the apocalyptic messages? How was Jesus' proclamation of the Kingdom related to the prophetic and the apocalyptic traditions? Was he a prophet or an apocalyptist? Therefore, we shall attempt first to analyze the prophetic hope of the Kingdom to de-

[1] See J. Bright, *The Kingdom of God* (1953).

termine its outstanding characteristics and then to see how the apocalyptic writings modified the Old Testament hope.

Although the expression "the Kingdom of God" does not occur in the Old Testament, the idea is found throughout the prophets.[2] God is frequently spoken of as the King, both of Israel (Exod. 15:18; Num. 23:21; Deut. 33:5; Isa. 43:15) and of all the earth. (II Kings 19:15; Isa. 6:5; Jer. 46:18; Ps. 29:10; 47:2; 93; 96:10; 97:1 ff.; 99: 1–4; 145: 11 ff.). Although God is now the King, other references speak of a day when he shall become King and shall rule over his people.[3] This brief glimpse of the idea of God's kingship provides the outline for the entire Old Testament concept. While God is King over all the earth, he is in a special way the King of his people, Israel. God's rule is therefore something realized in Israel's history. However, it is only partially and imperfectly realized. Therefore, the prophets look forward to a day when God's rule will be fully experienced, not by Israel alone but by all the world. Our main concern is with the Kingdom of God as a hope. Indeed, Bright defines the Kingdom of God as the rule of God over his people, and particularly the vindication of that rule and people in glory at the end of history.[4]

A DYNAMIC HOPE

The first and outstanding characteristic of the Old Testament concept is that it is theocentric and dynamic. It is the rule of God. Furthermore, the emphasis is not upon the state of affairs or the final order of things but upon the fact that God will rule. The state of affairs to be finally introduced is but the inevitable result of the final vindication of the divine rule.

The centrality of this abstract or dynamic character of the Kingdom of God is illustrated by the fact that the Hebrew word *malkuth* bears primarily the dynamic rather than the concrete meaning, and refers first to a reign, dominion, or rule and only secondarily to the

---

[2] P. Volz in *Festschrift für Georg Beer* (A. Weiser, ed.; 1935), p. 72.
[3] Cf. Isa. 24:23; 33:22; 52:7; Zeph. 3:15; Obad. 21; Zech. 14:9 ff. See also G. von Rad in *TWNT*, I, p. 567.
[4] *The Kingdom of God* (1953), p. 18.

realm over which a reign is exercised. Even when *malkuth* is used of human kingdoms, the primary reference is to the rule or reign of a king. We frequently meet the expression, "in the . . . the year of the kingdom of . . ." i.e., of the reign of a certain king.[5] Back of the actual reign of a king stands the authority which he exercises. When we read that Solomon's "kingdom was firmly established" (I Kings 2:12), we are to understand that his authority to reign was settled. The kingdom of Saul was turned over to David (I Chron. 12:23), i.e., the authority which had been Saul's was given to David; and as a result of having received regal authority, David became king. When the "royal position" (*malkuth*) of Vashti was given to Esther (Esther 1:19), she received the authority to be queen. This abstract idea of *malkuth* is evident when it is found in parallelism with such abstract concepts as power, might, glory, dominion (Dan. 2:37; 4:34; 7:14).[6]

When *malkuth* is used of God, it almost always refers to his authority or to his rule as the heavenly King. "They shall speak of the glory of thy kingdom and tell of thy power. . . . Thy kingdom is an everlasting kingdom, and thy dominion endures throughout all generations" (Ps. 145:11, 13). "The Lord has established his throne in the heavens, and his kingdom rules over all" (Ps. 103:19).

The dynamic concept of God as King is closely related to the concept of God who visits his people to accomplish his royal purposes among men. This is vividly illustrated by the so-called "enthronement" psalms.

> Say among the nations, "The Lord reigns!
>   Yea, the world is established, it shall never be moved;
>   he will judge the peoples with equity."
> Let the heavens be glad, and let the earth rejoice;
>   let the sea roar, and all that fills it;
>   let the field exult, and everything in it!

---

[5] See I Chron. 26:31; II Chron. 3:2; 15:10; Ezra 4:5; 7:1; 8:1; Esther 2:16; Jer. 52:31; Dan. 1:1; 2:1; 8:1. (This is not exhaustive.) In some places, *malkuth* is translated "reign." See II Chron. 29:19; Ezra 4:5, 6; Neh. 12:22; Jer. 49:34.

[6] We must also recognize that *malkuth* can be used to designate the realm over which a king reigns. See, e.g., II Chron. 20:30; Esther 3:6; Dan. 9:1; 11:9; Jer. 10:7. This fact will be important in the analysis of the New Testament concept.

Then shall all the trees of the wood sing for joy
    before the Lord, for he comes,
    for he comes to judge the earth.
He will judge the world with righteousness,
    and the peoples with his truth.

                      Psalm 96:10–13

The cause of rejoicing is not the fact that God sits enthroned as King
in the heavens, exalted high above the earth, but that God will come
and visit the earth to judge men and to establish his rule effectively
among men who do not now acknowledge it. This note of the King
coming to rule is re-echoed in Psalm 98:8–9:

Let the floods clap their hands;
    let the hills sing for joy together
before the Lord, for he comes
    to rule the earth.
He will judge the world with righteousness,
    and the peoples with equity.[7]

This idea of "the God who comes"[8] is one of the central characteristics of the Old Testament teaching about God, and it links together history and eschatology. The whole history of Israel, from the
birth of the nation at Mount Sinai to her final redemption in the
Kingdom of God, can be viewed in light of the divine visitations. God
visited his people in the wilderness to call them into being and thus
became their King.

The Lord came from Sinai,
    and dawned from Seir upon us;
    he shone forth from Mount Paran,

    [7] S. Mowinckel has interpreted these enthronement psalms in terms of a New
Year's festival with an alleged annual "enthronement" of Yahweh, after the
analogy of ancient eastern myths of the death, resurrection, and enthronement of
the chief god. See *Psalmenstudien*, II (1922); *He That Cometh* (1956), pp.
80 ff; W. R. Taylor and W. S. McCullough in *IB*, IV, pp. 502 ff. However, as
Snaith has pointed out, this interpretation rests upon certain *religionsgeschichtliche* presuppositions rather than upon historical knowledge or sound exegesis.
See N. H. Snaith, *The Distinctive Ideas of the Old Testament* (1944), pp. 18–
19; C. R. North, *The Old Testament Interpretation of History* (1946), pp.
121–125; and especially N. H. Snaith, *The Jewish New Year Festival* (1947),
pp. 204 ff.
    [8] See Georges Pidoux, *Le Dieu qui vient* (1947), for a study of this theme.

> he came from the ten thousands of holy ones,
> with flaming fire at his right hand. . . .
> Thus the Lord became king in Jeshurun.
>   Deuteronomy 33:2, 5

This initial coming of God was described as a mighty theophany. When the creator God visited the earth, his creation was shaken before his power and glory.

> Lord, when thou didst go forth from Seir,
> when thou didst march from the region of Edom,
> the earth trembled,
> and the heavens dropped,
> yea, the clouds dropped water.
> The mountains quaked before the Lord,
> yon Sinai before the Lord, the God of Israel.
>   Judges 5:4–5 (Cf. Psalm 68:7–8)

In the concluding prayer in Habakkuk, the author consoles himself in the face of evil times by the recollection of God's wonderful visitations in the past, particularly when "God came from Teman, and the Holy One from Mount Paran."

> The mountains saw thee, and writhed. . . .
> The sun and moon stood still in their habitation. . . .
> Thou didst bestride the earth in fury,
> thou didst trample the nations in anger
> Thou wentest forth for the salvation of thy people,
> for the salvation of thy anointed.
>   Habakkuk 3:3, 10, 11, 12–13

This is obviously poetic language, but it is not merely poetry. When God visited Israel at Sinai, the Jews believed that the place literally was shaken. A quake shook the earth and the mountain echoed with thunder and flashed with lightnings. There were also a fearful divine fire and a long trumpet blast which were more than ordinary phenomena (Exod. 19:16 ff.).[9]

---

[9] There is no evidence of volcanic activity at Mount Sinai. See J. Morgenstern in *JR*, I (1921), p. 241. For this reason, W. J. Phythian-Adams assumes that the site of Horeb is in Midian, east of the Gulf of Akaba. (*The Call of Israel* [1934], pp. 140–154).

This description of the initial theophanic visitation at Sinai reflects a theology of the relationship of God to his world and his people. God is transcendent above the earth; yet he does not remain aloof in heaven but comes to visit his people to bless and to judge. The world is God's creation, and as such it is by nature finite and transient, standing in a relationship of subordination to God. These descriptions of the shaking of the earth when God comes reflect not only the glory and majesty of God but the utter dependence of the creation upon its creator.

Similar language can be used in a purely poetical manner to describe the wonder of any divine deliverance from danger. When God's servant was in despair of his life, he called upon the Lord. God heard him and enabled him to escape. However, the psalmist praises God for his deliverance as though a mighty theophany had occurred.

> From his temple he heard my voice
>> and my cry to him reached his ears.
> Then the earth reeled and rocked;
>> the foundations also of the mountains trembled
>> and quaked, because he was angry.
> Smoke went up from his nostrils,
>> and devouring fire from his mouth;
>> glowing coals flamed forth from him.
> He bowed the heavens, and came down;
>> thick darkness was under his feet. . . .
> Out of the brightness before him
>> there broke through his clouds
>> hailstones and coals of fire. . . .
> Then the channels of the sea were seen
>> and the foundations of the world were laid bare,
>> at thy rebuke, O Lord,
>> at the blast of the breath of thy nostrils.
>> Psalm 18:7–15

In such a psalm, the imagery of the visitations at Sinai is applied in purely poetic terms to a visitation of God by which he enables his servant to escape the threat of death.

Such theophanic language can be used to describe historical judgments upon his people. Micah foretells the utter destruction of Samaria (1:6) and of Jerusalem (3:12) in symbolic language.

> For behold, the Lord is coming forth out of his place,
>   and will come down and tread upon the high places of the earth.
> And the mountains will melt under him and the valleys will be cleft,
>   like wax before the fire, like waters poured down a steep place.
> Micah 1:3–4

Some writers interpret these words as a secondary eschatological interpolation; but no compelling reason prevents us from understanding them in their context as a symbolic portrayal of God's judgments in history, even as Psalm 18 describes symbolically God's deliverance of the individual.

The final salvation is frequently described as a divine visitation. Zechariah foresees "a day of the Lord" when all nations will be gathered in battle against Jerusalem, when "the Lord will go forth and fight against those nations." "Then the Lord your God will come, and all the holy ones with him" (Zech. 14:3, 5). Israel will be "visited by the Lord of hosts" (Isa. 29:6) and delivered from her enemies. "Behold, your God will come with vengeance, with the recompense of God. He will come and save you" (Isa. 35:4). "And he will come to Zion as Redeemer, to those in Jacob who turn from transgression, says the Lord" (Isa. 59:20). God's coming will also mean judgment. "For behold, the Lord is coming forth out of his place to punish the inhabitants of the earth for their iniquity" (Isa. 26:21; cf. Isa. 2:21; 63:1–6; 64:1 ff.; 65:15–16; Zeph. 3:8; Zech. 14:3). This final coming of God will mean the salvation of the Gentiles as well as of Israel. "Sing and rejoice, O daughter of Zion; for lo, I come and I will dwell in the midst of you, says the Lord. And many nations shall join themselves to the Lord in that day, and shall be my people; and I will dwell in the midst of you" (Zech. 2:10–11; cf. Isa. 66:18 ff.).

Back of this language is a distinct theology of the God who comes. God who visited Israel in Egypt to make them his people, who has visited them again and again in their history, must finally come to them in the future to judge wickedness and to establish his Kingdom.

Israel's hope is thus rooted in history, or rather in the God who works in history. It is widely recognized that the Hebrew sense of history is unique in the ancient Semitic world. The other Semitic religions were nature religions and did not develop a sense of history; but the Hebrew faith developed an interest in history because of its concept of God whose activity was to be experienced in history.[10] The fundamental ground of the Old Testament hope is its faith in God who reveals himself dynamically in history. "There is no sure ground for hope in a future whether for mankind or for its individual members, which does not involve faith in a God who reveals Himself in history, and is the guarantor that the revelation will be vindicated. Such a God was Yahweh in the faith of Israel, and such a conception was unique in pre-Christian times. . . . The Biblical conception of the Kingdom of God is unique because it springs from a unique conception of God Himself."[11] God is both Israel's King and the King of all the earth, ruling over all. However, there are special times of visitation when his royal purposes find concrete expression, the most important of which will be the final visitation to consummate his will and to bring salvation.

An Eschatological Hope

It follows that Israel's hope of the Kingdom of God is an eschatological hope, and that eschatology is a necessary corollary to Israel's view of God. The older Wellhausenian criticism insisted that eschatology was a late development which emerged only in postexilic times. On the basis of this assumption, the authenticity of eschatological passages in the pre-exilic prophets was discounted. Recently the pendulum has been swinging in the other direction and the fundamental Israelitic character of eschatology recognized.[12] An increasing number of scholars can be cited who recognize that it was

[10] See M. Noth, *Gesammelte Studien zum Alten Testament* (1957), p. 249.

[11] H. W. Robinson, *Inspiration and Revelation in the Old Testament* (1946), pp. 32 f. Quoted by permission of the Clarendon Press.

[12] See O. Baab, *The Theology of the Old Testament* (1949), p. 179; P. Volz, in *Festschrift für Georg Beer*, A. Weiser, ed. 1935), p. 76; J. Bright, *Int*, V (1951), pp. 3–26.

the concept of God who had been concerned with Israel in redemptive history which gave rise to the eschatological hope.[13]

Some scholars object to the use of the word "eschatological" to describe the Old Testament hope. They insist that eschatology, properly speaking, cannot exist apart from the idea of a great drama of the end time in which the age of this world ends and a new eternal age of salvation is introduced.[14] In other words, "eschatology" requires the idea of the two ages, and this idea, according to J. Lindblom, is found in the Old Testament only in Isaiah 65-66.[15]

This raises the much debated question of the nature and definition of history and eschatology. The discussion is confusing because of the diverse use of the terms "eschatology" and "apocalyptic" made by various scholars. Mowinckel, following the view of Volz and Bousset, has given classical expression to the theory which finds two entirely diverse types of hope in Hebrew-Jewish literature, one native to Hebrew thought and the other emerging from extra-Hebrew influences. Perhaps the terms "prophetic" and "apocalyptic" are best suited to designate these two types of hope. The "prophetic" hope is rooted in history. God is the Lord of history and will bring history to a consummation on this earth. The Kingdom will be achieved within history by historical events which will see the rise of a Davidic king who will rule over a restored Israel, bringing peace to all the earth. This truly Hebraic prophetic hope is historical, earthly, and nationalistic in that the messianic salvation is accomplished through Israel.

This prophetic hope was not realized. The return of the Jews to Palestine from Babylon did not produce the Kingdom of God. Instead of God's rule, Israel suffered the rule of one evil nation after

[13] Set G. E. Wright, *IB*, I, p. 372; *God Who Acts* (1952), p. 51; J. Bright, *The Kingdom of God* (1952), pp. 29 f.; A. C. Knudson, *The Religious Teaching of the Old Testament* (1918), pp. 352 ff.; G. Pidoux, *Le Dieu qui vient* (1947), p. 51; E. Jacob, *Theology of the Old Testament* (1958), pp. 317 ff.; W. Eichrodt, *Theology of the Old Testament* (1961), I, pp. 498 ff.; H. W. Robinson, *Inspiration and Revelation in the Old Testament* (1946), pp. 28-33; T. C. Vriezen, *An Outline of Old Testament Theology* (1958), p. 229.

[14] G. Hölscher, *Die Ursprünge der jüdischen Eschatologie* (1925), p. 3.

[15] See J. Lindblom, *The Servant Songs in Deutero-Isaiah* (1951), p. 96; S. Mowinckel, *He That Cometh* (1956), p. 125.

another. This led to despair for the coming of the Kingdom within history. History appeared to be so dominated by evil that it could no longer be thought of as the scene of God's Kingdom. Therefore the prophetic hope for an earthly kingdom within history was displaced by the apocalyptic hope of a kingdom beyond history. This transformation arose in part under the influence of Persian and Iranian dualism. History was doomed. The Kingdom would come only by suprahistorical powers breaking into history and inaugurating a transcendental nonearthly order. The earthly Davidic Messiah is replaced by a heavenly transcendental Son of Man who is to come with the clouds to initiate the new order.[16] These two types of eschatology—the prophetic and the apocalyptic—are not the result of a natural development but are two different kinds of thought. Mowinckel considers any effort to unite these two eschatologies to be "a retrograde step in historical scholarship."[17]

A confusing factor in this discussion is, as we have already indicated, the different use of terms by these several scholars. Mowinckel, although he uses the term "eschatology" to describe the early Jewish hope, insists along with Lindblom that eschatology properly speaking requires some sort of dualism involving a catastrophic transformation of the present order (see p. 53, n. 15). He speaks of the "early Jewish hope" and insists there is no preprophetic or prophetic eschatology. On the other hand, Bousset, Volz, and Bultmann use the term "eschatology" of the early nationalistic hope. Bultmann distinguishes between nationalist and cosmic eschatology; and Bousset uses the term "apocalyptic" for the dualistic view which Mowinckel calls eschatology. It is not clear how Mowinckel would distinguish between eschatology, properly speaking, and apocalyptic eschatology. For clarity's sake, we shall follow the Bousset-Volz-Bultmann terminology rather than Mowinckel's, and consider as a

[16] See W. Bousset, Die Religion des Judentums im späthellenistischen Zeitalter (1926), Chaps. 12, 13; P. Volz, Die Eschatologie der jüdischen Gemeinde (1934), Chap. 23. It may also be found in W. O. E. Oesterley and T. H. Robinson, Hebrew Religion Its Origin and Development (1937), Chap. 39; R. Bultmann, Primitive Christianity in Its Contemporary Setting (1956), pp. 79–86; and especially in S. Mowinckel, He That Cometh (1956), Chaps. 8–10.
[17] S. Mowinckel, He That Cometh (1956), p. 267.

proper eschatology those prophetic views which conceive of the final consummation of God's salvation within the framework of history.[18]

This concept of two different kinds of eschatology, one earthly and the other dualistic, leads to the question of whether or not the Kingdom of God is to be conceived of within history or beyond history. Some scholars have argued that for history to have real meaning, the Kingdom of God must be realized within history and must be produced by strictly historical events. If the Kingdom of God can be achieved only by God breaking into history from outside history, then history itself really has no goal. We may recognize the hand of God in history, but this belongs altogether to the realm of faith and interpretation. God works in and through history and never breaks the nexus of historical causation. God can be seen in the evolutionary processes believed to be at work in history.[19]

According to this modern terminology, the so-called prophetic eschatology is "within history" while the apocalyptic eschatology is "beyond history," not simply because the Kingdom itself will be beyond history but because it can be achieved only by a catastrophic inbreaking of God, not by historical events.

Not all scholars have been convinced by this analysis. We are fortunate in having two different studies of this problem which come to strikingly similar conclusions. Stanley B. Frost has made a detailed study of Old Testament apocalyptic; and whether or not one follows his critical treatment of the prophetic writings, his conclusions about the form of the future hope are impressive. Frost finds four different concepts of the future in Hebrew-Jewish thought which he labels the Better Age, the Golden Age, the Future Age, and the Age to Come. The first or Better Age is a purely "historical" expectation of a good time which will arise out of the normal flow of events bringing peace and prosperity to Israel in terms of ordinary

[18] J Lindblom later admitted the legitimacy of the term "eschatology" in StTh, VI (1953), pp. 79–114. He recognized the fact of two ages, if not the terminology, in the pre-exilic prophets in Prophecy in Ancient Israel (1962), pp. 360, 364, 367. Fohrer recognizes a prophetic concept of two ages, but not in a dualistic sense. See Georg Fohrer, TLZ, LXXXV (1960), col. 401–420.

[19] See C. C. McCown, in HTR, XXXVIII (1945), pp. 151–175 for an excellent statement of this position.

experience. This was the popular expectation in Amos' day and is not really eschatological but preprophetic.[20] The fourth type—that of an Age to Come—is a transcendental order of a suprahistorical world. This view Frost finds only in the later development of Jewish apocalyptic, not in the Old Testament. The hope entertained by the prophets is that of a Golden Age (Amos, Zephaniah, Jeremiah) or of a Future Age (Ezekiel). The Golden Age results from "a cataclysmic irruption into history, and its finality is such that there are no after-effects. History is indeed at an end. Life continues, certainly, and in this world, but it is an entirely new quality of life."[21] The Future Age involves an even greater contrast with the present order, but it is still existence on the earth and not in a transcendental heavenly realm.

T. C. Vriezen comes to the same outline of development independently. He describes the four types of the future hope by the terms "pre-eschatological," "proto-eschatological," "actual-eschatological," and "transcendental-eschatological." The hope of purely historical earthly blessings was the popular hope of Amos' day and is pre-eschatological. The transcendentalizing eschatology is that of a developed dualism but is not found in the prophets, only in post-canonical writings. The "proto-eschatology" of Isaiah and his contemporaries is "historical and at the same time supra-historical. It takes place within the framework of history but is caused by forces that transcend history, so that what is formed is a new order of things in which the glory and the Spirit of God (Isa. 11) reveals itself."[22] "Actual-eschatology" is found in Deutero-Isaiah and differs from "proto-eschatology" in that the contrast between the older and the new is more distinct.

These two analyses indicate that the hope of a kingdom which would issue in a renewal of the world and which could be introduced

[20] S. B. Frost, Old Testament Apocalyptic (1952), pp. 48, 114, 236 f.
[21] Ibid., p. 48.
[22] T. C. Vriezen, "Prophecy and Eschatology," Supplements to Vetus Testamentum, I (1953), p. 222. A very different development is found by C. Steuernagel in Festschrift Alfred Bertholet (W. Baumgartner, et al., eds.; 1950), pp. 478–487. He discusses the development in terms of national, individual, and universal eschatology.

only by suprahistorical forces, i.e., by the direct act of God, is firmly rooted in the pre-exilic prophets. This may be called a truly eschatological hope, for it will mean the Eschaton—the age of the consummation of God's redemptive purpose. As scholars like Lindblom have insisted, there is therefore no reason why eschatology by definition must involve the doctrine of two ages.

The Israelites of Amos' day looked for a kingdom which would arise within history and be effected by historical forces. The popular expectation was that of a day of success, blessing, and prosperity for Israel when the glory of David's kingdom would be restored and Israel would achieve complete victory over her foes. This is the only Old Testament concept of the Kingdom which is strictly "this-worldly" and "historical"; but it was not shared by the prophets.[23] In fact, Amos condemned this as a false view. The Day of the Lord will be darkness and not light, judgment and not vindication, wrath and not blessing (Amos 5:18–20). The Day of the Lord which Amos announced will bring a disruption of the physical order, i.e., a cosmic catastrophe caused by God himself. Under the weight of divine judgment, the earth will be shaken and turned to chaos. The whole earth will become a sea, rising and falling like the Nile. The Day will even witness a heavenly catastrophe. The sun will go down at noon shrouding the earth in darkness at midday (Amos 8:7–9; 9:5–6). That more than natural disasters are indicated is evidenced by the fire which first devours the sea and then the land (Amos 7:4). This is no uncontrolled forest fire but "apocalyptic" fire.[24] Some scholars see no more than poetic fantasy in this language,[25] but others recognize real eschatology. "This is not to be dismissed as poetic exuberance. What Amos seems to envisage is convulsions of nature on something like a cosmic scale. It is genuine eschatology."[26] Frost is convinced that Amos does not announce a day rising out

---

[23] T. C. Vriezen, op. cit., p. 226; S. B. Frost, Old Testament Apocalyptic, p. 237.

[24] See A. C. Knudson, The Religious Teaching of the Old Testament (1918), p. 359.

[25] J. Lindblom, StTh, VI (1953), p. 102.

[26] C. R. North, The Old Testament Interpretation of History (1946), pp. 126 f.

of history but an eschatology involving a cataclysmic irruption into history which will bring history to its end.[27] Both John Bright and Walter Eichrodt[28] believe that even the popular expectation of the Day of Yahweh is eschatological, i.e., involving an inbreaking of God into history to judge his foes and to establish his rule.

If this interpretation of the eschatology of Amos is basically correct, we must conclude that the earliest prophetic eschatology expected the Day of the Lord to be a catastrophic visitation of God, breaking into history to manifest his rule in judgment as well as in salvation, and involving a disruption of the present order of both history and nature. These elements are even more clearly portrayed in another early prophet, Zephaniah. Koehler, who recognizes only casual cosmic elements in Amos, sees Zephaniah as the first true prophet of the judgment of the Lord. The Day of the Lord will mean the destruction of the whole earth, including all its creatures. Nevertheless, a remnant escapes unharmed to enjoy God's ultimate salvation.[29]

From this brief survey of two of the pre-exilic prophets, an important point emerges. The prophetic expectation cannot be described as "historical" or "this-worldly" in the sense that it looks for the Kingdom of God to be the product of historical forces. The source of God's Kingdom is suprahistorical; God himself must visit his people. Even in the oldest conceptions, God's kingship could come to pass absolutely only at the cost of a great change which would mark the end of the present state of things and the establishment of something new. "There is no eschatology without rupture."[30] In the careful words of H. H. Rowley, the Day of the Lord was conceived "as the time of the divine breaking into history in

---

[27] S. B. Frost, op. cit., p. 48.

[28] J. Bright, The Kingdom of God (1953), p. 60; see also "Faith and Destiny," Int, V (1951), pp. 9 ff.; W. Eichrodt, Theology of the Old Testament (1961), I, p. 479. Kuhl thinks Amos expected the end of the age (C. Kuhl, The Prophets of Israel [1960], p. 63). For a very different interpretation, see J. D. W. Watts, Vision and Prophecy in Amos (1958), pp. 68–84.

[29] L. Koehler, Old Testament Theology (1957), pp. 222 f.

[30] E. Jacob, Theology of the Old Testament (1958), p. 318.

spectacular fashion. While God was believed to be always active on the plane of history, using Nature and men to fulfil his ends, the Day of the Lord was thought of as a day of more direct and clearly manifest action." The prophetic predictions "were of a future not causally linked with the present."[31] History will not produce the Kingdom, not even history as the instrument of the divine activity. Only the direct visitation of God can bring the divine purpose to its consummation and transform the present order into the Kingdom of God.

This means that our modern way of speaking of the Kingdom in history or beyond history tends to obscure the biblical perspective. It makes too sharp a break between history and eschatology. In the Old Testament, the cleavage between history and eschatology is never radical. The God who will manifest himself in a mighty theophany at the end of history has already manifested himself during the course of history.[32] The final visitation may be properly called eschatological, for whatever form of existence results from this final visitation, it is conceived of as *final*; i.e., it brings God's redemptive purpose to its ultimate consummation.

An Earthly Hope

Although the Old Testament hope may be characterized as an eschatological hope, it also remains an earthly hope. The biblical idea of redemption always includes the earth. Hebrew thought saw an essential unity between man and nature. The prophets do not think of the earth as merely the indifferent theater on which man carries out his normal task but as the expression of the divine glory.[33] The Old Testament nowhere holds forth the hope of a bodiless, nonmaterial, purely "spiritual" redemption as did Greek thought.[34] The earth is the divinely ordained scene of human existence. Further-

---

[31] H. H. Rowley, *The Growth of the Old Testament* (1950), p. 179.
[32] E. Jacob, *Theology of the Old Testament* (1958), pp. 318 f.
[33] Adam C. Welch, *Kings and Prophets of Israel* (1952), pp. 254 f.
[34] Cf. J. Pedersen, *Israel, Its Life and Culture*, I–II (1926), p. 334.

more, the earth has been involved in the evils which sin has incurred. There is an interrelation of nature with the moral life of man;[35] therefore the earth must also share in God's final redemption. The human heart, human society, and all of nature must be purged of the effects of evil, that God's glory may be perfectly manifested in his creation.

This is true of the most advanced picture of the future in the Old Testament. "For behold, I create new heavens and a new earth; and the former things shall not be remembered or come into mind" (Isa. 65:17; cf. 66:22). A new universe is to be created which will replace the old. This is no new thought but is the summation of a whole aspect of prophetic theology.[36] But the new order in Isaiah is that of a new *earth*, and the description in these chapters of life in the Kingdom is one of material blessings.

Back of the eschatology is the prophet's view of the earth and man's relation to it. The earth is something more than the mere stage of human existence. Man and the world together belong to the order of creation; and in a real sense of the word, the world participates in man's fate. The world is affected by man's sin. The world was designed to reflect the glory of God and to provide the setting for a happy life; but because of sin, evil has infected the world. This intimate relationship is sometimes expressed poetically. Because of human wickedness, "the land mourns, and all who dwell in it languish, and also the beasts of the field and the birds of the air and even the fish of the sea are taken away" (Hos. 4:3). The divine judgment falls not only on man but on the world. This however is not merely poetry but reflects in poetic form the prophetic interpretation of the world and evil.

So radical is the effect of sin in the world that the final redemption can be achieved only by a mighty visitation of God. The blend-

[35] H. W. Robinson, *Inspiration and Revelation in the Old Testament* (1946), pp. 30 f.
[36] Cf. J. Skinner, *The Book of the Prophet Isaiah XL–LXVI* (1917), p. 240. This is the apogee of the concept of a transformation of nature to attain full harmony with a redeemed Israel. See Isa. 11:6–9; 29:17; 30:23 ff.; 32:15, 35, etc.

ing of this idea of the need of a sin-cursed creation for redemption with the concept of the transcendence and glory of God provides the particular form of the eschatological visitation.

When God visits men in history, the earth is shaken (see p. 45); and when God finally visits the earth, both for judgment and for salvation, not only will human society be shaken but the very structure of the world will be disrupted. "The heavens will vanish like smoke, the earth will wear out like a garment" (Isa. 51:6). God will punish the wicked for their iniquity and the heavens will tremble and the earth be shaken out of its place (Isa. 13:13). God will vent his indignation upon the wicked nations; then "all the hosts of heaven shall be dissolved and the heavens shall be rolled together as a scroll; and all their host shall fade away, as the leaf fadeth from off the vine, and as a fading leaf from the fig-tree" (Isa. 34:4). At the prospect of judgment, the land will tremble, it will rise and fall like the River of Egypt, the sun will be darkened at noonday (Amos 8:8-9). God will shake the heavens and the earth, the sea and the dry land as well as all the nations (Hag. 2:7). As redemption includes the transformation of the earth, so will God's judgment fall not only upon the nations of men but also upon the world. This is no mere poetic symbolism but concrete realism.[37]

The dissolution of the natural order is not designed to accomplish its destruction but to make way for a new perfect order arising out of the old imperfect one. God will create new heavens and a new earth (Isa. 65:17, 66:22) where there will be untroubled joy, prosperity, peace, and righteousness. The final visitation of God will mean the redemption of the world; for a redeemed earth is the scene of the future Kingdom of God. The prophets again and again look forward to the deliverance of the creation "from the bondage of corruption," and the description is often couched in simple physical terms. The wilderness will become fruitful (Isa. 32:15), the desert will blossom (Isa. 35:2), sorrow and sighing will flee away (Isa. 35:10). The burning sands will be cooled and the dry places be

[37] Cf. H. W. Robinson, *Inspiration and Revelation in the Old Testament* (1946), pp. 29-30.

springs of water (Isa. 35:7); peace will return to the animal world so that all injury and destruction is done away (Isa. 11:9); and all this results because the earth becomes full of the knowledge of God (Isa. 11:9).

The question arises of the extent to which such language is to be taken literally or symbolically. We have already discovered that the language of divine theophany which looks back to God's visitation at Sinai can be used poetically both of visitations to deliver his servant from personal danger and of historical visitations to bring judgment upon an erring people (see pp. 50 ff.). Does this not give us reason to interpret all such language about the eschatological shaking of the world, collapse of the heavens, etc., as poetical language used to depict the indescribable glory of the final theophany? The importance of this question can be seen by the fact that this terminology provides the conceptual material for the "apocalyptic" of the New Testament eschatology[38] with its view of a cosmic catastrophe bringing this age to a close and introducing the age to come. Is such language anything more than traditional language of Old Testament poetry used to describe the majesty of God?

It is impossible to deny that a poetical element exists in such "apocalyptic" language. The fact that this theophanic language can be employed in an altogether symbolical manner to assert the glory and majesty of God and his transcendence over his creation (Ps. 18; Mic. 1) should warn us against any wooden literalness of understanding. However, the theology which underlies this terminology makes it equally impossible to reduce this language altogether to poetry. The theophanic language describing the eschatological visitation sets forth not only the glory and majesty of God and the subordination and dependence of his creation upon its Creator; it is also an expression of a profound theology of creation and man's place in creation. Man is a creature and as such stands in a real solidarity with all creation. Both man and nature are dependent upon God for their very existence. However, man stands apart in

[38] See Mark 13:24 and parallels; Acts 2:19-20; II Pet. 3:11-13; Rev. 6:12-17; 20:11; 21:1.

that he was created in the image of God and therefore enjoys a relationship to God different from that of all other creatures. This does not mean that man will ever transcend creaturehood. Indeed, the very root of sin is the unwillingness to acknowledge the reality and the implications of creaturehood. The fact that man is a physical creature is not the measure of his sinfulness and therefore a state from which he must be delivered. Rather, the acceptance of his creaturehood and the confession of complete and utter dependence upon the Creator God are essential to man's true existence. Man only truly knows himself and realizes his true self when he realizes that he is a creature and accepts the humble role of one whose very life is dependent upon God's faithfulness and whose chief joy it is to serve and worship his Creator. The root of sin is found in the purpose of man to transcend creaturehood, to exalt himself above God, to refuse to give his Creator the worship and obedience that are his due.

Salvation for man does not mean deliverance from creaturehood, for it is not an evil thing but an essential and permanent element of man's true being. Salvation does not mean escape from bodily, creaturely existence. On the contrary, ultimate redemption will mean the redemption of the whole man. For this reason, the resurrection of the body is an integral part of the biblical hope.[39]

The corollary of this is that creation in its entirety must share in the blessings of redemption. There is no Greek dualism or Gnosticism in the Old Testament hope. The world is not evil per se and therefore a realm from which man must escape to find his true life. When God created the world, he saw that it was good (Gen. 1:31). The goodness of nature has indeed been marred by sin. The earth is cursed for man's sake, bearing thorns and thistles, and condemning man to a life of sweat and toil. This does not, however, suggest

[39] The Old Testament has little to say about resurrection, for it is more concerned with God's purposes for his people in history than with the fate of the individual. However, the teaching of the resurrection of the body found both in Judaism and in the New Testament is a logical consequence of the prophetic theology of man. Cf. T. C. Vriezen, *An Outline of Old Testament Theology* (1958), p. 230. For the teaching of the resurrection, see Robert Martin-Achard, *From Death to Life* (1960).

any intrinsic moral evil in nature. It does not mean that creation has fallen from goodness to evil, so that it has become offensive to its Creator. The world was created for God's glory (Ps. 19:1); and the ultimate goal and destiny of creation, along with man, is to glorify and praise the Creator (Ps. 98:7-9). The world is not a temporary stage upon which man acts out the drama of his mortal existence; neither is it the reality of sin and evil from which man must be rescued. The world was and remains God's world and therefore is destined to play a role in the consummation of God's redemptive purpose.

However, the curse which lies upon nature because of man's sin means that it cannot be the scene of the final realization of God's Kingdom apart from a radical transformation; and the new age of the Kingdom will therefore be so different as to constitute a new order of things. The Kingdom cannot be produced by the normal flow of events but, as Stanley Frost has insisted, only by a cataclysmic irruption of God into history; and the resultant order will be something which is concrete and earthly and yet at the same time supramundane. As Eichrodt has said, "the expected world-order is different in kind from the present one, and this long before the expressions 'the present age' and 'the age to come' had been invented."[40]

HISTORY AND ESCHATOLOGY

The hope of the Old Testament is also a historically orientated hope. By this, we mean to say not only that the establishment of God's reign is seen as the consummation of his working in history, but that the ultimate eschatological hope is directly related to the immediate historical future. The modern mind is interested in chronology, in sequence, in time. The prophetic mind usually was not concerned with such questions but took its stand in the present and viewed the future as a great canvas of God's redemptive working in terms of height and breadth but lacking the clear dimension of

[40] W. Eichrodt, Theology of the Old Testament (1961), p. 491. See also E. Jacob, Theology of the Old Testament (1958), p. 318.

depth. The prophets usually saw in the background the final eschatological visitation of God; but since they primarily concerned themselves with God's will for his people in the present, they viewed the immediate future in terms of the ultimate future without strict chronological differentiation and thus proclaimed the ultimate will of God for his people here and now.

A strictly analytical approach might try to separate these two elements in the Old Testament perspective—the hope of the immediate future, and the hope for the ultimate consummation—and to set one over against the other as two different kinds of hope. Such a critical analytical approach would only serve to obscure the Old Testament perspective. The prophets have a *single hope* which encompasses both the immediate historical and the ultimate eschatological future. The reason for this (to us) strange lack of chronological concern is the theocentric character of Israel's hope. Their hope was not in the future but in God; and the God who would act in the near future to further his redemptive purpose would also ultimately act to bring his purpose to its consummation. Therefore, the prophets usually have a single, though a complex, hope.

Another way of expressing this perspective is to say that the future stands in tension with the present. Eschatology is not an end in itself, standing in detachment upon the horizons of time. Eschatology finds its significance primarily in its relationship to history, for both are concerned chiefly with the will of God for his people. The prophets usually took their stand in the midst of an actual historical situation and addressed themselves to it. They proclaimed God's will for the ultimate future, that in its light they might proclaim God's will for his people here and now. The immediate future is interpreted in terms of God's ultimate purpose. The hope of the Kingdom was not a subject for detached study or for speculative conjecture. Nor was it even a subject of importance primarily for its own sake. The prophets were not philosophers or theologians; they were preachers of the will of God and were burdened for the relationship of Israel to God. This does not mean that the predictive

aspect of prophecy should be minimized so that the prophets become little more than moralists.[41] Prediction played a large and important role in the prophetic message. The question is that of the
prophetic center of gravity or focus of concern. This was not the
future per se but rather the will of God and the fate of his people,
especially in their present experience. God who will ultimately bring
his people into the Kingdom is the God who is now concerned with
them and their present sinfulness.

This historical concern is everywhere manifest. The prophets
usually name themselves and address their oracles to Israel or Judah,
sometimes dating their oracles by the year of the ruling king. Their
main objective is to interpret the present in light of the future.
Their oracles are shot through with references to historical persons,
events, and nations. When specific future events are predicted, the
prophets' main concern is to tell Israel how to act at that time in
view of the divinely ordained future.

The prophets often anticipate a divine visitation in the immediate
future; therefore, they speak of the Day of the Lord. Amos' contemporaries entertained bright hopes of political security and eco-
nomic prosperity, which they called the Day of the Lord. Amos
shattered this shallow nonreligious hope with the announcement
that the future holds disaster rather than security. Judgment will
fall upon Damascus and the neighboring peoples; but it will also
fall upon Judah and Israel for their sins. Fire will destroy Jerusalem
(Amos 2:5), and Assyria and Egypt will raze Israel (3:9–11). This
will be a divine visitation (4:12). "The Lord roars from Zion and
utters his voice from Jerusalem" (1:2). It is therefore the Day of
the Lord (5:18–20). God had indeed visited Israel in Egypt; and
for this very reason he must bring a corrective judgment upon them
(3:2).

Yet as Amos gazes into the future, he sees behind the impending
event a further visitation: the eschatological Day of the Lord. The

---

[41] See the excellent remarks of A. S. Peake in *The Servant of Jahweh and
Other Lectures* (1931), p. 83; H. H. Rowley, *The Relevance of Apocalyptic*
(1947), p. 13.

future holds a day of universal judgment (Amos 7:4; 8:8–9; 9:5), and beyond that a day of salvation when the house of David will be revived, the earth become a blessing, and Israel restored (9:11–15).[42]

These two visitations, the near and the far, or, as we may for convenience call them, the historical and the eschatological, are not differentiated in time. In fact, sometimes the two blend together as though they were one day. Isaiah 13 calls the day of the visitation of Babylon the Day of the Lord. The Lord is mustering a host for battle (13:4–6), he will stir up the Medes against Babylon (13:17). Therefore, men are to "wail, for the day of the Lord is near; as destruction from the Almighty it will come!" (13:6.) This historical Day of the Lord is painted against the backdrop of the eschatological Day of the Lord. The Day of the Lord will bring disaster to the earth and a disruption of the heavenly order (13:9–13). Judgment will fall both upon the world of nature and upon men (13:7) when God punishes the world for its evil and the wicked for their iniquity (13:11). Here is a picture of universal judgment. The Day of the Lord is the historical judgment of Babylon; the Day of the Lord is the eschatological judgment of mankind; but the two are seen as though they were one day, one visitation of God.

Zephaniah describes the Day of the Lord (1:7, 14) as a historical disaster at the hands of some unnamed foe (1:10–12, 16–17; 2:5–15); but he also describes it in terms of a worldwide catastrophe in which all creatures are swept off the face of the earth (1:2–3) so that nothing remains (1:18). Yet out of universal conflagration emerges a redeemed remnant (2:3, 7, 9), and beyond judgment is salvation both for Israel (3:11–20) and for the Gentiles (3:9–10).

---

[42] Many scholars feel that Amos 9:8b–15 is not authentic because the message of hope stands in such sharp contrast to the note of judgment in 9:1–4. However, the words of John Bright are here relevant: "True, he [God] called Israel to be the people of his rule, and Israel had egregiously failed and fallen under condemnation. But that fact could not in prophet theology cancel out the victory of God, for that would be to allow that the failure of man is also the failure of God. And no prophet would have dreamed of saying such a thing" (*The Kingdom of God* [1953], p. 87. Quoted by permission of Abingdon Press). So while the sharpness of the different points of view in Amos 9 must be admitted, the final optimistic note can equally well be the last word of the prophet expressing his ultimate confidence in God in spite of Israel's failure.

George Adam Smith describes Zephaniah as "the first shades of Apocalypse."[43] A strict analytical and critical treatment of this prophecy tries to separate the historical from the eschatological and to attribute the latter to a later tradition. Norman K. Gottwald thinks that Zephaniah thought of a historical disaster, but the later development of the theme carried it into suprahistorical realms where the sacrifical feast became part of the events of the end of the world.[44] However, this severe analytical treatment sacrifices an essential element in the prophetic viewpoint: the tension between eschatology and history. We must not try to force the prophets into twentieth-century thought-forms. They were able to view the immediate historical future against the background of the ultimate eschatological goal, for both embodied the coming of Israel's God to judge and to save his people. The focus of attention is the acting of God, not the chronology of the future.

Joel prophesies the visitation of the Day of the Lord as a fearful plague of locusts and drought (1:4–12) and also as a universal eschatological judgment (2:10–11; 3:11–15). It is practically impossible to determine where the description of the natural disaster ends and that of the eschatological enemies begins. Beyond judgment is salvation. Israel, endowed with the gift of God's Spirit (2: 28–29) is seen restored to the land, enjoying the blessings of a redeemed earth (3:16–21). Whether Joel is an early or a late book, this tension between eschatology and history is an essential element in the prophetic perspective.

In all of these prophecies, history and eschatology are so blended together as to be practically indistinguishable. Sometimes, however, the eschatological Day stands in the background on the distant horizon.[45] "In the latter days" Isaiah sees the final era of righteousness and peace (Isa. 2:2 ff.). "In the latter days" Israel will turn to the Lord and David their king (Hos. 3:5). "In the latter days" Israel will be restored, only to be assailed by the evil hosts of Gog

[43] An Exposition of the Bible (1907), IV, p. 574.
[44] A Light to the Nations (1959), p. 333.
[45] See H. H. Rowley, The Unity of the Bible (1953), p. 110.

(Ezek. 38:16). "The days are coming" when God will restore the fortunes of Israel with security and blessing (Amos 9:13 ff.). "The days are coming" when a righteous Branch will spring forth from David to execute justice and righteousness; Judah will be saved and Jerusalem dwell securely (Jer. 33:16). "The days are coming" when God will make a new covenant with Israel and with Judah, writing his law upon their heart and bringing them into a perfect knowledge of himself (Jer. 31:31 ff.). "At that time" God will restore the fortunes of Judah among all the people of the earth (Zeph. 3:20). "In that day" God will visit the earth in judgment (Isa. 2:20 f.). "In that day" God will restore his people that they may serve the Lord and David their king (Jer. 30:8 f.). "In that day" God will reign over them forever (Mic. 4:6 ff.).

This indefinite terminology is used also of historical visitations in the nearer future;[46] and this fact serves only to emphasize the tension between history and eschatology. God is the Lord of history. His lordship is manifested by historical visitations for judgment and deliverance and by an eschatological visitation for final judgment and deliverance. God is the King who comes and who will come. The future is related to the present because both present and future visitations are acts of the same God on behalf of his people. The present is viewed in light of the future; and the proclamation of the future visitations of God, both historical and eschatological, are designed to bring God's people into conformity with the divine will in the present.

These several aspects of the Old Testament hope are closely interrelated. This can be splendidly illustrated by the words of Edmond Jacob:

Although the cosmic aspect holds an important place in Old Testament eschatological concepts, it is not the determining factor: the idea of the end of the world is always secondary to that of Yahweh's coming and Yahweh does not come because the world is going to end, but his coming

[46] Cf. Jer. 46:10; Ezek. 7:19; 13:5; 30:2-3; Obad. 15 for the Day of the Lord; Amos 4:2; Jer. 7:32; 19:6; 48:12; 51:47, 52 for "days are coming;" Mic. 2:4; Isa. 3:18; 5:30; 7:18, 20, 21, 23; Jer. 4:9; 48:41; 50:30; Ezek. 7:6, 7, 10, 12 for "the day" or "in that day."

brings, among other things, the end of the world or more exactly the end of an age, which will be followed by a new period of the world. And as Yahweh is the God who creates life, the catastrophic aspect of eschatology could never be the last word of his coming. The essential place is occupied by the notions of a new creation and restoration. That is why the cleavage between history and eschatology is never radical, for on one side the God who will reveal himself by a grandiose theophany at the end of time has already manifested himself and does not cease manifesting himself in the course of history; and on the other side all historical events are already charged with eternal significance.[47]

AN ETHICAL HOPE

A final characteristic of the prophetic promise is its ethical emphasis. Israel always stands in an ethical tension between the present and the future. The future is a day of hope and promise only for those who are faithful to God; and therefore a constant ethical demand is laid upon Israel to turn from her sins and to submit to God. The main objective of prophecy in the recital of past history and the prediction of future events is the ethical and religious demand made upon Israel to get right with God in the present. Indeed, long passages in the prophetic writings are devoid of both historical recital and prediction but challenge Israel with the immediate will of God. When the future is portrayed, whether in terms of judgment or redemption, it is to enable God's people to repent and so avoid the threatening judgment and to be encouraged by the divine promise of blessing for righteous conduct.

This ethical character of prophecy may be pointedly illustrated by the profound ethical and religious concern of the most "apocalyptic" portions of the Old Testament. Ezekiel is frequently criticized for his narrow nationalism and fantastic apocalypticism. Yet he has been characterized as one of the greatest spiritual figures of all times[48] and is included by Waterman among the greatest ethical prophets.[49]

[47] *Theology of the Old Testament* (1958), pp. 318 f.
[48] W. F. Albright, *From the Stone Age to Christianity* (1946), p. 248.
[49] LeRoy Waterman, *The Religion of Jesus* (1952), pp. 22, 27, 32. Water-

To be sure, Ezekiel's primary eschatological concern is with Israel's future. Israel regenerated and purified (Ezek. 36:25-27) is to be restored to the land (11:17-20) and the two kingdoms to be reunited (34:23 ff.; 37:24 ff.). Under the rule of a Davidic king (34:23; 37:24-25) with a restored temple (40 ff.), she will enjoy the blessings of a universal, eternal kingdom of peace and righteousness (37:26-28; 36:28-30). This however is not really "particularism," for participation in the Kingdom is grounded on moral and religious principles and not upon the fact of Israelitic descent. Ezekiel taught as perhaps no other prophet the freedom and responsibility of the individual (11:17-20; 18:23, 30-32; 33:11). No man would be a recipient of God's blessing because he was a member of the chosen people. Every man was personally responsible to God and would live or die not because he was an Israelite, but because of his righteousness or his sin. While Ezekiel may not have made the application himself, such a teaching certainly suggests implicitly a universal religion. By this emphasis, Ezekiel laid "the foundation of all moral living."[50]

Isaiah 24-27 has such a catastrophic, i.e., apocalyptic, type of eschatology that many critics hold that Isaiah could not have written it but that it must have been written much later, even as late as the third century B.C. Yet the prophetic ethical emphasis is dominant. When God visits the earth in wrath (26:20 f.), a great catastrophe of judgment will fall upon the physical order (24:1, 17-20) and a new order of blessing will emerge (27:2-5). God will then spread a rich banquet for all people and will remove from them the veil of mourning (25:6-7). "He will swallow up death forever, and the Lord God will wipe away tears from all faces, and the reproach of his people he will take away from the earth; for the Lord has spoken" (25:8). However, this promise is not extended to Israel as such but only to a regenerated people. Judgment is to fall upon both priest and people (24:2) because the laws, statutes, and covenant have been

man argues that prophetic and apocalyptic are two mutually exclusive types of religion.

[50] G. A. Cooke, A Critical and Exegetical Commentary on the Book of Ezekiel (1936), p. xxx.

violated (24:5). Salvation is to come to Judah (24:23), but only to a
Judah which has become a righteous nation and keeps faith (26:2).
In the Kingdom, a remnant of the nations which has escaped the
great catastrophe brings homage to God. All antagonism comes to an
end; Zion becomes the center of blessing for all the world.[51] George
Adam Smith was right when he said that these chapters "stand in
the front of evangelical prophecy. In their experience of religion, their
characterizations of God's people, their expressions of faith, their
missionary hopes and hopes of immortality, they are very rich and
edifying."[52]

These illustrations drawn from the most apocalyptic strata of the
prophetic writings suffice to demonstrate that the primary concern
of the prophets is ethical. They are sensitive to the sin and the
faithlessness of Israel. They see God's judgment falling upon Israel
both in the present historical situation and in the future eschatological day. They foresee a restoration, but only of a people which
has been purified and made righteous. Their message both of woe
and of weal is addressed to Israel that the people may be warned
of their sinfulness and turn to God. Eschatology is ethically and
religiously conditioned.

Perhaps the most significant result of the ethical concern of the
prophets is their conviction that it will not be Israel as such that
enters into the eschatological Kingdom of God but only a believing,
purified remnant. This remnant concept points up the basic ethical
character of the Old Testament hope and is of great importance for
the New Testament concept of the church and Israel.[53]

The Israel of the restoration which will experience the final salvation will be only a fragment or remnant of the nation as a whole.
Amos likens the Israel of the past to a brand plucked from the
burning, and the Israel of the future will be like a few scraps of a

[51] A. F. Kirkpatrick, The Doctrine of the Prophets (1910), pp. 486 ff.
[52] An Exposition of the Bible (1907), III, pp. 723 f.
[53] See H. H. Rowley, The Faith of Israel (1956), pp. 117 f.; The Biblical
Doctrine of Election (1950), pp. 70 ff.; E. Jacob, Theology of the Old Testament (1958), pp. 323 f.; J. Bright, The Kingdom of God (1953), pp. 89–92,
passim; V. Herntrich, TWNT, IV, pp. 200–215; G. H. Davies, TWBB, pp.
188–191.

sheep saved from the lion's mouth (Amos 3:12). Isaiah named one of his sons Shearjashub, "A remnant shall return" (Isa. 7:3; see 11: 11-16). Micah uses the phrase, "the remnant of Jacob," as practically synonymous for Israel (Mic. 5:7-8). Jeremiah foretells the reign of the righteous Branch of David when Judah and Israel shall be saved; but this saved Israel is but a remnant of the flock which has been scattered afar (Jer. 23:3-6; see also 31:7).

This future Israel will consist of a believing and faithful remnant. It is difficult to decide whether the prophets anticipate the restoration as a result of the repentance of the remnant, or whether their restoration to the land is the ground of their repentance. In any case, the restored remnant will be forgiven of their sins (Mic. 7:18-19) and will turn to the Lord (Isa. 10:20-23) in mourning and repentance (Zech. 12:10 ff.). Isaiah likens the destruction of a faithless nation to a fallen tree. There remains standing, however, the stump of the tree; "the holy seed is its stump" (Isa. 6:13). "In that day the branch of the Lord shall be beautiful and glorious, and the fruit of the land shall be the pride and glory of the survivors of Israel. And he who is left in Zion and remains in Jerusalem will be called holy, everyone who has been recorded for life in Jerusalem, when the Lord shall have washed away the filth of the daughters of Zion and cleansed the blood stains of Jerusalem from its midst by a spirit of judgment and by a spirit of burning" (Isa. 4:2-4).

The redeemed of the future will experience the eschatological salvation not because they are Israelites but because they are faithful, holy, righteous. Back of this expectation lies the deeper concept, seldom explicit in the Old Testament but constantly implicit, that the true Israel is of the spirit rather than of the flesh. In fact, the entire Old Testament history illustrated the Pauline statement that "not all who are descended from Israel belong to Israel" (Rom. 9:6). Only the remnant of Noah and his family were saved from the flood. Isaac and his seed alone inherited the promises given to Abraham. Joshua and Caleb alone of all Israel entered into the promised land. Elijah was told of seven thousand faithful who had not bowed to Baal. Jeremiah distinguishes between those who are circumcised only in flesh and those who are circumcised in heart (Jer. 4:4; see also Deut. 10:15–16). Here plainly is the concept of an Israel within Israel, of a spiritual Israel within national Israel. As the faithful people within the faithless nation, the remnant does not constitute a separate people. It does, however, as John Bright has pointed out, constitute a "church" within the nation. A distinction begins to be made between the physical Israel and the true Israel, between the actual Israel and the ideal Israel.[54] The distinction rests not upon nationality or cult or race, but upon faith. It is fundamentally a spiritual relationship.

The Israel which will experience salvation is the "church" rather than the nation, the spiritual rather than the physical Israel. The national and physical elements are not sloughed off, but they are subordinated to the spiritual factors.

There is a close relationship between the ethical concern of the prophets and their eschatological perspective. The prophets were not primarily concerned about the time of the eschatological redemption, nor were they primarily concerned with that redemption in itself. They were concerned with the state of God's people in their day and with God's will for his people. It is because of this ethical concern that they have a perspective which, to the modern critical mind, seems confused and even erroneous. Frequently, the prophets sound a note of imminence which, from the point of view of analytic chronology, seems quite wrong. They speak of the nearness of the Day of the Lord (Isa. 13:9; Zeph. 1:7, 14; Joel 1:15, 3: 14; Obad. 15) as though the end of the world lay immediately ahead.

In the Old Testament, this note of imminence is an essential element in the prophetic perspective and must not be forced into modern ideas of chronology but must be interpreted in its own setting. The Day of the Lord for the prophets was *both* the immediate act of God expected in history and the ultimate eschatological visitation. The prophets did not usually distinguish between these two aspects of the Day of the Lord, for it was the same God who would act. The two events are viewed as though they were one.

[54] J. Bright, *The Kingdom of God* (1953), p. 94.

Furthermore, the prophets were not primarily concerned with the question of chronology but with the ethical impact of the future upon the present. Therefore the warning of the nearness of the Day of the Lord is more a note of ethical exhortation than it is a chronological reference. The question of whether they were guilty of a chronological error is therefore the wrong question and fails to appreciate their way of thinking. God *did* act. The Day of the Lord *did* come; and yet, the Day of the Lord continued to be an eschatological event in the future. This tension between the immediate and the ultimate future, between history and eschatology, stands at the heart of the ethical concern of the prophetic perspective. For the important thing is not what is going to happen and when it will happen, but the will of God, who is Lord of both the far and the near future, for his people in the present.

3 The Apocalyptic Interpretation of the Promise

The centuries which followed the restoration from Babylon involved the Jewish people in a historical and theological dilemma whose dark meaning they could not easily interpret. The prophets had proclaimed God's judgments in history upon Israel for her apostasy and disobedience and had held out the hope of repentance, conversion, and the Kingdom of God. When the Jews returned to their land, they renounced their former idolatry, giving themselves devotedly in obedience to the law as never before, separating themselves from sinful alliances with their pagan neighbors (Neh. 8–10). Never had Israel displayed more heroic devotion to the law than in the days of the Maccabees when many devout Jews gladly suffered torture and martyrdom rather than betray their devotion to God and the law (II Macc. 5–7).

However, in spite of Israel's faithfulness, God's Kingdom did not come. Instead came the kingdom of the Seleucids and the determination to turn the Jews away from their fanatical devotion to the law and to force them to adopt Greek habits. This bloody period was followed by a century of Jewish independence; but the increasing worldliness and Greek-loving ways of the Hasmonacan rulers proved that this was not the Kingdom of God. Finally, with the appearance of Pompey in Palestine in 63 B.C., hopes for Jewish sovereignty were crushed under the iron foot of Rome. During the New Testament period, the sight of Roman standards in Jerusalem was a vivid reminder to every devout Jew that while the Kingdom of God might exist in heaven, the kingdom of Rome ruled on earth.

The enigma of the rule of wicked pagan nations instead of God over his righteous people is expressed in the pathetic cry of a first-century A.D. apocalyptist. "If the world has indeed been created for us, why do we not possess our world as an inheritance?" (IV Ezra 6:59.) The hard fact was that the promises of the prophets appeared to be frustrated. Israel was no longer an apostate backsliding people; she was devoted to her God and obedient to his law. She spurned idolatry and meticulously separated herself from uncleanness. The irrational conduct of devout Jews in the practice of their unreasonable religion became an object of ridicule among their pagan neighbors.[1] Still the Kingdom did not come. History was shot through with evils for which there was no prophetic explanation. This perplexing fact demanded a new interpretation of the hope of the Kingdom; and the apocalyptic writings provided such a reinterpretation.

The word "apocalyptic" is derived from the New Testament Apocalypse 1:1 and is applied by modern scholars to a particular type of Jewish writing produced between 200 B.C. and A.D. 100. Most discussions of "apocalyptic" fail to point out that the word is used to describe two different historical phenomena: a genre of literature, and the particular kind of eschatology embodied in this literature.[2]

A preliminary question is that of the religious milieu of this literature. Until recent years, we possessed practically no historical information to answer this question, and scholars differed radically as

---

[1] Juvenal, Satires, XIV, 96 ff.
[2] This distinction is recognized by H. H. Rowley, The Relevance of Apocalyptic (1947), p. 23; W. Bousset in The New Schaff-Herzog Encyclopedia, I, pp. 209–210; E. Lohmeyer in RGG (2nd ed.), I, col. 402–404. Rowley, unfortunately, does not carry out the distinction in his description of the characteristics of apocalyptic.

to the role of these writings in first-century Judaism.[3] Extensive new information about first-century Judaism has come to hand in the so-called Qumran literature, but new problems have also been raised. One fact is clear: the Qumran community prized the apocalyptic writings. This is proved by the fact that fragments of the books themselves or of the sources of several of the apocalypses have been found. This includes fragments of ten manuscripts of Jubilees, fragments of ten manuscripts of four of the five parts of Enoch, and fragments of sources of the Testaments of Levi and of Naphtali.[4] This fact has led some scholars to conclude that the Qumran community, or rather, the proto-Essenes of which it was one community, produced and preserved the apocalyptic literature, and that these writings should be interpreted in the *Sitz in Leben* of the thought of this community.[5] However, H. Ringgren admits only the possibility of an Essenic source for the apocalyptic writings;[6] and while there are marked similarities between the eschatological ideas of the apocalypses and the other Qumran literature, there are also striking differences.[7] Perhaps this problem could be solved if we had sufficient control over these writings to reconstruct the two-hundred-year history of the Essene movement. However, only fragments of the apocalypses or their sources have been found at Qumran, and Cross

---

[3] W. F. Albright (*From the Stone Age to Christianity* [1946], p. 287) held that Jewry swarmed with apocalyptists, while G. F. Moore (*Judaism*, I, p. 127) thought that they were known only by a small circle of religious enthusiasts who were practically ignored by the masses of the people and their religious leaders. See the sound observations by W. D. Davies, *Christian Origins and Judaism* (1962), pp. 19–30; also Joshua Bloch, *On the Apocalyptic in Judaism* (1952).

[4] See J. T. Milik, *Ten Years of Discovery in the Wilderness of Judaea* (1959), pp. 32–35.

[5] See F. M. Cross, Jr., *The Ancient Library of Qumran and Modern Biblical Studies* (1957), pp. 147 ff.; W. Foerster, *Neutestamentliche Zeitgeschichte* (1959), pp. 78–84; H. H. Rowley, *Jewish Apocalyptic and the Dead Sea Scrolls* (1957).

[6] "Jüdische Apokalyptik" in RGG (3rd ed.), I, col. 464.

[7] See Millar Burrows, *The Dead Sea Scrolls* (1955), p. 261. Some of these similarities and differences will be pointed out in the discussion which follows. See the conclusion of W. S. LaSor that "the eschatology of Qumran was messianic rather than apocalyptic." *Studies and Essays in Honor of Abraham A. Neuman* (Meir Ben-Horin et al., eds.; 1962), p. 364.

believes that the apocalypses in their present form as well as other later apocalyptic materials, e.g., II Baruch, the Similitudes of Enoch, II Enoch, IV Ezra, the Assumption of Moses, the Testaments of the Twelve Patriarchs, et al., have not been found at Qumran.[8] Therefore we can hardly conclude uncritically that the views found in the present form of the apocalypses represent the views of the Essenes. We shall therefore deal with the apocalypses as they stand and await further light upon their historical milieu.

As a genre of literature, apocalyptic is notable for several features which set it apart from prophetic literature.[9] There is, however, no sharp break between these two types. Isaiah 24–27 is often called an apocalypse because it shares a distinct catastrophic form of eschatology; but it lacks most of the other characteristics of apocalyptic. Joel and Zechariah 9–14 lay a stronger emphasis on the cataclysmic character of apocalyptic eschatology than does much of the prophetic literature. The book of Daniel is usually called the first of the apocalypses; but in view of the fact that it shows prophetic traits which are lacking in the other apocalypses, Daniel must be contrasted as well as compared with the noncanonical writings, for it stands between the prophetic and the fully developed apocalyptic writings.

REVELATORY CHARACTER

The first characteristic of apocalyptic as a literary genre is suggested by the word itself: it is revelatory in a special and technical

---

[8] F. M. Cross, Jr., *The Ancient Library of Qumran and Modern Biblical Studies* (1957), p. 150.

[9] For some of the standard summaries of these characteristics, see in addition to the titles mentioned in note 2 the following: H. W. Robinson in *A Companion to the Bible* (T. W. Manson, ed.; 1939), pp. 307 f.; A. C. Zenos in *Hasting's Dictionary of Christ and the Gospels*, I, pp. 79–94; R. H. Charles in *HDB*, I, pp. 109–110; also in *Encyclopaedia Biblica*, I, col. 213 ff.; Leslie Fuller in *The Abingdon Bible Commentary* (1929), pp. 188–190; I. T. Beckwith, *The Apocalypse of John* (1919), pp. 166–197; P. Volz, *Die Eschatologie der judischen Gemeinde im neutestamentlichen Zeitalter* (1934), pp. 4–10; J. Paterson, *The Goodly Fellowship of the Prophets*, pp. 256–270; H. Ringgren in *RGG* (3rd ed.), I, col. 464–466; J. B. Frey, "Apocalyptique," *Supplement au Dictionnaire de la Bible* (1926), I, col. 325–354. The list of characteristics differs in the several analyses. The present author comes to several independent conclusions.

sense. We may understand the genius of apocalyptic literature by comparing and contrasting its concept of revelation with that of the prophets. For the prophets, the central content of revelation was the will of God, and the chief means of revelation was the word of the Lord. The prophets foretold God's action in the future, that in its light they might reinforce the present demands of the divine will. Furthermore, while the prophets received revelations through dreams and visions (e.g., Isa. 6; Ezek. 1; Jer. 24), these were not their main "stock in trade." "The word of the Lord," the dynamic message of the living God, was the center of their experience. Dreams and visions were never an end in themselves but were accompanied by an explanatory word. "All apparitions are verbal and revelatory. . . . the visual part vanishes, the word remains. That is true of nearly all visions. Revelation in visions is also verbal revelation."[10] Often the word came without dream or vision but as a powerful inner voice laying hold of the prophet. The word of God "is in my heart as it were a burning fire shut up in my bones, and I am weary with holding it in and I cannot" (Jer. 20:9).

With the apocalyptists, the center of interest has shifted. The living word of the Lord has given way altogether to revelations and visions.[11] God no longer speaks by his Spirit to the prophet. The seer learns the solution to the problem of evil and the coming of God's Kingdom through dreams, visions, or through heavenly journeys with angelic guides. By means of these media the apocalyptist discovers the secrets of the hidden world, the reason for the suffering of the righteous on earth, and when and how the Kingdom will come.

Consonant with this is the consciousness in Judaism that the living voice of God through the prophets was no longer heard. This

[10] L. Koehler, Old Testament Theology (1957), p. 103. See also T. C. Vriezen, An Outline of Old Testament Theology (1958), pp. 233–253.

[11] It is significant that this phrase, "the word of the Lord," occurs frequently in such Old Testament "apocalyptic" books as Zechariah and Ezekiel but almost never in the noncanonical apocalypses as a means of revelation. For the word of God in the apocalypses, see e.g., En. 14:24; 59:2; 61:9; 69:29; 102:1; 104:9; 106: 13; Apoc. Bar. 10:1. In this, Daniel is closer to the apocalypses than to the prophets.

is reflected in the history of the Maccabean times (I Macc. 4:46; 9:27; and 14:41), in Josephus[12] and in the rabbinic literature.[13] The emphasis which the Qumran community placed upon the inspiration of the Holy Spirit[14] cannot be understood as a revival of the prophetic gift, for the Qumran sectaries did not receive a word direct from the Lord but believed themselves to be inspired by the Holy Spirit to find the true hidden meaning in the Old Testament Scriptures. Thus we read in the Commentary on Habakkuk, "And God told Habakkuk to write down the things which will come to pass in the last generation, but the consummation of time He made not known to him. And as for that which He said, *That he may read it easily that reads it*, the explanation (*pesher*) of this concerns the Teacher of Righteousness to whom God made known all the Mysteries (*razim*) of the words of His servants the Prophets."[15] God had revealed his secrets (*razim*) to the prophets, but the true explanation or exposition (*pesher*) of these secrets was reserved by God until the end time when the Holy Spirit would enable the Teacher of Righteousness, the founder of the Qumran community, by inspiration to penetrate these mysteries and thus to understand and teach the events of the end time.[16] "The revelation pictured in the Hymns is in terms of its contents the same as the knowledge which can be gained through study of the law and the prophets."[17]

This "apocalyptic exegesis"[18] which found the secrets of the end

---

[12] *Adv. Apion*, I, 8.

[13] See the references in Eduard Schweizer, *BKW: Spirit of God* (1961), p. 13; (See Kittel's *TWNT*, VI, pp. 383–384); Strack and Billerbeck, *Kommentar*, I, p. 127 ff.; G. F. Moore, *Judaism*, I, p. 237. The rabbis believed that God did on occasion speak through a heavenly voice (*bath qol*); but this was only a substitute for the absence of the direct word of God from the Holy Spirit (Strack and Billerbeck, *Kommentar*, I, p. 125).

[14] See Hymns 12:11–13; M. Mansoor, *The Thanksgiving Hymns* (1961), p. 174.

[15] See A. Dupont-Sommer, *The Essene Writings from Qumran* (1961), p. 262. By permission of Basil Blackwell, Oxford.

[16] See F. F. Bruce, *Biblical Exegesis in the Qumran Texts* (1959), pp. 7–17.

[17] Otto Betz, *Offenbarung und Schriftforschung in der Qumransekte* (1960), p. 118.

[18] The term is that of F. M. Cross, Jr., *The Ancient Library of Qumran and Modern Biblical Studies* (1957), p. 82.

time in an inspired interpretation of the law and the prophets is very different from the revelations of the apocalypses. The Qumran teachers sought a true understanding of the revelation given long ago, whereas the apocalyptists announced new revelations directly from God.[19] They were concerned to explain the tragic evil of their own times and to offer hope for its final resolution. Enoch, for instance, is shown that the fearful evil among men is due to the fallen angels who disclosed to men secrets of unrighteousness which led to universal corruption (En. 9:6). The solution to the problem of evil will not be found in this age but only at the coming of the Lord "with ten thousands of His holy ones to execute judgment upon all and to destroy all the ungodly" (En. 1:9). Secrets of the heavenly world and secrets of the eschatological denouement are the two themes about which the apocalyptists declare new revelations received by visions, dreams, or by journeys to the heavens.

We should note that some of the books usually called apocalyptic are not true apocalypses in that they are not revelations of this apocalyptic sort. The Testaments of the Twelve Patriarchs contains eschatology of an apocalyptic character, but the literary form of the book as a whole excludes it from the genre of apocalyptic. Each of the twelve patriarchs gives a brief résumé of his life, makes a moral application, and usually offers a brief prediction of the future of his descendants. In form the book is imitative prophecy rather than apocalyptic. Its primary concern is ethical rather than eschatological, and it contains a universalism which is alien to the usual spirit of the apocalypses. We would agree with Glasson that this book ought not to be included in the apocalyptic genre.[20]

The Psalms of Solomon are not apocalyptic, i.e., revelatory, but are patterned after the Old Testament Psalms. Since two of the psalms anticipate the coming of Messiah and the Kingdom of God (Ps. of Sol. 17, 18), they are usually included in the survey of Jewish apocalyptic literature. The Sibylline Oracles put into the

[19] Millar Burrows, The Dead Sea Scrolls (1955), p. 261.
[20] T. F. Glasson in London Quarterly and Holborn Review (1952), pp. 104–110.

mouth of a pagan prophetess predictions about the future including the coming of the Kingdom, and therefore in the broadest sense of the word they may be included in the apocalyptic type. However, eschatology plays a very small role in the oracles, and they should be classed as apologetic rather than apocalyptic literature.

These last three books illustrate the fact that apocalyptic literature and apocalyptic eschatology are not identical. The apocalyptic type of eschatology found expression in literary forms which were not apocalyptic in character.

ARTIFICIAL NATURE

A second characteristic of apocalyptic literature is the imitative and artificial nature of its revelations. This stands in contrast to the visions of the canonical prophets which involved genuine subjective experiences. Theology traditionally has recognized a transcendent factor in the prophetic experiences which sometimes operated through the media of psychological visions but sometimes transcended them. Many scholars attempt to explain these experiences exclusively in terms of psychological experience and often appeal to the realm of the abnormal; but there remains an element which defies control.[21] Whatever the explanation, prophets often experienced visions and dreams and then proclaimed the Word of the Lord to the people. Other prophets displayed little of the ecstatic element but spoke from deep inner conviction borne in upon them by the Word of God.

An entirely different atmosphere pervades apocalyptic literature. Visions and dreams have become a form of literature. While a few of the apocalyptists may have experienced some sort of subjective experience as a result of brooding over the problem of evil,[22] Porter was correct in saying that "the visions described in the apocalypses

[21] See the survey of recent criticism by O. Eissfeldt in *The Old Testament and Modern Study* (H. H. Rowley, ed.; 1951), pp. 134-145. See also the relevant chapters in J. Lindblom, *Prophecy in Ancient Israel* (1962), and Abraham J. Heschel, *The Prophets* (1962).

[22] See G. H. Box, *The Ezra-Apocalypse* (1912), p. lxvii.

are beyond doubt in the majority of cases not real visions at all, but literary fictions."[23] This is not to deny that the apocalyptists, like the prophets, believed that they had a real message from God to deliver to the suffering faithful.[24] There is, however, a great difference. The prophets, out of real experiences, confronted the people with the will of God, reinforcing the challenge with announcements of God's purposes for the future. The apocalyptists, brooding over unfulfilled promises of the prophets and the evils of their own times, used vision as a literary device to assure an imminent deliverance. The prophets were essentially preachers of righteousness to the nation. We do not know that the apocalyptists engaged in any kind of public ministry. They were authors, not preachers. Thus the apocalyptists in imitation of the visions of the prophetic literature transposed subjective vision into a literary genre.

Pseudonymity

A third characteristic of this literature is pseudonymity. Usually, the apocalyptists employed the transparent fiction of using the name of an Old Testament saint as a means of validating their revelations. Many critics feel that the real authors did not intend to deceive their readers by this devout fiction. But if the prevailing interpretation of the reason for pseudonymity is valid, the authors expected their pious fraud to be taken seriously. How could such revelations gain a hearing? The age of prophecy was over; God no longer spoke through the living voice. Since therefore the apocalyptist could not speak as a prophet, "thus saith the Lord," he borrowed an Old Testament saint and attributed the visions to him, that the writing might receive authority from the prophetic name.

In this connection, we must observe that Daniel is not really pseudonymous, for Daniel is not an Old Testament saint whose name could be used to give authority to a book. Apart from the stories in the book of Daniel, he is a nonentity. This fact lends

---

[23] F. C. Porter, *The Messages of the Apocalyptical Writers* (1905), pp. 40 f.
[24] See H. H. Rowley, *The Relevance of Apocalyptic* (1947), p. 14.

credence to the view that, whatever the date of composition of the book of Daniel, it embodies traditions of a historical person who lived in the time of the captivity.[25]

PSEUDO-PROPHECY

A fourth literary characteristic of the apocalypses is pseudo-prophecy. The apocalyptist not only borrowed an Old Testament saint as the alleged author of his book; he also rewrote the history of Israel from the time of the alleged author to his own time but cast it in the form of prophecy.

The prophets were men known to their audiences, and they took their stand in their own historical situation and proclaimed their message to their own generation against the background of the coming Kingdom of God. Each prophetic writing reflects the events of its own time which the critic must study to determine the date of the book; but historical events were foretold which yet lay in the future. The apocalyptists, on the other hand, often took their stand in the distant past and rewrote history down to their own times as though it were prophecy, attributing the pseudo-prophecy to the pseudo-author. It is frequently possible to follow the course of the alleged prophecy down to the actual author's own time, when the predictions of historical events become vague and the Kingdom is expected to come. The obvious advantage of this technique was that it allowed the author to reinterpret history in terms of his particular interest, to explain the reasons for the prevalence of evil and the sufferings of the righteous, and to assure the faithful that deliverance was at hand and the Kingdom about to come.

SYMBOLISM

A final characteristic of the apocalyptic genre is the use of symbolism in declaring the will of God for his people. This goes back

---

[25] Professor Rowley modifies the usual theory of pseudonymity, apparently in recognition of the fact that Daniel is not truly pseudonymous (*The Relevance of Apocalyptic* [1947], pp. 37 f.).

to the prophets. To illustrate Israel's corruption, Jeremiah buried a linen cloth until it was spoiled (Jer. 13:1–11). His vision of two baskets of figs illustrated God's future purpose for his people (Jer. 24). Ezekiel's vision of the resurrection of a valley full of bones pictured the future return of Israel to national life (Ezek. 37). Hosea's tragic marital experience was a divinely commanded symbol for God's relationship to his adulterous people (Hos. 1). With Zechariah, symbolic visions reach a new dimension. The first six chapters contain eight visions, each involving developed symbolism. The last vision is of four chariots with red, black, white, and dappled-gray horses which came from between two mountains of bronze to patrol the four corners of the earth (Zech. 6:1–8). These chariots are symbolic of the accomplishment of God's will in all the earth. They are not designed to be identified with specific historical events or personages. Furthermore, the visions in these six chapters are concerned more with contemporary events than with the future. The eschatological chapters of Zechariah (9–14) have less of symbolism than the earlier chapters.

In the use of symbolism, Daniel goes beyond the other prophets. He employs symbolism to represent events in history. The great image of gold, silver, brass, and iron represents four successive nations in history before the coming of God's Kingdom (Dan. 2)', as do the four beasts in Daniel 7. This device is greatly elaborated in the subsequent apocalypses. In Enoch's dream-vision (En. 85–90), the course of history is retold in symbolism of a veritable menagerie. Ezra's vision of an eagle with twelve wings, three heads, and eight opposing wings represents historical events connected with Rome (IV Ezra 11). Such symbolism is not always employed. Enoch's apocalypse of weeks (En. 91:12–17; 93:1–10) and the Assumption of Moses trace the course of history without the use of apocalyptic symbolism.

We must now consider the characteristics of apocalyptic eschatology. The world-view expressed in the apocalyptic literature is a distinct philosophy of history.[26] It provided an explanation for the apparent frustration of the prophetic promises, the delay of God's Kingdom, and the domination of history by evil in spite of the faithful observance of the law by the righteous.

DUALISM

The first characteristic of apocalyptic eschatology is its dualism. This term can be confusing for it is used in the study of ancient religions to designate several different kinds of thought.[27] For the sake of clarity, these must be summarized. (a) There is a simple ethical dualism, found in the Old Testament, which contrasts righteousness with unrighteousness, life with death (Deut. 30:19). (b) A physical-metaphysical dualism takes two forms. In biblical thought, the Creator stands over against his creation; but the creation remains God's world and therefore is never viewed as evil per se. In Platonic thought, this metaphysical dualism takes a more absolute form, contrasting the noumenal world and the phenomenal world. In later Gnostic thought, the phenomenal world is the sphere of darkness, evil, and sin. (c) There is a cosmological dualism which sees two ultimate principles of good and evil, or light and darkness, in the universe struggling with each other. In Zoroastrianism, this cosmic dualism embodies the principles of good and evil—light and darkness—in the evil spirit Ahriman and the good spirit Ahura Mazda (Ormazd). While these are coeval in origin, they are not coeternal, for ultimately light will overcome and destroy darkness. (d) An eschatological dualism contrasts a present time of evil, suffering, and death with a future time of righteousness and life. Developed Zoroastrian doctrine taught that Saoshyant, a hero born of the seed of Zoroaster and therefore not a god, would raise all the dead,

---

[26] See F. C. Burkitt, *Jewish and Christian Apocalypses* (1914), pp. 32 f.

[27] See G. Mensching in *RGG* (3rd ed.), II, col. 272–274; R. Marcus in *Biblical Research*, I (1957), p. 34; H. W. Huppenbauer, *Der Mensch zwischen zwei Welten* (1959), pp. 103–115. These authors do not agree exactly in their analyses of the several types of dualism, and they use differing terminology.

bringing them into a blessed immortality which was described in terms of the perfection of earthly life.[28] The consummation was thus a final rehabilitation of the entire race. Meanwhile, Ormazd would bring about the final defeat of Ahriman. Thus in Zoroastrianism, cosmological dualism issued in an eschatological dualism.

The study of dualism in Jewish thought has received new impetus from the discovery of the Qumran literature. H. W. Huppenbauer's book, Der Mensch zwischen zwei Welten, is entirely devoted to the question of dualism in this literature. Two outstanding types of dualism appear in the Jewish literature. The physical-metaphysical dualism of the Greek type needs little discussion, for apocalyptic dualism usually remains in the Jewish tradition of creation and never becomes a Greek dualism in which creation is the sphere of evil.[29] The dualism of Jewish literature, both apocalypses and the Qumran writings, combines a cosmological dualism which sees the world in the grip of two conflicting spirits, God and Satan, who is also called Belial, Beliar, and Mastema, with an eschatological dualism which limits the struggle between these two powers to this age and sees the complete triumph of God in the age to come. Many scholars assume that this development of dualistic thought in Judaism is the result of Zoroastrian and/or Gnostic influences. Indeed, we have already noted that some scholars feel that these alien influences introduced a type of eschatology into Jewish thoughtwhich was essentially different from the genuine Hebrew hope (see pp. 53 ff.). However, this is an assumption which cannot be taken for granted. The Zoroastrian eschatology, outlined above, is found in the Bundahishn, which is later than Muhammad and may or may not embody pre-Christian ideas. In any case, as George Foot Moore has pointed out, such alleged influences if they occurred only served to sharpen concepts already intrinsic in Jewish thought.[30]

[28] See R. C. Zaehner, The Teachings of the Magi (1956), Chap. 10; The Dawn and Twilight of Zoroastrianism (1961), Chap. 15.

[29] Possible hints of this Greek influence may be seen in Jub. 23:31; En. 103:3–4 and Wisd. of Sol. 3:1–4; 8:13.

[30] Judaism, II, pp. 394 f. Moulton thinks that "most of the parallels between the higher doctrines of the two religions are pure coincidences" (J. H. Moulton, Early Zoroastrianism [1913], p. 309). See also the judicious remarks by Ralph

Therefore, our problem is to try to determine the relationship between the dualism in the Jewish literature, particularly in the apocalypses, and in the prophetic writings.

The prophets were conscious of the contrast between God's world and the world of nature and history. While nature and history were under the divine sovereignty, both lay under the curse of sin and the burden of evil. God's Kingdom would be established only by an inbreaking of God into history which would result in both a moral and a physical transformation of the present order.

The problem of undeserved, unexplained evil in historical experience led the apocalyptists to extend and sharpen this contrast between man's world and God's world, and between the present sinful order and the future redeemed order of God's Kingdom. They developed the concept of evil spirits and Satan, already found in the Old Testament,[31] to the point of a sharp dualism, which never became absolute. Neither the apocalypses nor the Qumran literature abandon essential monotheism. God has both created Belial and will finally destroy him.[32] However, the apocalyptists often felt that the only explanation for the radical evil in the world is the rule of evil spirits. The Testament of Dan describes the present as "the kingdom of the enemy" (6:4). The Manual of Discipline speaks of this age as the time of "the dominion of Belial" (1:17, 23; 2:19) as does the War Scroll (14:9). This overthrow of evil and the establishment of God's Kingdom can be accomplished only by a cataclysmic inbreaking of God. The most vivid picture of this apocalyptic visitation is found in the Similitudes of Enoch[33] in which the end is

---

Marcus (*Biblical Research*, I [1957], p. 45, n. 89) who quotes M. P. Nilsson that this problem is "that at once most obscure and most difficult problem in the religious history of this period."

[31] See H. H. Rowley, *The Faith of Israel* (1956), p. 80; T. C. Vriezen, *An Outline of Old Testament Theology* (1958), p. 156; E. Jacob, *Theology of the Old Testament* (1958), pp. 70-72.

[32] See War Scroll 13:11.

[33] The date of the Similitudes has been reopened by the fact that this is the only part of Enoch of which fragments have not been found in the Qumran literature. This fact has led many scholars to the conclusion that the Similitudes in their present form are the product of a Jewish-Christian community. However, Burrows expresses reservations at this point (*More Light on the Dead Sea*

brought about by the glorious coming of a heavenly Son of Man when the present order is transformed into the glorious order of the Kingdom of God.

There is, however, no necessary relationship between an elaborate angelology and this more "transcendental" form of the Kingdom. This is proved by the fact that in the first part of Enoch, where great emphasis is placed upon the mischief caused by the fallen angels, the Kingdom is pictured as an earthly order (10:16–22), whereas in the Similitudes and in IV Ezra, where there is the most pronounced eschatological dualism, the fallen angels play a very small role.[34]

This dualistic eschatology gradually developed the terminology of "this age" and "the age to come." This terminology is implicit in Enoch, but it emerges explicitly only in IV Ezra, Baruch, the Pirke Aboth, and the New Testament.[35] However, as Volz points out, the concept is surely older than the terminology, and we may think of the dualistic concept of the two ages before the explicit terminology emerges.

Scrolls [1958], pp. 71 f.); and to the present author, it still remains a fact that there is nothing in the Similitudes which could not have arisen in a Jewish milieu. The Similitudes "may well have been a separate work, . . . unknown at Qumran and only later combined with other parts of the book" (Burrows, loc. cit.). See also H. H. Rowley, Jewish Apocalyptic and the Dead Sea Scrolls (1957), pp. 8–9.

[34] The elaborate angelology of En. 65–69 belongs to a Book of Noah (See R. H. Charles, The Book of Enoch [1912], pp. 129 ff.) Fragments of a book of Noah have been found at Qumran (See D. Barthélemy and J. T. Milik, Discoveries in the Judean Desert [1955], I, pp. 84–86.)

[35] En. 16:1, "the age shall be consummated"; 48:7, "this world of unrighteousness"; 71:15, "he proclaims unto thee peace in the name of the world to come"; IV Ezra 7:50, "The Most High has made not one Age but two"; 7:113, "The Day of Judgment shall be the end of this age and the beginning of the eternal age that is to come"; 8:1, "This age the Most High has made for many, but the age to come for few"; see also Apoc. Bar. 14:13; 15:7; Pirke Aboth 4:1, 21, 22; 6:4, 7. The earliest of these references do not appear to be earlier than the last of the first century A.D. For other references, see P. Volz, Die Eschatologie der jüdischen Gemeinde [1934], p. 65. Volz cites a possible reference to Hillel (ca. 30 B.C.), but this is not certain. Since IV Ezra belongs late in the first century A.D., it would appear that this dualistic terminology of the two ages appears first in our Gospels; and if, as seems most likely, it was used by Jesus, his use is the earliest recorded instance of the terminology.

Indeed, the idea goes back to the Old Testament. The coming of the Kingdom of God will mean a transformation of the present order which is often so radical that the result is a new order. It is impossible to trace a gradual evolution from a simple earthly concept of the Kingdom to a radically different transcendental concept. Nor is there a single eschatology, nor a single line of development, but rather several different eschatologies. Jubilees and Enoch 1–36 picture an earthly kingdom with no Messiah. The kingdom in Enoch 1–36 is pictured in materialistic terms. The righteous will live and beget thousands of children; the earth will become fruitful and yield wine in abundance and grain a thousandfold; and uncleanness will be purged from the earth and all nations will worship God (10:16–22). The Psalms of Solomon 17–18 pictures a Davidic Messiah arising from among men, but he is supernaturally endowed to destroy his enemies and to inaugurate an earthly kingdom with Jerusalem as its capital.

The Similitudes of Enoch 37–71 (see pp. 89 f., above) has a different messianic personage: a pre-existent supernatural Son of Man who has been kept in heaven since creation, who will sit on the throne of his glory (En. 47:3; 51:3; 62:5) to judge the living and the resurrected dead (51:1–5). While the resurrection is described in transcendental language (62:16), the redeemed will dwell upon a transformed earth. "I will transform the earth and make it a blessing; and I will cause mine elect ones to dwell upon it" (45:5). "In those days shall the mountains leap like rams, . . . and the earth shall rejoice, and the righteous shall dwell upon it, and the elect shall walk thereon" (51:4–5). This is not transcendental dualism but a radically developed prophetism along the lines of Isaiah 65:17 and 66:22.

A transcendental eschatology is found in the fifth book of Enoch (92–105). The final redemption will witness a new heaven but not a new earth (91:16). The righteous are raised from Sheol (92:3–5) but not in bodily resurrection. The portals of heaven will be open to them (104:2), and they will become companions of the hosts of heaven (104:6). "The spirits of you who have died in righteousness shall live and rejoice, and their spirits shall not perish" (103:4).

This brief survey suggests that different apocalyptists dwelt upon various Old Testament pictures of the future, some emphasizing one aspect and others another aspect. Some prophets had described the future in familiar earthly terms, while Isaiah 65 and 66 looked for a new order so different that it was called a new heaven and a new earth. Some apocalyptists emphasized the earthly aspect of the Old Testament hope, sometimes in very sensuous terms. Others, pondering the implications of a new heaven and a new earth, tried to picture what this transformed order would be like. Two first-century A.D. apocalypses combined the ideas of an earthly kingdom followed by a new creation (IV Ezra 7; Apoc. Bar. 29–30). Charles has well said that these conceptions are in germ and principle as old as Isaiah 65 and 66.[36]

The problem of eschatological dualism and the character of the age to come is placed in sharp focus by the eschatology of the Qumran literature. While the terminology of the two ages does not occur,[37] the Qumran community was sure that it was living in the end times and that the Kingdom of God would shortly be established. Hippolytus tells us that the Essenes believed that the world would be destroyed by fire at the end of time,[38] and this teaching is found in the Qumran writings.[39] Logically, one might think that the only form of a kingdom which could follow such a conflagration would be a transcendental heavenly order; but logic does not determine apocalyptic thought. Out of the universal conflagration will emerge a renewed earthly order. A Commentary on Psalm 37 says, "they will possess the sublime Mountain of Isra[el] and will

[36] R. H. Charles, *The Apocalypse of Baruch* (1896), p. 81. These two forms of the kingdom are found also in rabbinic terminology and are called "the days of the Messiah" and "the age to come." For the entire question, see Joseph Klausner, *The Messianic Idea in Israel* (1955), pp. 339–348, 354–365, 408–419. See also W. D. Davies, *The Setting of the Sermon on the Mount* (1964), pp. 115, 121, for the roots of the concept of the two ages in Isa. 65 and 66.

[37] H. W. Huppenbauer, *Der Mensch zwischen zwei Welten* (1959), p. 111, n. 471.

[38] *Refutation*, 9, 22.

[39] Hymns 3:19–39.

taste [everlasting] delights [in] his holiness."[40] The Hymns (13:12) speak of the new creation after the existing things have been destroyed.[41] Fragments found in caves 1, 4 and 5 appear to have contained a detailed description of a restored temple to be built on earth which would be miraculously renewed.[42]

We conclude that, with the possible exception of Enoch 91–105, a truly transcendental dualism is not found in the Jewish literature. The Kingdom in the age to come is a new and transformed order, but it is a renewed earth; and the life of the age to come means earthly existence freed from all corruption and evil. The pictures of this redeemed order can be accounted for in terms of reflection upon the implication of Isaiah's promise of new heavens and a new earth.

HISTORY AND ESCHATOLOGY

A second characteristic of apocalyptic eschatology is its nonprophetic view of history. The primary concern of the prophets was with God's dealings with Israel in their present historical situation. They constantly referred to Israel's history in order to illustrate God's gracious ways and Israel's faithlessness, and announced God's judgments in the immediate future. They also saw in the background the eschatological Day of the Lord when the divine purpose would be fulfilled. However, both the past and the future are usually cited because of their relevance for the present. The prophetic message is addressed to Israel in a specific historical situation, and the present and the future are held together in an eschatological tension.

The apocalyptists lost this tension between history and eschatology. The present and the future are quite unrelated. The apocalyptists could not understand the prophetic interpretation of present

---

[40] Dupont-Sommer's translation in *The Essene Writings from Qumran* (1961), p. 272. See F. M. Cross, Jr., *The Ancient Library of Qumran and Modern Biblical Studies* (1957), p. 62, n. 53.

[41] See also Manual of Discipline 4:25.

[42] M. Mansoor, *The Thanksgiving Hymns* (1961), p. 178. See also Millar Burrows, *More Light on the Dead Sea Scrolls* (1958), p. 351; Matthew Black, *The Scrolls and Christian Origins* (1961), p. 136.

historical experience as God's judgment upon his people for their apostasy, for Israel was no longer faithless.

Has another nation known thee besides Israel? Or what tribes have so believed thy covenants as these tribes of Jacob? Yet their reward has not appeared and their labor has borne no fruit! For I have traveled widely among the nations and have seen that they abound in wealth, though they are unmindful of thy commandments. Now therefore weigh in a balance our iniquities and those of the inhabitants of the world; and so it will be found which way the turn of the scale will incline. When have the inhabitants of the earth not sinned in thy sight? Or what nation has kept thy commandments so well? Thou mayest indeed find individual men who have kept thy commandments, but nations thou wilt not find.

IV Ezra 3:32–36

These words vividly picture the apocalyptists' problem. Israel has received and kept God's law; why then are God's people suffering under the heel of godless pagans? This cannot be God's doing. The only answer given is that God's ways are inscrutable. There is no other answer. "And how can one who is already worn out by the corrupt world understand incorruption?" (IV Ezra 4:11.) Ezra's response is one of utter despair. "It would be better for us not to be here than to come here and live in ungodliness, and to suffer and not understand why" (IV Ezra 4:12). The only solution offered is that God will yet act to rectify the evil of the present. This age will finally come to its end, and God will inaugurate the new age of righteousness. However, this final redemptive act of God has no bearing upon the present. God is no longer redemptively active in the present. God is the God who will come (IV Ezra 5:56; 6:18; 9:2); he is no longer God who comes to his people in history. The apocalyptists do not view the coming of the Kingdom as the final act of God who is constantly acting in history. On the contrary, their writings offer a theological solution in explanation of the failure of God to bring deliverance to his afflicted people. These books are therefore not truly historical documents but theological treatises attempting to solve the enigma of history which can no longer be interpreted in prophetic terms.[43]

[43] See F. M. Cross's comment that in the Qumran literature "prophecy be-

In its view of history, Daniel is close to the prophets. The first part of the book stands entirely apart from later apocalypses in that it relates allegedly historical events and God's care for his servants in history. Daniel directly addresses the king to teach him that "the Most High rules the kingdom of men, and gives it to whom he will, and sets over it the lowliest of men" (Dan. 4:17; see 5:21). It was God who had invested Nebuchadnezzar with his regal power (2:37); and it was God who humbled the king until he learned the lesson that "the Most High rules the kingdom of men and gives it to whom he will" (4:32). The God of Daniel is both the God of history and the God of the consummation.

PESSIMISM

An important element in this loss of the prophetic concept of history is a third characteristic, which we may call "pessimism." Some scholars object to the use of this term.[44] We agree with these authors that it is erroneous to call the apocalyptists pessimists in their ultimate outlook, for they never lost their confidence that God would finally triumph. They possessed an ultimate optimism which was born of an unshakable faith. Indeed, the very purpose of their writings was to assure God's people that God had not really forsaken them.

This, however, is not what we mean by pessimism. The apocalyptists reflect pessimism about this age. The blessings of the Kingdom cannot be experienced in the present, for this age is abandoned to evil and suffering. Such a theology was forced upon devout Jews as the only possible explanation for their evil plight. Israel was obedient to the law and yet did not find deliverance. The solution to the problem of evil was thrown altogether into the future. The present is

---

came eschatology" (*The Ancient Library of Qumran and Modern Biblical Studies* [1957], p. 55, n. 35a). A different note is sounded in the Zadokite Fragments where the appearance of the Teacher of Righteousness and the rise of the community is attributed to God's acting in history (1:7; 2:9; 8:3; ed. R. H. Charles).

[44] Adam C. Welch, *Visions of the End* (1922), pp. 43 f.; H. H. Rowley, *The Relevance of Apocalyptic* (1947), p. 36.

irremediably evil; and the righteous can only submit patiently to suffering, sustained by the assurance that deliverance will surely come when the evil age is over and the new age of the Kingdom arrives.

This apocalyptic pessimism must be illustrated. In Enoch 6, the evil character of the age is attributed to fallen angels. The earth is overrun by evil and corrupted by the fallen angels. God has not, however, ultimately relinquished his sovereignty. Jewish theology could never tolerate such a thought. God continues to rule nature (2:1; 5:1, 2; 84:3). He has power over all things (9:5). He is the King of the ages (12:3, 22:14; 25:7), King over all kings (63:4), God of the whole world (84:2). Yet he has become essentially a "deistic" God. While God sees and permits evil, he allows it to exercise its influence on earth without restraint. After recounting the fearful evil the fallen angels have wrought, contrary to the purpose of God, Enoch complains, "And Thou knowest all things before they come to pass, and Thou seest these things and Thou doest suffer them, and Thou dost not say to us what we are to do to them in regard to these" (9:11). Evil has got out of hand, but God has no word for his people in their fearful plight, except the promise of final deliverance.

Again, the hopelessly evil character of the age is illustrated by a passage in the Similitudes of Enoch. When Wisdom descended from her dwelling place in heaven to dwell with men, she found no place but had to return to heaven and take her seat among the angels to await the messianic times. However, "unrighteousness went forth from her chambers; Whom she sought not she found, and dwelt with them" (En. 42:3; cf. 48:1, 91:10; 94:5).

Again in the Dream-Visions of Enoch, God personally guided the experiences of Israel throughout its history until the Babylonian captivity. Then God withdrew his personal leadership, forsook the temple, and surrendered his people to wild beasts to be torn and devoured. God "remained unmoved, though He saw it, and rejoiced that they were devoured and swallowed and robbed, and left them to be devoured in the hand of all the beasts" (En. 89:58). Then God turned the fortunes of the nation over to seventy shepherds, instructing them as to the number of Jews who might be slain. However, the shepherds were self-willed and faithless, ignoring the divine directive and permitting fearful evils to befall God's people. When reports of the evil conduct of the shepherds were brought to God, he laid them aside and remained unmoved and aloof (89:71, 75). A record was made of the angels' faithlessness that they might be punished on the day of judgment when Israel would be delivered. Between the years 586–165 B.C., God was conceived to be inactive in the fortunes of Israel. God's people found themselves at the mercy of faithless angels. No deliverance could be expected before the messianic era.

Finally, this pessimism is vividly portrayed in IV Ezra. This book does indeed retain a formal doctrine of God's activity in history. Israel's sufferings have come not from evil angels but from God's hand (3:27, 30; 5:28) because of her sins (3:25). Theologically, Ezra must admit that Israel is a sinful people; yet precisely at this point lies his problem. Israel alone has received God's law and kept it (6:55–59), while the Gentiles have rejected it (3:31–34; 7:20–24). Therefore, because God has spared the ungodly and preserved his enemies but has destroyed his people (3:30), Ezra is faced with an insoluble problem which issues in abject despair. He wishes he had never been born (4:12), for the righteous who suffer undeservingly are worse off than the dumb beasts who cannot think about their fate (7:66). The only hope lies in the future. By divine decree, there are two ages: the present age is hopelessly evil, but the future age will witness the solution to the problem of evil (4:26–32; 7:50; 8:1–3). The righteous therefore must now patiently resign themselves to evil in the confidence of a solution in the age to come and are not to be disturbed because the masses perish. God himself is not moved by the death of the wicked (7:60, 61, 131; 8:38, 55). This age is evil; hope belongs altogether to the age to come.

Daniel stands apart from the later apocalypses in that this pessimistic note is strikingly absent. If the focus of the last half of the book is the coming of God's Kingdom, it is not because the author despairs of God's acts in history. On the contrary, God's deliverances in history are apparent. He delivered his servants from the fiery furnace, demonstrating to Nebuchadnezzar that he was God. He delivered Daniel from the lions, convincing Darius of the glory of his dominion. It was God who set Nebuchadnezzar on his throne (Dan. 2:37) and removed Belshazzar (5:24-28). The God of Daniel, whose sovereignty will in the latter days shatter all other sovereignties (2: 44), manifests his sovereignty in historical acts. God is both Lord of the end and of present history. Indeed, God's name is to be blessed forever because "he changes times and seasons; he removes kings and sets up kings" (2:21). The succession of kingdoms is overruled and ordered by the Most High who "rules the kingdom of men and gives it to whom he will" (4:25). A central theme of the book is that God is the living God, whose "kingdom shall never be destroyed, and his dominion shall be to the end. He delivers and rescues, he works signs and wonders in heaven and on earth" (Dan. 6:26). God never abandons the stage of history; he remains Lord of all. Indeed, it is because he remains the Lord of history that he will finally establish his Kingdom on the earth.

DETERMINISM

A fourth characteristic is determinism. The course of this age is predetermined, and must run its course to completion. The Kingdom does not come even though the righteous deserve it, because certain fixed periods must first unfold. Therefore, the Kingdom must await the appointed time. Little emphasis is placed upon a sovereign God who is acting through these appointed times to carry out his purposes. Rather, God himself is awaiting the passing of the times which he has decreed. "For he has weighed the age in the balance, and measured the times by measure, and numbered the times by number; and he will not move nor arouse them until that measure is fulfilled."[45] The entire course of human history is prerecorded in heavenly books (En. 81:1-3; 103:1-2).

---

[45] IV Ezra 4:36-37. See also En. 81:2 and the note by R. H. Charles, *The Book of Enoch* (1912), pp. 91 f.

Since the time of the end is fixed, the present age is often thought of as divided into certain determined periods. The Dream-Visions of Enoch divide time, from the captivity to the end, into seventy periods during which Israel is given to the care of seventy shepherds (En. 89:72; 90:1, 5). Only when the seventy periods have passed can the end come. The apocalypses usually asume that the fixed periods have nearly run out, and therefore the end is about to come.

ETHICAL PASSIVITY

A final characteristic may be called ethical passivity. The apocalyptists are not motivated by strong moral or evangelical urgency. The prophets continually appealed to Israel to repent and to turn from their sins to God. Judgment is to fall upon a sinful nation, but the Kingdom will one day come for a righteous remnant. The problem of the apocalyptists was created by their conviction that Israel was the righteous remnant—but did not inherit the Kingdom. The apocalyptic and rabbinic definitions of righteousness are basically the same: obedience to the law. This is clearly illustrated in IV Ezra and the Apocalypse of Baruch.[46] Therefore the apocalyptists devoted very little space to ethical exhortation. The two notable exceptions are the Testaments of the Twelve Patriarchs and the last part of Enoch (92–105). The Testaments have a strong ethical emphasis with a noteworthy stress on inward righteousness and the ethic of love; but this sets the book apart from the usual atmosphere of apocalyptic literature. The book is not in fact apocalyptic in form (see p. 82).[47] The last section of Enoch defines righteousness in terms of obedience to the law (99:2, 14) and has little apocalyptic in the strict sense of the word. The scholars[48] who insist upon a strong ethical emphasis in apocalyptic literature draw most of their illustrations from the two

[46] See H. M. Hughes, The Ethics of Jewish Apocryphal Literature (n d.), pp. 125–133. This position is supported by W. D. Davies in his essay, "Apocalyptic and Pharisaism" in Christian Origins and Judaism (1962), p. 22.

[47] Ibid., pp. 51–62.

[48] R. H. Charles, A Critical History of the Doctrine of a Future Life in Israel, in Judaism, and in Christianity (2nd ed.; 1913), pp. 190–193; H. H. Rowley, The Relevance of Apocalyptic (1947), pp. 172 f.

canonical apocalypses and from the Testaments of the Twelve
Patriarchs. However, precisely this difference in ethical concern is one
of the factors which distinguishes Daniel and Revelation from other
apocalypses.[49]

Ethical exhortation is lacking because there is a loss of a sense of
sinfulness. The problem of the apocalyptists is found in the fact that
the true Israel does keep the law and therefore is righteous, and yet
is still permitted to suffer. IV Ezra seems to be an exception to this
statement, for the author at several points expresses a profound sense
of sinfulness (4:12; 7:118). This however is counterbalanced by a
sense of the righteousness of God's people who have received the
law (3:32; 5:29; 8:29), have kept it (3:35; 7:45) and therefore have
a treasury of works before God (6:5; 7:77; 8:33). Ezra's problem is
a theological one. The biblical interpretation of the destruction of
Jerusalem should lead to a recognition of the sinfulness of God's
people, for only great sin could merit such a fearful judgment. Reflecting on this principle, Ezra is thrown into confusion. Israel must
be guilty of great sin; the prophetic interpretation of recent history
demands this conclusion. This is Ezra's inherited theology. And yet,
as a matter of fact, Israel is not sinful! She has kept the law. This
problem created a tension in the author's mind which led to deep
despair (7:118) and a pitiful cry to God to deal with his people in
terms of grace (8:6). Thus Ezra's conviction of sin is more theoretical theology than a deep conviction. Throughout the book we
meet the contrast between the righteous few who have kept the law
(Israel) and the mass of men who perish but about whose fate God
is unconcerned (6:56; 7:61; 7:131; 8:38).

Here is another point where Daniel stands closer to the prophets
than to the later apocalyptists. He does not claim deliverance for
Israel because they are God's covenant people and therefore merit the
divine blessing. God's covenant is conditional and God's blessings
can be enjoyed only by "those who love him and keep his commandments" (Dan. 9:4). Daniel has an acute consciousness of sin; and
his prayer breathes the ethical earnestness of the prophets. Israel is

[49] See G. E. Ladd, EQ, XXIX (1957), pp. 98–100.

not righteous; she has forsaken the law and ignored the prophets (9:5 f.) and is deservedly suffering because of her sinfulness. Daniel can only plead the mercy of God as the ground of forgiveness (9:17 f.). This ethical emphasis extends even to the heathen. Daniel exhorts the king to "break off your sins by practicing righteousness, and your iniquities by showing mercy to the oppressed, that there may perhaps be a lengthening of your tranquility" (4:27). Here is the prophetic note: If the king will turn to the Lord, he will experience the divine blessing. God has a due regard for the free decisions of men and renders to them their fate in conformity to their conduct. This is a note missing in Jewish apocalyptic.

It is time to summarize our findings. The apocalyptic eschatology can be understood as a historical development of the prophetic eschatology as the latter is interpreted against the background of the historical evils of the post-Maccabean times. Both prophetic and apocalyptic eschatology can conceive of the establishment of the Kingdom only by an inbreaking of God; both are essentially catastrophic. In both, the Kingdom will be a new and transformed order, redeemed from all corruption and evil. The apocalyptic dualism results from a sharpening of concepts found in the prophets.

However, apocalyptic eschatology has lost the dynamic concept of God who is redemptively active in history. The apocalyptists, contrary to the prophets, despaired of history, feeling that it was completely dominated by evil. Hope was reposed only in the future. The harsh experiences of the last two centuries B.C. left the apocalyptists pessimistic of any divine visitation in history. God would visit his people to deliver them from evil only at the end of history. Thus the prophetic tension between eschatology and history was lost. God is alone the God of the future; he is God of the present only in a theoretical sense. Redemptive history becomes altogether eschatology; and eschatology has become a guarantee of ultimate salvation, not an ethical message to bring God's people face to face with the will of God.

PART III

THE FULFILLMENT OF THE PROMISE

4 Fulfillment without Consummation

"In those days came John the Baptist, preaching in the wilderness of Judea, 'Repent, for the kingdom of heaven is at hand'" (Matt. 3:1 f.). John's appearance found a hearty response among the Jews. Messianic movements had arisen in those days, but most of them were political in character.[1] The Qumran sect had withdrawn from Jewish society to seek new revelations of the divine will; but these revelations came not from prophets who announced, "Thus saith the Lord," but from an inspired and therefore correct exposition of the law and the prophets. The sect looked forward to the fulfillment of Deuteronomy 18:18 when a prophet would arise who would bring fresh revelations from God. Until that time, "they shall not depart from the whole counsel of the Torah."[2] The apocalyptists, pondering

[1] See W. R. Farmer, *Maccabees, Zealots and Josephus* (1956); T. W. Manson, *The Servant-Messiah* (1953).

[2] *Manual of Discipline* 9:9. (See William Hugh Brownlee, *The Dead Sea Manual of Discipline* [1951], *in loc.*) Some scholars believe that the Righteous Teacher was himself designated the prophet; but this passage, like I Macc. 4:44, places the appearance of the prophet in the future. See Oscar Cullmann, *The Christology of the New Testament* (1959), pp. 19–21; A. Dupont-Sommer, *The Essene Writings from Qumran* (1961), pp. 94–95, n. 3; F. M. Cross, Jr.,

the prophets and brooding over the evils of current history, wrote messages of encouragement to assure the righteous that though they seemed forsaken, God would soon intervene to save them and bring the promised day of salvation.

In John the Baptist, the word of God once more was proclaimed. John appeared as a prophet in fulfillment of the prediction in Isaiah 40:3. His camel's hair garb and leather girdle were doubtless intended to recall the dress of Elijah (II Kings 1:8). Luke asserts that "the word of God came to John . . . in the wilderness" (Luke 3:2). The people saw in John a new prophet (Mark 11:32) inspired by the Holy Spirit.

Here was a new thing. God had once again spoken. The prophetic Spirit was once more active in Israel. It does not require a vivid imagination to picture what excitement the appearance of John must have caused throughout Israel. The scanty notices in our Gospels hardly do justice to the impact of his appearance as a new prophet rather than as a political revolutionary or separatist or writing apocalyptist. For John revived the role of the ancient prophets. He did not claim the authority of an Old Testament saint. He did not recite apocalyptic disclosures to unravel the enigma of the plight of God's people. He did not proclaim a sure salvation and imminent deliverance for Israel. He offered no timetable of eschatological events, and he painted no pictures of the new order. In these matters he stands apart from the apocalyptists and in line with the prophets. It is not impossible that John was for a time a member of the Qumran community "in the wilderness" (Mark 1:4); but if so, he left it because the Holy Spirit moved in him in a new way. He could no longer be satisfied with esoteric exegesis, even though the Qumran sectaries believed they were inspired of the Spirit to find the true meaning of Scripture.[3]

Qumran had no prophetic word directly from God, nor did it have

---

The Ancient Library of Qumran and Modern Biblical Studies (1957), pp. 168–169.

[3] See above, pp. 81 ff. for a discussion of Qumran. See J. A. T. Robinson, Twelve New Testament Studies (1962), pp. 11–27.

a message for Israel as a whole. Its residents were concerned only to find the meaning of Scripture for their own separatist group. John, on the other hand, like the prophets of old, had a message directly from God for all Israel. His message consisted of the announcement that God was about to act. God would again visit his people. The Kingdom of God was at hand, and it would be inaugurated by a messianic personage who is designated only as the Coming One. It is an evidence of the historical credibility of our records that John does not call him the Messiah—a title we would expect if the historical tradition had been as completely reworked by Christian faith as many form critics believe. The main mission of the Coming One would be to separate men. The righteous he would baptize with the Spirit; the wicked he would baptize with fire (Matt. 3:11; Luke 3:16).

The integrity of John's proclamation has often been questioned. The form of John's reference to the baptism of the Spirit is thought to reflect the later Christian experience of Pentecost, and John's proclamation has been interpreted as an announcement only of judgment.[4] However, both the eschatological outpouring of the Spirit (Isa. 44:3-5; Isa. 32:15; Ezek. 37:14, 36:27; Joel 2:28-32) and the eschatological judgment with fire (Mal. 4:1; Isa. 30:27 f., 33; Nah. 1:6) are prophetic concepts, although only the latter is developed at length in the apocalyptic literature. Furthermore, this twofold character of the messianic mission is interpreted in the Q saying (Matt. 3:12 = Luke 3:17). The Coming One will purge his threshing floor, gathering the grain into the barn (salvation) but destroying the chaff with fire (judgment). The fact that the fire is "unquenchable" shows that it is an eschatological concept. If it is objected that the baptism of the Spirit in the Old Testament is not seen as a work of the Messiah,[5] it should be pointed out that neither is judgment by fire a messianic function. Malachi, who pictures most vividly the fiery judgment, has no Messiah. Isaiah 32:1 pictures the messianic King; but he neither bestows the gift of the Spirit (32:15) nor brings a fiery judgment (30:27, 33). If John could attribute one function to

---

[4] See Carl H. Kraeling, *John the Baptist* (1951), pp. 58 ff.
[5] Vincent Taylor, *The Gospel according to St. Mark* (1952), p. 157.

the Coming One, he could also attribute the other.[6] There is, therefore, no adequate reason for rejecting the twofold prophetic announcement of John.

Furthermore, while John speaks as a prophet announcing the fulfillment of the Old Testament promise, the content of his announcement goes a step beyond the earlier prophets in that the Coming One
is the agent of the messianic salvation and judgment. In the Old
Testament, the messianic King does not establish God's rule in the
world; he reigns after God has effectively set up his reign.

It is important to note that John has a dynamic concept of the
Kingdom of God. The Kingdom has come near. These words, interpreted in their context, mean that God is about to act. God will
visit his people for salvation and for judgment. The primary emphasis
of John's proclamation is not upon the approach of the messianic
age nor on the age to come. In fact, John offers no picture of the
state of things to be introduced by Messiah. The Kingdom is rather
the act of God which will bring judgment upon the present order.
The divine act has a negative as well as a positive aspect; the Kingdom of God means both salvation and judgment.

John offered no timetable of the eschatological events. He gave no
indication of the relationship of these two messianic acts of the
Coming One. His message may be paraphrased thus: "The Kingdom
of God is at hand, God is about to visit his people. This divine
visitation will be accomplished by a Coming One who will be the
agent of the eschatological salvation and judgment." It appears that
John expected this twofold messianic work to take place in a single
eschatological event. We shall see later that John himself failed to
understand how Jesus fulfilled this prophecy. (See pp. 158 ff.) From
prison, John sent emissaries with the question whether Jesus was indeed the Coming One or whether another was to be expected who
would actually carry out the eschatological salvation (Matt. 11:2-3).
John believed that the eschatological salvation and judgment would
take place in the near future, even though in typical prophetic fashion

---

[6] See C. E. B. Cranfield, The Gospel according to Saint Mark (1959), pp.
49-51.

he provided no calendar by which these events could be calculated.[7]

John stands apart from contemporary Jewish teachers by his ethical concern. The coming Kingdom is the coming supernatural event; yet it is profoundly ethical in character. Judaism believed that the Kingdom of God would bring salvation to Israel and judgment to her enemies. "For the Most High will arise, the Eternal God alone, and He will appear to punish the Gentiles. . . . Then thou, O Israel, shalt be happy, And thou shalt mount upon the necks and wings of the eagle. . . . And God will exalt thee" (Asmp. of Moses 10:7–9).[8] In a few places (En. 50:1–3; 90:30; 91:14) salvation is extended to Gentiles who repent; but this is rare. More typical is the word, "I will rejoice over the few [Israelites] that shall be saved. . . . And I will not grieve over the multitude of them [Gentiles] that perish" (IV Ezra 7:61 f.). The Qumran community believed that they alone would inherit the Kingdom of God and would be enabled by the reinforcement of embattled angels to destroy all their enemies, including the apostate Jews, in a final eschatological war.[9] John announced that the coming of God's Kingdom means that judgment must begin at the house of God. He flatly rejected Jewish particularism and the ethical passivism which had so often characterized the apocalyptic writings. Jewish ancestry was no guarantee of salvation. Rigid adherence to the scribal tradition assured nothing. John demanded repentance, not in the Jewish sense of accepting the yoke of the law, but in an ethical sense: an acknowledgment of sinfulness and changed conduct. Evidence of such repentance was baptism in water. The source of this rite is a much debated question;[10]

[7] John's message as recorded by John's Gospel (John 1:29) sounds a different note: "Behold, the Lamb of God, who takes away the sin of the world." If this is not interpretation, we can only conclude from a comparison of John with the Synoptics that this was a word of prophetic insight whose implications John himself did not understand.

[8] The eagle is a possible reference to Rome.

[9] See the "War of the Sons of Light against the Sons of Darkness," translated in A. Dupont-Sommer, The Essene Writings from Qumran (1961), Chap. 5.

[10] See H. H. Rowley in Hebrew Union College Annual, XV (1940), pp. 313–334; and "The Baptism of John and the Qumran Sect" in New Testament Essays (A. J. B. Higgins, ed.; 1959), pp. 218–229.

but the most likely solution is that John deliberately adapted Jewish proselyte baptism, thereby saying in effect that Jews stood on the same level with the Gentiles in view of the coming messianic visitation.[11] The Jew had no advantage; he must experience personal repentance as though he were no son of Abraham.

THE FULFILLMENT IN JESUS

"Now after John was arrested, Jesus came into Galilee, preaching the gospel of God, and saying, 'The time is fulfilled, and the kingdom of God is at hand; repent, and believe in the gospel!'" (Mark 1:14, 15.) Mathew's report is even more concise, "Repent, for the kingdom of heaven is at hand."[12]

Our Gospels summarize the preaching of the Baptist and of Jesus in the same words: "Repent, for the kingdom of heaven is at hand" (Matt. 3:2; 4:17). It would be easy to conclude that their message was essentially the same: the proclamation of an imminent eschatological event, the immediate fulfillment of the apocalyptic hope of the visitation of God to inaugurate the Kingdom of God in the age to come.

However similar the wording may be, modern scholarship acknowledges a fundamental difference between the two messages. As we have already seen, Günther Bornkamm recognizes that between John and Jesus "there is a difference like that between the eleventh and twelfth hours. For Jesus calls: the shift in the aeons is here, the kingdom of God is already dawning. . . . It is happening now in

---

[11] T. W. Manson, *The Servant-Messiah* (1953), pp. 44 f.

[12] No difference of meaning is to be seen between "kingdom of God" and "kingdom of heaven" (Greek: the kingdom of the heavens) although the latter may place somewhat more emphasis upon the transcendental source and character of the Kingdom. It is the Kingdom which comes from heaven and enters this world (H. D. Wendland, *Eschatologie* [1931], p. 15). The difference of expression is linguistic, reflecting the Semitic and Greek elements in the Gospel tradition. "The kingdom of the heavens" is a Semitic idiom which would be meaningless to the Greek ear. Matthew alone has the Semitic idiom (34 times) except for some manuscript tradition in John 3:4. "Kingdom of God" is found everywhere in Mark and Luke as well as in Matthew 12:28; 19:24 (?); 21:31, 43. Probably Jesus favored the semitic form of the expression, thus following the usual rabbinic form.

Jesus' words and deeds."[13] Such a conclusion is not to be determined from the terminology alone but from a study of its meaning against the total message and mission of Jesus.

The difference between John and Jesus is suggested by Mark's formulation which interprets Jesus' message to mean that "the time is fulfilled" (Mark 1:15). Jesus did not merely proclaim, as did John, the imminence of divine visitation; he asserted that this visitation was in actual progress, that God was already visiting his people. The hope of the prophets was being fulfilled.

This note of fulfillment is the truly distinctive element in Jesus' message which sets him apart from Judaism. It occurs again and again in the Gospels. Luke introduces Jesus' ministry by recording his sermon in Nazareth whose main theme is fulfillment. Jesus read from Isaiah a promise which looked forward to the messianic salvation. "The Spirit of the Lord is upon me, because he has anointed me to preach good news to the poor. He has sent me to proclaim release to the captives and recovering of sight to the blind, to set at liberty those who are oppressed, to proclaim the acceptable year of the Lord" (Luke 4:18–19). Then he amazed his audience by the assertion, "Today this scripture has been fulfilled in your hearing" (Luke 4:21).

Here was an amazing claim. John had announced an imminent visitation of God which would mean the fulfillment of the eschatological hope and the coming of the messianic age. Jesus proclaimed that this promise was actually being fulfilled. This is no apocalyptic Kingdom but a present salvation. Jesus did not promise his hearers a better future or assure that they would soon enter the Kingdom. Rather he boldly announced that the Kingdom (Herrschaft) of God had come to them. The presence of the Kingdom was "a happening, an event, the gracious action of God."[14] The promise was fulfilled in the action of Jesus: in his proclamation of good news to the poor, release to captives, restoring sight to the blind, freeing those who were

---

[13] *Jesus of Nazareth* (1960), p. 67; see *Jesus von Nazaret* (1956), p. 61; cf. above, pp. 35 ff.

[14] G. Bornkamm, *Jesus of Nazareth* (1960), p. 77.

oppressed. This was no new theology or new idea or new promise; it was a new event in history. "The wretched hear the good news, the prison doors are open, the oppressed breathe the air of freedom, blind pilgrims see the light, the day of salvation is here."[15]

This was an unexpected and astonishing announcement, and the first reaction of the audience was a favorable one; but they marveled that one of their neighbors—one whom they had known from child-hood—could proclaim such a message of the grace of God. Jesus was not trained as a rabbi; he was only a layman. How then could he presume to announce the coming of the messianic age?[16]

The note of fulfillment is again sounded in Jesus' answer to the question about fasting. Jesus explained why he and his disciples did not follow the usual Jewish custom of fasting with the words, "Can the wedding guests fast while the bridegroom is with them? As long as they have the bridegroom with them, they cannot fast" (Mark 2: 19). The metaphor of the bridegroom was not a contemporary messianic expression; but the relationship of Israel to God was described in terms of marriage (Hos. 2:20; Ezek. 16:8 ff.), and sometimes the messianic salvation was depicted in similar terms (see Hos. 2:19–20; Isa. 54:1 ff.; 62:4 f.). The marriage feast thus became a metaphor in Judaism for the messianic consummation;[17] and even though Jeremias believes that the messianic significance of the bridegroom metaphor does not go back to Jesus because his audience would not have

[15] J. Jeremias, *The Parables of Jesus* (1954), p. 94. Jeremias recognizes these as authentic words of Jesus. In his earlier work, *Jesus als Weltvollender* (1930), Jeremias used this incident in Nazareth as the first illustration of Jesus as the "Weltvollender in der Niedrigkeit" (pp. 12 ff.). See also the detailed analysis by N. B. Stonehouse, *The Witness of Luke to Christ* (1951), pp. 76–85. "The coming kingdom of God . . . begins to come to realization through his mighty deeds" (p. 85). G. Duncan, *Jesus, Son of Man* (1949), p. 38: "The age of promise has, for Jesus, given place to one of fulfillment."

[16] J. Jeremias, *Jesus' Promise to the Nations* (1958), pp. 44 f. See also A. R. C. Leaney, *A Commentary on the Gospel according to St. Luke* (1958), p. 119. Jeremias thinks the crowd was angered because Jesus omitted the word of judgment upon the Gentiles. For a different interpretation, see J. W. Bowman, *The Intention of Jesus* (1943), pp. 92–97, who thinks "words of grace" refers to the manner of Jesus' preaching, not to the message.

[17] See J. Jeremias, *TWNT*, IV, p. 1094; Strack and Billerbeck, *Kommentar*, I, p. 517.

understood it in these terms, he admits that Jesus did announce the presence of the messianic time of salvation. It would be meaningless for the disciples to fast "who are already in enjoyment of the New Age!"[18] The time of fulfillment is here.

A saying found in different contexts in Matthew and Luke echoes this central note of the fulfillment of the Old Testament hope. "Blessed are the eyes which see what you see! For I tell you that many prophets and kings desired to see what you see, and did not see it, and to hear what you hear, and did not hear it" (Luke 10:23–24 = Matt. 13:16–17). Since neither Mark nor Luke includes this saying in his account of the parables, it is likely that Matthew has placed it in a new context; but this critical question is not important for our purpose. Both Matthew and Luke associate this saying with the Kingdom of God, and both agree that it means that the hope of former generations has become experience. Many prophets and kings looked forward to something; but they looked in vain, for it did not come to them. What they longed for has now come to men; and this can be nothing less than the promised messianic salvation.[19]

Fulfillment is again asserted in Jesus' answer to John's perplexity concerning the correctness of his message about the Coming One. Jesus replied in words which echo the promise of the messianic salvation in Isaiah 35:5–6, "Go and tell John what you hear and see: the blind receive their sight and the lame walk, lepers are cleansed and the deaf hear, and the dead are raised up, and the poor have good news preached to them" (Matt. 11:4–5; cf. Luke 7:22). In these words Jesus claims that the blessings of the messianic salvation are present. There is indeed reason for John's perplexity, for the fulfillment is not taking place along expected lines. The eschatological consummation does not appear to be on the horizon. The point of Jesus' answer is that fulfillment is taking place without the escha-

---

[18] J. Jeremias, The Parables of Jesus (1954), p. 42, n. 82. See also Jesus als Weltvollender (1930), pp. 21 ff. See V. Taylor, The Gospel according to St. Mark (1952), pp. 210 f., for a defense of the messianic use of the bridegroom metaphor by Jesus.

[19] See T. W. Manson, The Sayings of Jesus (1949), p. 80; W. G. Kümmel, Promise and Fulfilment (1957), p. 112.

tological consummation. Therefore Jesus pronounced a special beatitude upon those who are not offended by the character of the messianic fulfillment (Matt. 11:6). The fulfillment is indeed taking place, but in unexpected terms. The promise of the last days and of the eschatological salvation is being fulfilled even now.[20]

FULFILLMENT WITHOUT CONSUMMATION

The preceding discussion is not exhaustive but has selected several of the most important passages which indicate a present fulfillment of the Old Testament hope. The entire ministry of Jesus must be interpreted in terms of this fact, for the fulfillment consists not in a new teaching or a new manner of life or new concepts of God, but in a new event. Something happened in the person and ministry of Jesus which constituted the fulfillment of the Old Testament promise. Our study therefore cannot be limited to the words of Jesus but must also take into account his entire mission.

However, this message of fulfillment is accompanied by a view of the Kingdom of God which is futuristic and eschatological. Side by side with these sayings of a fulfillment in history are equally important sayings about a future apocalyptic coming of the Kingdom. This eschatological message may best be illustrated not by several proof texts but by the fundamental dualistic structure of Jesus' teaching. The Gospels constantly represent Jesus as teaching that the consummation of the Old Testament promise of God's Kingdom, which is in process of fulfillment, will occur only in the age to come.

We have found that a dualistic structure was implicit in the eschatology of the prophets because they saw the present order, including both nature and history, marred by evil; and they therefore looked for a new order to be brought about by a redemptive inbreaking of God. This new order would be freed from all evil and would involve the redemption both of God's people and of the earth on which they

---

[20] W. G. Kümmel, *Promise and Fulfilment* (1957), pp. 111 f. Kümmel, however, goes too far in speaking of "the presence of the messianic consummation" (*Heilsvollendung*). The Gospels do not confuse fulfillment and consummation. This passage is discussed in greater detail below, pp. 158 ff.

dwelt. This implicit dualism became explicit to a greater or less degree in the various writings of the intertestamental period until it acquired the technical terminology of "this age" and "the age to come" in IV Ezra and the rabbinic tradition.

Both the dualistic structure and the dualistic terminology of the two ages are placed in the mouth of Jesus by the evangelists. Furthermore, the two-age terminology appears in every stratum of the Gospel tradition except Q.[21] The terminology of the two ages is also found in the Epistles of Paul.[22] These data suggest several very interesting facts. The earliest certain literary sources for this dualistic terminology are the epistles of Paul;[23] and if our Gospels accurately preserve the language of Jesus' teaching, he may have been the first to use this terminology.[24]

The most important of these sayings, from a critical point of view, is that of Mark 10:30. When the young man asked Jesus how he might inherit eternal life (Mark 10:17), he had no thought of life as a present possession in the Johannine sense. He was concerned about his future destiny, the life of the age to come. Probably he had in mind the words in Daniel when "many of those who sleep in the dust of the earth shall awake, some to everlasting life, and some to shame and everlasting contempt" (Dan. 12:2). In the subsequent discussion with his disciples, Jesus equated eternal life with the Kingdom of God (Mark 10:23-25), and also with the age to come. In this age,[25] his disciples will enjoy certain rewards in return for the sacrifice

---

[21] Mark (Mark 4:19; 10:30), M (Matt. 13:39-40; 28:20), L (Luke 16:8), Matt. 24:3; 12:32, and Luke 20:34-35.

[22] See Gal. 1:4; Rom. 12:2; I Cor. 1:20; 2:6, 8; 3:18; II Cor. 4:4; Eph. 1: 21. For a discussion of the Pauline dualism, see G. E. Ladd in EQ, XXX (1958), pp. 75-84.

[23] "The witnesses [from the rabbinic writings] before 70 A.D. are very infrequent and uncertain" (H. Sasse in TWNT, I, p. 207).

[24] We must recognize the possibility that this terminology existed in rabbinic Judaism and that Paul brought it into the Christian tradition. However, for this there is no proof. It is more likely, in view of the appearance of the terminology in our sources, that it came into the Christian tradition through Jesus' teaching, and Paul uses this same terminology which was also emerging simultaneously in rabbinic idiom.

[25] The word is kairos, meaning "time." This seems to be the only place in Jewish or Christian literature where kairos is used in place of aion in the idiom

they are called upon to make, but they are also to expect persecutions (Mark 10:30). The supreme gift, eternal life, belongs to the age to come. So far as this saying is concerned, apart from the age to come God's people will not experience eternal life.

The dualistic terminology also appears in Mark 4:19 in the parable of the sower. "The cares of the age," the concern for security, wealth, and recognition, which characterize this age so oppose the word of the Kingdom of God that it can be choked and become unfruitful. The character of this age is hostile to the Kingdom of God.

A saying in Luke's special source contrasts "the sons of this age" with "the sons of light" (Luke 16:8). While these expressions have no parallel in the rabbinic writings, we find "the sons of light" contrasted with "the sons of darkness" in the Qumran literature. Although it appears infrequently in the Synoptics (Matt. 5:14; Luke 22:53), in John the contrast between light and darkness becomes a central theme of Jesus' teaching. The idiom is parallel to "the sons of the kingdom" and "the sons of the evil one" in Matthew 13:38.

In Luke's account of Jesus' discussion with the Sadducees about the resurrection, Luke adds this dualistic terminology to his Marcan source. "The sons of this age marry and are given in marriage; but those who are accounted worthy to attain to that age and to the resurrection from the dead . . ." (Luke 20:34-35) will no longer die but will be imperishable like the angels. If this is a secondary saying, it seems to represent the thought of Jesus. Death belongs to this age, and therefore marriage is an absolutely necessary institution. But the age to come will be the age of eternal life when men will no longer die but will enter upon a new level of immortal existence.

Matthew alone records the expression, "the consummation of the

---

"this age," but it is used elsewhere in the New Testament in an eschatological context where it is synonymous with *aion*; Heb. 9:9 (*enestos kairos*) and in Rom. 3:26; 8:18; 11:5; II Cor. 8:14 (*ho nun kairos*). (See H. Sasse in *TWNT*, I, p. 206; G. Delling in *TWNT*, III, p. 463). The interchange between *aion* and *kairos* as well as *kosmos* is further illustrated by the use of *saeculum, tempus*, and *mundus* in IV Ezra (see H. Sasse, *TWNT*, I, p. 206; Strack & Billerbeck, *Kommentar*, IV, pp. 844 ff.). The methodological problem recently raised by James Barr (*Biblical Words for Time* [1962]) need not concern us here.

age." This age will be terminated by the Parousia of the Son of Man (Matt. 24:3), by the judgment of men (13:39 f.) when the righteous will be separated from the wicked (13:49). The same expression occurs in the promise of the risen Jesus assuring his disciples of his presence with them to the consummation of the age (Matt. 28:20), i.e., until his Parousia and the coming of the Kingdom of God in the new age.

Many scholars believe that the Gospels do not correctly record the words of Jesus and that he could not have used the two-age terminology. While it is clear that several uses of the phrase are secondary, there is no convincing reason to conclude that the terminology does not in fact go back to Jesus. G. Dalman says, "It is clear that the ideas, 'this age,' 'the future age,' *if Jesus used them at all,* were not of importance in His vocabulary. . . . The idea of the 'sovereignty of God' filled the place of that of the 'future age.' "[26] This is a surprising statement in view of the fact that he had already said, "the true affinity of the idea of the sovereignty of God, as taught by Jesus, is to be found, not so much in the Jewish conception of *malkuth shamayim* as in the idea of the 'future age,' or that of the 'life of the future age.' "[27] However, if the *idea* of the two ages is found in Jesus' teachings, we should admit the probability of the terminology unless strong reasons prevent it. Dalman is right, as we shall see in the next chapter, that the Kingdom of God is primarily the sovereignty of God; but this sovereign rule of God will be eschatologically manifested, bringing this age to its end and inaugurating the age to come into which God's people will enter.

Bultmann regards the terminology as secondary but recognizes the integrity of the thought pattern expressed in the two ages.[28] Taylor also admits that the substance of Mark 10:30 is authentic although he feels that the precise form of expression is later.[29] However, it is

[26] *The Words of Jesus* (1909), p. 148. See also the long note in W. G. Kümmel, *Promise and Fulfilment* (1957), p. 49.
[27] G. Dalman, *The Words of Jesus* (1909), p. 135.
[28] *Jesus and the Word* (1934), p. 156.
[29] *The Gospel according to St. Mark* (1952), p. 435.

difficult to feel the force of Vincent Taylor's objection to the linking of eternal life with the age to come in Mark 10:30, for it is at this very point that the significance of the terminology and of the thought pattern underlying it is to be found. In the words of T. W. Manson, who was not inclined to "play up" eschatological concepts, "Parousia and Judgment mark the division between the present age and the age to come. They usher in what is described as 'The Kingdom of God' or as 'life.' These two terms appear to be used interchangeably."[30] One might add, both the Kingdom of God and eternal life belong to the age to come. We must agree with Cranfield that the objection to linking eternal life with the age to come in Jesus' teaching is valid only if the eschatological element in his teaching is very much less important than it seems to be.[31]

A further element in the dualism of Jesus' teachings is the role of Satan in this age. The roots of the idea of Satan are to be seen in Job 1, when one of the "sons of God" impugns Job's sincerity before the Lord and is permitted to bring upon him all sorts of evils. This evil spirit not only is the accuser of the saints but also can intrude his influence into human affairs.[32] This rudimentary idea of a supernatural spirit who opposes the well-being of God's people was developed in later Judaism to an elaborate demonology with hosts of fallen evil angels, sometimes with and sometimes without a head; and it appears in the New Testament in a far more restrained form than in much of the Jewish literature.[33]

Paul characterizes this situation by speaking of Satan as the "god of this age" whose object it is to keep men under his control by holding them in darkness of unbelief (II Cor. 4:4). This pattern is reflected in Jesus' temptation when Satan showed him in imagination all the nations of the world in a moment of time and said, "To you I will give all this authority and their glory; for it has been delivered to me, and I give it to whom I will" (Luke 4:6). Such a saying cannot be taken in an ultimate sense; there is no absolute Persian

---

[30] *The Teaching of Jesus* (1935), p. 276.
[31] *The Gospel according to Saint Mark* (1959), p. 333.
[32] See G. von Rad, *TWNT*, II, pp. 42 ff.
[33] For the Old Testament teaching of Satan, see above, p. 89, n. 31.

dualism in the Bible. God forever remains the "King of the ages" (I Tim. 1:17). However, throughout the entire New Testament, including the teachings of Jesus, this age is viewed as an age in which Satan has been permitted in the sovereign purpose of God to exercise a tragic sway over men. He is referred to as a strongly armed man who guards his house (Mark 3:27). Men must be saved from his power (Matt. 6:13).[34] He may take possession of the wills of men and cause them to perpetrate monstrous evil, as in the case of Judas' betrayal of the Lord (Luke 22:3). He is eager to bring testings upon Jesus' disciples (Luke 22:31) and constantly aims to frustrate the working of the Kingdom of God among men (Mark 4:14; Matt. 13:39). Disease may be described as a bondage to Satan (Luke 13:16). Matthew 12:26 (= Luke 11:18) speaks of Satan's kingdom or realm, and the demons who are able to take possession of men are his "angels" (Matt. 25:41). The tragedy of men who are outside the blessings of God's Kingdom is described by the phrase, "sons of the evil one" (Matt. 13:38). This does not refer to particular sinfulness but only to the fact that so far as the controlling principle of life is concerned, it is satanic in source rather than of God.

Only the age to come will witness the destruction of Satan. While no description of the place or portrayal of the event occurs in the Gospels, as it does often in apocalyptic literature,[35] there is an eternal fire which is prepared for the Devil and his angels (Matt. 25:41; cf. Rev. 20:10). Reference to this judgment is found in Mark 1:24 when the demons ask Jesus if he has come to destroy them. That there are so few references in our Gospels to the eschatological destruction of the Devil is due to the important fact that the focus of interest is not the future but the present. Nevertheless, the pattern is clear. Satan is the "god of this age." Until God destroys Satan and his power, the new age cannot come; or better, when the Kingdom of God comes, Satan will be destroyed, and this age of evil and death will give way to the age to come and eternal life.

Professor Manson correctly described the significance of this dual-

---

[34] Tou ponerou probably should be translated, "from the evil one" as RSV mg.
[35] For example, En. 21:7–10; 54:1–6; 56:1–5; 90:24–27.

istic structure. "The essential thing for the understanding both of the Ministry of Jesus and the theology of Paul is the doctrine of the two kingdoms: the Kingdom of God and the kingdom of Satan. All the evils under which men suffer, and all the evils which they commit, may be regarded as the manifestation in history of the power of the evil kingdom. All men's hopes for the future—the future of the world or of the individual—are bound up with the triumph of the Kingdom of God over the kingdom of Satan. That, when it comes, is the coming of the Kingdom of God in power."[36] Manson goes on to say that the distinctive thing about Jesus is that in some real sense the Kingdom of God had come, even though in an unexpected way. "What we call the Ministry of Jesus is the Rule of God."[37]

This is precisely the central problem in the theology of the Gospels. The Kingdom of God is the future eschatological victory over Satan, yet it is also present event. How can the Kingdom of God be both future and present? How can a future apocalyptic order be conceived of as present in history? How are we to conceive of Jesus' mission as introducing the time of fulfillment of the Old Testament hope, while the time of consummation remains in the future?

Many scholars have felt that they must choose one center of emphasis and exclude the other as secondary. Those who follow Consistent Eschatology insist that Jesus meant that the age of fulfillment was near, so near that its signs and powers could be felt; but that the Kingdom itself was not present. Others have reinterpreted eschatology or have attributed it to early Christian misunderstanding of Jesus' message of an altogether realized eschatology. However, both emphases—the present and the future—play an important role in Jesus' teaching. The age of fulfillment is not only near; it is actually present. Nevertheless, the time of apocalyptic consummation remains in the future. One of the most important tasks of modern biblical theology has been the search for the key to this problem of how the

---

[36] T. W. Manson in *Law and Religion* (E. I. J. Rosenthal, ed.; 1938), p. 128. For the theological significance of the doctrine of Satan see below, p. 334.
[37] *Ibid.*, p. 129.

Kingdom can be both future and present so that both sets of sayings—those of present fulfillment and those of future consummation—can be preserved. We believe the solution to this problem is to be found in the dynamic meaning of the Kingdom of God.

5 The Kingdom: Reign or Realm?

New Testament scholars generally agree that the burden of Jesus' message was the Kingdom of God (Mark 1:15; Matt. 4:17). The same message was entrusted to the twelve disciples (Matt. 10:7) and to a band of seventy on a later mission (Luke 10:9, 11). The critical problem arises from the fact that Jesus nowhere defined what he meant by the phrase. We must therefore assume either that the content of the phrase was so commonly understood by the people as to need no definition or that the meaning of Jesus' proclamation is to be interpreted in terms of his total mission and conduct. We have already determined that Jesus' message was marked by two important emphases. The messianic salvation foretold by the prophets was being fulfilled in his person and mission; but there remained an eschatological consummation when the messianic salvation would be perfectly accomplished in the age to come. Against this background, we must examine the use of the "Kingdom of God" in the Gospels to discover its meaning in Jesus' message.

THE GOSPEL DATA

The difficulty of the problem will be seen when the Gospel data are briefly surveyed. The Kingdom of God appears in diverse contexts. We may isolate at least four distinct uses of the phrase. First, in a few places, the Kingdom of God bears clearly the abstract meaning of reign or rule. This has been recognized by the translators of the Revised Standard Version who render *basileia* by "kingly power" in Luke 19:12, 15; 23:42, and by "kingship" in John 18:36. A second group of sayings refers to the Kingdom as a future apocalyptic order into which the righteous will enter at the end of the age. In such sayings, the Kingdom of God is interchangeable with the age to come (Mark 9:47; 10:23–25; 14:25; Matt. 8:11 = Luke 13:28). In a third group, the Kingdom is something present among men. The most notable sayings are Mark 10:15 where the Kingdom is something men must now receive; Matthew 6:33 = Luke 12:31 where the Kingdom is something to be sought; Matthew 11:12 and 12:28 where the Kingdom is a power active in the world; and Luke 17:21 where the Kingdom is plainly asserted to be present within or among men.[1] In a fourth group, the Kingdom is represented as a present realm or sphere into which men are now entering (Matt. 11:11 = Luke 16:16; Matt. 21:31; 23:13; cf. Luke 11:52).

Many critics select one meaning of the Kingdom of God and try to interpret all other sayings in terms of one central emphasis lest the unity of the concept be lost and there result an unfortunate decomposition of it.[2] Those who accept Consistent Eschatology interpret the sayings about the presence of the Kingdom either as secondary or as referring to the present signs of the Kingdom but not to the Kingdom itself. Those who find the central truth in the present Kingdom often evade the force of the eschatological sayings by attributing them to an early Christian apocalyptic misunderstanding of Jesus' pure spiritual message, or by interpreting them in symbolic terms. However, Jesus taught a present fulfillment in the setting of future consummation. The question therefore arises whether it is not possible that these several types of sayings may reflect diverse facets of a single but complex idea. What is the

---

[1] For a discussion of Matt. 11:12, see below, pp. 159 ff.; for Matt. 12:28, see pp. 140 f.; for Luke 17:21, see p. 228, n. 25.

[2] S. Aalen, *NTS*, VIII (1962), p. 215.

central idea in the Kingdom of God? Is it the reign of God, or the realm over which he reigns? Is it possible that it can be both? And if so, what is the relationship between these two elements?

THE QUESTION IN RECENT CRITICISM

The difficulty of this question is illustrated by the diverse conclusions to which recent scholars have come. Furthermore, it is not enough merely to solve this initial problem, for both concepts—reign and realm—have been employed in the interest both of Consistent Eschatology and of noneschatological views. Therefore, we must ask not only whether the Kingdom of God is God's reign or the realm over which he reigns, but also about the relationship of the reign and realm to the present and the future.

Followers of Consistent Eschatology have interpreted the Kingdom of God both as God's reign and as the realm of his reign. Bultmann thinks that the Kingdom is the eschatological act of God by which he will inaugurate the new age. He asserts that this essential meaning of a miraculous, world-transforming divine act by definition excludes any idea of a present kingdom.[3] Others who follow Consistent Eschatology see the Kingdom not as the divine eschatological visitation, the final inbreaking of God's reign, but as the new order of the age to come. Maurice Goguel defined it as "a new order which will be realized by an act of God."[4] Consistent Eschatology can interpret the Kingdom of God either as the final eschatological visitation or as the new order introduced by this divine event.

Both interpretations raise a serious problem which the strict historian will feel is irrelevant but which theology must honestly face. Both views interpret the sayings which seem to speak of the Kingdom as something present not of the actual presence of the Kingdom

[3] *Theology of the New Testament* (1951), I, p. 22. The same view is found in M. Dibelius, *Jesus* (1949), pp. 64–88, and R. H. Fuller, *Mission*, pp. 20–49.

[4] *The Life of Jesus* (1933), pp. 563; see also pp. 312, 565. This same view is found in the articles on Jesus Christ and the Kingdom of God by H. Conzelmann in RGG (3rd ed.), III, col. 641–646; V, col. 912–918.

but of its imminence. The eschatological event is so close that its powers can be felt. In fact, Jesus saw God's reign already in progress, already breaking in, already dawning.[5] The signs of the Kingdom prove its proximity. They do not prove that the Kingdom is present but that it is so very close that God is already beginning to transform the curse of this present existence. The splendor of the coming Kingdom is already shining; its powers are already present, but not the Kingdom itself.[6]

In such interpretations, the imminence of the Kingdom is the central fact in Jesus' message. Amos N. Wilder goes so far as to say that few will disagree with Schweitzer on the main point, viz., that Jesus taught an imminent judgment and world renovation.[7]

This question involves far more than the problem of whether Jesus could be in error and make a mistake about the time of the future Kingdom. If, as is widely held today, Jesus was in error in the *main emphasis* of his message, if he was mistaken as to the *central purpose* of his mission—to proclaim and to prepare men for an imminent end of the world—it is difficult to understand how the other elements in his religious message remain trustworthy. Furthermore, if the very imminence of the future Kingdom was already producing the present signs of its inbreaking, but if in fact Jesus was quite in error about the coming of this future Kingdom, it is difficult to see how the present signs and powers of the future Kingdom can retain any validity or worth. They would be signs produced by a delusion and therefore must themselves be illusory. To imagine that one sees on the horizon the rosy blush of the breaking dawn and in its faint light sets out upon a journey only to wander in the darkness of midnight is utter deception. Therefore both the nature and the time of the Kingdom remain central problems in the study of Jesus' ministry. If Schweitzer was correct in his analysis of Jesus'

[5] R. Bultmann, *Theology of the New Testament* (1951), p. 7; M. Dibelius, *Jesus* (1949), p. 69.

[6] M. Dibelius, *Jesus* (1949), pp. 78 f., 89 f.; R. H. Fuller, *Mission*, pp. 34 ff. See also the views of E. F. Scott, M. Enslin, S. J. Case, E. Dinkler, etc., above, pp. 8 ff.

[7] *Eschatology and Ethics in the Teaching of Jesus* (1950), p. 38.

message, he was right in the conclusion that the historical Jesus was the victim of a gross error and can have little relevance for the twentieth century. Indeed, "we must be prepared to find that the historical knowledge of the personality and life of Jesus will not be a help, but perhaps even an offence to religion."[8] "It still looks as though a monstrous illusion lies at the basis of the whole mission of Jesus."[9]

The Kingdom of God has been interpreted as a realm in an utterly noneschatological way. This has recently been attempted by Aalen who rejects the dynamic idea of God's reign. He admits this dynamic eschatological use in Judaism but points out that in an eschatological context, God's Kingdom is spoken of as appearing or being revealed. Jesus speaks of its coming, not of its appearing. In Judaism, this involves an epiphany of God; but Jesus' language conveys an altogether different idea. Jesus' teachings always bear affinity to a local sphere, designating an area, like a house, a city, or a feast, into which one enters. Aalen rules against an eschatological order, arguing that in Jewish thought, the world to come must not be understood as an apocalyptic term. The primary idea of the Kingdom of God is the sphere of redemption and salvation, and this new realm of salvation Jesus brought to men in history. The Kingdom is the good realm where the realities of redemption are granted and received, and has become a present reality on the scene of history.[10]

While we must agree that the Kingdom is a realm of salvation, it is significant that the Kingdom of God as the dynamic rule or

[8] A. Schweitzer, *The Quest of the Historical Jesus* (1911), p. 399. What Schweitzer means by "the abiding and eternal in Jesus [which] is absolutely independent of historical knowledge" is capable of all sorts of "Gnostic" interpretations.

[9] M. Dibelius, *Jesus* (1949), p. 70. The author is aware that some scholars would admit that Jesus was the victim of such a delusion, but would find the Christian gospel in the Kerygma, not in the message of the historical Jesus. However, such a divorce of Jesus from the gospel creates greater problems than it solves; and even the disciples of Bultmann are seeking ways to make the historical Jesus relevant for Christian faith. For the relationship of the Kingdom of God in the mission of Jesus and in the Kerygma, see below, pp. 270 ff.

[10] S. Aalen, *NTS*, VIII (1962), pp. 215–240.

reign of God has become the most widely accepted definition of the concept.[11] However, diverse use has been made of this dynamic interpretation of the concept. Some have understood it to be the reign of God in the human heart and therefore timeless and beyond localization.[12] Such an interpretation follows Harnack's theology and tends to do away altogether with the eschatological dualism which we have found basic in Jesus' teachings. Others understand this dynamic interpretation in terms which involve an eschatological tension between the present and the future (see pp. 38–39, n. 161).

The need for deciding whether the Kingdom of God means reign or realm is illustrated by Kümmel's outstanding study, *Promise and Fulfilment*. Kümmel has been described as the scholar who has come closer than any other exegete to a "genuine synthesis of realized and futurist eschatology in the teaching of our Lord."[13] In spite of its exegetical and scholarly excellence, Kümmel's study leaves the reader with a difficult problem of understanding in just what sense

[11] See Liddell, Scott, and Jones, *A Greek-English Lexicon* (1940), *in loc.*; J. H. Moulton and G. Milligan, *The Vocabulary of the Greek Testament* (1930), *in loc.*; W. F. Arndt and F. W. Gingrich, *A Greek-English Lexicon of the New Testament* (1957), p. 134; K. L. Schmidt, *TWNT*, I, pp. 579 ff.; E. Klostermann, *Das Matthäusevangelium* (1927), p. 35; G. Dalman, *The Words of Jesus* (1909), pp. 91 ff.; J. Schniewind, *Das Evangelium nach Matthäus* (1950), pp. 23 ff.; G. S. Duncan, *Jesus, Son of Man* (1949), pp. 45 ff.; A. M. Hunter, *The Work and Words of Jesus* (1950), pp. 68 ff.; A. E. J. Rawlinson, *St. Mark* (1925), p. 13; C. J. Cadoux, *The Historic Mission of Jesus* (n.d.), pp. 111 ff.; V. Taylor, *The Gospel according to St. Mark* (1952), p. 114 and references; J. Bright, *The Kingdom of God* (1953), p. 197; S. E. Johnson, *The Gospel according to St. Mark* (1960), p. 42; F. V. Filson, *The Gospel according to St. Matthew* (1960), p. 32; G. E. Wright and R. H. Fuller, *The Book of the Acts of God* (1957), p. 240; R. Schnackenburg, *Gottes Herrschaft und Reich* (1959); Alan Richardson in *A Theological Word Book of the Bible* (Alan Richardson, ed.; 1950), pp. 119 f. Some of the older works expressly deny any extensive application of this dynamic concept to the Gospels. Cf. J. H. Thayer, *A Greek-English Lexicon of the New Testament* (1887), p. 97, where the primary emphasis is placed on a perfect order of things in which a new society would enjoy the blessings of eternal salvation; H. Cremer, *Biblico-Theological Lexicon of New Testament Greek* (1895), pp. 132 ff., 659 ff. where "reign" is allowed only in Luke 1:33; I Cor. 15:24; Luke 23:42; Matt. 16:28. The new understanding may be seen in the article in the eleventh edition of Cremer's *Wörterbuch* (Julius Kögel, ed.; 1923).

[12] See the interpretations of T. W. Manson, C. J. Cadoux, E. J. Goodspeed, *et al.*, above, pp. 12 ff.

[13] G. R. Beasley-Murray, *Jesus and the Future* (1954), p. 103.

the Kingdom of God is present in Jesus; and this arises in part out of Kümmel's failure to define precisely what the Kingdom of God is. What does he mean by the Eschaton?[14] Is it the divine eschatological event, or is it the new order to be established by this event— the age to come? Kümmel uses language which lends itself to both interpretations. He speaks of the Eschaton in terms of the beginning of God's reign,[15] as the activity of the Kingdom of God,[16] as an event.[17] But he appears more often to speak of the Eschaton as the eschatological order of salvation. To be sure, he does not think that Jesus employed the dualistic terminology of the two ages;[18] but he speaks of the Kingdom of God "coming into existence,"[19] and as a future realm to be entered.[20] Further, the coming of the Kingdom meant the end of the old aeon;[21] and this implies that the Eschaton is the new aeon which is about to appear.

However, if the Eschaton is the eschatological order of salvation, how are we to conceive of its powers being present in the person of Jesus in such terms that one can actually assert that the Kingdom of God itself is present?[22] If the Kingdom of God by definition is the rule of God, we can understand how God can manifest his rule in the person and mission of Jesus and again at the end of the age. But if the Kingdom by definition is the eschatological order, it is difficult to understand how the Kingdom itself can be both present

14 W. G. Kümmel, *Promise and Fulfilment* (1957), pp. 25, 49, 105, 143.
15 *Ibid.*, p. 91.
16 *Ibid.*, pp. 124, 153.
17 *Ibid.*, pp. 53, 111.
18 *Ibid.*, p. 49, n. 98.
19 *Ibid.*, p. 25.
20 *Ibid.*, pp. 28, 52.
21 *Ibid.*, pp. 121, 124.
22 The following are typical quotations from Kümmel: "The Kingdom of God has already become effective in advance in Jesus" (p. 35). "It is the meaning of the mission of Jesus, when announcing the *approach* of the Kingdom of God, to make this future at the same time already now a present reality" (p. 109). "The present possesses a definite eschatological character on account of the breaking in of the coming Kingdom through Jesus in the present" (p. 136). "The coming Kingdom of God [is] realizing itself already in his person, his actions, his message" (p. 153). "In Jesus the Kingdom of God came into being and in him it will be consummated" (p. 155). Quoted by permission; London: S. C. M. Press. Distributed in U.S.A. by Allenson's, Naperville, Illinois.

and future. One of Kümmel's own students has correctly pointed out that what is present in his interpretation is not the Kingdom itself but only the imminence of the Kingdom.[23] When Kümmel discusses the meaning of Jesus' eschatological proclamation about the proximity of the Kingdom, he says that it "clearly derives its special meaning in Jesus' mouth through this unusual proclamation of the presence of the future eschatological consummation." "It is the meaning of the mission of Jesus, when announcing the approach of the Kingdom of God, to make this future at the same time already now a present reality."[24] In other words, the Kingdom is so near that the old aeon is at an end because the Kingdom of God is now appearing.[25] The imminence of the Kingdom means that men are confronted with the end of history as it advances toward the goal set by God.[26] In his concluding summary, Kümmel appears to shift his ground to maintain that the note of imminence can be separated from the note of futurity without impairing Jesus' message. Imminence becomes only the necessary form in which the certainty of the coming of the Kingdom expresses itself, while the element of futurity is essential and indispensable. Apparently we are to understand this message of imminence as an expression of Jesus' certainty of the eschatological consummation in terms of the powers of the future Kingdom actually displaying themselves in Jesus' person and mission;[27] that is, the end is so near that its powers are already displaying themselves.

This analysis of Kümmel's work points up the necessity of defining more precisely the relationship between the concepts of reign and realm in Jesus' message of the Kingdom; for it remains unclear, if the Kingdom is the eschatological realm of salvation, in what sense the Kingdom itself can be present. Furthermore, we are again confronted with the importance of the question of imminence. If the presence of the powers of the Kingdom in Jesus' ministry is but

[23] E. Grässer, Das Problem der Parusieverzögerung (1957), p. 7.
[24] W. G. Kümmel, Promise and Fulfilment (1957), pp. 108, 109.
[25] Ibid., p. 121.
[26] Ibid., p. 152.
[27] Ibid., pp. 151–153.

a reflex of his sense of the imminence of the Kingdom, how can this note of imminence be detached from his message without impairing its entire validity? For if the powers of the Kingdom are present and active because the Kingdom is thought to be very near when in fact the Kingdom is not near at all, then the message of the presence of the powers of the Kingdom must itself be illusory, for it rests upon an illusion.

AN ABSTRACT MEANING

The majority of exegetes have recognized that the central meaning of basileia, as of the Hebrew word malkuth, is the abstract or dynamic idea of reign, rule, or dominion rather than the concrete idea of realm. "The bond that binds them [the two Testaments] together is the dynamic concept of the rule of God."[28] We have discovered this to be the central use of the word in the Old Testament; but we have also shown that malkuth can be both the reign of a king and the realm over which he reigns (see p. 47, n. 6). The fact that there is nothing incongruous in these two facets of the concept but that they are two inseparable parts of a single complex idea can be illustrated from the profane use of the word. The author of Esther can use malkuth to designate both the reign to which Esther has come as queen (Esther 4:14) and the realm over which her husband was king (3:6, 8).

It is surprising to discover that "the Kingdom of God" is seldom found in the apocalyptic writings or in the other literature of the intertestamental period. Furthermore, when the phrase or its variants occur, they refer to God's reign, not to the realm over which he reigns, nor to the new age. In the Psalms of Solomon (17:23 ff.), "kingdom" is not used of the messianic order to be established by the Lord's Anointed; it is God's rule. "For the might of our God is forever with mercy, and the kingdom of our God is forever over the nations in judgment" (Ps. of Sol. 17:4). God's special rule is over

---

[28] J. Bright, The Kingdom of God (1953), p. 197. See also, above, p. 127, n. 11.

Israel (Ps. of Sol. 5:21). When the righteous man is shown God's kingdom (Wisd. of Sol. 10:10), he was given "knowledge of holy things," and was enabled to understand the workings of the divine providence. When Benjamin tells his children that because of their future sins, "the kingdom of the Lord shall not be among you" (Test. Ben. 9:1), he means that they will lose the divinely authorized right to rule.

Occasionally God's Kingdom is spoken of as an eschatological event. When God breaks into history to punish the wicked and save Israel, "then His kingdom shall appear throughout all His creation" (Asmp. Moses 10:1). God's rule will be manifested and established in all the world. The Sibylline Oracles describes this eschatological event in the words, "then the mightiest kingdom of the immortal king over men shall appear" (3:47 f.). In such passages, God's Kingdom is not the new age but the effective manifestation of his rule in all the world so that the eschatological order is established.[29]

The rabbinic usage is most instructive. God's Kingdom, his sovereignty, is an eternal fact. "His kingly sovereignty endures for ever and ever."[30] However, God's sovereignty on earth began when Abraham submitted himself to the divine rule. "Before our father Abraham came into the world, God was, as it were, only the king of heaven; but when Abraham came, he made Him to be king over heaven and earth." After Mount Sinai, God's sovereignty was manifested on earth in Israel. The Israelites experienced the Kingdom of God by obedience to the law. The daily repetition of the Shema with the reading of Deuteronomy 6:4–10 was regarded as a repeated taking upon oneself of the yoke of the sovereignty of God. When a Gentile became a Jewish proselyte and adopted the law, he thereby took upon himself the sovereignty of heaven.

---

[29] The Qumran literature adds nothing to our study but does illustrate that *malkuth* can designate both "rule" (1QSb: Adjunct to Rule of the Community, 3:5; 5:21; War Scroll 19:8; see also "royal" in War Scroll 12:7; 1QSb 4:26; 4Q Patriarchal Blessings 2:4) and "realm" (War Scroll 12:15; 19:7).

[30] See G. Dalman, *The Words of Jesus* (1909), pp. 91–101, for this and the following illustrations. See also K. G. Kuhn in *BKW: Basileia* (1957), pp. 13 ff.; G. F. Moore, *Judaism*, II, pp. 371–376; Strack and Billerbeck, *Kommentar*, I, pp. 172–184.

However, God's Kingdom is yet to appear. In a future day, "his kingdom will be manifest in all his creation. And then the Devil will have an end, and with him sorrow will be removed. . . . For the Heavenly One will arise from his royal throne, and come forth from his holy habitation, with indignation and wrath for his sons." This appearing of God's Kingdom will mean the shaking of the physical world. The order of the earth, sun, moon, and stars will be disrupted. "For the Most High will arise, the Eternal God alone; and he will come openly to take vengeance on the Gentiles, and destroy all their idols. Then happy wilt thou be, O Israel! and thou wilt mount above the neck and wings of the eagle . . . and God will exalt thee and make thee to cleave to the heaven of the stars, to the place of their habitation. And thou will look from the highest (place) and wilst see thy enemies in the dust, and wilt recognize them and rejoice, and wilt give thanks and confess thy Creator."[31] This appearing of God's sovereignty is frequently reflected in rabbinic literature. An ancient prayer concludes with the petition, "and may he [God] set up his sovereignty in your lifetime, and in your days, and in the lifetime of the whole house of Israel, [yea] speedily, and in a time that is near."

Malkuth is God's sovereignty, God's rule. God's rule *de jure* exists universally over the heavens and earth; but *de facto*, it exists in this age only when men submit themselves to the divine rule. The initiative in bringing God's Kingdom to earth rests with men. However, God's Kingdom will also appear eschatologically; and then God will establish his sovereignty *de facto* in all the earth. Before this eschatological event, God's *malkuth* may be more accurately described as an abstract rather than as a dynamic concept. It is always "there," waiting for men to accept it and submit to it. However, it does not "come" until the end of the age.[32]

In summary, God's Kingdom in Jewish literature has almost al-

---

[31] Asmp. Moses 10. Manson's translation. See *JTS*, XLVI (1945), pp. 42–45. Cf. Apoc. Bar. 49:7: "Then shall the principate of my Messiah be revealed."

[32] Professor Aalen makes a sharp distinction between the concepts of God's Kingdom "appearing" and "coming"; but this seems difficult to sustain (S. Aalen, *NTS*, VIII (1962), p. 221).

ways the abstract meaning of God's rule. Only infrequently is it used of the sphere or realm over which he rules. The rule of God becomes a dynamic concept in its eschatological context when God will cause his rule to appear in all the earth.

If Jesus' proclamation of the Kingdom is understood strictly against this background, Bultmann and Dibelius have the correct interpretation. Jesus came proclaiming that the eschatological visitation of God is about to occur; the final effective establishment of his reign is about to take place; and this will result in the breaking off of history and the inauguration of the age to come. Jesus proclaimed that what the Old Testament prophesied and the Jewish writers hoped for was about to take place: the final eschatological visitation of the King.

However, it is gratuitous to assume that Jesus must be interpreted strictly in terms of his Jewish background; for even those who employ this approach admit that there are elements of novelty in Jesus' teaching. A number of scholars have contrasted Jesus' eschatological teaching with typical Jewish apocalyptic speculation (see pp. 6, 30). At another important point, Jesus departed from the apocalypses and the rabbinic writings. Contrary to both, Jesus used the term, "the Kingdom of God" to designate the eschatological salvation of the age to come. In Judaism, the Kingdom of God is never a realm into which men enter.[33] If there are important points of originality in Jesus' teachings, we must allow for the possibility that the burden of his message is not to be interpreted strictly in terms of its Jewish milieu but may involve originality at the central point. Therefore, we must seek for the meaning of Jesus' proclamation of the Kingdom in terms of his entire message.

THE ABSTRACT USE IN THE NEW TESTAMENT

We have found two central emphases in Jesus' message: present fulfillment and future eschatological consummation. We have now to consider more closely the terminology about the Kingdom of

[33] E. Percy, *Die Botschaft Jesu* (1953), pp. 21–22; S. Aalen, *NTS*, VIII (1962), p. 220.

God to determine whether or not it conveys this same tension of fulfillment and consummation.

First of all, we may note that there are several places outside of the Gospels where *basileia* means reign and not realm. The one self-confessed apocalypse in the New Testament speaks of ten kings "who have not yet received royal power (*basileia*), but they are to receive authority as kings for one hour" (Rev. 17:12; cf. vs. 17). In the one saying in the New Testament where *basileia* is unquestionably used of a society of men, the redeemed are called a "kingdom" not because they constitute the kingdom over whom Christ reigns but because "they shall reign on the earth" (Rev. 5:10). They are called a kingdom because they will share the royal reign. Again, when the kingdom[34] of the world becomes the Kingdom of our Lord and his Christ (Rev. 11:15), the authority, the rule exercised by men will pass into the hands of Christ, and "he shall reign forever and ever." This is clear in the announcement of the voice proclaiming the consummation: "Now the salvation and the power and the kingdom of our God and the authority of his Christ have come" (Rev. 12:10). The "coming" of the Kingdom is the open, visible, universal extension of God's rule and authority issuing in the new age.

The same abstract concept is to be found in Paul's classic passage about the Kingdom of God. At the very end, Christ "delivers the kingdom to God the Father after destroying every rule and every authority and power. For he must reign until he has put all his enemies under his feet" (I Cor. 15:24 f.). Then "the Son himself will also be subjected to him who put all things under him, that God may be everything to everyone" (I Cor. 15:28). Christ is to reign, to exercise his kingly authority, until all enemies are brought under his sway. Then he will relinquish his kingly rule to the Father.

When, after his resurrection, the disciples asked Jesus if he would "at this time restore the kingdom to Israel" (Acts 1:6), they were concerned first of all about the sovereignty of Israel as the covenant people over the Gentiles. Again, the abstract quality is uppermost.

[34] The AV "kingdoms" is incorrect; only one source of authority is in view.

THE ABSTRACT USAGE IN THE GOSPELS

We have deliberately chosen passages outside the Gospels to illustrate the abstract meaning of *basileia*. We cannot uncritically assume that the Gospels follow the same usage; but we have at least found a background of contemporary usage against which the Gospel usage may be examined.

First, we may note several sayings where God's Kingdom is an eschatological event. The announcement to Mary that "the Lord God will give to him the throne of his father David; and he will reign over the house of Jacob forever; and of his kingdom there will be no end" (Luke 1:32–33) illustrates the abstract use in an eschatological context. Jesus will be the one in whom the promises of the rule of a Davidic messianic king are to be fulfilled.

The dynamic eschatological meaning of God's Kingdom is illustrated by the preaching of John the Baptist (see pp. 105 ff.). John described what he meant by the coming of the Kingdom in dynamic terms: a baptism with the Spirit and a baptism with fire—salvation and judgment. The Kingdom means a mighty act of God through the Coming One, resulting in the final separation of the righteous and the wicked.

This abstract eschatological concept is illustrated in the parable of the pounds, which corrected the popular expectation that the Kingdom of God was about to appear (Luke 19:11). The people thought that God was about to disclose his royal power and establish his glorious reign. It is not clear whether they expected the appearance of God's reign to be in apocalyptic power or military conquest. Jesus answered with a parable of a nobleman who went into a far country to receive "kingly power and then return" (Luke 19:12). The parable is to be understood against the background of recent Jewish history. Josephus tells us that when Herod the Great died, he divided his realm among his sons.[35] When Archelaus set out to Rome to seek confirmation by the Roman senate of his rule

---

[35] *The Jewish War*, II, 6; *Antiquities*, XVII, 8–11.

over Judea, he was followed by an embassy of Jews protesting his appointment. The "kingdom" in question was not a realm or a people but the right to reign as king. According to this passage, Jesus speaks of the Kingdom of God in terms of the exercise of divine royal power.

This dynamic eschatological meaning is found in the question of the Pharisees about the coming of the Kingdom of God (Luke 17: 20). They were concerned about the mighty act of the heavenly Kingdom to crush the Roman might, punish the Gentiles, exalt Israel, and establish God's reign in all the world. This was doubtless in the mind of the dying thief who asked Jesus to remember him when "you come in your kingly power" (Luke 23:42). The thief recognized something of royal dignity in Jesus' conduct; he believed that the man dying at his side in humiliation would one day assume a position of authority and power.

The use of Kingdom as an eschatological reign is evident in other sayings of Jesus. When Jesus told his disciples, "As my Father appointed a kingdom for me, so do I appoint for you" (Luke 22:29), the "kingdom" promised is "royal rank."[36] This promise has an eschatological reference, for the disciples are to exercise their rule by sitting "on thrones, judging the twelve tribes of Israel" (Luke 22:30). The disciples have experienced humiliation in the world; but the day will come when the authority, the Kingdom will be theirs.

The petition in the "Lord's Prayer" for the coming of God's Kingdom is a prayer for the perfect realization of God's will (Matt. 6:10). This coming of the Kingdom is undoubtedly eschatological;[37] but it is a divine act, not a future realm. This petition has its parallel in the Jewish prayer, "May he establish his Kingdom during your life

---

[36] W. F. Arndt and F. W. Gingrich, A Greek-English Lexicon of the New Testament (1957), p. 134; C. J. Cadoux, The Historic Mission of Jesus (n.d.), p. 290.

[37] C. J. Cadoux, The Historic Mission of Jesus (n.d.), p. 201; W. G. Kümmel, Promise and Fulfilment (1957), p. 25; H. K. McArthur, Understanding the Sermon on the Mount (1960), p. 88; T. W. Manson, The Sayings of Jesus (1949), p. 169.

and during your days."[38] This looks to the future perfect establishment of God's rule in the world. It is an act of God resulting in the eschatological order of the new age.

There is a different group of sayings in which the Kingdom is God's rule viewed as a present reality, not as an eschatological event. The Kingdom is something which men can seek here and now (Matt. 6:33 = Luke 12:31). Harvey K. McArthur says more than the text warrants when he designates this passage as explicit eschatology.[39] Both Filson and Schniewind point out that to those who seek God's Kingdom, other things which pertain to this life will be added in addition. Therefore the quest for the Kingdom will be fulfilled at least in part in this present life where food, drink, and clothing are real needs.[40] Furthermore, the Kingdom is something which is to be received here and now (Mark 10:15; Luke 18:17; Matt. 18:3). What must be received is not a realm, present or future, but a reign, God's reign, and the blessings which accompany it. To receive the Kingdom of God is to accept the yoke of God's sovereignty.[41] This again is similar to rabbinic sayings about taking upon oneself the malkuth of heaven. By this, the rabbis meant scrupulous observance of the law, for the will of God was embodied in the Torah. Jesus' words had a different meaning. He contrasted the presence of the Kingdom with this Jewish view of its presence. Acceptance of the Kingdom of God in rabbinic terms was the way of the "wise and prudent," i.e., those who followed the teachings of the rabbinic schools.[42] Jesus swept away this legalistic learning and taught that God's reign may be accepted by the simple and the childlike; and one must submit to God's reign in complete childlike obedience and trustful receptiveness.[43]

---

[38] G. Dalman, The Words of Jesus (1909), p. 99. Even C. H. Dodd admits the analogy. See The Parables of the Kingdom (1935), p. 42.

[39] Understanding the Sermon on the Mount (1960), pp. 89 f.

[40] J. Schniewind, Das Evangelium nach Matthäus (1937), p. 95; F. V. Filson, The Gospel according to St. Matthew (1960), p. 34.

[41] S. E. Johnson, The Gospel according to St. Mark (1960), p. 172.

[42] C. H. Dodd, The Parables of the Kingdom (1935), pp. 41 f.

[43] E. Lohmeyer (Das Evangelium des Markus [1937], p. 204) and W. G.

The idea of the Kingdom as a present blessing to be received is also reflected in the parables of the treasure and the pearl (Matt. 13:44–46). The most natural exegesis of these two parables is that the Kingdom is something which can be found and experienced in this age. "He who accepts God's Reign is ready to give up anything else for it." "He owns nothing else in the world, but he has the pearl! This is not sacrifice, as people ordinarily think of the word— it is the satisfaction of having what is most worth while, the achievement of heart's desire."⁴⁴

In summary, we find that the abstract use of *basileia* in the Gospels is very similar to rabbinic Judaism. The Kingdom is God's rule which men can and must receive in the present; but God's rule will also be eschatologically manifested in the future. Some modern interpreters find little more in Jesus' teachings than this rabbinic pattern of a present reign in the lives of men and future eschatological reign. The only difference is in the character of God's present reign. For Judaism, it was obedience to the law; while for Jesus, it was obedience to a new ethic of love and discipleship to his person.

THE KINGDOM COMES IN THIS AGE

There is however another element in Jesus' teaching which sets it in contrast to Judaism. We have seen that Jesus taught that be-

---

Kümmel (*Promise and Fulfilment* [1957], p. 126) reject this verse because it is without parallel in the Gospels, and they therefore feel that the expression must be considered to have been influenced by the language of the church. But where is there any parallel to this language in the rest of the New Testament? The Kingdom in Acts and the Epistles is usually eschatological. When it is a present reality, it may be preached (Acts 8:12; 19:8; 28:23, 31), entered (Col. 1:13), or manifested (I Cor. 4:20); but nowhere do we read that it must be received. There is therefore no adequate reason to take this saying as a creation of the church. Furthermore, the idea is found in Luke 10:8–11 where reception of the disciples is equivalent to reception of the Kingdom and vice versa. Furthermore, Mark 9:37 (= Matt. 18:5, Luke 9:48) says that to receive a little one in Jesus' name is equivalent to receiving Jesus, and to receive Jesus is to receive God. Taylor thinks that there can be no question about the genuineness of Mark 10:15. (See V. Taylor, *The Gospel according to St. Mark* [1952], p. 424.)

⁴⁴ S. E. Johnson, *Jesus in His Own Times* (1958), pp. 118 f.

fore the eschatological consummation, an actual fulfillment of the Old Testament hope was occurring in his own person and mission. This same note of present fulfillment is found in sayings about a present coming and working of the Kingdom in the world. This brings us to our central thesis: that *before the eschatological appearing of God's Kingdom at the end of the age, God's Kingdom has become dynamically active among men in Jesus' person and mission.* The Kingdom in this age is not merely the abstract concept of God's universal rule to which men must submit; it is rather a dynamic power at work among men. This is not only the element which sets our Lord's teaching most distinctively apart from Judaism; *it is the heart of his proclamation and the key to his entire mission.* Before the apocalyptic coming of God's Kingdom and the final manifestation of his rule to bring in the new age, God has manifested his rule, his Kingdom, to bring to men in advance of the eschatological era the blessings of his redemptive reign. There is no philological or historical or exegetical reason why God's Kingdom, God's rule, cannot manifest itself in two different ways at two different times to accomplish the same ultimate redemptive end. The rabbis had such a twofold concept of God's *malkuth.* God's reign could be accepted in this age, and it would appear dynamically at the end of the age. Jesus followed this basic pattern but went beyond the rabbis by teaching that God's kingly reign was manifesting itself dynamically in this age in his own person and mission before its eschatological appearing.

This thesis is not to be established merely by a few proof texts but by a careful appraisal of Jesus' total ministry and teaching. However, any thesis must rest upon careful exegesis of particular passages. As a point of departure, we shall consider one saying in which the Kingdom of God is unambiguously affirmed to be dynamically present among men in this age, and then go on to develop the thesis in larger terms of Jesus' message and mission.

Referring to his exorcism of demons, Jesus said, "If it is by the Spirit of God that I cast out demons, then the kingdom of God has come (*ephthasen*) upon you" (Matt. 12:28 = Luke 11:20). An analysis of the entire passage will be undertaken in the next chapter. Here we need only notice that our Lord speaks unequivocally of a present coming of the Kingdom. The older meaning of the Greek verb (*phthano*), "to come first, to precede," is found in I Thessalonians 4:15. At the Parousia of Christ, the living will not "get ahead" of those who have died and reach the presence of Christ before their sleeping fellows; both the dead and the living will be taken up together to be with the Lord. Some exegetes have attempted to apply this meaning of "precede" to Matthew 12:28 by arguing that the verb means imminence to the point of contact without providing participation in the ensuing experience. The word is thus taken to be almost synonymous with *eggiken* and means that the Kingdom has "drawn near," even to the very point of contact; but the experience which draws near is still in the future. Matthew 12:28 might be translated, "the Kingdom of God has just reached you."[45]

This interpretation has been used to support modified Consistent Eschatology. Dibelius interprets this saying to mean that the Kingdom is so near that its powers are already at work, but the Kingdom itself remains future. What is manifested is the *proximity* of the Kingdom. "God is already beginning to transform the curse of this present existence, which appears in sickness and other dark fatalities, into blessing."[46]

Several facts are to be noted about this interpretation. First, we must repeat that if the works of Jesus are signs of the nearness of the Kingdom and not of its actual presence, we cannot avoid the theological problem which casts Jesus' entire message and mission under a cloud. If the powers which Jesus thought were at work in and through him were based upon an illusory sense of the nearness of the Kingdom of God, then those very powers themselves must

---

[45] Cf. K. Clark, *JBL*, LIX (1940), pp. 367–383. Clark is concerned to refute Dodd's interpretation that *eggiken* means "has come."

[46] M. Dibelius, *Jesus* (1949), pp. 78 f. Similarly R. Bultmann, *Theology of the New Testament* (1951), I, p. 7; B. T. D. Smith, *The Parables of the Synoptic Gospels* (1937), pp. 78, 93; R. H. Fuller, *Mission*, pp. 25 ff.; W. Michaelis, *Das Evangelium nach Matthäus* (1949) II, pp. 26 f.; C. Guignebert, *Jesus* (1935), p. 338; C. T. Craig, *IB*, VII, p. 148.

also be illusory. It is difficult to see how the integrity of Jesus' person and message can be rescued from the charge of complete delusion.

Second, we must agree with Dibelius that this statement of the coming of the Kingdom cannot mean that the Kingdom of God has come in the fullest sense of the term. Kümmel really goes too far when he speaks of "the presence of the eschatological consummation" and says that with Jesus' appearance, "the old aeon is at an end."[47] Both the eschatological consummation and the end of the old aeon remain events in the future. Dibelius is right that it was obvious that the world was not being transformed; the old age continued.[48]

Third, it is most significant that Dibelius is forced exegetically to admit the presence of the Kingdom although he denies its presence theologically. " 'But if it is by the finger of God I expel the evil spirits, then God's Kingdom has already made its presence known among you' (Luke 11:19, 20). In this saying too, whose wording permits the translation, 'God's Kingdom has come even to you,' it is not said that God's Kingdom is already there—of such a statement, these expulsions taken alone would really have been no proof!—but that in the abundance of such wonderful events it announced its proximity. Hence the demon expulsions are also signs of the coming Kingdom."[49] Here is a patent contradiction: "God's Kingdom has come even to you"; "it is not said that God's Kingdom is already there." If the Kingdom has in some way reached men, then it is present; but if it is only near, then it has not yet reached them; it has only *almost* reached them. If in fact, as Dibelius claims, the evils of present existence are in process of being transformed, it can be nothing else but the powers of the Kingdom, and therefore the Kingdom of God itself—if the Kingdom of God by definition is the dynamic reign and rule of God.

[47] *Promise and Fulfilment* (1957), pp. 108, 121.
[48] M. Dibelius, *Jesus* (1949), p. 88.
[49] *Ibid.*, pp. 78 f. Copyright 1949, W. L. Jenkins. The Westminster Press. Used by permission.

Finally, the dynamic interpretation of the Kingdom of God is required by the passage. *Ephthasen eph' humas* means in some sense actual presence, not merely proximity. Romans 9:31 says that although Israel followed the law of righteousness, they did not reach the law, i.e., attain the end—righteousness—which was the goal of the law. In II Corinthians 10:14, Paul says that he was the first "to come all the way to you" with the gospel of Christ. In these words, Paul describes his personal presence in Corinth, not his approach to that city. In Philippians 3:16 Paul exhorts his readers to hold true to what they have attained, to be faithful to the level of experience at which they have actually arrived. In these passages the idea is involved of reaching a goal, of attaining an end, not of coming close to it or of approaching it.

A difficult use of the word occurs in I Thessalonians 2:16. Referring to the Jews who killed the Lord Jesus and opposed his followers, Paul announces their doom with the words, God's wrath "has come upon them" at last. This saying has recently been taken to prove that the word is proleptic in meaning and that Paul means that God's eschatological wrath is so certain that he can speak of it as though it had already come.[50]

To this, two things must be said. This interpretation admits that *ephthasen* means "has come." The proleptic element is found not in the meaning of the verb but in the use made of it. Second, it must be admitted that Paul can speak of eschatological realities as though the believer's eschatological glorification had already taken place (Rom. 8:30).

However, this is probably not the meaning of I Thessalonians 2:16, for wrath is not always a future eschatological entity. When Paul speaks of eschatological wrath in I Thessalonians 1:10, he adds a limiting word, the *coming* wrath. In Romans 2:5 wrath is eschatological; but in Romans 1:18 it is a present reality now revealed against men. Therefore, we must conclude that wrath in I Thessalonians 2:16 means that God's wrath *now* rests upon the Jewish

---

[50] R. H. Fuller, *Mission*, p. 26.

nation. The Revised Standard Version has correctly translated the verse.[51]

Another important fact has not often been observed. If *ephthasen eph' humas* bears the older proleptic sense and means, "to come first, to precede," it designates not merely proximity but actual arrival, although of a premature character. "The Kingdom of God has arrived in advance upon you." This meaning would support the present thesis: that before the eschatological coming of God's Kingdom, an actual coming of the Kingdom has occurred in history; but the character of its arrival could be characterized as premature. In advance of its eschatological coming, the Kingdom has come unexpectedly into history to work among men. Interpreted in this way, *ephthasen* means an actual arrival and real presence but of a premature and unexpected sort. This is, however, the less likely meaning of the word.

In view of this evidence of the meaning of *ephthasen*, we must translate Matthew 12:28 with the Revised Standard Version, "The kingdom of God has come upon you." In some real sense of the word, the Kingdom is itself present. It is not merely the signs of the Kingdom or the powers of the Kingdom, but the Kingdom itself which is said to be present. Kümmel is entirely right in rejecting all efforts to minimize or evade the plain meaning of the saying.[52] Kümmel is also right in recognizing that the Kingdom is present in

---

[51] The meaning of *ephthasen* is further illustrated in the Greek Old Testament. II Chron. 28:9 speaks of a rage "which has reached up to heaven" (*ephthaken*). Song of Sol. 2:12, "The time of singing has come" (*ephthaken*). Dan. 6:24, "before they reached (*ephthasan*, 6:25, Theodotion) the bottom of the den the lions overpowered them." Dan. 7:13, "Behold, with the clouds of heaven there came one like a son of man, and he came to (*ephthasen heos*, Theodotion) the Ancient of Days." Dan. 7:22, "The time came (*ephthasen*, Theodotion) when the saints received the kingdom." In all of these sayings, something actually arrives, not merely comes close.

[52] *Promise and Fulfilment* (1957), p. 107. There is no necessity of reviewing the debate between Professor Dodd and his critics over the relationship between *ephthasen* and *eggiken*. The debate is outlined and the literature cited in W. G. Kümmel, *op. cit.*, pp. 105–109. We need not understand *ephthasen* to imply that the Kingdom has come in its fullness, as Dodd's Realized Eschatology has construed it.

the person and activity of Jesus. It remains to be asked, What was present? How are we to understand the presence of the Kingdom of God? Dibelius is correct in insisting that the eschatological order is not present, but rather the powers of the Kingdom of God. What was present was divine power, the activity of the Spirit of God, the working of God himself. Men were being delivered from the powers of evil; demons were being cast out by a greater power. Jesus asserted that this meant that the Kingdom of God itself was present.

Exegesis can do justice to this saying only when the Kingdom of God is interpreted in terms of its dynamic meaning: the reign or rule of God. God's Kingdom, his reign, will come at the end of the age in a mighty irruption into history inaugurating the perfect order of the age to come. But God's Kingdom, his reign, has already come into history in the person and mission of Jesus. The presence of God's Kingdom means the dynamic presence of his reign. It means that God is no longer waiting for men to submit to his reign but has taken the initiative and has invaded history in a new and unexpected way. The Kingdom of God is not merely an abstract concept that God is the eternal King and rules over all; it is also a dynamic concept of the acting God. God's reign which will come at the end of the age to accomplish God's redemptive purpose in the world has also come into the midst of human history in the person and mission of Jesus. God the heavenly King, who will act mightily tomorrow is also acting today in Jesus. It is the same God, the same rule, the same Kingdom dynamically at work among men.

This saying sets Jesus' teaching about the Kingdom of God in sharp contrast to rabbinic thought. The rabbis conceived of God's reign as being continually present de jure; but it becomes a present reality de facto in this age only when men take the initiative and bow to God's reign. This they do by accepting the yoke of the law. God has given the expression of his will in the Torah. When men submit in obedience to the law, they take upon them the yoke of the Kingdom, i.e., they submit to his reign. God's rule is extended de facto in the earth to the extent that men become subservient to his will as it is embodied in the law. In this view, the Kingdom itself may be said to be inactive. Jewish literature has nothing to say about the coming of the Kingdom in this age. The initiative in the realization of the Kingdom is in the hands of men. God has committed to Israel the law, and it is the responsibility of Israel to mediate the law to men. The initiative is on the human side. God's Kingdom will come, i.e., God will take the initiative only at the end of the age. Then God will mightily display his power and manifest his Kingdom in all the earth. Then sin and evil will be swept away and the will of God will reign without the hindrance of evil in any form.

Jesus' saying in Matthew 12:28 stands apart from Jewish thought. He asserted that now, in this age, before the arrival of the age to come, God has acted. In the present age, God's Kingdom is unexpectedly manifesting itself among men in his own person. God's Kingdom has come, not to usher in the new age, but to work in an unexpected way within history. The reign of God which will indeed one day establish the new age has become redemptively active among men in this age. God has taken the initiative.

Here is the key by which we can understand the diverse sayings of our Lord about the Kingdom; and it remains to work out this basic approach in detail and to attempt an interpretation of Jesus' total ministry by use of this concept of the Kingdom as God's activity. G. Gloege wrote, "The Kingdom of God (Gottesherrschaft) is never something which can to some extent be separated from God, but is only a more pregnant expression for God himself."[53] In Jesus, God has become present among men and redemptively active. In its dynamic meaning, the Kingdom of God is God himself, not merely ruling in the universe but actively establishing his rule among men.

We may now gain a fresh understanding of our Lord's words, "The Kingdom of God has drawn near." Formally, Jesus' message and that of John the Baptist are the same: "God is about to act." The meaning of both statements is to be understood from their contexts. John understood that God was about to act in his apocalyptic work of salvation and judgment. The meaning of Jesus' state-

[53] Reich Gottes und Kirche im Neuen Testament (1929), p. 36.

ment is quite different. It is our thesis that what he meant was: *God is about to act in a work of salvation and judgment which is not the apocalyptic manifestation but which is a necessary precedent to it.*

The question may be raised whether the meaning of *eggiken* does not render this interpretation impossible and refer to some event which, as Kümmel has demonstrated, is near but has not yet come?[54] Since there is undeniably an eschatological use of *eggiken* and *eggus*,[55] does this not require us to interpret Jesus' announcement about the nearness of the Kingdom strictly of the temporal nearness of the eschatological day?

The answer to this is found in what we have earlier called the prophetic tension between history and eschatology. In our analysis of the Day of the Lord in the prophets, we found that the term designated both an immediate historical visitation and the ultimate eschatological event; but the prophets did not attempt to make a sharp chronological differentiation between the two. The historical and the eschatological were viewed as one day because the prophetic focus of attention was not the chronology of God's redemptive working, but the God who works redemptively in history and eschatology (see pp. 64 ff.). One might say that the historical is realized eschatology, and the eschatological is consummated history. A striking difference between the apocalyptists and the prophets is found precisely at this point: the apocalyptists lost this essential tension between history and eschatology. History was dominated by evil; the Kingdom of God belonged solely to the future. God was no longer working redemptively in history.

Jesus stands apart from the apocalyptists in his recovery of the prophetic tension between history and eschatology. By "the Kingdom of God," he designated both the fulfillment of the prophetic hope in the historical present in his own person and mission and the eschatological consummation of the prophetic hope at the end of

54 *Promise and Fulfilment* (1957), pp. 19–25.
55 For *eggiken*, see Rom. 13:12; Heb. 10:25; Jas. 5:8; I Pet. 4:7; *eggus*, Rom. 13:11; Rev. 1:3; 22:10.

the age. He can do this because both the historical present and the eschatological future are visitations of the same God, manifestations of the same divine rule to accomplish the same redemptive purpose. Therefore, to understand the proclamation "The Kingdom of God has drawn near" to mean "The end of the world is about to take place" is altogether too simple an interpretation because it fails to grasp an essential element in the prophetic message of Jesus and forces upon him modern analytic categories of thinking rather than interpreting the statement in terms of its own prophetic setting. The Kingdom of God *did* draw near; God *did* visit his people. The age of fulfillment of the prophetic hope dawned upon Israel in the mission of Jesus. But the day of final consummation still remained in the future, at the end of history.

One last objection to our central thesis remains to be considered. Hans Windisch has made a sharp distinction between historical and theological exegesis and has argued that historical exegesis of the Gospels, which tries to discover what was meant by a given text in its own historical context, must insist that the Kingdom of God meant to Jesus what it meant to the Jews: the new apocalyptic order.[56] From the point of view of historical exegesis, Jesus' message has little relevance for today, for the imminent apocalyptic order which Jesus proclaimed did not come. Theological exegesis can make use of the rabbinic concept of the Kingdom of God as the reign or rule of God, and by this device make the Kingdom of God relevant for today. By this use of theological exegesis, the message of Jesus which was historically erroneous[57] may be reinterpreted in terms which are theologically relevant and meaningful for the modern man. If Windisch is correct, the thesis of the present study is quite unhistorical.

However, the rabbinic teaching about the Kingdom of God as the reign or rule of God is as much a fact of history and an element in

---

[56] H. Windisch, *The Meaning of the Sermon on the Mount* (1951), pp. 28, 62, 193.

[57] Windisch does not express himself in such terms, but this is what is involved in his position. See Windisch, *op. cit.*, Chap. 4, esp. pp. 199 ff.

Jesus' religious environment as apocalyptic concepts. Furthermore, it is a historical fact that "the Kingdom of God," when it occurs even in the apocalyptic writings, refers to the manifestation of God's rule and not to the new apocalyptic order. Finally, it is a far too rigid application of a critical historical methodology to ignore the possibility that Jesus may have proclaimed a message about the Kingdom of God which radically transcended his environment. We have tried to show that the conceptual milieu of Jesus' message is the prophetic hope and not apocalyptic concepts. Therefore the interpretation of the Kingdom of God as God's reign or rule is to be understood as the correct historical meaning of Jesus' proclamation.[58]

---

[58] See G. E. Ladd, "The Kingdom of God: Reign or Realm?" *JBL*, LXXXI (1962), pp. 230–238.

6 The Kingdom Present as Dynamic Power

In the preceding chapter, we attempted to establish exegetically on the basis of Matthew 12:28 that Jesus taught that the Kingdom of God in a real sense was present in fulfillment of the prophetic hope, while the age of consummation remained future. The presence of the Kingdom of God was seen as God's dynamic reign invading the present age without transforming it into the age to come. This thesis must now be supported by a consideration of other sayings interpreted in the context of Jesus' person and ministry as a whole.

THE BINDING OF SATAN

We must first investigate the setting of Matthew 12:28. The exorcism of demons was one of the most characteristic activities of Jesus' ministry. At the very outset, Mark strikes the note of exorcism as one of the motifs of Jesus' ministry (Mark 1:23–28). The mission of the twelve (Mark 6:7) and of the seventy as well (Luke 10:17) emphasizes this same motif. J. M. Robinson has seen in these exorcisms a

149

cosmic struggle in history to inaugurate the eschatological reign of God.[1]

The meaning of this conflict must be interpreted against the background of *Heilsgeschichte*. From the Old Testament perspective, the coming of God's Kingdom would mean the defeat of Israel's enemies and the godless nations. The motif of an eschatological war frequently appears in the prophets (Mic. 4:11–13; Zeph. 3:8; Isa. 31:4–9; Ezek. 38, 39; Joel 3:9–15; Zech. 12:1–9; 14:1–3). This hope of victory over human enemies was preserved in Jewish thought and became one of the central motifs in popular hopes of the coming of the Kingdom. An unknown writer in the first century B.C. prays for the coming of the Lord's Anointed to restore the fortunes of Israel, purge Jerusalem of the hated Romans, and exalt the Holy City so that nations will come from the ends of the earth to see her glory (Ps. of Sol. 17:23–27, 32–33). Another unknown apocalyptist looks for a theophany to punish the Gentiles, destroy their idols, and exalt Israel to her place in the sun (Asmp. Moses 10:7–8). The recent discovery of the literature of the Qumran community, which includes an account of the eschatological war between the Sons of Light (the Qumran sectaries) and the Sons of Darkness, accentuates the Jewish understanding of the Kingdom of God in terms of politico-national victory.[2] Against this background, we can understand the desire of the people to make Jesus their King after he had displayed miraculous power in multiplying the loaves and fishes (John 6:15). Against a royal military leader so endowed by God, victory could be assured for Israel over the Romans.

Jesus reinterpreted the prophetic hope in terms of a spiritual rather than a military conflict. The coming of the Kingdom as an eschatological event will mean nothing less than the destruction of the Devil and his angels in eternal fire (Matt. 25:41) at the Parousia of the Son of Man. This conflict between good and evil, light and darkness, God and Satan is a fundamental element in the dualistic struc-

[1] James M. Robinson, *The Problem of History in Mark* (1957), p. 38; cf. pp. 31, 42.

[2] See W. R. Farmer, *Maccabees, Zealots and Josephus* (1956), which includes a translation of the War Scroll and a discussion of the question.

ture of Jesus' teachings (see pp. 118 ff.). The chief opponents of God's Kingdom are spiritual, and the victory of the Kingdom of God is first of all a spiritual victory. Whether or not the modern man feels he must "demythologize" it, an inescapable element in the biblical concept of redemption is that man must be saved from spiritual powers which are beyond his ability to conquer. The ultimate coming of God's Kingdom and the universal establishment of his reign will mean nothing less than the destruction of the very principle of evil in the spiritual realm.

The meaning of Jesus' exorcism of demons in its relationship to the Kingdom of God is precisely this: that before the eschatological conquest of God's Kingdom over evil and the destruction of Satan, the Kingdom of God has invaded the realm of Satan to deal him a preliminary but decisive defeat.

This fact is pictured in the saying about the strong man. In explanation of the exorcisms by the power of God's Kingdom, Jesus said, "Or how can one enter a strong man's house and plunder his goods, unless he first binds the strong man? Then indeed he may plunder his house" (Matt. 12:29). Luke's version of the saying emphasizes the conflict motif even more vividly: "When a strong man, fully armed, guards his own palace, his goods are in peace; but when one stronger than he assails him and overcomes him, he takes away his armor in which he trusted and divides his spoil" (Luke 11:21–22).

This saying reflects the implicit eschatological dualism underlying the Gospels which becomes explicit at numerous points. Satan is a strong man. His palace or house is "this present evil age" (Gal. 1:4), and his "goods" are men and women under his evil influence. However, he has not been left in peace to manage his affairs. A stronger, Jesus, has assailed and overcome him. This victory over Satan is the same whether it be described as a binding of the strong man (Matthew) or stripping him of his armor (Luke). In metaphorical language Jesus interprets his own mission among men as an invasion of Satan's kingdom (Matt. 12:26) for the purpose of assaulting the Evil One, overcoming him, and despoiling him of his goods. The last mentioned end is the deliverance of men from the power of satanic evil, which finds its most dramatic expression in the exorcism of demons.

That these exorcisms are not an end in themselves or the final goal of God's Kingdom is proved by Jesus' warning that exorcism is not enough. To do no more than free a man from satanic bondage is like emptying a house of its occupant. A new tenant must move in and take possession or no final good has been accomplished; only a vacuum has been created (Matt. 12:43–45; Luke 11:24–26). Unless a life is possessed by the power of God, its deliverance from Satan can be only temporary. Thus the exorcism of demons is only the outward visible aspect of an inner spiritual reality: the deliverance of human personality from evil that it may be possessed by God.

This conquest over Satan by the power of the Kingdom of God is accomplished *in this age, before the coming of the eschatological Kingdom*. We need not think of this victory of the Kingdom as a *complete* defeat of Satan. Indeed, this idea can hardly be entertained, for Satan continued to be active in the subsequent ministry of Jesus (Mark 8:33; Luke 22:3; 22:31). As Oscar Cullmann has so quaintly put it, we may think of Satan as bound with a rope which can be lengthened or shortened.[3] The figures of the binding and disarming of Satan are metaphors describing a spiritual reality. The powers of God's Kingdom have invaded human history. The power of evil has been defeated. Since this evil power is at work in human experience, the victory of God's Kingdom over spiritual evil must take place on the level of human history. It is, as Robinson has put it, a cosmic struggle in history (see p. 150, n. 1).

Two minor problems are raised by the passage under discussion. Does not Matthew 12:29 seem to place the victory over Satan before the exorcisms? If so, when did it occur and of what did it consist? Some scholars see here a reference either to a mythical fall of Satan in heaven[4] or to the victory Jesus won over Satan in his temptation.[5]

---

[3] *The State in the New Testament* (1956), p. 69.
[4] R. Otto, *The Kingdom of God and the Son of Man* (1943), pp. 97–103.
[5] W. Grundmann, *TWNT*, III, p. 404; T. Zahn, *Das Evangelium des Matthäus* (1922), p. 460; J. Jeremias, *The Parables of Jesus* (1954), p. 98.

However, the "binding" of Satan is metaphorical language and we do not need to search for a single decisive event. R. Leivestad is right in saying that "the simplest explanation is that the exorcisms themselves are regarded as a victorious combat with the devil and his kingdom. Whenever a demon is cast out from a body, it signifies that Satan has been defeated and spoiled of his goods."[6]

Another problem is raised by Matthew 12:27. The Pharisees recognized in Jesus supernatural power but accused him of being in league with Satan himself. Jesus replied that this was an impossible notion, for it would mean that Satan's house was divided against itself in civil strife. Then he added, "And if I cast out demons by Beelzebub by whom do your sons cast them out? Therefore they shall be your judges." These words naturally raise the question, Why are the exorcisms by Jewish magicians[7] not to be interpreted as evidence of the power of the Kingdom of God?[8]

The answer to this apparent difficulty is twofold. Jesus' words appear to be an *argumentum ad hominem*. He is meeting the Pharisees on their own terms and not expressing a personal judgment about the validity of other exorcisms. The only pertinent facts are that the Pharisees attributed Jesus' exorcisms to satanic power but accepted the validity of other exorcisms by their fellow Jews. This, says Jesus, is self-contradictory. If the Pharisees think Jesus' power is satanic, they ought for consistency's sake to see the same satanic power in Jewish exorcisms.

Furthermore, there was a distinct difference between Jewish exorcisms and those by Jesus. It was not merely the fact of Jesus' ability to exorcise demons that impressed the Pharisees; it was the manner in which he did it. With a single command he cast out demons. They were helpless before his word. It was not exorcism itself but the authority of Jesus' conduct which amazed the Jews (Mark 1:27). In

---

[6] *Christ the Conqueror* (1954), p. 47. See also A. Fridrichsen, *Theology*, XXII (1931), p. 127: "In each act of exorcism Jesus saw a defeat of Satan." See also E. Hoskyns and N. Davey, *The Riddle of the New Testament* (1949), p. 121.

[7] Cf. Acts 19:13; Josephus, *Antiquities*, VIII, 2, 5.

[8] W. G. Kümmel, *Promise and Fulfilment* (1957), p. 106; E. Klostermann, *Das Matthäusevangelium* (1927), p. 109.

contrast to this, Jewish exorcism involved the exercise of magical practices as the famous account in Josephus shows (see p. 153, n. 7).

Another fact is pertinent. Jewish exorcism was not a common practice. The Talmud has little to say about it. The victory over Satan by the Kingdom of God was shown by the difference in the scope and character of Jesus' exorcisms in comparison to the Jewish practice.

THE FALL OF SATAN

The presence of the Kingdom of God in advance of the age to come to overthrow the rule of evil is again illustrated by the mission of the Seventy who were sent out to proclaim the Kingdom of God and to heal the sick (Luke 10:9). Returning to Jesus, they reported joyfully that they had found themselves in possession of a surprising power over the demons. To this Jesus replied, "I saw Satan fall like lightning from heaven" (Luke 10:18).

This passage is studded with difficulties. Did Jesus have a vision of the fall of Satan, or was he speaking figuratively? J. Weiss held that these words report an ecstatic experience in which Jesus saw in vision the overthrow of Satan and thereby was convinced that the coming of the eschatological Kingdom was imminent.[9] That Jesus refers to an ecstatic vision which included the fall of Satan in the form of the phenomenon of light has been accepted by many exegetes.[10] Rudolf Otto builds his interpretation of Jesus around this theory of vision, but not in the interests of Weiss's futuristic eschatology. Jesus had seen a vision of the victory of the Kingdom of God over Satan in heaven. This heavenly victory released a great tidal wave of power which swept down to the earth. Jesus felt himself caught up in this surge of eschatological power. His ministry was a manifestation of

[9] *Die Schriften des Neuen Testaments* (4th ed., 1929), I, p. 446.

[10] W. G. Kümmel, *Promise and Fulfilment* (1957), p. 113, and literature in n. 27. Also T. W. Manson, *The Sayings of Jesus* (1949), p. 258; S. M. Gilmour, *IB*, VIII, p. 189; W. Manson, *The Gospel of Luke* (1930), p. 126; C. K. Barrett, *The Holy Spirit and the Gospel Tradition* (1947), pp. 63 f.; A. B. Higgins, *ET*, LVII (1945–46), p. 293; C. A. Webster, *ET*, LVII (1945–46), pp. 52 f.; A. R. C. Leaney, *The Gospel according to Luke* (1958), p. 179.

this movement. Therefore "it is not Jesus who brings the kingdom . . . , the kingdom brings him with it."[11]

Otto's dynamic interpretation of the Kingdom of God has led him to many accurate insights. It is indeed impossible to interpret the New Testament teaching about the Kingdom of God except against the background of a great spiritual struggle. The doctrine of demonic powers is no mere "surd" or irrational element without obvious functions in Jesus' teachings as a whole, as some have tried to maintain.[12] The Kingdom of God is no timeless abstract concept of the universal will of God which "comes" only as men receive it. In this case the initiative would be man's, not God's. This would be good rabbinic teaching, but it is not the New Testament idea. The Kingdom is God's dynamic power, and it must "come" because there are real spiritual enemies which oppose it, both human and superhuman. The "coming" of God's Kingdom means the invasion of the power of Satan and the overthrow of his kingdom. Otto is right to this extent: the coming of the Kingdom in Jesus must be interpreted in terms of a great struggle between mighty spiritual powers. K. G. Kuhn has re-echoed this idea: "The Then of the coming of the kingdom of God cannot be separated from the Now of the battle against the kingdom of Satan. Inasmuch as Jesus breaks the power of Satan with his word and with his deeds the kingdom of God is actually made manifest. . . . The kingdom of God is a concept neither of the apocalyptic future nor of a static present—but a dynamic eschatological event."[13]

However, Otto interprets the Gospels too much in terms of religionsgeschichtliche presuppositions and not sufficiently in terms of themselves. Bowman has emphasized an equally important aspect of the problem. Satan's fall refers not to an event in the eternal order alone but to the coming of the Kingdom on the historical plane.[14] Here is an essential fact in the Gospel: the suprahistorical and the historical are inseparably wedded in Heilsgeschichte. We may not separate the victory of God's Kingdom from the person of Jesus, as

[11] R. Otto, The Kingdom of God and the Son of Man (1943), p. 103.
[12] J. W. Bowman, The Religion of Maturity (1948), p. 258.
[13] In The Scrolls and the New Testament (K. Stendahl, ed.; 1958), p. 111.
[14] J. W. Bowman, The Religion of Maturity (1948), p. 257.

Otto does, and see his ministry as a sort of reflex from the overflow of heavenly power. The New Testament locates the Kingdom in Jesus' person and ministry. Jesus brought the Kingdom. Apart from Jesus, there would have been no Kingdom. The victory over demons is a victory in the spiritual realm; but it took place because Jesus came on the plane of history to overthrow evil and deliver men from bondage.

Therefore, in view of the fact that we have no other evidence that Jesus experienced ecstatic visions, and since the word for "seeing" in Luke 10:17 does not require a vision as its object,[15] we must join those who interpret this saying about the vision of Satan's fall figuratively.[16]

This conclusion does not solve the problem. If this saying does not refer to a vision, the question remains, When did the fall of Satan occur? T. Zahn argues strongly for a defeat of Satan at Jesus' temptation. He insists that the fall of Satan must be an event prior to the disciples' mission which enabled them to perform exorcisms.[17] This is unlikely. At the temptation, Satan attacked Jesus; but sayings like those of Luke 10:18 and Matthew 12:28 represent Satan being attacked by Jesus.[18] The sayings are quite meaningful when interpreted in terms of a spiritual defeat over Satan in the very fact of Jesus' ministry.

Some scholars have interpreted Luke 10:18 in the interests of the eschatological view. The success of the Seventy is seen as a sign of the approach of Satan's final overthrow at the eschatological consummation. With vivid prophetic imagination, Jesus sees this end as an already accomplished fact. The certainty of the coming of the Kingdom is so overwhelming, the signs of its impendingness are so sure

---

[15] W. Michaelis, *TWNT*, V, p. 345, n. 161.

[16] K. H. Rengstorf, *Das Evangelium nach Lukas* (1949), p. 133; J. Schmid, *Das Evangelium des Lukas* (1951), p. 153; N. Geldenhuys, *Commentary on the Gospel of Luke* (1950), pp. 302, 305; C. G. Montefiore, *The Synoptic Gospels* (1927), II, pp. 461 f.; R. Leivestad, *Christ the Conqueror* (1954), p. 49.

[17] *Das Evangelium des Lukas* (1913), pp. 420 f. Cf. C. J. Cadoux, *The Historic Mission of Jesus* (n.d.), p. 66; H. B. Swete, *The Gospel according to St. Mark* (1927), p. 67; J. Jeremias, *The Parables of Jesus* (1954), p. 98.

[18] David Bosch, *Die Heidenmission in der Zukunftsschau Jesu* (1959), p. 50; E. Percy, *Die Botschaft Jesu* (1953), p. 183.

that it is said to have occurred or to be occurring already.[19] Fuller refers to the vision in Revelation 12:9 to support his contention that Jesus referred to an eschatological event. However, the heavenly war in Revelation 12 may not refer to an eschatological event at all but may paint a vivid picture in mythological language of the victory already wrought by Christ over Satan. The exclusion of Satan from heaven is a redemptive event; it means the defeat of "the accuser of our brethren" who conquer Satan by the blood of the Lamb (Rev. 12:10–11). Therefore, Revelation 12 and Luke 10:18 seem to refer to the same victory over Satan's kingdom accomplished by the Kingdom of God in Jesus.[20] Here is just the point: the victory over Satan which Jewish thought placed altogether at the end of the age has in some sense happened in history in the mission of Jesus.

We conclude that Jesus saw in the successful mission of the Seventy an evidence of the defeat of Satan. It is beside the point to ask precisely when Satan was cast down, even as we may not ask when Satan was bound (Matt. 12:29). The Fourth Gospel conceives of the death of Jesus as the time of Satan's defeat (John 12:31; 16:11; cf. Heb. 2:14); and as we shall see, the Synoptics represent the death of Jesus as an essential fact in the coming of the Kingdom. It is the entire mission of Jesus which brings about Satan's defeat. We do not need to decide whether Satan's fall is thought of as preceding the mission of the Seventy or as taking place in their very mission. The objection that we cannot conceive of the disciples causing the overthrow of Satan[21] is met by the fact that it was not the disciples themselves but only the authority committed to them by Jesus (Luke 10:19) which effected Satan's fall. They exercised their power only in Jesus' name. Their authority was a delegated authority. Bowman is right in insisting that this passage teaches that the power of God's Kingdom has entered into human history through the ministry of his disciples.[22] The deeper significance of these exorcisms is seen in Luke

[19] R. H. Fuller, *Mission*, p. 27; A. Richardson, *An Introduction to the Theology of the New Testament* (1958), p. 208.
[20] See W. Foerster, *TWNT*, II, p. 79.
[21] T. Zahn, *Das Evangelium des Lukas* (1913), p. 420.
[22] *The Religion of Maturity* (1948), pp. 244 f.; cf. also T. W. Manson, *The*

10:20 where the disciples are told to rejoice above all because their names are written in heaven. Defeat of the forces of evil is but a means to an end. The warfare of the Kingdom only makes room for the peace of the Kingdom. The destruction of evil is part and parcel of the salvation of mankind. The true reason for joy is the salvation that is being achieved.[23] This is achieved because the Kingdom of God has broken the power of evil.

THE DYNAMIC WORKING OF THE KINGDOM

This understanding of the Kingdom of God as the dynamic working of God's rule in the world in advance of the eschatological consummation provides the context for the understanding of another saying which, taken by itself, is very difficult. We have already found in Matthew 11:2–6 evidence that Jesus' ministry had inaugurated the time of messianic fulfillment (see pp. 113 f.). The age of messianic salvation promised by Isaiah has come, although in an unexpected form. There was good reason for John to be perplexed. If Jesus was indeed the Coming One, his messianic works were not introducing the eschatological judgment and bringing the age to come as John had expected. Nevertheless, Jesus' reference to the promise in Isaiah 35 made a clear claim that he had brought the messianic salvation; but then he added the words, "Blessed is he who takes no offense at me" (Matt. 11:6). In other words, John's disciples were to reassure him that Jesus was the Messiah, but that his messianic mission differed from John's expectations. There was reason to stumble; and Jesus therefore pronounced a special beatitude upon those who could recognize the fulfillment of the prophetic hope even though the form of the fulfillment was quite unforeseen.

When the emissaries departed, Jesus added a word of explanation to the crowd. The age of the law and the prophets had come to its

---

Sayings of Jesus (1949), pp. 258 f.; J. Bright, The Kingdom of God (1953), p. 231; D. Bosch, Die Heidenmission in der Zukunftsschau Jesu (1959), p. 50; S. M. Gilmour, IB, VIII, p. 189.

[23] T. W. Manson, The Sayings of Jesus (1949), pp. 258 f.; W. Manson, Studiorum Novi Testamenti Societas: Bulletin, III (1952), p. 13.

end with John. Since John, a new era had been inaugurated.[24] This new age is characterized by this fact: "From the days of John the Baptist until now the kingdom of heaven *biazetai*, and men of violence take it by force (*biastai harpazousin auten*)" (Matt. 11:12).

This saying involves a twofold problem. Does it witness to the presence of the Kingdom of God? If so in what sense of the word? How is the Kingdom to be understood? The problem lies in the fact that the verb *biazetai* can be understood either as a middle voice, "to exercise force," or as a passive, "to be treated forcibly." If it is passive it can be interpreted in several ways:

1. The Kingdom of heaven is forcibly seized by its friends. An eager crowd enthusiastically lays hold of it and takes it by storm.[25] This is a likely rendering, but it has not received much support by recent commentators. In this interpretation, the second half of the verse repeats the same thought, and the *biastai* are good men who violently· lay hold of the Kingdom.

2. Schweitzer, followed by M. Werner,[26] holds that the saying refers to the movement of repentance which Jesus expected his preaching to arouse among the people. This repentance in Israel would drag the eschatological Kingdom from heaven and compel its coming. Such an idea, however, does not fit the fundamental character of the eschatological Kingdom. It is pure miracle and entirely in God's hands. Man cannot compel or prevent its coming. It is true that some later rabbis taught that the coming of the Kingdom could be hastened by the repentance and faithfulness of Israel.[27] However, this teaching was not so much an eschatological hope as it was a means of trying to promote a revival of religion to bring the people into obedience to the law.

---

[24] For further discussion of this new era, see Chap. 8.

[25] See J. H. Thayer, A Greek-English Lexicon (1886), and the commentaries by A. Plummer, H. A. W. Meyer, H. Alford, R. A. Micklem. Also, R. Leivestad, Christ the Conqueror (1954), pp. 31 f.

[26] A. Schweitzer, The Quest of the Historical Jesus (1911), pp. 355 f.; The Mystery of the Kingdom of God (1913), pp. 110–112; M. Werner, The Formation of Christian Dogma (1957), pp. 70 f.

[27] Strack and Billerbeck, Kommentar, I, pp. 599 f.; G. F. Moore, Judaism, II, pp. 350 f.

3. The phrase is taken by some to refer to the misguided efforts of the zealots to establish a national-political earthly kingdom by force. Violent men are *trying* to seize the kingdom and to compel its coming by illegitimate means. These words of Jesus contain an implied condemnation of the erroneous views of the revolutionary zealots.[28] Two strong objections face this interpretation. There was no reason for Jesus to introduce a word about the zealot movement in his reply to the messengers from John, or for Matthew to include such a word in this context. Furthermore, Jesus' reference is to something novel which has been taking place only since the days of John the Baptist, whereas the revolutionary movements in behalf of an earthly kingdom go back much earlier.[29]

4. Some scholars have seen in these words reference to a spiritual battle. Jesus proclaimed an eschatological Kingdom whose coming was so near that its powers could be felt; the great eschatological event was already set in motion. However, its coming was being resisted by evil spiritual powers, "the rulers of this age," "the hosts of darkness."[30] This interpretation involves a real difficulty. The Gospels do indeed represent Jesus as engaged in a struggle with evil of supernatural proportions. Satan is the enemy of God's Kingdom and does all he can to frustrate its work among men (Matt. 13:19; 13:39). However, we do not discover the idea of Satan attacking the Kingdom of

[28] See the commentaries by T. H. Robinson, A. H. McNeile, B. T. D. Smith, C. G. Montefiore; see also J. Klausner, *Jesus of Nazareth* (1925), p. 206; O. Cullmann, *The State in the New Testament* (1956), pp. 20 f.; G. Bornkamm, *Jesus of Nazareth* (1960), p. 66; J. Weiss, *Die Predigt Jesu vom Reiche Jesu* (2nd ed.; 1900), pp. 195-197; G. Gloege, *Reich Gottes und Kirche im Neuen Testament* (1929), p. 132; D. Bosch, *Die Heidenmission in der Zukunftsschau Jesu* (1959), p. 44.

[29] G. Schrenk, *TWNT*, I, p. 610.

[30] See M. Dibelius, *Die urchristliche Überlieferung von Johannes dem Täufer* (1911), pp. 24-29; *Jesus* (1949), pp. 68 f.; C. H. Kraeling, *John the Baptist* (1951), pp. 156 f.; A. N. Wilder, *Eschatology and Ethics in the Teaching of Jesus* (1950), pp. 58, 149-150, 182; W. Manson, *Studiorum Novi Testamenti Societas; Bulletin*, III, p. 13; A. Richardson, *An Introduction to the Theology of the New Testament* (1958), p. 210; A. Fridrichsen in *Theology*, XXII (1931), p. 128. W. G. Kümmel, *Promise and Fulfilment* (1957), p. 123, considers this one of the two possible meanings.

God or exercising his power against the Kingdom itself. He can only wage his war against the sons of the Kingdom. In the conflict motif between Satan and the Kingdom of God, God is the aggressor; Satan is on the defensive. Satan does indeed tempt Jesus; but the satanic role of tempter is a different motif from Satan as tormentor.[31] In the conflict motif, it is the Kingdom of God which attacks the kingdom of Satan.[32] Whenever Jesus speaks of the conflict with Satan and his demons, it is always in terms of their defeat. The stronger invades the house of the strong man (Matt. 12:28). Satan is toppled from heaven (Luke 10:18). Demons quail before Jesus' presence (Mark 1:24). It is contrary to this basic motif to think of the Kingdom of God itself, whether in its eschatological appearing or as an invasion into this age, as actually experiencing violence at the hands of evil spirits. Kümmel is right when he says, "Within the framework of Jesus' preaching there can be no thought of practicing violence against God."[33]

5. One of the most widely accepted interpretations is that the Kingdom suffers violence in the persons of its servants when they are maltreated by the enemies of God's Kingdom. The Kingdom of God suffers violence in that violent men seek to rob other men of the Kingdom of God.[34] Herod is one of the *biastai* and John the Baptist suffered violence at his hands. Support for this interpretation is sought in such sayings as "The evil one comes and snatches away (*harparzei*) what is sown in his heart" (Matt. 13:19); "You shut the kingdom of heaven against men" (Matt. 23:13). However, our saying differs from these. It says nothing about doing violence against men but against the Kingdom of God. If Jesus meant that "sons of the Kingdom" suffered violence, we would expect him to make it

---

[31] R. Leivestad, *Christ the Conqueror* (1954), p. 52.

[32] This is true in the mythological war in Rev. 12. Michael and his angels wage war against Satan.

[33] *Promise and Fulfilment* (1957), p. 123.

[34] See G. Dalman, *The Words of Jesus* (1909), pp. 141 f.; G. Schrenk, *TWNT*, I, p. 610. W. Michaelis, *Der Herr verzieht nicht die Verheissung* (1942), pp. 69 f.; W. G. Kümmel, *Promise and Fulfilment* (1957), p. 123; H. D. Wendland, *Eschatologie*, pp. 47 f.; R. H. Fuller, *Mission*, p. 32; F. V. Filson, *The Gospel according to St. Matthew* (1960), pp. 138 f.

clear. We should not resort to the interpolation of explanatory words unless no other meaning is possible. Furthermore this meaning of harpazein is not established.[35]

6. These five possible interpretations treat biazetai as a passive, and each is beset with difficulties. However, biazetai may equally well be taken as a middle voice and translated, the Kingdom of heaven "exercises its force" or "makes its way powerfully" in the world (RSV mg). This rendering of the verb is most consistent with the dynamic view of the Kingdom of God. There is no philological hindrance to this rendering.[36] The exegetical question must be decided from the context.

Two objections are raised against this interpretation. First, some scholars insist that biazetai must be understood in terms of the following phrase which speaks of the action of biastai upon the Kingdom. The second phrase must be taken as an expansion of the first. The violence in question in biazetai is explained not as the action of the Kingdom but of violent men (biastai) against the Kingdom.[37] Second, the word biastai cannot easily bear a good meaning but designates violent, evil action. Therefore, biazetai must mean that the Kingdom is in some sense suffering violence from evil men.[38]

These are indeed compelling arguments: Kümmel considers them conclusive.[39] They are not, however, unanswerable. To deal with the second objection first, biastai is not a common enough word for us to be certain that it must refer to evil men. Clement of Alexandria felt no difficulty in understanding biastai to mean good men who seize the Kingdom. "Nor does the kingdom of God belong to sleepers and sluggards, but 'the men of force seize it.' This is the only good force, to force God, and seize life from God . . . for God welcomes being

[35] W. Foerster, TWNT, I, p. 472.

[36] See A. Deissmann, Bible Studies (1901), p. 258; G. Schrenk, TWNT, I, p. 609, n. 3; E. Percy, Die Botschaft Jesu (1953), p. 196, n. 7; W. F. Arndt and F. W. Gingrich, A Greek-English Lexicon of the New Testament (1957), in loc.

[37] R. H. Fuller, Mission, pp. 31–32.

[38] Schrenk, TWNT, I, pp. 608–610.

[39] Promise and Fulfilment (1957), p. 122.

worsted in such contests."[40] Since Jesus used radical metaphors involving physical violence to describe the reaction of men to the Kingdom, it is consistent with his teaching to interpret *biastai* in terms of the radical reaction of those who receive the Kingdom.

As to the former objection, there is no reason why the two parts of the sentence must describe the same thing, viz., the treatment of the Kingdom by the violent. In fact, the passage makes better sense when the two halves of the sentence are taken to be complementary. To say that "the Kingdom of heaven suffers violence and violent men assault it" is redundancy.[41] To say, "The Kingdom of heaven acts powerfully and requires a powerful reaction" makes much better sense.[42] It was this factor which set Jesus' teaching apart from rabbinic Judaism. The rabbis taught that men should take upon them the yoke of the Kingdom and accept the law as the norm of God's will. Jesus taught that because God has acted, because the dynamic power of his Kingdom has invaded the world, men are to respond with a radical reaction. "And if your hand causes you to sin, cut it off; . . . and if your eye causes you to sin, pluck it out; it is better for you to enter the kingdom of God with one eye than with two eyes to be thrown into hell" (Mark 9:43, 45, 47). These are acts of violence required of those who would enter the Kingdom.

In other sayings, Jesus demanded violent conduct of those who

---

[40] *The Rich Man's Salvation*, XXI (Butterworth's translation: *Loeb Classical Library*: Clement of Alexandria, p. 315). See also Origen's use of the word in A. E. Brooke, *The Commentary of Origen on St. John's Gospel* (1896), I, p. 133.

[41] T. Zahn, *Das Evangelium des Matthäus* (1922), p. 427.

[42] This interpretation is supported by T. Zahn, *loc. cit.*; R. Otto, *The Kingdom of God and the Son of Man* (1943), pp. 108 ff.; N. B. Stonehouse, *The Witness of Matthew and Mark to Christ* (1944), pp. 247-248; T. W. Manson, *The Sayings of Jesus* (1949), pp. 134-135; G. Duncan, *Jesus, Son of Man* (1949), p. 100; E. Percy, *Die Botschaft Jesu* (1953), p. 196; S. E. Johnson, *IB*, VII, pp. 382-383; A. T. Cadoux, *The Theology of Jesus* (1940), p. 249; M. Black, *ET*, LXIII (1952), p. 290; R. Schnackenburg, *Gottes Herrschaft und Reich* (1959), p. 90; A. M. Hunter, *Introducing New Testament Theology* (1957), p. 18. T. W. Manson at first interpreted this saying as a warning against revolutionary zealots (*The Teaching of Jesus* [1935], p. 124, n. 2), but under the influence of Otto withdrew this in favor of the dynamic interpretation (*Ibid.*, p. 331).

would be his disciples. "If any one comes to me and does not hate his own father and mother and wife and children and brothers and sisters, yes, and even his own life, he cannot be my disciple" (Luke 14:26). He said that he came not to bring peace but a sword (Matt. 10:34). In his parables, he taught that a man should be willing to surrender everything he possesses to secure the Kingdom of God (Matt. 13:44 ff.). He told a rich man that he must rid himself of all his earthly possessions to enter into the Kingdom (Mark 10:21). The presence of the Kingdom demands radical, violent conduct. Men cannot passively await the coming of the eschatological Kingdom as the apocalyptists taught. On the contrary, the Kingdom has come to them, and they are actively, aggressively, forcefully to seize it. This idea could not be delineated more spiritedly than by the acute word-play on *biazetai* and *biastai*.[43]

This dynamic interpretation is supported by the fact that Luke understood it in this way. He renders this saying, "The good news of the kingdom of God is preached, and every one enters it violently" (*eis auten biazetai*) (Luke 16:16). While the form of the Lucan saying is secondary and difficult to reproduce in Aramaic, it embodies the same fundamental idea as Matthew 11:12.[44] The same three elements appear in both sayings: the violent response of men to the Kingdom of God; the contrast between the action of the Kingdom and the reaction of men; and the dynamic working of the Kingdom.

THE DYNAMIC WORD OF THE KINGDOM

This saying in Luke brings us to another evidence for the present dynamic working of the Kingdom of God. It was present and active in the word and authority of Jesus. This is seen particularly in the words "gospel" (*euaggelion*), "to preach the gospel" (*euaggelizes-thai*), and "to preach" (*keryssein*). Jesus' message about the Kingdom of God was not merely instruction or prophecy or promise; it was the proclamation of good news. It was gospel. The prophets had

[43] R. Otto, *The Kingdom of God and the Son of Man* (1943), p. 112.
[44] G. Friedrich, *TWNT*, II, p. 715.

promised a time when the good news would be proclaimed that God was visiting his people. "Behold, the Lord God comes with might, and his arm rules for him" (Isa. 40:9–10). A herald would appear upon the mountains publishing peace, announcing good tidings of salvation, saying to Zion, "Your God reigns. . . . The Lord has bared his holy arm before the eyes of all the nations; and all the ends of the earth shall see the salvation of our God" (Isa. 52:7, 10; cf. Isa. 41:27; 60:6; Nah. 1:15). This promised day will be heralded by one anointed by the Spirit of the Lord "to bring good tidings to the afflicted, to bind up the broken-hearted, to proclaim liberty to the captives, and the opening of the prison to those who are bound; to proclaim the year of the Lord's favor, and the day of vengeance of our God; to comfort all who mourn" (Isa. 61:1–2). These good tidings are nothing less than the visitation of God to bring to his people the messianic salvation.

In the synagogue at Nazareth, Jesus claimed that this gospel was no longer hope but event (Luke 4:18). The time of fulfillment had come. Jesus had been anointed to preach good news (euaggelisasthai) to the poor, to proclaim (keryxai) release to the captives, to proclaim (keryxai) the acceptable year of the Lord. In the proclamation of the gospel, promise had become fulfillment.

The Kingdom was present not only in deed but also in word. The word which Jesus proclaimed itself brought to pass that which it proclaimed: release for captives, recovery for the blind, freeing of the oppressed.[45] In the passage in Matthew 11, the items in the present messianic salvation appear to be arranged in ascending order of significance: blind see, lame walk, lepers are cleansed, deaf hear, the dead are raised, and the poor hear the good news (euaggelizontai). In this last phrase, the sentence reaches its climax. "The message creates the new era (die neue Zeit), it makes possible the signs of the messianic fulfillment. The word brings about the Kingdom of God."[46] The gospel is itself the greatest of the messianic signs. The gospel was not a new teaching; it was itself event. Preaching and heal-

---

[45] G. Friedrich, TWNT, III, p. 705.
[46] G. Friedrich, TWNT, II, p. 715; cf. also E. Bammel, TWNT, VI, p. 903.

ing: these were the two signs of the presence of the Kingdom. This explains why Luke (16:16) renders Matthew's *biazetai* (11:13) by the word *euaggelizetai*. "The Kingdom exercises its power" and "the Kingdom is preached" express the same idea: the dynamic presence of the Kingdom in the deeds and words of Jesus.

Closely associated with the fact of preaching and of proclaiming the gospel is Jesus' authority. His word was not mere human speech; it was a word with authority. The Jews' amazement at Jesus' power over demons was not the mere fact of exorcism but the manner of his exorcisms. "What is this? A new teaching! With authority he commands even the unclean spirits, and they obey him" (Mark 1:27). The novelty in Jesus' teaching did not consist in its form or content but in its power. He spoke, and things happened. He commanded as one who was master of demons, and they obeyed his word.

This authority of his word set Jesus apart from the scribes. The first impression Jesus' teaching made on the people was his difference from the scribes (Mark 1:22). The scribes were conveyors of tradition. A praiseworthy scribe is "a plastered cistern which loseth not a drop" of the traditions of the elders,[47] but faithfully preserves and teaches it to the next generation. Although similarities may be traced between the teachings of Jesus and the scribes, they belonged to different religious worlds. The scribes taught and nothing happened. Jesus spoke and demons fled, storms were settled (Mark 4:39), dead were raised (Mark 5:41), sins forgiven (Mark 2:5). Jesus did not merely promise forgiveness of sins; this could always be done. His authority consisted in the power to accomplish what he proclaimed. That the unique element in Jesus' words and deeds was this authority is proved by the fact that it was this which the scribes challenged (Mark 2:7; 11:28). His authority in deeds and words was nothing less than the presence of the Kingdom of God.[48]

The presence of the Kingdom in Jesus' words explains his imperious manner of speaking. All four Gospels witness to a character-

[47] Pirke Aboth 2:10.
[48] W. Foerster, *TWNT*, II, p. 566.

istic speech form: "Amen, I say to you."[49] "Amen" is used in the Old Testament as a solemn formula to confirm the validity of an oath (Num. 5:22; Deut. 27:15–26), to give assent to an announcement (I Kings 1:36), or as a doxology. Jesus' use of the word to introduce a statement is without parallel in rabbinic usage.[50] Jesus used the expression as the equivalent of an oath, paralleling the Old Testament expression, "As I live, saith the Lord."[51] Jesus' usage is without analogy because in his person and words the Kingdom of God manifested its presence and authority. H. Schlier is right: this one little word contains in nuce the whole of Christology.[52]

This is why Jesus' words possess eternal validity (Mark 13:31). His words will decide the final destiny of men (Mark 8:38; Matt. 7:24–26). Furthermore, the form of the saying in Mark 8:38 ("whoever is ashamed of me and of my words") shows that Jesus' person is inseparable from his words. The scribes stood apart from their teaching; their teachings were greater than their persons. They were vehicles of tradition. But Jesus' words are inseparable from his person. He himself is the message he proclaims.

This is why Jesus swept aside the entire corpus of the rabbinic oral interpretation. He set his authority absolutely over against the rabbinic teaching. "You have heard that it was said to the men of old . . . but I say to you" (Matt. 5, passim). He even claimed authority to reinterpret the true meaning of the law itself. He did not annul the law. On the contrary, he condemned the scribal traditions because they did this very thing, emptying the word of God of its true intent (Mark 7:13). Jesus reinterpreted the role of the law by asserting that observance of merely ceremonial rules of purity could not accomplish God's purpose in the law, for purity was a matter of the heart rather than of the hands. Mark adds to Jesus'

---

[49] Thirty times in Matthew, 13 in Mark, 6 in Luke, 25 in John. Luke substitutes other expressions, such as "truly"; John doubles the "Amen." The force of the word cannot be rendered in English.

[50] D. Daube, The New Testament and Rabbinic Judaism (1956), p. 388.

[51] C. E. B. Cranfield, The Gospel according to Saint Mark (1959), p. 140.

[52] TWNT, I, p. 341.

words the interpretative comment, "Thus he declared all foods clean" (Mark 7:19). Thus Jesus claimed for his words an authority equal to that of the word of God itself.

Seen against this background, Jesus stands apart even from the prophets. The prophetic "thus saith the Lord" is not the same as "Amen, I say unto you." Efforts to interpret Jesus' person and mission largely in terms of the prophetic office fall far short of the demands of the Gospels. His authoritative word is the word of one who knows that the authority of God is present in his own person.[53] The prophet announced the coming of the Kingdom; Jesus embodied its presence and power in his own mission. This was the new element in the gospel which set Jesus apart from Judaism.[54]

This dynamic presence of the Kingdom in Jesus' words explains why the Gospels emphasize the word of the Kingdom. On three significant occasions, Mark summarizes the entire mission of Jesus by the expression, "he was preaching the word to them." The first reference describes the initial stages of the ministry in Capernaum (Mark 2:2), and "speaking the word" is equivalent to "preaching the gospel of the kingdom" (Matt. 4:23) and "preaching the good news of the kingdom of God" (Luke 4:43). The gospel is present in Jesus' word.[55]

In only one place do the evangelists represent Jesus himself as referring to his teaching as "the word." In the interpretation of the parable of the sower, Mark has Jesus say eight times (Mark 4:14 ff.) that the sower sows the word in men,[56] which can be snatched away, or produce only spurious growth,[57] or be choked. This word must be received by men that it may take root and grow and produce fruit. Both Matthew and Luke embellish Mark's simple term by explana-

---

[53] G. Kittel, TWNT, IV, p. 128.

[54] O. Cullmann, The Christology of the New Testament (1959), pp. 46 f.

[55] See also Mark 4:33; 8:32. On the latter verse see E. Klostermann, Das Markusevangelium (1926), p. 95; "ton logon probably = the word, the Gospel, hardly the thing as 1:45, 9:10."

[56] Eis autous, Mark 4:15. Matthew (13:19) and Luke (8:12) both have "in their heart."

[57] Possibly the perplexing alternation in the language between the seed and those in whom the seed is sown, in Mark 4:14-15, is to be explained as indicating that one cannot think of the word of the Kingdom itself as withering and dying.

tory phrases: "the word of the kingdom" (Matt. 13:19) and "the word of God" (Luke 8:11).[58] In view of the twofold fact that the expression is nowhere else found on Jesus' lips but only in the interpretation of the parable of the sower, it is often maintained that this usage is not original but reflects primitive Christian idiom.[59] While this is possible, it is equally possible that Mark correctly reproduces Jesus' idiom, for the idiom corresponds to the fact which is the presence of the Kingdom of God in Jesus' words and in his gospel.[60]

The Kingdom is God's redemptive rule, now present in the person, deeds, and words of Jesus. The message of the parable of the sower is found in precisely this fact: that the coming of the Kingdom of God, which was expected by both apocalyptic and rabbinic Judaism to be a world-shattering divine visitation, has occurred in the proclamation of good news, in words which in and of themselves are weak and powerless. The present working of the Kingdom, like seed, does not enjoy uniform success. Only in those who receive it does it bear fruit. In others, it can be fruitless and futile. Yet this is the Kingdom of God present and active in the word of the gospel. Kittel is right in pointing out that the question of whether the precise wording of the parable is genuine or a Christian product is of secondary significance. The essential question is whether the parable correctly reproduces Jesus' meaning. This question in turn rests on the more fundamental question of Jesus' sense of mission and authority. The truth embodied in the Marcan language about the sowing of the word is funda-

---

[58] Luke uses this expression in 5:1; 8:21; 11:28.

[59] G. Kittel, *TWNT*, IV, p. 123; J. Jeremias, *The Parables of Jesus* (1954), p. 61. V. Taylor, *The Gospel according to St. Mark* (1952), p. 259 and C. E. B. Cranfield, *The Gospel according to Saint Mark* (1959), p. 162, leave the question open.

[60] Fr. Büchsel maintains that the future eschatological Kingdom is present primarily in Jesus' word. Büchsel defines the Kingdom as the form of existence which will arise when God, through the final judgment, has broken all resistance to his reign so that his will alone prevails. Jesus' word brings men into a right relationship with God so that they will survive the final judgment and enter into the Kingdom (*Theologie des Neuen Testaments* [1937], pp. 36-42; *Jesus: Verkündigung und Geschichte* [1947], pp. 42–53). While this interpretation oversimplifies the present meaning of the Kingdom, it is valid as far as it goes.

mentally the same as that expressed in Jesus' words, "I say to you" (Matt. 5:22), in his words of condemnation over the cities (Matt. 11:20 ff.), in the message about the Baptist (Matt. 11:4 ff.), and in the authority of the word addressed to the paralytic (Matt. 9:2 ff.).[61] The question is not the authenticity of this or that saying, but the accuracy of the portrait of Jesus as a whole. Biblical critics realize increasingly that the search for a purely "historical" Jesus who can be explained in terms of ordinary human experience is futile. The most "advanced" circle of German criticism has now engaged in a new quest for the historical Jesus,[62] based upon new concepts of history. The most striking characteristic of this new portrait of Jesus is his authority (Vollmacht), which is in turn the expression of the consciousness of God and of the immediateness of the divine will which in the person of Jesus becomes "unmediated event." "The Gospels call this patent immediacy of Jesus' sovereign power his 'authority.' They apply this word to his teaching. . . . They use it also for the power of his healing word. The word 'authority' certainly contains already the mystery of Jesus' personality and influence, as understood by faith. It therefore transcends the merely 'historical' (historisch) sphere. Yet it denotes a reality which appertains to the historical (geschichtlich) Jesus and is prior to any interpretation."[63] This, so far as it goes, we believe to be correct. In Jesus' person, in his deeds, in his words, the Kingdom of God and its blessings are present and dynamically active among men.

---

[61] G. Kittel, TWNT, IV, p. 124. See the same thought in G. Friedrich, TWNT, II, pp. 725 f.

[62] See J. M. Robinson. A New Quest of the Historical Jesus (1959).

[63] G. Bornkamm, Jesus of Nazareth (1960), p. 60.

7 The Kingdom Present as the Divine Activity

The dynamic understanding of the basileia tou theou has been drawn first from a linguistic and exegetical study of the meaning and use of the term itself. This dynamic interpretation is further illustrated by the theology of the Gospels, strictly speaking, i.e., by their doctrine of God.

The Kingdom is God's Kingdom, not man's: basileia tou theou. The emphasis falls on the second word, not the first; it is the Kingdom of God. "The fact with which we have to reckon at all times is that in the teaching of Jesus his conception of God determines everything, including the conceptions of the Kingdom and the Messiah."[1] If the Kingdom is the rule of God, then every aspect of the Kingdom must be derived from the character and action of God. The presence of the Kingdom is to be understood from the nature of God's present activity; and the future of the Kingdom is the redemptive manifestation of his kingly rule at the end of the age.

[1] T. W. Manson, The Teaching of Jesus (1935), p. 211. This approach was emphasized by A. Schlatter, Die Geschichte des Christus (1923), pp. 140 ff., and has been worked out with strongest emphasis by G. Gloege, Reich Gottes und Kirche im Neuen Testament (1929). See also H. D. Wendland, Die Eschatologie des Reiches Gottes bei Jesu (1931), whose basic point of departure is "Gottesgedanke und Gottesherrschaft."

This was also true in Judaism. God's Kingdom was God's over-all sovereign rule. He never ceased to be the God whose kingly providence ultimately superintended all existence. Furthermore, God's rule could always and everywhere be known through the law; and God would act to establish his Kingdom at the end of the age. Jesus' proclamation of the presence of the Kingdom means that God has become redemptively active in history on behalf of his people. This does not empty the eschatological aspect of the Kingdom of its content, for the God who was acting in history in the person and mission of Jesus will again act at the end of the age to manifest his glory and saving power. Both the present and future display God's Kingdom, for both present and future are the scene of the redemptive acting of God.

THE SEEKING GOD

This thesis is supported by a study of the particular concept of God found in Jesus' teachings. Here we find a striking fact: the novel element in Jesus' proclamation of the Kingdom is paralleled by a new element in his teaching about God: viz., that God is the seeking God. We do not mean to suggest that it was Jesus' purpose to impart a new theoretical truth about God. God is One who is to be experienced, not a teaching to be imparted. This does not exclude the question of what concept of God is reflected in and through Jesus' teaching and ministry.

Critics have debated whether Jesus only purified the contemporary Jewish idea of God[2] or brought a new teaching.[3] This debate appears to be largely one of terminology, depending upon the definition of "new." Certainly there is continuity between Jesus' thought of God and that of the Old Testament and late Judaism. P. Feine is quite correct in saying that Jesus did not purpose to bring a new message about God, for his God is the God revealed in the Old Testament—

[2] R. Bultmann, *Jesus and the Word* (1926), Chap. 4.
[3] II. D. Wendland, *Eschatologie*, pp. 10 ff.

the God of Abraham, Isaac, and Jacob (Mark 12:26), the almighty Lord of heaven and earth (Matt. 11:25, 5:34 f.) who declared his holy will in Moses and the prophets (Matt. 5:17; John 5:44 ff.).[4] We may say, however, that in one sense the God of late Judaism was not the God of the Old Testament. The God of the prophets was constantly active in history both to judge and to save his people; the God of late Judaism had withdrawn from the evil world and was no longer redemptively working in history.[5] One final redemptive act was expected at the end of the age; but meanwhile, God stood aloof from history.

Jesus' message of the Kingdom proclaimed that God not only will finally act, but that God was now again acting redemptively in history. In fact, God had entered into history in a way and to a degree not known by the prophets. The fulfillment of the Old Testament promises was taking place; the messianic salvation was present; the Kingdom of God had come near. God was visiting his people. This is why Wendland says that Jesus did not bring a new teaching about God, but a new reality,[6] the reality of a God who is concerned about sinners. In Jesus, God has taken the initiative to seek out the sinner, to bring lost men into the blessing of his reign. He was, in short, the seeking God.

Some scholars interpret Jesus' view of the Kingdom along the lines of rabbinic thought, except that the role of the law is replaced by Jesus' religious experience. The heart of the Kingdom of God was Jesus' inner experience of God as Father. His mission was to share this experience with men. As men enter into Jesus' experience of God, the Kingdom of God, his rule, "comes" to them. As increasingly large circles of men enter into this experience, God's Kingdom grows and is extended in the world.[7]

[4] *Die Theologie des Neuen Testaments* (8th ed.; 1951), p. 15.
[5] See the essay by W. G. Kümmel in *Judaica*, I (1945), pp. 40–68. Bultmann's way of expressing this same phenomenon is, "The God of the future is not really God of the present" (*Jesus and the World* [1934], p. 148).
[6] H. D. Wendland, *Eschatologie*, p. 10.
[7] Cf. H. E. W. Turner, *Jesus Master and Lord* (1953), pp. 256–260. The earlier interpretation of T. W. Manson does not differ greatly from this pattern,

While there is an important element in this interpretation which must be preserved, it is inadequate because it overlooks the dynamic character of the Kingdom of God. At the very heart of our Lord's message and mission was embodied the reality of God as seeking love. God was no longer waiting for the lost to forsake his sins; God was seeking out the sinner.

This fact was the center of Jesus' conflict with the Pharisees. Their definition of righteousness and their understanding of God raised rigid barriers between the "righteous" and "sinners." This latter term is used in a threefold way in the Gospels.[8] It designates Gentiles who did not worship the God of Israel (Mark 14:41; Luke 6:32 ff.; cf. Matt. 5:47). It designates also the many Jews living in conscious disobedience to the law, such as the woman who anointed Jesus in the house of Simon (Luke 7:37, 39) and Zacchaeus the tax collector who had defrauded many (Luke 19:7 f.). Probably the phrase "tax collectors and sinners" includes such immoral persons, for we read of "tax collectors and harlots" in Matthew 21:31, 32. Tax collectors were despised not only because they were agents of a Gentile government but because of their rapacity and low morals.[9] However, "sinners" refers primarily to a third group consisting of the mass of the people who simply ignored the oral scribal traditions. These traditions, later codified in the Mishnah, possessed to the scribes and the Pharisees the same authority as the law of Moses. Therefore "the people of the land" (Am ha-Arez) who recognized only the written law were despised as sinners (John 7:49). The Pharisaic definition of righteousness included not only correct ethical conduct but also obedience to innumerable rules for ceremonial purity and Sabbath observances. The Pharisees raised rigid barriers between themselves,

---

as he himself admits (The Teaching of Jesus [1935], p. 201). The difference between Jesus and Judaism is that Jesus realized God's will on earth in a new way and brought other men into the same experience, thus creating "the Son of Man"—the society of those who follow the Messiah and take upon themselves the yoke which he bears.

[8] K. H. Rengstorf, TWNT, I, pp. 331 f.

[9] See references in V. Taylor, The Gospel according to St. Mark (1952), p. 204.

the righteous, and the "sinners" with whom they felt they could have no contact without defiling themselves.

Jesus angered the religious leaders not only by ignoring these barriers but by making his association with "sinners" a religious issue. He criticized the Pharisees because their interpretation of God and righteousness actually raised a barrier of religious pride between themselves and God (Luke 18:10 ff.), causing them to lose sight of the true spiritual virtues (Matt. 9:13; 12:7; 23:23) and actually preventing sinners from coming to God (Matt. 23:13). Jesus swept aside the rules of formal righteousness because they were in violation of the essential character of God. He taught that God was more concerned with the sinner than with external rules. God showed this concern by taking the initiative to seek out lost sinners and to bring them into fellowship with himself.

This fact was embodied in Jesus' own mission. When he was criticized by the Pharisees for violating their standards of righteousness and associating with sinners, he replied that it was his mission to minister to sinners (Mark 2:15–17). It is those who know they are sick who need a physician. Jesus must bring the saving good news of the Kingdom to such sinners. He does not deny that they are sinners, nor does he make light of their guilt. Rather he points to their need and ministers to it.

The great truth of God seeking out the sinner is set forth at length in Luke 15 in three parables given to silence the criticism that Jesus welcomed sinners in the intimacy of table fellowship. He said that it was the divine purpose to search out the sheep that had strayed; to seek the coin that had been lost; to welcome the prodigal into the family even though he did not merit forgiveness. In each parable there is a divine initiative: the shepherd searches for sheep; the woman sweeps the house for the coin; the father longs for the prodigal's return. The central character in the parable of the "prodigal son" is not the son but the longing father. The parable illustrates primarily not the prodigality of man but the love and grace of God.

Jewish scholars admit that this concern for the sinner was something new. Abrahams insists that Pharisaism taught that God was always ready to take the first step; yet he admits that the initiative was usually left to the sinner to turn to God.[10] Montefiore recognizes that the "greatness and originality" of Jesus opened "a new chapter in men's attitudes towards sin and sinners" because he sought out sinners rather than avoiding them.[11] This concern for sinners is something entirely unheard of in Judaism[12] and contrasts strikingly with such sentiments as those expressed in IV Ezra, where the author, grieving over the small number of the righteous, is told, "For indeed I will not concern myself about the fashioning of those who have sinned, or about their death, their judgment, or their destruction; but I will rejoice over the creation of the righteous, over their pilgrimage also, and their salvation" (8:38 f.). The heart of the "good news" about the Kingdom is that God has taken the initiative to seek and to save that which was lost.

THE INVITING GOD

The God who seeks is also the God who invites. Jesus pictured the eschatological salvation in terms of a banquet or feast to which many guests were invited (Matt. 22:1 ff.; Luke 14:16 ff.; cf. Matt. 8:11). Against this background we may understand the frequent table fellowship between Jesus and his followers as an acted parable representing an offer of and summons to the blessings of the Kingdom of God.[13] Table fellowship to the Jew was a most intimate relationship, and it played an important role in Jesus' ministry (Mark 2:15). The Pharisees were offended because he ate with sinners (Luke 15:2). He was called "a glutton and a drunkard, a friend of tax collectors and sinners" (Matt. 11:19). The word "call" means

[10] I. Abrahams, Studies in Pharisaism and the Gospels (First Series, 1917), p. 58.
[11] C. G. Montefiore, The Synoptic Gospels (1927), I, p. 55. The validity of Montefiore's observation stands even though his view that Jesus looked upon these sinners as the children of God is to be questioned. It is not because men are God's children that Jesus sought out the sinner, but because God would make them his children.
[12] H. D. Wendland, Eschatologie, p. 11.
[13] Cf. G. Bornkamm, Jesus of Nazareth (1960), p. 81.

invite. "To invite sinners to the Great Banquet of the Kingdom was precisely the Lord's mission."[14]

Jesus called men to repentance, but the summons was also an invitation. In fact, the character of Jesus' summons to repentance as invitation sets his call apart from the Jewish teaching. In Judaism, the doctrine of repentance held a place of greatest importance for it was one of the means by which salvation was to be obtained.[15] Repentance was understood largely in terms of the law and meant, negatively, breaking off evil works and offenses against the law and, positively, obedience of the law as the expression of the divine will. The "yoke of the law" could also be called the "yoke of repentance." The order of events is: man repents, God forgives. The human action must precede the divine. "According to Jewish teaching, the forgiveness of sins depends upon the sinner, for there is no question of a mediator."[16]

Jesus' demand for repentance was not merely a summons to men to forsake their sin and to turn to God; it was rather a call to respond to the divine invitation and was conditioned by this invitation which was itself nothing less than a gift of God's Kingdom. This distinguished Jesus' call to repentance from that of John the Baptist. John called upon men to forsake their sins in view of the coming day of judgment; Jesus called on men to accept an invitation.[17]

This is illustrated by the parables of the pearl and the treasure (Matt. 13:44-46). The Kingdom of heaven which is now offered to men is of such inestimable value that nothing should be permitted to stand in the way of obtaining it. To interpret these parables of the future eschatological Kingdom makes them colorless. No Jew needed that lesson. The whole point of these parables is that the presence of Jesus offers the blessing of the Kingdom to men now.

[14] A. E. J. Rawlinson, St. Mark (1925), p. 29.
[15] See W. O. E. Oesterley and G. H. Box, The Religion and Worship of the Synagogue (1907), pp. 245 ff.; G. F. Moore, Judaism, I, pp. 507-534; J. Behm in TWNT, IV, pp. 991 ff. Moore describes repentance as "the Jewish doctrine of salvation" (op. cit., p. 500).
[16] Oesterley and Box, The Religion and Worship of the Synagogue (1907), p. 247.
[17] See G. Bornkamm, Jesus of Nazareth (1960), pp. 82 f.

Repentance means to receive this proffered gift of God and to lay aside excuses which might seem to be more or less legitimate (Luke 14:16 ff., Matt. 22:1 ff.). This summons to repentance is not laid upon men because God is about to do something in the future, whether near or remote; it is conditioned by the fact that God is now acting. "This very call to repentance speaks, too, of a decision and an action on God's part first."[18] In fact, we may say that the very summons to repentance is itself the action of God's Kingdom.

The gracious character of repentance is vividly illustrated in our Lord's words, "Unless you turn [i.e., repent] and become like children, you will never enter the kingdom of heaven" (Matt. 18:3). What is required here cannot be accomplished by human endeavor. To become a child means to be in oneself helpless, to come into a condition of complete dependence on God, to be ready to let God work. "The children of the heavenly Father to whom Jesus preached are completely receptive toward God. He gives to them what they cannot give to themselves. That is true also of repentance. It is God's gift and yet does not cease to be a demand. It is both at the same time."[19]

Jesus' message of the Kingdom of God is the announcement by word and deed that God is acting and manifesting dynamically his redemptive will in history. God is seeking out sinners; he is inviting them to enter into the messianic blessing; he is demanding of them a favorable response to his gracious offer. God has again spoken. A new prophet has appeared, indeed one who is more than a prophet, one who brings to men the very blessing he promises.

THE FATHERLY GOD

God is seeking out sinners and inviting them to submit themselves to his reign that he might be their Father. An inseparable relationship exists between the Kingdom of God and his Fatherhood; and it is particularly notable that this affinity between the two concepts

---

[18] *Ibid.*, p. 83.
[19] J. Behm, *TWNT*, IV, p. 998.

appears most frequently in an eschatological setting. In the eschatological salvation, the righteous will enter into the Kingdom of their Father (Matt. 13:43). It is the Father who has prepared for the blessed this eschatological inheritance of the Kingdom (Matt. 25:34). It is the Father who will bestow upon Jesus' disciples the gift of the Kingdom (Luke 12:32). The highest gift of God's Fatherhood is participation in God's sovereignty which is to be exercised over all the world. In that day, Jesus will enjoy a renewed fellowship with his disciples in the Father's Kingdom (Matt. 26:29). Since the greatest joy as children of God is that of sharing the blessings of the Kingdom, Jesus taught his disciples to pray, "Our Father who art in heaven, . . . thy kingdom come" (Matt. 6:9, 10). Clearly Kingship and Fatherhood are closely related concepts.[20]

These eschatological sayings illustrate one important fact about God's Fatherhood. It is a blessing and a relationship which cannot be enjoyed by all men but only by those who enter the eschatological Kingdom. The concept of Fatherhood is qualified by that of the Kingdom. It is as the Father that God will grant men entrance into the eschatological Kingdom; and it follows that those who do not enter that Kingdom will not enjoy the relationship to God as their Father.

The gift of Fatherhood belongs not only to the eschatological consummation; it is also a present gift. Furthermore, the future blessing of the Kingdom is dependent upon a present relationship. This is shown from the fact that Jesus taught his disciples to call God their Father and to look upon him as such. But even in this present relationship, Fatherhood is inseparable from the Kingdom. Those who know God as their Father are those for whom the highest good in life is the Kingdom of God and its righteousness (Matt. 6:32, 33; Luke 12:30).

This raises the important question of the source and nature of Jesus' teaching about the Fatherhood of God. The concept has its roots in the Old Testament where Fatherhood is a way of describing the covenant relationship between God and Israel. Israel is God's

[20] G. Schrenk, TWNT, V, pp. 995 f.

firstborn son because of this covenant (Exod. 4:22). God is therefore frequently conceived as the Father of the nation (Deut. 32:6;
Isa. 64:8; Mal. 2:10). This is not a relationship which is grounded
in nature[21] but was created by the divine initiative. Although God
was the Father of the nation as a whole, when Israel became faithless, God's Fatherhood was limited to the faithful remnant of the
righteous within Israel (Ps. 103:13; Mal. 3:17). In the post-canonical
literature, God's Fatherhood was particularly stressed with reference
to the individual (Sir. 23:1; Wisd. of Sol. 2:16). The full meaning
of Fatherhood is eschatological and will be experienced in the Kingdom of God (Ps. of Sol. 17:30 Jub. 1:24). In the rabbinical literature,
the Fatherhood of God is an ethical relationship between God and
Israel.[22]

The old liberal view of the Kingdom of God seized upon this
concept of Fatherhood in Jesus' teaching and made it the determinative theme, interpreting it in universal terms. Jesus allegedly took
up the Jewish teaching of God's Fatherhood, deepened and en-
riched it, extending it to all men. God is Father to all men because
he is perfect in love, and love is the sum of all his moral perfections.
God is the universal Father because he always remains what he
ought to be.[23]

Recent criticism has recognized that "in spite of what is commonly supposed, there is no ground whatever for asserting that Jesus
taught a doctrine of 'the Fatherhood of God and the Brotherhood
of man.' "[24] Two facts emerge from a study of the terminology. (a)
Jesus never grouped himself together with his disciples as the sons
of God. The usage in John 20:17 is only more explicit than that in
the Synoptics: "I am ascending to my Father and your Father, to
my God and your God." Jesus' messianic sonship is different from

---

[21] Paul has a doctrine of God's universal Fatherhood resting upon the fact of
creation (Acts 17:28–29), which represents a different line of thought.

[22] See T. W. Manson, The Teaching of Jesus (1935), pp. 89–92.

[23] See G. B. Stevens, The Theology of the New Testament (1906), pp. 65 ff.;
W. Beyschlag, New Testament Theology (1895), I, pp. 79 ff.; T. Rees, "God,"
ISBE, II pp. 1260 ff.; G. H. Gilbert, "Father," DCG, I, pp. 580 ff.

[24] H. F. D. Sparks in Studies in the Gospels (D. E. Nineham, ed., 1955), p.
260.

the sonship of his disciples. (*b*) Jesus never applied the category of sonship to any but his disciples. Men become sons of God by recognizing his messianic sonship.[25]

A universal Fatherhood of God has been seen in Jesus' saying, "Love your enemies and pray for those who persecute you, so that you may be sons of your Father who is in heaven; for he makes his sun rise on the evil and on the good, and sends rain on the just and on the unjust" (Matt. 5:44 f.). This saying has been interpreted to mean that love for one's enemies is required because God is the universal Father and Jesus' disciples must love all men because God loves all men as his children. This interpretation reads something into the saying. Actually, God is viewed only as the Father of Jesus' disciples. The goodness of God in sending rain to all men, good and evil alike, is not to be confused with the divine Fatherhood. The same exegesis should lead to the conclusion that God is also the Father of all creatures. "Look at the birds of the air; they neither sow nor reap nor gather into barns, and yet your heavenly Father feeds them" (Matt. 6:26). It is not as Father that God cares for the birds, and it is not as Father that God bestows his creaturely blessings on those who are not his children. The Fatherhood of God belongs to those who have responded to the divine seeking-love and have submitted themselves to God's Kingdom. God seeks men, not because he is their Father, but because he would become their Father.

The universal Fatherhood of God has also been seen in the parable of the prodigal son (Luke 15:11–24). The prodigal has been interpreted to teach that every man is by nature a son of God and needs only to return where he belongs. This ignores the fact that a parable is a story drawn from daily life whose purpose is to set forth a basic truth and whose details cannot be pressed (see pp. 219 ff.). It is an improper exegesis to say that this parable teaches

---

[25] For this teaching of "limited sonship" see H. F. D. Sparks in *Studies in the Gospels* (D. E. Nineham, ed.; 1955), pp. 241–262; G. S. Duncan, *Jesus, Son of Man* (1949), pp. 43–45; T. W. Manson, *The Teaching of Jesus* (1935), pp. 98, 102; J. Moffatt, *Love in the New Testament* (1929), p. 70; A. M. Hunter, *Introducing New Testament Theology* (1957), pp. 31 f.

that men are by nature children of God as it would be to say that dumb beasts (Luke 15:1–7) are also sons of God. The central truth of all three parables is that of the yearning God. God is like one who seeks for the lost sheep, who searches for the lost coin, who longs for the return of the prodigal. This is a parable about the Father, not about the son. The one element which all three parables embody about the lost is that the lost sheep *belongs* in the fold; the lost coin *belongs* in the housewife's possession; the son *belongs* in his father's house. Man's proper place is in the house of the Father.

This certainly teaches the potential universal Fatherhood of God but not an actual Fatherhood. While the son was in the strange land, his sonship was an empty thing, void of content. However, he belonged in the Father's house; and "when he came to himself," he returned where he belonged. So is God not only willing but longing to receive all who will come to themselves and turn to the Father, that they may enter into the enjoyment of the Father's blessings.

While there is a close relationship between God's Kingdom and his Fatherhood, T. W. Manson appears to have gone too far in saying, "The Kingship and the Fatherhood are one and the same thing looked at from different points of view."[26] Manson draws this conclusion because he understands the Kingdom in its essence as "the Reign of God, a personal relation between God and the individual, and there is no point in asking whether it is present or future, just as there is no point in asking whether the Fatherhood of God is present or future. It is something independent of temporal and spatial relations. It is a standing claim made by God on the loyalty and obedience of man. From time to time individuals admit this claim and accept the sovereignty of God. This is what is meant by the phrase, 'receive the Kingdom of God'. . . ."[27]

---

[26] T. W. Manson, *The Teaching of Jesus* (1935), p. 163. Quoted by permission of the Cambridge University Press.

[27] *Ibid.*, p. 135. Duncan follows Manson: "In His proclamation of God's Kingdom, as in His message of the divine Fatherhood, Jesus had in mind the establishment of a right relationship between men and God" (*Jesus, Son of Man* [1949], p. 45).

Such a statement preserves an important truth. The Kingdom of God includes the relationship of men to God; and therefore the Fatherhood of God is a concept inseparable from his Kingship. But such an identification omits two important aspects of the Kingdom; its dynamic character and its eschatological consummation. Manson's view of the Kingdom is very close to the rabbinic concept, with the exception that the right relationship to God is mediated through Jesus instead of through the law. One accepts the yoke of Jesus (Matt. 11:29) instead of the yoke of the Torah and thus becomes a son of the Kingdom (see p. 173, n. 7).

The Kingdom of God includes man's relationship to God, but it is larger than this. The Kingdom of God has come in the mission of Jesus to defeat evil and to deliver men from its power. The Kingdom of God comes (Matt. 12:28); it exercises its power among men (Matt. 11:12). It means not only the restoration of individuals to a right spiritual relationship with God, but will ultimately include the redemption of the entire man, even his physical being and his very environment. Therefore exorcisms and healings are signs of the Kingdom's power and presence.

For this same reason, the Kingdom of God has a necessary eschatological dimension when evil will not only be defeated but abolished, and when the evils of the present age will give way to the perfected salvation of the age to come. If the Kingdom is limited to the spiritual relation of men to God, the consummation of the Kingdom could be achieved by the final inclusion of all men in the Kingdom when every last individual on earth has accepted God's rule. In several statements, Manson's view of the consummated Kingdom seems to exclude eschatology.[28] Such statements result from a neglect of the dynamic character of God's rule in Christ. It is a more comprehensive concept than that of Fatherhood; and it would be more accurate to say that the Kingdom of God gives to men the gift of sonship and brings them into a relationship with God as their Father.[29]

[28] See the quotation from Manson above, pp. 12 f.
[29] H. D. Wendland, *Eschatologie*, p. 66.

Nevertheless, these two concepts cannot be separated. At the heart of the Kingdom of God in its eschatological consummation will be the enjoyment of perfect fellowship with God as the heavenly Father; and this new relationship Jesus brought to men in their historical experience. In Jesus' mission God is seeking men to bring them under his fatherly care that he might finally bestow upon them the blessings of his eschatological rule. The enrichment and deepening of the content of Fatherhood in contrast to the concept in Judaism is due to the present activity of the Kingdom of God. God's redemptive action among men has the end of bringing them into a new and more intimate relationship with himself.

THE JUDGING GOD

While God seeks the sinner offering him the gift of the Kingdom, he remains a God of retributive righteousness to those who reject the gracious offer. His concern for the lost does not dissipate the divine holiness into a benign kindliness. God is seeking love; he is also *holy* love. He is the *heavenly* Father. His name is to be hallowed (Matt. 6:9). Therefore, those who reject the offer of his Kingdom must stand under his judgment.

Indeed, the very fact that God is seeking love throws man into a predicament. Man *must* respond to this overture of love; otherwise a greater condemnation awaits him. Bultmann speaks of God who has come near to men as "the Demander."[30] When confronted by the person of Jesus, a man stands before God and must make a decision. The outcome will be either the salvation of the Kingdom or judgment.

This note of retributive righteousness sounds repeatedly in Jesus' proclamation of the Kingdom. In the preaching of the Baptist, the coming of the eschatological Kingdom will mean salvation for the righteous but a fiery judgment for the unrighteous (Matt. 3:12). Jesus taught the same thing. The obverse of inheriting the Kingdom

[30] *Der Fordernde.* Cf. R. Bultmann, *Theology of the New Testament* (1951), I, p. 24.

will be to suffer the punishment of everlasting fire (Matt. 25:34, 41).
To those who refused to enter the Kingdom and who tried to prevent others from entering (Matt. 23:13), Jesus said, "You serpents,
you brood of vipers, how are you to escape the sentence of hell?"
(Matt. 23:33.) The power of the Kingdom was present and active
in Jesus to deliver men from bondage to evil, and God not only
offers free forgiveness to the penitent but even seeks out the sinners
to bring them to himself. When a man has become so blind that he
cannot distinguish between the power of God's Kingdom and the
working of the Devil but thinks that the Kingdom of God is
demonic, that person can never be forgiven; he is guilty of an
eternal sin (Mark 3:29). A fearful doom awaits those who try to
turn believers away from the Kingdom of God (Matt. 18:6). The
great truth of God as seeking love does not nullify the righteousness
and justice of God. The meaning of God's Kingdom is both salvation and judgment.

This eschatological judgment of God's Kingdom is in principle
decided in Jesus' mission among men. As men react to Jesus and
his proclamation, their eschatological doom is determined (Mark
8:38; Matt. 10:32–33). When Jesus' disciples visited various cities
proclaiming the Kingdom and were rejected, they were to wipe the
dust from their feet in an acted parable of judgment;[31] and their
announcement "Nevertheless know this, that the kingdom of God
has come near" becomes a threat instead of a promise. Fearful judgment awaits such a town.

Jesus also pronounced judgment upon cities where he had preached
and performed the works of the Kingdom: Chorazin, Bethsaida,
Capernaum (Matt. 11:20–24; Luke 10:13–15). The nature of the
judgment pronounced on Capernaum is not altogether clear. Luke
(10:14) like Matthew (11:22) describes the judgment which will

---

[31] This gesture in rabbinic thought indicated that the persons concerned were
thereafter to be viewed as heathen and all intercourse broken off (Strack and
Billerbeck, Kommentar, I, p. 581). The context of the act seems to suggest that
the towns concerned would be forever after aliens to the Kingdom of God and
would be no part of the true Israel, the "sons of the kingdom" who accept it.
Theirs would be judgment instead of blessing.

befall Chorazin and Bethsaida in eschatological terms. But both Luke (10:15) and Matthew (11:23) speak of Capernaum's judgment in less eschatological terms, saying merely that this proud city, which was the center of Jesus' Galilean ministry and had heard the message of the Kingdom repeatedly, would be brought down to Hades. Even though Matthew adds an eschatological note (Matt. 11:24), it is evident that he understood this saying to refer to a judgment in history, for he adds that if the works of the Kingdom seen in the streets of Capernaum had been performed in Sodom, "it would have remained until this day" (Matt. 11:23). In this judgment of Capernaum, Jesus uses the taunt song directed against Babylon in Isaiah 14:13-15, even though he does not quote it directly.[32]

Here is an important note recorded by both Matthew and Luke: The judgment for rejecting the Kingdom occurs in history as well as at the eschatological day. Capernaum which was lifted up with worldly pride would be dragged down to the lowest level of shame. Capernaum would suffer the same fate as Sodom: extinction. Here is the relevance of the allusion to Isaiah 14; Capernaum, like Babylon, would be dragged down to ruin. Jesus, like the prophets, could view the divine visitation for judgment in historical as well as eschatological terms. The destruction of Capernaum would be the judgment of the Kingdom of God.

This is not the only time Jesus spoke of judgment in historical terms. A number of sayings pronounce judgment upon Jerusalem and its inhabitants for their spiritual blindness and failure to recognize the proffered messianic salvation. Jesus wept over Jerusalem because it had rejected the offer of the Kingdom (Matt. 23:37-39 = Luke 13:34-35). The metaphor of a hen gathering her brood is drawn from the Old Testament (Deut. 32:11; Ps. 17:8; 36:7); and the Jew who converts a Gentile is said to bring him under the wings of the shekhinah (the presence of God).[33] "The sense is the quite

[32] F. V. Filson, The Gospel according to St. Matthew (1960), p. 141; T. W. Manson, Sayings, p. 77.
[33] Strack and Billerbeck, Kommentar, I, p. 943.

simple one of bringing men into the Kingdom of God."[34] Rejection of this invitation will mean that "your house is forsaken and desolate." It is not clear whether "your house" refers to the temple or to the Jewish commonwealth, but the sense is the same, for the temple and the Jewish commonwealth stand and fall together. Because the offer of the Kingdom has been rejected, Jerusalem which the Jews expected to be the capital of the redeemed world, and the temple, the only sanctuary of mankind, are to be forsaken by God and to become a desolation.

This idea is repeated in Luke 19:41–44. Jesus wept over Jerusalem because she did not recognize "the time of your visitation." In this word (episkope) is reflected the prophetic idea of the God who comes to visit his people.[35] In this saying, God has graciously visited Jerusalem in the mission of Jesus to bring peace. The Kingdom of God had drawn near to Israel in grace and mercy. But Israel rejected the offer of mercy and chose the road that led to disaster.[36] The catastrophe is a historical visitation bringing death and destruction to the city.

We do not need to survey other sayings about the historical judgment which is to overtake Jerusalem (Luke 21:20–24; 23:27–31) and the temple (Mark 13:2; cf. 14:58; 15:29). Wilder is right when he says that Jesus can look at the future in two different ways. He can describe the coming visitation sometimes in terms of an imminent historical catastrophe and sometimes as an apocalyptic transcendental event.[37] Both the historical and the eschatological are divine visitations bringing upon Israel judgment for having rejected the Kingdom of God. God has once again become active in history. He has visited his people in the mission of Jesus to bring them the blessings of his Kingdom. But when the offer is spurned, a visitation of judgment will

---

[34] T. W. Manson, The Sayings of Jesus (1949), p. 127.

[35] Episkope is used in the LXX in this sense in such passages as Isa. 10:3; 23:17; 24:22; 29:6.

[36] T. W. Manson, The Sayings of Jesus (1949), pp. 321 f.

[37] A. N. Wilder, Eschatology and Ethics in the Teaching of Jesus (1950), Chap. 3.

follow: both a judgment in history and an eschatological judgment at the end. Both are judgments of God's kingly rule.

THE KINGDOM: SUPERNATURAL

If the Kingdom of God is the divine redemptive act of seeking the lost, bringing salvation to those who receive it but judgment to those who reject it, a final conclusion must be drawn: the Kingdom is altogether God's deed and not man's work. It is self-evident that the eschatological manifestation of the Kingdom will be altogether God's act. It is "pure wonder." It will transcend all previous human experience and will be so different from the events of human history that modern scholars use the expression "beyond history" to describe it.

However, this same Kingdom of God has come into history in the person and mission of Jesus. The redemptive rule of God which will shatter the mold of history, creating the eschatological order, has entered into history in advance of the eschatological event. This coming of the Kingdom in Jesus is the redemptive activity of the same God directed toward a common redemptive end. Although it is active within history, it is also essentially miracle. Many modernizing interpretations of the Kingdom of God failed to appreciate this fact. Some scholars equate the Kingdom of God with the ideal good to be realized in a spiritual universal Kingdom.[38] Others identify the Kingdom with the idea of inevitable progress or evolution.[39] Against such views, the Gospels represent the Kingdom of God as God's redemptive activity, God's saving will in action. It is not an abstract principle, even the "principle of the divine rule,"[40] for such a concept is too philosophical and too readily separated from the activity

---

[38] A. B. Bruce, *The Kingdom of God* (1890). "All who live in the spirit of love the Son of Man recognizes as Christians unawares, and therefore as heirs of the kingdom" (p. 318). See G. Lundström, *The Kingdom of God in the Teaching of Jesus* (1963), Chaps. 1–3, for Ritschl's interpretation and the "Social Gospel."

[39] See W. Manson, *Christ's View of the Kingdom of God* (1918). This is very different from the view found in his later book, *Jesus, the Messiah* (1946).

[40] J. Orr, *HDB*, II, p. 852. See also *The Christian View of God and the World* (1897), pp. 349–361.

of God. The Kingdom of God is God's redemptive working in history. It cannot be identified with history, nor is it merely God's
working in and through historical events in general. It is more than
this; it is God's supernatural breaking into history in the person of
Jesus. The coming of the Kingdom into history as well as its eschatological consummation is miracle—God's deed.

This is the central teaching of the parable of the seed growing by
itself (Mark 4:26–29). We must be reminded that the parables are
not allegories and that the details of the parables are not essential
to their central message (see Chap. 10). The identity of the sower
and the reaper should not constitute a problem,[41] for the message
of the parable has to do with the activity of the Kingdom and not
with the identity of the sower. That a man sows seed means no more
than that seed is sown. The sleeping and rising of the sower means
only that man cannot contribute to the life and growth of the seed.
The element of growth has often been made the central truth in
the parable, and great significance has been seen in the stages of
growth: the blade, the ear, and finally the full grain. This has been
taken to illustrate the analogy between the natural world and the
Kingdom of God. Just as there are laws of growth resident within
nature, so there are laws of spiritual growth through which the
Kingdom must pass until the tiny seed of the gospel has brought
forth a great harvest. The interpretation of gradual growth has been
espoused by representatives of many theological positions.[42]

[41] Cf. W. G. Kümmel, Promise and Fulfilment (1957), p. 128. Trench was
troubled by this problem (R. C. Trench, Notes on the Parables of Our Lord
[1872], pp. 287 f.), and the interpretation of the parable has sometimes been
made to depend on its solution. If Jesus is the sower, he must be the reaper; and
how could it be said of him that he was ignorant of the growth of the seed?
F. C. Grant (IB, VII, pp. 705 f.) feels that vs. 29 must be an "apocalyptic
appendage" to the parable because it confuses the picture. In the parable the
sower is also the reaper; but in vs. 29 God who is the harvester could not have
been the farmer. Such criticisms ignore the character of parables, assuming that
they are allegories rather than parables.
[42] A. B. Bruce, The Parabolic Teaching of Christ (1882), pp. 117 ff.; H. B.
Swete, The Parables of the Kingdom (1920), pp. 16 ff.; W. O. E. Oesterley,
The Gospel Parables (1936), p. 71; J. Orr, HDB, II, pp. 852–854; C. J. Cadoux,
The Historic Mission of Jesus (n.d.), pp. 113–114; T. W. Manson, The Teaching
of Jesus (1935), p. 133; G. C. Morgan, The Parables and Metaphors of Our
Lord (1943), pp. 145 ff.

However, three facts oppose this interpretation. In his nonparabolic teachings, Jesus nowhere set forth the idea of gradualness and growth of the Kingdom. If this were an essential element in his teaching, he must have made it clear, since the gradual growth of God's Kingdom was an utterly novel idea to first-century Jews. Second, the concept of sowing and planting is frequently found in Christian and Jewish literature but is never used to illustrate gradualness and development.[43] Third, the metaphor of sowing and reaping is used in Christian literature to illustrate the supernatural.[44]

C. H. Dodd understands the parable to teach the present crisis of the Kingdom in the ministry of Jesus. The period of growth was the previous activity of God in the history of Israel which had reached its climax with the coming of Jesus. The harvest had become ripe; all that waited was the actual ingathering.[45] This view assumes that the eschatological coloring in the idea of the harvest is due to the church's misunderstanding of Jesus and not to Jesus himself; but Dodd has admitted that he underrated the eschatological element in Jesus' teaching.[46] Furthermore, Matthew 11:12 (cf. Luke 16:16) contrasts sharply the time of the prophets and the time of the Kingdom, and contradicts the idea of the Kingdom passing through a long period of growth in Old Testament times, only to come to its harvest in Jesus' time.[47] The time of the prophets is not the time of the growth of the Kingdom, but is distinguished from the Kingdom.

The clue to the meaning of the parable was discovered by the eschatological school, although we feel that the consistent eschatological interpretation must be modified to fit the total context of

[43] See N. A. Dahl, StTh, V (1952), pp. 140–147, for references.

[44] See I Cor. 15:35 ff.; II Cor. 9:6; Gal. 6:7–8; I Clement 24. Clement uses the phenomenon of growth in nature as a proof of the resurrection, which is altogether supernatural.

[45] C. H. Dodd, The Parables of the Kingdom (1936), pp. 178–180; V. Taylor, The Gospel according to St. Mark (1952), p. 266; A. T. Cadoux, The Theology of Jesus (1940), p. 36; A. M. Hunter, Introducing New Testament Theology (1957), p. 30.

[46] The Coming of Christ (1951), p. 16.

[47] W. G. Kümmel, Promise and Fulfilment (1957), p. 129.

Jesus' message. The Kingdom is seen as the eschatological event which is utterly independent of all human effort. J. Weiss felt the parable taught that Jesus had nothing to do with the coming of the Kingdom. He could not foresee it; only God could bring it. Man can do nothing but wait.[48] Many other interpreters have found the truth of the parable in the utter independence of the future eschatological harvest of all human activity.[49]

This is certainly an indispensable truth about the Kingdom. However, this interpretation is as one-sided as that of Realized Eschatology, for it neglects the central and unique element in Jesus' message—the presence of the Kingdom in his own mission. It fails therefore to relate Jesus' ministry to the eschatological coming of the Kingdom except as an advance announcement.[50] The most obvious difficulty with a strictly futuristic interpretation is that it is colorless; no Jew needed to be told that the eschatological consummation of the Kingdom was a miracle. It could be nothing but a supernatural act of God.

It is not allegorizing to insist that there is in the parable a necessary relationship between sowing and harvest.[51] In some sense or other, the ministry of Jesus involved the "seed" of the Kingdom which would one day come in fullness of harvest. The seed was being sown; a harvest would one day come. Both are manifestations of God's Kingdom. "The present hiddenness and ambiguousness of

[48] J. Weiss, Die Schriften des Neuen Testaments (4th ed.; 1929), I, pp. 115 f.

[49] Cf. W. G. Kümmel, Promise and Fulfilment (1957), pp. 128 f.; B. T. D. Smith, The Parables of the Synoptic Gospels (1937), pp. 129 ff.; M. Dibelius, Jesus (1949), pp. 66-67; C. G. Montefiore, The Synoptic Gospels (1927), I, pp. 130 f.; B. H. Branscomb, The Gospel of Mark (1937), p. 83; R. Bultmann, Jesus and the Word (1934), pp. 36 f.; A. E. Barnett, Understanding the Parables of Our Lord (1940), pp. 51-54; E. Klostermann, Das Markusevangelium (1926), p. 50; A. E. J. Rawlinson, St. Mark (1925), p. 56; J. Jeremias, The Parables of Jesus (1954), pp. 91 ff. F. C. Grant (IB, VII, pp. 704 f.) finds the single point in the certainty of harvest.

[50] A. Schweitzer felt this problem and offered a novel explanation to avoid it. The preaching of Jesus must compel the coming of the Kingdom (The Quest of the Historical Jesus [1911], pp. 355 f.).

[51] This is strongly emphasized by C. Masson, Les Paraboles de Marc IV (1945), p. 42. See also J. Schniewind, Das Evangelium nach Markus (1937), p. 81.

the kingdom of God [will] be succeeded by its glorious manifestation."[52]

Here is the central truth of the parable. Seedtime and harvest: both are the work of God. Both are essentially supernatural. The earth bears fruit of itself. The seed has resident within it powers which man does not place there and which utterly transcend anything he can do. Man can sow the seed, but the Kingdom itself is God's deed.

This interpretation pays adequate attention to the historical setting of our Lord's ministry. His mission was to bring to men the fulfillment of the messianic salvation, while the apocalyptic consummation remained in the future. Such an event was unheard of. Precisely here was to be found the predicament of Jesus' hearers: how could *this* be the supernatural Kingdom of God? Jesus made no display of apocalyptic glory. He refused to act as a conquering Davidic king, supernaturally endowed to crush Israel's enemies. How could the Kingdom be present in one whose only weapon was his word, whose only victory was over demons and Satan and sickness?

The unexpected presence of the supernatural Kingdom is the central message of the parable in its historical setting. The Kingdom of God which will one day bring an apocalyptic harvest is present; but it is like a seed rather than the harvest. Yet the seed is related to the harvest; and the life of the seed is itself the act of God—supernatural. While men sleep, the earth produces fruit *automate*. The supernatural act of God which will one day be disclosed in glory is active and at work in a new and unexpected form, in Jesus of Nazareth. In him is taking place a supernatural work of God.[53]

---

[52] C. E. B. Cranfield, *The Gospel according to Saint Mark* (1959), p. 168. For other interpretations recognizing the tension between future and present, see E. Percy, *Die Botschaft Jesu* (1953), pp. 203–206; R. Otto, *The Kingdom of God and the Son of Man* (1943), p. 123; W. Manson, *Jesus, the Messiah* (1946), p. 75; N. A. Dahl, *StTh*, V (1952), pp. 145–150; G. Bornkamm, *Jesus of Nazareth* (1960), pp. 73–74; A. M. Hunter, *Interpreting the Parables* (1960), p. 45. Several of these scholars emphasize the factor of growth in a way that does not seem compatible with the basic idea of the reign of God; see, e.g., Otto and Hunter.

[53] This supernatural dimension of the Kingdom of God which has invaded history in the person of Jesus creates an insoluble problem for the historian as

The supernatural character of the present Kingdom is confirmed by the words found in association with it. A number of verbs are used with the Kingdom itself as the subject. The Kingdom can draw near to men (Matt. 3:2; 4:17; Mark 1:15; etc.); it can come (Matt. 6:10; Luke 17:20; etc.), arrive (Matt. 12:28), appear (Luke 19:11), be active (Matt. 11:12). God can give the Kingdom to men (Matt. 21:43; Luke 12:32), but men do not give the Kingdom to one another. Further, God can take the Kingdom away from men (Matt. 21:43), but men do not take it away from one another, although they can prevent others from entering it. Men can enter the Kingdom (Matt. 5:20; 7:21; Mark 9:47; 10:23; etc.), but they are never said to erect it or to build it. Men can receive the Kingdom (Mark 10:15; Luke 18:17), inherit it (Matt. 25:34), and possess it (Matt. 5:4), but they are never said to establish it. Men can reject the Kingdom, i.e., refuse to receive it (Luke 10:11) or enter it (Matt. 23:13), but they cannot destroy it. They can look for it (Luke 23:51), pray for its coming (Matt. 6:10), and seek it (Matt. 6:33; Luke 12:31), but they cannot bring it. Men may be in the Kingdom (Matt. 5:19; 8:11; Luke 13:29; etc.), but we are not told that the Kingdom grows. Men can do things for the sake of the Kingdom (Matt. 19:12; Luke 18:29), but they are not said to act upon the Kingdom itself. Men can preach the Kingdom (Matt. 10:7; Luke 10:9), but only God can give it to men (Luke 12:32).

The character of the Kingdom reflected in these expressions is summed up in a saying preserved in John's Gospel: "My *basileia* is not of this world; if my *basileia* were of this world, my servants would fight, that I might not be handed over to the Jews; but my kingdom is not from the world" (John 18:36). The Revised Standard Version is correct in translating *basileia* "kingship." The source and the character of Jesus' Kingdom is from a higher order than this world; it comes from God and not from this world. The King-

---

historian, for he knows nothing of supernatural events; he can deal only with purely natural occurrences. The evidence of the supernatural is inexplicable to the historian. This is why the person of Jesus presents a continuing problem for historical scholarship, for the essential fact of his person and mission transcends historical explanation.

dom is the outworking of the divine will; it is the act of God himself. It is related to men and can work in and through men; but it never becomes subject to men. It remains God's Kingdom. It is significant that although men must receive the Kingdom, this individual human act of reception is not described as a coming of the Kingdom. The Kingdom does not come as men receive it. The ground of the demand that men receive the Kingdom rests in the fact that in Jesus, the Kingdom has come into history. God has done a new thing. He has visited his people in Jesus' mission, bringing to them the messianic salvation. The divine act requires a human response, even though it remains a divine act.

8 The Kingdom Present as the New Age of Salvation

In our survey of the secular use of *malkuth* in the Old Testament, we discovered that the word was used both of the reign of a king and of the realm over which he exercised his rule (see pp. 46 f.). There should therefore be no philological or logical reason why the Kingdom of God may not be conceived of both as the reign of God and as the realm in which his reign is experienced.

THE REALM OF SALVATION

This is in fact what we find in the Gospels. The fundamental meaning of the Kingdom of God is God's rule or reign. We have argued that the truly distinctive element in Jesus' teaching is that before God manifests his kingly reign in glory, his reign has invaded human history in advance of the eschatological consummation.

However, not all uses of *basileia* can be adequately explained by this dynamic concept. Many sayings picture the Kingdom as an eschatological realm into which men enter.[1] This is an idea which

---

[1] See Mark 9:47; Mark 10:15 = Luke 18:17; Matt. 18:3; Mark 10:23 = Matt. 19:23 = Luke 18:24; Mark 14:25 = Matt. 26:29; Matt. 5:19, 20; 7:21;

Jesus shared with contemporary Judaism, for it was a central element in the prophetic hope. The eschatological manifestation of God's rule will destroy all evil and will issue in a new eschatological realm of salvation. However, Jesus' terminology for expressing this idea differed from that of contemporary Judaism. Jesus could speak of entering either the Kingdom of God or the age to come; and both were in some sense synonymous with eternal life (Mark 10: 17–30). Judaism spoke of entering the age to come, and of inheriting it.[2] This eschatological realm of salvation was not called "the Kingdom of God." Judaism retained the dynamic meaning of the term (see pp. 130 ff.).[3]

Jesus not only departed from usual idiom by speaking of the Kingdom of God as an eschatological realm; he used the term also to designate a realm of salvation which is present.[4] This is not surprising. If the eschatological coming of God's Kingdom issues in a realm of salvation in which his people enjoy the blessings of his reign, and if God's Kingdom has in fact already manifested itself in the mission of Jesus, we might expect that this would issue in a realm in which men may experience the blessings of God's present rule.

The clearest illustration is a detached logion in Luke 16:16: "The law and the prophets were until John; since then the good news of the kingdom of God is preached, and every one enters it violently." The interpretation of this verse must await a discussion of the parallel saying in Matthew 11:12, for Luke has apparently simplified and interpreted a difficult saying in Matthew. However, we may now indicate that the saying in Luke embodies three elements: one era (that of the law and prophets) had ended with John; since then a new activity had been taking place—the proclamation of the King-

---

8:11; 20:21; 25:34; Luke 14:15; 22:29–30. See also C. J. Cadoux, *The Historic Mission of Jesus* (n.d.), pp. 197 f.

[2] See, for instance, Apoc. Bar. 14:13; 51:3.

[3] See also Strack and Billerbeck, *Kommentar*, I, pp. 181 ff.; E. Percy, *Die Botschaft Jesu* (1953), p. 22; R. Schnackenburg, *Gottes Herrschaft und Reich* (1963), p. 62.

[4] The recent study by S. Aalen in *NTS*, VIII (1962), pp. 215–240, takes this meaning to be the normative element in Jesus' message.

dom; the result was that men were entering the Kingdom, conceived as a new realm of salvation.

Other sayings carry the same thought of entering the Kingdom as a present realm. "The tax collectors and the harlots go into the kingdom of God before you," the rebellious priests and elders (Matt. 21:31). To the scribes and the Pharisees, Jesus said, "You shut the kingdom of heaven against men; for you neither enter yourselves, nor allow those who would enter to go in" (Matt. 23:13). A similar saying is found in Luke 11:52, which does not mention the Kingdom but obviously refers to it. "Woe to you lawyers! for you have taken away the key of knowledge; you did not enter yourselves, and you hindered those who were entering." This same idea appears in the saying to a scribe who responded to Jesus' teaching: "You are not far from the kingdom of God" (Mark 12:34). In Matthew 11:11, Jesus says that the one who is (now) in the Kingdom of heaven is greater than John the Baptist.

Many scholars insist that these sayings should not be allowed their apparent present reference but should be interpreted in terms of the unquestionable eschatological passages. Since Aramaic has no future tense, such "neutral" sayings where the Kingdom might be interpreted as a present realm should for consistency's sake be understood to refer to the future eschatological realm.[5] Matthew 21:31 means no more than that the tax collectors and harlots are on the way toward the Kingdom and have an advantage over the religious leaders or will enter the Kingdom ahead of them.[6]

This, however, is too easy a solution. It is arbitrary to insist that all sayings about entry into the Kingdom are eschatological[7] unless it is established that the eschatological concept exclusively dominated Jesus' thinking; and this is precisely the question at issue. If, however, the Kingdom is also the present activity of God's kingly reign,

[5] See W. Michaelis, Taüfer, Jesus, Urgemeinde (1928), pp. 64–73; H. Windisch in ZNTW, XXVII (1928), pp. 163–192.

[6] J. Weiss, Die Predigt Jesu vom Reiche Gottes (1892), p. 15; A. H. McNeile, The Gospel according to St. Matthew (1915), p. 306; C. T. Craig, IB, VII, p. 148; R. Bultmann, Jesus and the Word (1934), p. 204; S. M. Gilmour, The Gospel Jesus Preached (1957), p. 56.

[7] J. Jeremias, The Parables of Jesus (1954), p. 100, n. 53.

there must be those who receive the divine rule in the present. It would be natural to speak of their entrance into the sphere of its blessings, and the present tense suggests this meaning.[8] So when Jesus told the scribe that he was not far from the Kingdom, it is artificial (künstlich) to take the meaning to be, "The future rule of God is approaching and you belong to it."[9] Taylor is right in saying that the imagery of this saying is spatial, picturing a domain in which God's will is done and his rule supreme. The scribe stands on the threshold,[10] because he is ready to respond to the demand of God's will embodied in the person and teaching of Jesus and expressed in the law of love.

The woe against the scribes and the Pharisees for shutting the Kingdom of heaven against man (Matt. 23:13) could conceivably be interpreted of a future kingdom; but the emphasis is on something which was occurring then and there. They were preventing from entering the Kingdom men who were inclined to enter and were in process of doing so (tous eiserchomenous). They both refused to become disciples and they sought to turn men away and to prevent them from receiving the rule of God which Jesus proclaimed and from entering into its blessings.

The saying in Luke 11:52 has the same meaning as Matthew 23:13. The "key of knowledge" is not mere intellectual perception but is the knowledge of God disclosed in the Old Testament revelation.[11] The revelation in Israel's history should provide the key for men to understand the revelation in Jesus' person and mission and enable them to enter the Kingdom which he proclaimed. The Pharisees have frustrated this divine purpose and have in effect lost the key.

The most natural interpretation of the saying about the tax collectors and harlots entering the Kingdom ahead of the priests and elders is of a present activity (Matt. 21:31). It receives its coloration from Jesus' words about John and the Kingdom in Matthew 11. As we shall see, John himself stood on the threshold of the new era of

---

[8] F. V. Filson, The Gospel according to St. Matthew (1960), p. 34.
[9] J. Schniewind, Das Evangelium nach Markus (1952), p. 162.
[10] V. Taylor, The Gospel according to St. Mark (1952), p. 489.
[11] T. W. Manson, The Sayings of Jesus (1949), p. 103.

salvation. While there were disciples of John who apparently never became disciples of Jesus (Mark 2:18; Acts 19:3), the harlots and tax collectors to whom Jesus refers in Matthew 21:31 are those who believed John and then later became Jesus' disciples. These, in contrast to John, are said to be "in the kingdom of heaven" (Matt. 11: 11) because they have received the rule of God proclaimed by Jesus. Therefore they may be said already to enter into the Kingdom of God while the elders stand aside. The point of the saying is that "even the sight of the outcasts streaming into the Kingdom has not changed their attitude."[12]

The most important passage about the Kingdom as the new era of salvation is Matthew 11:11–13, and it is associated with one of the most important sayings about the Kingdom as the present dynamic activity of God in the world (see pp. 158 ff.). Jesus spoke of John as a great prophet, yet as more than a prophet, for he was the fulfillment of Malachi 3:1 (Matt. 11:10) which foretold a divine visitation. Before the great and terrible day of the Lord comes (Mal. 4:5–6), Elijah would appear to bring conversion to Israel lest they fall under the divine judgment.

Jesus asserted that the prophecy of Malachi was fulfilled in John the Baptist. John was Elijah, sent to warn Israel of the approaching Day of the Lord. However, the fulfillment of the prophecy was not self-evident. Jesus said, "If you are willing to accept it" (Matt. 11:14). There was something enigmatic about the nature of the fulfillment. It was not self-explanatory; it could not be recognized by all. A willing heart was required to recognize that John was Elijah. "He who has ears to hear, let him hear" (Matt. 11:15). Not all have ears; not all can hear. Therefore, many did not recognize John for the Elijah he was, but "did whatever they pleased" (Mark 9:13), putting him to death. The fulfillment of the Elijah prophecy was taking place in terms other than those expected, and spiritual responsiveness was necessary to recognize the fulfillment.

Nevertheless, said Jesus, Elijah has come; therefore something which belongs to the Day of the Lord is present. The restoration of

<hr>

[12] F. V. Filson, *The Gospel according to St. Matthew* (1960), p. 227.

all things (Mark 9:12) is under way. This term (apokathistemi-apokatastasis) had come to have a technical meaning designating the restoration of Israel to her promised blessings.[13] Jesus asserted that the day of restoration meant the religious renewal of the people in terms of repentance and forgiveness.[14]

It is in light of this unexpected fulfillment of the Elijah prophecy and the spiritual renovation he presaged that we are to interpret the difficult saying in Matthew 11:11: "Truly, I say unto you, among those born of women there has arisen no one greater than John the Baptist; yet he who is least in the kingdom of heaven is greater than he." What does it mean to be in the Kingdom of heaven?

Some scholars treat this saying as a product of the later Christian community. Jackson and Lake argue that a saying which seems to exclude John from the Kingdom could not have arisen in a Jewish environment, and in fact is "meaningless here except in the sense of the Christian church."[15] Other scholars, endeavoring to avoid this difficulty, translate the saying, "There has arisen no one greater than John the Baptist; yet he who in the [future] kingdom of heaven is least [will be] greater than John [is now]."[16]

These are not the only alternatives. No reference to the church is called for, and an eschatological reference in this context is unnecessary and out of place. It is unnecessary because it is a self-evident truth which needs no affirmation. No Jew needed to be told that the blessings of the age to come would be infinitely greater than those of the present age. It is out of place because the problem under discussion was not the character and blessings of the age to come but the person and mission of Jesus. Was he the Coming One? Was John right in identifying Jesus as the one who would introduce the

---

[13] See Jer. 16:15; 24:6; Hos. 11:11; Ezek. 16:55; Acts 3:21. See also A. Oepke, TWNT, I, p. 388.

[14] J. Jeremias, TWNT, II, p. 940.

[15] F. J. Foakes Jackson and K. Lake, Beginnings of Christianity (1920), I, p. 331. W. G. Kümmel (Promise and Fulfilment [1957], p. 125, n. 75) also thinks Matt. 11:11b is a Christian creation because it disparages John.

[16] See A. H. McNeile, The Gospel according to St. Matthew (1915), p. 154; E. Klostermann, Das Matthäusevangelium (1927), p. 97; F. Dibelius, ZNTW, XI (1910), pp. 190 ff.

Kingdom of God? Precisely here was John's problem: the eschatological salvation and judgment he had proclaimed were not being fulfilled in Jesus. Jesus' answer in Matthew 11:4–6 assured John's disciples that the messianic salvation was present and in process of fulfillment, but in unexpected terms. The reference, therefore, to those "in the Kingdom of heaven" is to those who were experiencing the messianic salvation, proclaimed and performed by Jesus. It was a greater thing to hear the good news and to receive the healing and life of the messianic salvation than to be a prophet as great as John the Baptist.

This interpretation is supported by three facts admitted by most exegetes. (1) Matthew 11:11 contrasts those in the Kingdom with John. (2) Verse 12 says that since the days of John, something is happening that has to do with the Kingdom of God.[17] (3) Verse 13 says that an age has ended with John—the age of the law and the prophets. Therefore we must conclude that (a) John brought to its end the era of the law and the prophets; (b) since John, a new era has begun; and (c) this new era is called the Kingdom of God.[18]

---

[17] Apo can be exclusive, meaning "since." See Matt. 1:17 ("since the deportation," vs. 12); Luke 2:36. Some scholars think that John stands within the new order (E. Percy, Die Botschaft Jesu (1953), pp. 198–202; J. M. Robinson, A New Quest of the Historical Jesus (1959), p. 119; but see W. Foerster, TWNT, I, p. 472.

[18] The presence of the Kingdom of God as a new era of salvation is recognized by T. W. Manson, The Sayings of Jesus (1949), pp. 70, 134; C. H. Dodd, The Parables of the Kingdom (1936), p. 47; J. Bright, The Kingdom of God (1953), p. 197; E. Percy, Die Botschaft Jesu (1953), pp. 198–202; R. N. Flew, Jesus and His Church (1943), p. 26; W. Foerster, TWNT, I, p. 472. Other scholars who interpret biazetai as a passive agree that the passage teaches that a new era of the Kingdom was actually present. Cf. G. Schrenk, TWNT, I, p. 610; W. G. Kümmel, Promise and Fulfilment (1957), pp. 123–124; H. D. Wendland, Eschatologie, p. 48; F. V. Filson, The Gospel according to St. Matthew (1960), p. 138. A number of scholars see three periods: "until John," the time of the law and the prophets; the time of John, "from John . . . until now," a provisional period when the Kingdom is under attack; the time of Jesus [from now], the consummation when Satan is bound. See, with variations, M. Dibelius, Die urchristliche Überlieferung von Johannes dem Täufer (1911), pp. 24–29; A. N. Wilder, Eschatology and Ethics in the Teaching of Jesus (1950), p. 149, n. 5; D. Bosch, Die Heidenmission in der Zukunftsschau Jesu (1959), p. 45. This view is deduced from the expression "until now," which, it is assumed, required a third period beyond the "now." This does not follow, for "until now" need

This accords fully with the obvious conclusion that John stood outside of this new era of the Kingdom. The blessings which Isaiah saw in the eschatological salvation have come to men in history: healing, life, the gospel. These gifts of the Kingdom are now present. However, John did not experience them. We have no record that he or his disciples performed the miracles of the Kingdom. John stood on the threshold of fulfillment, announcing the new order. He brought to its climax the age of preparation. The fulfillment is so much greater than the preparation that the least who experiences the fulfillment is "greater" than John, "not by what the least in the Kingdom does for God . . . [but] in what God does for him here and now."[19] This is what it means to be "in the Kingdom." It has no reference to being in the church but in the new order of the messianic salvation.

This saying about being in the Kingdom is not really "neutral" but illuminates the other sayings about entering the Kingdom. God's Kingdom, his kingly rule, has become dynamically active in history, creating a new realm of blessing into which men may enter. This too is called the Kingdom of God. "According to 11 as it stands, the new era has already begun. The kingdom was virtually present. It is present, though in its full reality and manifestation it is still future."[20]

This interpretation of Matthew 11:11–13 is supported by Luke. "The law and the prophets were until John; since then the good news of the kingdom of God is preached, and every one enters it violently" (Luke 16:16). This verse is probably secondary to Matthew; and the question arises whether Luke has correctly understood and interpreted the saying. We find the same basic contrast between the period of the law and the prophets which ended with John and the period since John which is the time of the preaching of the Kingdom.

---

mean only a continuing situation with no intimation as to its end, as in I Cor. 4:13 and 8:7. Cf. E. Grässer, Das Problem der Parousieverzögerung (1957), p. 181.

[19] T. W. Manson, The Sayings of Jesus (1949), p. 70.

[20] C. G. Montefiore, The Synoptic Gospels (1927), II, p. 161. Montefiore, following Jackson and Lake, thinks that 11b is a "Christian" addition. This is highly unlikely, if only for the reason that we have no proof that the early church equated the Kingdom with the church.

In both sayings, some are "in the Kingdom." This does not mean "in the church"; the thought is much more primitive than that. To be in the Kingdom is to receive the gospel of the Kingdom and experience its salvation.[21]

Some scholars overinterpret the meaning of Matthew 11:13. Schniewind says, "Since John, 'the end' has already come! With John and Jesus, God's Kingdom has begun. The end of this aeon is here and the new aeon, the new world of God has begun."[22] Such an interpretation says more than the Gospels do, and it ignores the tension which exists between fulfillment and consummation. Jesus did not say that the old aeon was at an end but that the age of the law and the prophets was at an end. John's difficulty lay at precisely this point; the structure of the old age seemed undisturbed. How then could Jesus be Messiah? It was not the new aeon which had begun, but the blessings of the messianic salvation, the Kingdom of God, which had come to men within the old aeon. John had not learned how to distinguish between the messianic salvation and the new aeon; hence his perplexity.

Jesus intimated that there was an enigmatic element in the present fulfillment of the Old Testament expectation. "If you are willing to accept it . . . . ," "He who has ears . . ." (Matt. 11:14, 15). This coming of the messianic salvation was not something which compelled universal recognition and could be perceived by all men.

This is further indicated by the words, "Blessed is he who takes no offense at me" (Matt. 11:6). From one point of view, no one could be offended at Jesus. He was a Jewish teacher surrounded by his disciples. This was self-evident. Yet there was a dimension adhering to his person and mission which many did not perceive. Rather they

---

[21] K. H. Rengstorf, *Das Evangelium nach Lukas* (1949), p. 188; F. Hauck, *Das Evangelium des Lukas* (1934), p. 207; T. W. Manson, *The Sayings of Jesus* (1949), p. 134; W. Manson, *The Gospel of Luke* (1930), pp. 187 f.; R. Otto, *The Kingdom of God and the Son of Man* (1943), p. 111.

[22] *Das Evangelium nach Matthäus* (1950), p. 145. Cf. also W. G. Kümmel, *Promise and Fulfilment* (1957), p. 124, "The eschatological consummation is already in the present bringing the old aeon to an end"; G. Bornkamm, *Jesus of Nazareth* (1960), p. 67, "The shift in the aeons is here"; J. M. Robinson, *A New Quest of the Historical Jesus* (1959), p. 119.

stumbled over his claim. The coming of the Kingdom in Jesus was an event in history, yet it was no ordinary historical phenomenon. If the coming of the Kingdom of God into history was like the coming of the Roman rule which ended Jewish independence and inaugurated a new era and a new reign, all men living in Palestine would have to accept it whether they would or not. Any who were "offended" by the representative of Rome could resist by force of arms, but such resistance would be crushed. Submit or die; there was no other option unless it were that of carrying on subversive activities. But even so, the power of Rome was dominant. A new order had come which all had to acknowledge and submit to.

Not so was the coming of the Kingdom of God in Jesus. Some men were offended by it; they would not accept it. Some did not have ears and could not hear. For them, only the old order existed. They were blind to the new order and its blessings.

Furthermore, the blessings of the new order did not come to all men. Not all the blind received their sight; not all the lame were healed; not all lepers were cleansed; only a few dead were raised. Multitudes of deformed, sick, diseased, and dead men in Palestine were untouched by the life of the Kingdom of God. These signs of the Kingdom were only a token, not the fullness of the consummation. When the Eschaton comes and this age passes away, there will be no more deaf or blind or leprous or dead. Death will be swallowed up in life. Here is the mysterious fact about the Kingdom. Its blessings have entered the old age, introducing a new order of life which nevertheless does not bring the old order to its end for all men. The new order is not the age to come, the Eschaton, but is a new order hidden in the old age. However, the new order, hidden as it was, brought salvation to its recipients but judgment to those who rejected it (Matt. 11:20–24).

Thus Jesus introduced a previously unforeseen era of the Kingdom of God. The old order of the law and the prophets ended with John. The age to come, the eschatological consummation, still lay in the future. But meanwhile, a new order had begun which brought to men in the old age the blessings of the messianic salvation. This new order was not a worldly phenomenon encompassing all human existence. It was a new order hidden in the old age. Not all men who lived since John were in the new order, but only those who had ears to hear, who repented, who were not offended by Jesus. To be "in the Kingdom" meant to receive the messianic salvation and to enjoy its blessings even while living in the evil age of mortality and sin.

The Kingdom of God is therefore not only the dynamic rule of God revealing itself in history; it is also a new realm of blessing foretold by the prophets. Yet its fulfillment took place within history in a way neither the prophets nor contemporary Judaism envisaged.

THE KINGDOM AS A PRESENT GIFT

When we ask about the content of this new realm of blessing, we discover that basileia means not only the dynamic reign of God and the realm of salvation; it is also used to designate the gift of life and salvation. Here is another original element in Jesus' teaching. The Kingdom of God stands as a comprehensive term for all that the messianic salvation included.[23] Dalman recognized that the Kingdom in Jesus' teaching could be "a good which admits of being striven for, of being bestowed, of being possessed, and of being accepted."[24]

In the eschatological consummation, the Kingdom is something to be freely inherited by the righteous (Matt. 25:34). The word here designates neither the reign of God nor the age to come but the blessing of life which is the gift of God's rule in the coming age (Matt. 25:46). In answer to the young man's question about inheriting eternal life (Mark 10:17), Jesus spoke of entering the Kingdom (10:23–24) and receiving eternal life (10:30) as though they were synonymous concepts. The Kingdom is a gift which the Father is pleased to bestow upon the little flock of Jesus' disciples (Luke 12:32).

If God's Kingdom is the gift of life bestowed upon his people

[23] See Strack and Billerbeck, Kommentar I, p. 181; R. Schnackenburg, Gottes Herrschaft und Reich (1959), p. 62; G. Gloege, Reich Gottes und Kirche im Neuen Testament (1929), pp. 154 f.
[24] The Words of Jesus (1909), p. 121.

when he manifests his rule in eschatological glory, and if God's Kingdom is also God's rule invading history before the eschatological consummation, it follows that we may expect God's rule in the present to bring a preliminary blessing to his people. This is in fact what we find. The Kingdom is not only an eschatological gift belonging to the age to come; it is also a gift to be received in the old aeon.

This is reflected in numerous sayings. The Kingdom is like a treasure or a costly pearl whose possession outranks all other goods (Matt. 13:44–46; see p. 238). It is something to be sought here and now (Matt. 6:33; see p. 137) and to be received as children receive a gift (Mark 10:15 = Luke 18:16–17). In this saying the Kingdom is God's rule, but it includes the gift of his rule. The divine reign is not a fearful power before which men are compelled to bow, but a gift. Children exemplify the trustfulness and receptivity required of the "sons of the Kingdom." The Kingdom belongs to them not because their humility is a virtue which merits it, but because they are responsive. "The Kingdom belongs to such because they receive it as a gift; . . . [it] is the gift of the divine rule."[25] Matthew 19:14 echoes the same thought that the Kingdom of God is a present possession of the childlike. The promise that those who ask shall receive, and those who seek shall find (Matt. 7:7) is to be understood in this context. "The thing to be sought is the Kingdom of God, which, being found, is the satisfaction of all needs (Luke 12:31). The door to be knocked at is the door which gives entrance into the Kingdom of God."[26]

The Beatitudes view the Kingdom as a gift. The poor in spirit, those persecuted for righteousness' sake receive the gift (Matt. 5:3, 10). It is not easy to decide whether the Kingdom in these sayings is future or present. The Beatitudes certainly have an eschatological

[25] V. Taylor, The Gospel according to St. Mark (1952), p. 423. We differ with Taylor when he eliminates the eschatological significance of the last phrase. See also T. W. Manson, The Teaching of Jesus (1935), p. 135. Acceptance of God's present rule is the condition of entrance into the eschatological order.

[26] T. W. Manson, The Sayings of Jesus (1949), p. 81; cf. J. Schniewind, Das Evangelium nach Matthäus (1950), p. 99.

cast. The sayings about inheriting the earth, obtaining mercy (in the day of judgment), and seeing God are primarily eschatological. However, the main objective of the Beatitudes is to teach a present blessedness rather than to promise blessing in the consummation.[27] The comfort for those who grieve because of their spiritual poverty[28] is both present and future, as is the satisfaction of the hungry (Matt. 5:4, 6). The gift of the Kingdom, twice mentioned, probably includes both present and future. It is the eschatological salvation, and it is also the present blessedness which the Beatitudes expound.

THE GIFT OF SALVATION

The Kingdom as God's gift may be further illustrated by a study of the word "salvation." In the Gospels, the words "to save" and "salvation" refer both to an eschatological and to a present blessing.

Salvation is primarily an eschatological gift. In Jesus' answer to the rich young ruler about eternal life, salvation is synonymous with eternal life and entrance into the Kingdom of God in the age to come (Mark 10:17–30). This eschatological salvation is elsewhere described merely as a saving of one's [true] life in contrast with losing one's physical life (Mark 8:35; Matt. 10:39; Luke 17:33). This eschatological salvation can be described simply as entrance into (eternal) life (Mark 9:43; Matt. 25:46) or into the joy of the Lord (Matt. 25:21, 23).

This future salvation means two things: deliverance from mortality, and perfected fellowship with God. The Gospels do not say much about resurrection, but the saying in Luke 20:34–36 (cf. Mark 12: 24–27) makes it clear that eschatological salvation includes the whole man. Resurrection life will have something in common with the angels, viz., the possession of immortality. This immortal resurrection life is the life of the age to come (Luke 20:35). The evils

---

[27] Even Windisch admits this, although he attributes this meaning to theological exegesis (*The Meaning of the Sermon on the Mount* [1951], pp. 175 f.).
[28] See J. W. Bowman and R. W. Tapp, *The Gospel from the Mount* (1957), pp. 31 f.

of physical weakness, sickness, and death will be swallowed up in the life of the Kingdom of God (Matt. 25:34, 46).

Eschatological salvation means not only redemption of the body but also the restoration of communion between God and man which had been broken by sin. The pure in heart will see God (Matt. 5:8) and enter into the joy of their Lord (Matt. 25:21, 23). This eschatological consummation is usually described in pictures drawn from daily life. The harvest will take place and the grain be gathered into the barn (Matt. 13:30, 39; Mark 4:29; cf. Matt. 3:12; Rev. 14:15). The sheep will be separated from the goats and brought safely into the fold (Matt. 25:32). The most common picture is that of a feast or table fellowship. Jesus will drink wine again with his disciples in the Kingdom of God (Mark 14:25). They will eat and drink at Jesus' table in the Kingdom (Luke 22:30). Men will be gathered from all corners of the earth to sit at table with the Old Testament saints (Matt. 8:11–12; Luke 13:29). The consummation is likened to a wedding feast (Matt. 22:1–14; 25:1–12) and a banquet (Luke 14:16–24). All of these metaphors picture the restoration of communion between God and men which had been broken by sin.[29]

The religious dimension of the eschatological salvation is set in sharp contrast to what it means to be lost. The one Greek word (*apollumi*) carries two meanings: to destroy or kill, and to lose (passive: to be lost, to die or perish). Both meanings, to be destroyed and to perish, are used of the eschatological destruction (*apoleia*, Matt. 7:13). Not to be saved means to lose one's life (Mark 8:35; cf. Matt. 10:39; 16:25; Luke 9:24; 17:33); and to lose one's life is to lose everything (Mark 8:36), for one has lost himself (Luke 9:25). Thus to lose one's life is to be destroyed. It is within God's power to destroy not only the body but also the soul; and this destruction is described in terms of the fire of Gehenna (Matt. 10:28; Mark 9:42–48), eternal fire (Matt. 18:8; 25:41), and darkness (Matt. 8:12; 22:13; 25:30). Since fire and darkness are not homogeneous concepts, the central fact is not the form of this ultimate destruction but its religious significance. This is found in the words, "I

---

[29] J. Jeremias, *The Parables of Jesus* (1954), p. 154.

never knew you; depart from me, you evildoers" (Matt. 7:23; Luke 13:27). Here is the meaning of destruction: exclusion from the joys and pleasures of the presence of God in his Kingdom.

Jesus' mission to save the lost sheep of the house of Israel (Matt. 10:6; 15:24) stands against this eschatological background. Their "lostness" is both present and future, for they have strayed from God and have forfeited their lives. Because they are now lost, they stand under the threat of eternal destruction. The lost son was in fact dead; his "salvation" or restoration to his father's house meant restoration to life (Luke 15:24).

Jesus' mission to save the lost has a present as well as a future dimension. He sought the sinner not only to save him from future doom but to bring him into a present salvation. To a repentant Zacchaeus Jesus said, "Today salvation has come to this house. . . . For the Son of man came to seek and to save the lost" (Luke 19: 9–10). Against the background of the meaning of "lost," one can approve of the decision of Arndt and Gingrich, following Bauer, to list "lost" in Luke 19:10 under the meaning "eternal death."[30] The lost have not only gone astray but are in danger of perishing unless rescued. God promised through Ezekiel (34:16, 22), "I will seek the lost. . . . I will save my flock." This mission Jesus claimed to be fulfilling. The salvation Jesus brought to Zacchaeus was a present visitation, although its blessings reach into the future.

The parables of the lost sheep, the lost coin, and the lost son are not eschatological but describe a present salvation (Luke 15). The restoration of the lost son to the joy of his father's house illustrates the blessing of a present salvation which Jesus brought to Zacchaeus and to the tax collectors and sinners who welcomed his fellowship. The elder brother represented the Pharisees and the scribes. As they claimed to be the true Israel who alone obeyed the law of God, so the elder brother dwelt under his father's roof. But he too was lost, for he knew neither real fellowship with his father nor the joy of his father's house.

---

[30] W. F. Arndt and F. W. Gingrich, A Greek-English Lexicon of the New Testament (1957), p. 94.

This gift of present fellowship in anticipation of the eschatological consummation is the motif illustrated by the acted parable of table fellowship. The scribes were offended because Jesus joined in a dinner party with tax collectors and sinners (Mark 2:15 ff.). This was no ordinary meal but a feast. The Jews did not follow the Gentile custom of reclining at ordinary meals but sat at the table. Only on special occasions—parties, wedding feasts, or royal banquets—did the Jews recline.[31] The metaphor of a feast was a common Jewish picture of the eschatological salvation;[32] and the fellowship of Jesus with his disciples and those who followed them is to be understood as an anticipation of the joy and fellowship of the eschatological Kingdom. The religious significance of this meal is reflected in Jesus' word, "I came not to call the righteous, but sinners" (Mark 2:17). He was fulfilling his messianic mission when he gathered sinners into fellowship with himself.[33]

That this was no isolated instance is reflected in two other sayings. Luke records that one of the main grounds of criticism by the scribes and the Pharisees was the fact that Jesus received sinners and ate with them (Luke 15:1-2). All three parables which follow emphasize the fact of joy at the recovery of lost sinners. The central truth is the joy in heaven over one sinner who repents (Luke 15:7); but it is a joy which was anticipated on earth in the table fellowship of Jesus and the repentant sinners.

So typical of Jesus' ministry was this joyous fellowship that his critics accused him of being a glutton and a drunkard (Matt. 11:18). The same note of messianic joy is heard in Jesus' answer to the criticism that he and his disciples did not follow the example of the Pharisees in fasting. Fasting does not belong to the time of a wedding. The presence of the bridegroom calls for joy, not fasting (Mark 2:18-19). While we have no evidence that the metaphor of a bridegroom was applied to the Messiah in Judaism, the wedding feast

---

[31] See J. Jeremias, *The Eucharistic Words of Jesus* (1955), pp. 20-21 and references. The translation of RSV, "sat at table," renders the idea in modern idiom.

[32] G. F. Moore, *Judaism*, II, pp. 363 ff.

[33] J. Schniewind, *Das Evangelium nach Markus* (1952), p. 62.

was a symbol of the Kingdom of God.[34] During the seven days of the wedding festivities, the friends and guests of the bridegroom were excused from the observance of many serious religious duties that they might share in the festivities.[35] Jesus described his presence in the midst of his disciples by this messianic symbol of the wedding. The day of salvation has come, the wedding songs resound; there is no place for mourning, only for joy. Therefore Jesus' disciples cannot fast.[36]

The presence of the messianic salvation is also seen in Jesus' miracles of healing for which the Greek word meaning "to save" is used. The presence of the Kingdom of God in Jesus meant deliverance from hemorrhage (Mark 5:34), blindness (Mark 10:52), demon possession (Luke 8:36) and even death itself (Mark 5:23). Jesus claimed that these deliverances were evidences of the presence of the messianic salvation (Matt. 11:4–5). They were pledges of the life of the eschatological Kingdom which will finally mean immortality for the body. The Kingdom of God is concerned not only with men's souls but with the salvation of the whole man.

The limitation of these physical deliverances illustrates the nature of the present Kingdom in contrast to its future manifestation. In the eschatological Kingdom, all "who are accounted worthy to attain to that age" (Luke 20:35) will be saved from sickness and death in the immortal life of the resurrection. In the present working of the Kingdom, this saving power reached only a few. Not all the sick and crippled were saved, nor were all the dead raised. Only three instances of restoration to life are recorded in the Gospels. Men must come into direct contact with Jesus or his disciples to be healed (Mark 6:56). The saving power of the Kingdom was not yet universally operative. It was resident only in Jesus and in those whom he commissioned (Matt. 10:8; Luke 10:9).

However, not even all who came into contact with Jesus experienced the healing life of the Kingdom; this physical salvation re-

---

[34] See J. Jeremias, *TWNT*, IV, p. 1095.
[35] Strack and Billerbeck, *Kommentar*, I, p. 505.
[36] J. Jeremias, *The Parables of Jesus* (1954), p. 94; C. H. Dodd, *The Parables of the Kingdom* (1936), pp. 115 f.; H. Seesemann, *TWNT*, V, 164.

quired the response of faith. It did not work *ex opere operato*. "Your
faith has saved you" (Mark 5:34; 10:52). A spiritual response was
necessary to receive the physical blessing. The miracles of healing,
important as they were, were not an end in themselves. They did
not constitute the highest good of the messianic salvation. This fact
is illustrated by the arrangement of the phrases in Matthew 11:4–5.
Greater than deliverance of the blind and the lame, the lepers and
the deaf, even than raising the dead, was the preaching of the good
news to the poor.[37] This "gospel" was the very presence of Jesus
himself, and the joy and fellowship which he brought to the poor.

That salvation from physical sickness was only the external aspect
of spiritual salvation is shown by a saying about demon exorcism.
While this miracle was one of the most convincing evidences of the
presence of the Kingdom (Matt. 12:28), it was preliminary to God's
taking possession of the vacant dwelling. Otherwise, a man is like a
house which stands in good order, clean but empty (Matt. 12:44 =
Luke 11:25). Unless the power of God enters that life, the demon
can return bringing seven other demons with him, and the man
will be worse off that he was at first. Healings, demon exorcisms,
were the negative side of salvation; the positive side was the incom-
ing of the power and life of God.

The bond between physical salvation and its spiritual aspect is
illustrated by the healing of the ten lepers. All ten were "cleansed"
and "healed" (Luke 17:14 f.). To the one, a Samaritan who returned to express his gratitude, Jesus said, "Your faith has saved
you" (Luke 17:19). These are the same words used elsewhere of
healing. Are we to suppose that the other nine were not really healed?
Many commentators suspect confusion in the text. However, in
view of the fact that these same words are clearly used of "spiritual"
salvation (Luke 7:50), we may agree with those expositors who see
a greater blessing bestowed on the Samaritan than on the nine. His
"salvation" or wholeness was more than physical healing. It implied
a sound spiritual state.[38]

---

[37] G. Friedrich, *TWNT*, II, p. 715.
[38] See L. Ragg, *St. Luke* (1922), p. 228; W. F. Arndt, *The Gospel* accord-

That this present "salvation" is spiritual as well as physical is proved by the incident of the sinful woman in the house of Simon. Her tears and display of affection proved her repentance. To her Jesus said, "Your faith has saved you; go in peace" (Luke 7:50). No miracle of healing was performed. Her disease was altogether moral and spiritual. The meaning of her "salvation" is expounded in the words, "Your sins are forgiven" (Luke 7:48).

THE GIFT OF FORGIVENESS

This mention of forgiveness points to the deeper significance of the messianic salvation. According to Mark, the conflict between Jesus and the scribes began when Jesus claimed to forgive sins. Such a claim was nothing less than blasphemy, for only God had the right to forgive sins (Mark 2:7). On their own presuppositions, the scribes were right (Ps. 103:3; Isa. 43:25). In the prophets, forgiveness will be one of the blessings of the messianic age. The Lord who is judge, ruler, and king will save his people so that there will be no longer any sick, for the Lord will forgive all iniquity (Isa. 33:24). The saved remnant will be pardoned and forgiven, for their sins will be cast into the depths of the sea (Mic. 7:18–20). God will make a new covenant and will inscribe his law in the heart, granting a perfect fellowship with himself and the forgiveness of sins (Jer. 31:31–34; cf. also Ezek. 18:31; 36:22–28). A fountain will be opened for the house of David which will cleanse God's people from all sin (Zech. 13:1).

With one possible exception, this function was limited to God.[39] One prophecy tells of the servant of the Lord who will bear the iniquities of the people and give himself as an offering for sin (Isa. 53:11–12); but Judaism did not apply this prophecy to the Messiah until the third century and later.[40] There is no source known to us

---

ing to St. Luke (1956), p. 372; A. Schlatter, Die Evangelien nach Markus und Lukas (1947), p. 341.

[39] "Forgiveness is a prerogative of God which he shares with no other and deputes to none" (G. F. Moore, Judaism, I, p. 535).

[40] G. Quell in TWNT, II, p. 188.

in which the Messiah by virtue of his own authority promises to men the forgiveness of sins.[41] Furthermore, while God was believed to forgive sins, Judaism never solved the problem created by the tension between God's justice and his grace.[42] The righteous man was not one who had been freely pardoned by God, but the man whose merit outweighed his debt. Righteousness is the divine acquittal in the day of judgment, but this eschatological acquittal is determined by a theory of merit. A man's standing before God is settled by the balance between his good deeds and his transgressions. If the former outweigh the latter, he will be acquitted.[43]

Against this background, one can readily understand the amazement and dismay among the scribes when Jesus on his own authority pronounced the free forgiveness of sins. John the Baptist had promised forgiveness (Mark 1:4); Jesus fulfilled this promise. The healing of the paralytic was the external proof that "the Son of man has authority on earth to forgive sins" (Mark 2:10). The Son of Man was the heavenly figure in Daniel 7:13 representing the saints of the Most High, who would come with the clouds of heaven to bring the Kingdom of God, and to judge men. In this saying, Jesus claimed that he was this heavenly judge, but that he had appeared on earth among men exercising the divine prerogative to forgive sins.[44] This was the sign of the presence of the messianic salvation.

The centrality of the forgiveness of sins in the concept of the Kingdom of God is illustrated by the parable of forgiveness (Matt. 18:23–35). It sets forth the relationship between the divine and human forgiveness in the Kingdom of God. The divine forgiveness

[41] Strack and Billerbeck, Kommentar, I, p. 495.

[42] Note the struggle with this same problem by the modern Jewish scholar, J. Klausner, Jesus of Nazareth (1925), p. 379.

[43] See G. Schrenk, TWNT, II, pp. 198–199; Eng. trans., BKW: Righteousness (1951), pp. 31–33; W. O. E. Oesterley and G. H. Box, The Religion and Worship of the Synagogue (1907), pp. 244–251.

[44] See J. Schniewind, Das Evangelium nach Markus (1952), pp. 58 ff.; O. Cullmann, The Christology of the New Testament (1959), pp. 159 f. For other interpretations see C. E. B. Cranfield, The Gospel according to Saint Mark (1959), pp. 100 f. For the Son of Man in Judaism, see O. Cullmann, The Christology of the New Testament (1959), pp. 137 ff.

precedes and conditions human forgiveness. While Jeremias emphasizes the eschatological element of judgment, he recognizes that the parable teaches primarily God's mercy; for the eschatological judgment will be based on a prior experience of the gift of God's forgiveness.[45] The free gift of God's forgiveness lays upon men the demand of a forgiving spirit.

Jesus did not teach a new doctrine of forgiveness; he brought to lost sinners a new experience of forgiveness. He did not tell the woman in the house of Simon that God was forgiving her or explain to her the way she might find salvation; he pronounced her sins forgiven (Luke 7:48). This was her "salvation." Jesus did what he proclaimed. The presence of the Kingdom of God was not a new teaching about God; it was a new activity of God in the person of Jesus bringing to men as present experience what the prophets promised in the eschatological Kingdom.[46]

THE GIFT OF RIGHTEOUSNESS

Closely related to forgiveness is righteousness, for righteousness is not primarily an ethical quality but a right relationship; the divine acquittal from the guilt of sin.[47] To seek the Kingdom of God means to seek God's righteousness (Matt. 6:33); and to receive the Kingdom of God means to receive the accompanying righteousness.

Righteousness in Jewish thought was a human activity.[48] The rabbis taught that it was a human work consisting of obedience to the law and acts of mercy. Jesus taught that it was both God's demand and God's gift. A righteousness exceeding that of the scribes and the Pharisees was demanded for entrance into the eschatological Kingdom (Matt. 5:20). This righteousness includes freedom from anger, from lust, from retaliation (Matt. 5:21–48). If the attain-

[45] J. Jeremias, The Parables of Jesus (1954), pp. 147 f.
[46] H. D. Wendland, Eschatologie, pp. 65–66. See the excellent note on forgiveness in V. Taylor, The Gospel according to St. Mark (1952), pp. 200 f.
[47] G. Schrenk in TWNT, II, pp. 187, 197 f.; Eng. trans., BKW: Righteousness (1951), pp. 16 ff., 29 f., 52.
[48] G. Schrenk, TWNT, II, p. 198; Eng. trans., BKW: Righteousness (1951), p. 32.

ment of such a perfect righteousness is left to human effort, no one can acquire it; it must be God's gift.

Here is the very heart of Jesus' ethical teaching: the renunciation of self-attained righteousness and the willingness to become like children who have nothing and must receive everything. The scribes were unwilling to lay aside their pride in their righteousness to become nothing that they might receive the gift of God's righteousness. So long as they considered themselves to be righteous (Mark 2:17; Luke 18:9),[49] they felt no need of God's gift. In contrast to the self-righteous Pharisee stands the tax collector, who cast himself entirely upon God's mercy. He had nothing: no deeds of righteousness, no acts of merit. He was therefore open toward God. "This man went down to his house justified" (Luke 18:14), declared righteous by God. Obviously his righteousness was no attainment of his own, but the gift of God. The teaching of this parable is the same as the Pauline doctrine of free justification, with the exception that there is no mention of the cross.[50]

The righteousness of the Sermon on the Mount is also God's gift. The promise of satisfaction to those who hunger and thirst after righteousness (Matt. 5:6) is a promise to those who are conscious of their own unrighteousness but hunger and thirst to be right with God. "Righteousness is here not a matter of merit, as with the Jews, but a free gift of God to those who earnestly desire it."[51]

Thus the unforeseen presence of the eschatological salvation is illustrated in many aspects of Jesus' message and mission and is to be seen far beyond the actual terminology of the Kingdom of God. The mission of Jesus brought not a new teaching but a new event. It brought to men an actual foretaste of the eschatological salvation.

---

[49] While Jesus adopted the usual Jewish terminology of "the righteous" and "the unrighteous," his teachings "put a question mark after the word 'righteous,' as applied to themselves by men who were hypocritical, complacent and scornful of others" (G. Schrenk, TWNT, II, pp. 191 f.; Eng. trans., BKW: Righteousness [1951], p. 22).

[50] G. Schrenk, TWNT, II, p. 219; Eng. trans., BKW: Righteousness (1951), p. 60. See also J. Jeremias, The Parables of Jesus (1954), p. 114.

[51] G. Schrenk, TWNT, II, p. 200; Eng. trans., BKW: Righteousness (1951), p. 35.

Jesus did not promise the forgiveness of sins; he bestowed it. He did not simply assure men of the future fellowship of the Kingdom; he invited men into fellowship with himself as the bearer of the Kingdom. He did not merely promise them vindication in the day of judgment; he bestowed upon them a present righteousness. He not only taught an eschatological deliverance from physical evil; he went about demonstrating the redeeming power of the Kingdom, delivering men from sickness and even death.

This is the meaning of the presence of the Kingdom as a new era of salvation. To receive the Kingdom of God, to submit oneself to God's reign meant to receive the gift of the Kingdom and to enter into the enjoyment of its blessings. The age of fulfillment is present, but the time of consummation still awaits the age to come.

9 The Mystery of the Kingdom

The central thesis of this book is that the Kingdom of God is the redemptive reign of God dynamically active to establish his rule among men, and that this Kingdom, which will appear as an apocalyptic act at the end of the age, has already come into human history in the person and mission of Jesus to overcome evil, to deliver men from its power, and to bring them into the blessings of God's reign. The Kingdom of God involves two great moments: fulfillment within history, and consummation at the end of history. It is precisely this background which provides the setting for the parables of the Kingdom.

CANONS OF INTERPRETATION

Modern critical study has posited two canons for interpreting the parables which are necessary for a correct historical understanding. The first of these was enunciated by Jülicher, who established the essential principle that parables must not be interpreted as though they were allegories.[1] An allegory is an artificial story created by the

[1] A. Jülicher, *Die Gleichnisreden Jesu* (1910, 2 vols.).

author as a teaching medium. Since the details of an allegory are under the control of the author, it can be structured so that every detail bears a distinct and important meaning. A simple allegory is the story of the thistle and the cedar in II Kings 14:9–10.

A parable is a story drawn from everyday life to convey a moral or religious truth. Because the author does not create his story and therefore does not have control over the details, they are often of little importance to the truth conveyed by the story. A parable is designed to convey essentially a single truth rather than a complex of truths.

This principle can be clearly demonstrated in the parable of the unjust steward (Luke 16:1–13). If the details are pressed, this parable teaches that cleverness is better than honesty; but this is obviously impossible. Such details as the ninety-nine sheep (Luke 15: 4), ten coins (Luke 15:8) carry no particular significance. In the parable of the Good Samaritan, the allegorical meaning of the robbers, the priest and the Levite, the significance of oil and wine, the reason for two coins, the meaning of Jerusalem, Jericho, and the hotel are no more to be sought than is the identity of the donkey. We must therefore seek in each of the parables of the Kingdom a central truth.

However, the radical application of this distinction between parable and allegory can lead to equally radical results. Must we assume, with Jeremias, that all allegorization is due to the early church and not to Jesus?[2] Why could not Jesus have combined parables with some allegorical detail? "To maintain a rigid distinction between parable and allegory is quite impossible in dealing with material originating in Hebrew or Aramaic languages which have only one word [masal] to denote both things."[3] Goguel is right when he says,

---

[2] The Parables of Jesus (1954), pp. 32–70. Jeremias tries to prove that the interpretations of many of the parables, since they contain some allegory, must be secondary and due to the church rather than to Jesus. He tries to get behind the allegorical interpretations of the church to the original (lost) parabolic meaning intended by Jesus. Even if the church had a tendency toward allegory, this would not prove that Jesus did not use some allegory.

[3] C. E. B. Cranfield, The Gospel according to Saint Mark (1959), p. 159. See

"The teaching of Jesus is too living, and therefore too complex, for us to be able to lay down as a principle that it contains no element of allegory at all, and claim that every time a parable is presented as an allegory it must have been altered in this sense by a later tradition." But he goes too far when he adds, "Some of the parables, like those of the sower . . . are really allegories and indeed very transparent allegories."⁴ While the parable of the sower has some allegorical detail, it is not a true allegory, because the parable contains a single truth which is only reinforced by but not dependent upon the details. The number of soils is unimportant; the various reasons for the failure of the seed are unimportant. The one central truth is this: the word of the Kingdom is sown; sometimes it bears fruit, sometimes it does not. This truth, as we shall later show, is the most important fact in terms of the actual historical setting of Jesus' life and mission, and it is merely reinforced by the choice of four soils and the reasons for the ineffectiveness of the word of the Kingdom.

The second canon of criticism is that the parables must be understood in the historical life setting of Jesus' ministry and not in the life of the church. This means that it is not a sound historical approach to understand the parables as prophecies of the working of the gospel in the world or of the future of the church. Exegesis of the parables must be carried out in terms of Jesus' own mission in Palestine. This admission should not blind us to the fact that if analogies exist between Jesus' mission and the role of the word and the church in the world, important, even necessary, applications of the parables may be made to the later situation. However, we are here concerned to try to find the historical meaning of the parables in Jesus' ministry.

Jülicher's method was defective at this point because he found in the parables religious truths of general and universal application.

---

also the excellent remarks by A. M. Hunter, "Interpreting the Parables," *Int*, XIV (1960) pp. 442–443, and by M. Black, "The Parables as Allegory," *Bulletin of the John Rylands Library*, XLII (1960), pp. 273–287.

⁴ *The Life of Jesus* (1933), p. 290. Quoted by permission of the Macmillan Company.

Recent scholarship, especially the work of C. H. Dodd, has shown that the *Sitz im Leben* of the parables is Jesus' proclamation of the Kingdom of God. Jeremias considers this to be a breakthrough of historical criticism which introduced a new era in the interpretation of the parables.[5] However, he criticizes Dodd's one-sided emphasis which resulted in a contraction of eschatology, emptying it of its futuristic content. Jeremias proposes to correct Dodd's conclusions while accepting his method; and he attempts to discover the original message of the parables by recovering their primitive historical form. Jeremias suggests "an eschatology in process of realization."[6] Jesus' mission inaugurated an eschatological process which he expected would shortly carry through to its eschatological consummation.[7] The early church dissolved this single process into two events, and in so doing applied to the Parousia parables which originally had a noneschatological meaning.

However, Jeremias goes too far in taking as his main presupposition that the original meaning of the parables can be recovered only in terms of what they must have meant to Jesus' Jewish hearers. This assumes that the proper *Sitz im Leben* of the parables is Judaism, not the teachings of Jesus. This tends to limit the originality of Jesus. We must make allowance for the possibility that his teachings transcended Jewish ideas. Therefore the proper *Sitz im Leben* of the parables is the totality of Jesus' teachings, not Judaism.

The Mystery of the Kingdom

The parables as they stand are susceptible of an adequate historical interpretation in terms of the life-setting of Jesus without the assumption of such a radical transformation as Jeremias assumes. The historical *Sitz im Leben* of the parables is summed up in the single word "mystery." Mark summarized the message of the Kingdom parables by reporting the words of Jesus to his disciples: "To

[5] *The Parables of Jesus* (1954), p. 18.

[6] Jeremias' words are "sich realisierende Eschatologie." See *Die Gleichnisse Jesu* (1947), p. 114; *The Parables of Jesus* (1954), p. 159.

[7] See the summary of Jeremias' view above, pp. 26 ff.

you has been given the mystery of the kingdom of God, but for those outside everything is in parables; so that they may indeed see but not perceive, and may indeed hear but not understand; lest they turn again, and be forgiven" (Mark 4:11–12).[8] *The mystery of the Kingdom is the coming of the Kingdom into history in advance of its apocalyptic manifestation.* It is, in short, "fulfillment without consummation." This is the single truth illustrated by the several parables of Mark 4 and Matthew 13.

This conclusion is not self-evident and can be sustained only by a critical discussion of the meaning of *mysterion*, and by an analysis of the parables in light of this term. Some modern exegetes have seen direct influence of the Hellenistic mystery religions in which the mystery, according to Mark's theory, is esoteric religious truth shared only by the initiated and strictly withheld from all outsiders.[9] However, as we shall see, the idea has roots in the Old Testament and in contemporary Judaism; and as Cranfield has said, "to run off on a wild goose chase after the influence of the mystery religions to explain something so familiar in the Bible is fantastic."[10]

Others understand the mystery to refer in a general way to the truths which Jesus taught about God and his Kingdom. It is the working out of God's holy purpose which includes the world of nature and of self-conscious beings.

Its motive is love, its means service, and its end a state of things where the will of God is done on earth as in heaven. The sovereignty of God over nature is demonstrated not by the trampling march of supernatural power in some great cataclysm, but by his constant care over all his creatures, even the humblest. It is manifested in human life not by legions of angels sweeping forward to crush the forces of evil, but by the realisation in those who accept its rule of a strange power to overcome

[8] Matt. 13:11 and Luke 8:10 speak of the "mysteries" of the Kingdom. Mark's wording suggests a single truth, the others a truth embodied in several aspects. Cf. O. Piper in *Int*, I (1947), pp. 183–200.

[9] Cf. especially B. H. Branscomb, *The Gospel of Mark* (1937), pp. 78–79: "The idea is so exactly that of the Hellenistic religious world that its influence in the formation of the saying can hardly be denied." This explanation appears to be supported by A. E. J. Rawlinson, *St. Mark* (1925), p. 48; C. Guignebert, *Jesus* (1935), p. 256; S. E. Johnson, *IB*, VII, p. 410; and F. C. Grant, *IB*, VII, pp. 699 f.

[10] C. E. B. Cranfield, "St. Mark 4:1–34," *SJTh*, V (1952), p. 53.

evil with good. This power is recognized, by all who experience it, as the strongest thing in the world, and as something which must finally prevail. In other words, the throne of the universe is founded upon a Father's love. This is probably the clue to "the mystery of the Kingdom."[11]

While this interpretation embodies a substantial truth, it fails to do justice to the particular biblical and revelational significance of mysterion and to the unique historical setting of the mystery of the Kingdom in the history of redemption. It recognizes inadequately the Kingdom of God as event.

While the word mysterion is found in the Old Testament in Daniel, the idea of God disclosing his secrets to men is a familiar Old Testament concept.[12] In Daniel is found the background of the New Testament use of the word. God granted a dream to the king which was to him meaningless and whose meaning could be recognized only by revelation through a vision given to Daniel, God's inspired servant. The dream had to do with the mystery of God's eschatological purpose.[13]

The concept of mystery (raz) also appears in the Qumran literature. To the Teacher of Righteousness, "God made known all the mysteries of the words of his servants the prophets."[14] This means that God has given special illumination to the Teacher of Righteousness to find in the prophetic Scriptures their true and hidden meaning. These mysteries have to do both with the events the Qumran community expected to occur in the end time[15] and with the "divine unfathomable unalterable" decisions of God.[16]

[11] T. W. Manson, The Teaching of Jesus (1935), p. 170. Quoted by permission of The Cambridge University Press. See also G. Duncan, Jesus, Son of Man (1949), pp. 214, 217; W. Manson, The Gospel of Luke (1930), pp. 89-91.

[12] Cf. C. E. B. Cranfield, The Gospel according to Saint Mark (1959), p. 152; R. N. Flew, Jesus and His Church (1943), pp. 63 f.; R. E. Brown, CBQ, XX (1958), pp. 417-443.

[13] G. Bornkamm, TWNT, IV, p. 821.

[14] Commentary on Habakkuk, 7:1-5. The passages have been collected by E. Vogt in Biblica, XXXVII (1956), pp. 247-257. See also R. E. Brown, CBQ, XX (1958), pp. 417-443; Helmer Ringgren, The Faith of Qumran (1963), pp. 60-67.

[15] See F. F. Bruce, Biblical Exegesis in the Qumran Texts (1959), pp. 16, 66 f.

[16] J. Licht, Israel Exploration Journal, VI (1956), pp. 7-8.

There is an ample background for the idea of mystery in the Old Testament and in Jewish literature. While the term enters upon a new career in the New Testament,[17] it is not altogether novel but further develops the idea found in Daniel. Paul understood "mysteries" to be revealed secrets, divine purposes hidden from men for long ages but finally disclosed by revelation to all men (Rom. 16:25–26). A mystery is not something esoteric, proclaimed only to the initiated. Mystery designates "the secret thoughts, plans, and dispensations of God which are hidden from the human reason, as well as from all other comprehension below the divine level, and hence must be revealed to those for whom they are intended."[18] However, the mystery is proclaimed to all men even though it is understood only by those who believe. All men are summoned to faith; only those who respond really understand.

This interpretation of mystery reinforces the view of the Kingdom of God supported in this study. The mere fact that God proposes to bring his Kingdom is no secret; practically every Jewish apocalyptic writing reflects that expectation in one form or another. Those who follow Weiss' and Schweitzer's Consistent Eschatology quite fail to do justice to this fact.[19] That the Kingdom was to come in apocalyptic

---

[17] J. Armitage Robinson, *St. Paul's Epistle to the Ephesians* (1904), p. 240.

[18] W. F. Arndt and F. W. Gingrich, *A Greek-English Lexicon* (1957), p. 532. This basic understanding of "mystery" will be found also in B. S. Easton, *The Gospel according to St. Luke* (1926), p. 112; R. N. Flew, *Jesus and His Church* (1943), pp. 62 ff.; C. E. B. Cranfield, *SJTh*, V (1952), pp. 51 ff.; *The Gospel according to Saint Mark* (1959), pp. 152 ff.; V. Taylor, *The Gospel according to St. Mark* (1952), p. 255; C. Masson, *Les Paraboles de Marc IV* (1945), pp. 21–23; J. Schniewind, *Das Evangelium nach Markus* (1952), pp. 75 f.; Mundle, *RGG* (2nd ed.), IV, col. 1820; O. Piper, *Int* (1947), p. 187; G. Bornkamm, *TWNT*, IV, pp. 823–825; C. F. D. Moule, *The Epistles to the Colossians and to Philemon* (1957), pp. 80 ff.

[19] A. Schweitzer thinks the secret is how so great a harvest can come from so insignificant a beginning (*The Mystery of the Kingdom of God* [1913], pp. 108 f.). F. C. Burkitt interprets the mystery as the unexpected delay in the coming of the eschatological kingdom (*Jesus Christ* [1932], p. 29). W. C. Allen understands it to refer to truths about the Kingdom and its near approach (*The Gospel according to S. Matthew* [1913], p. 144) known only by the disciples. Klostermann explains the reference as a piece of early Christian polemic (*Das Markusevangelium* [1926], p. 47); and J. Weiss assigns the idea to the evangelist and insists that the modern interpreter should not be bound by it (*Die Schriften des Neuen Testaments* [2nd ed.; 1929], I, p. 112).

power was no secret; it was affirmed also by orthodox Jewish theology. The mystery is a new disclosure of God's purpose for the establishment of his Kingdom. The new truth, now given to men by revelation in the person and mission of Jesus, is that *the Kingdom which is to come finally in apocalyptic power, as foreseen in Daniel, has in fact entered into the world in advance in a hidden form to work secretly within and among men.*[20]

This is indeed a mystery, a new revelation. That there should be a coming of God's Kingdom in the way Jesus proclaimed, in a hidden, secret form, working quietly among men, was utterly novel to Jesus' contemporaries. The Old Testament gave no such promise. The coming of God's Kingdom would mean a mighty manifestation of divine power by which the godless nations of the earth would be broken to pieces and brought to an end (Dan. 2:44). These nations would be crushed by God's Kingdom, which would then fill the whole earth (Dan. 2:35). This was the Kingdom the Jews expected: a display of divine sovereignty that would overthrow Rome, sweep the godless Gentiles away, purge the earth of unrighteousness and evil, and exalt God's people, Israel, in their own land over all the nations of the earth (see Chap. 3). This was the expectation aroused in the hearts of the people by the announcement of John the Baptist and then by Jesus, "The Kingdom of God has come near." The passing reference in John 6:15 shows that the people wanted a messianic king; and had Jesus publicly proclaimed himself as the Messiah, the Lord's Anointed, whose purpose it was to initiate a political kingdom of power, the entire countryside would have been ready to follow him in rebellion against Rome to overthrow the rule of Caesar and establish the Kingdom of God.

This interpretation has the merit of doing justice to the undeniable

[20] Essentially this view is held by Flew, Cranfield, Masson, Schniewind, Mundle, Piper, Bornkamm (cf. n. 18 above) and W. Manson (*Jesus, the Messiah* [1946], p. 60). N. A. Dahl (*StTh*, V [1952], pp. 156 ff.) finds this truth in the parables but discounts the validity of Mark 4:11. Edwyn Hoskyns and Noel Davey (*The Riddle of the New Testament* [1949], p. 134) express it as "something hidden now which is to be revealed openly in the future." J. Jeremias (*The Parables of Jesus* [1954], p. 13): "a particular revelation, namely, the recognition of its present irruption."

eschatological element in the Gospels. The present aspect of the Kingdom neither replaces nor reinterprets the eschatological aspect; rather it supplements it. The same God who will manifest his Kingdom at the end of history in apocalyptic glory is now exercising that same kingly power in the person of Jesus to carry forward his redemptive purposes within history.

Thus the coming of the Kingdom in history is a real fulfillment of the Old Testament expectation. This secret of the Kingdom now revealed was what many prophets and righteous men longed to see but did not experience (Matt. 10:17). The Kingdom for whose coming they longed has now become experience.[21]

This raises one of the most strongly contested elements in the parabolic teaching. Could Jesus have used parables in order to conceal the truth he intended to convey (Mark 4:12)? Or did Jesus resort to the parabolic method because of the spiritual dullness of his hearers (Matt. 13:13)? The difference in the wording of the two Gospels may be due to divergent renditions of Jesus' Aramaic terminology; or the construction found in Mark's Gospel, which is the common construction of purpose, may here designate cause rather than purpose.[22] In either case, the final result is essentially the same. If Jesus resorted to parables because many of his hearers were spiritually blind, the parabolic teaching served the purpose of more completely veiling his teaching from them. The fundamental facts are not changed.

Many modern exegetes reject this idea as utterly unworthy of Jesus.[23] However, this is no new thought. Mark 4:12 says no more than Isaiah 6. The word of God forces men to decision, and the same

---

[21] Luke records this same saying in a different context but affirms the same truth, viz., that God has made known to those who possess spiritual sensitivity the fact that in the mission of the Seventy and the display of Kingdom power (Luke 10:17), the Kingdom of God has come near (10:9). This again is a fact which centers in the person of Jesus (Luke 10:22). Whether Matthew and Luke have employed this saying in different contexts, or whether Jesus repeated it on various occasions, the saying interprets the significance of the mystery of the Kingdom and the defeat of Satan (Luke 10:17); they are two aspects of the same fact.

[22] Cf. V. Taylor, *The Gospel according to St. Mark* (1952), p. 257.

[23] "On any interpretation of the parable [of the sower] this is simply absurd" (T. W. Manson, *The Teaching of Jesus* [1935], p. 76).

word creates life and imposes death; it converts and it hardens (cf. Isa. 28:13; Jer. 23:29). The same truth is repeated in the New Testament. The word brings both salvation and destruction (Heb. 4:12; I Pet. 2:8; Acts 5:3 ff.; John 12:40; Acts 28:26). This idea is by no means limited to Paul's discussion of election in Romans 9–11. In this teaching Jesus stands in the succession of the prophets and the apostles.[24]

The idea of revelation which is perceptible only to those who are spiritually responsive is not limited to this saying. A classic passage is that of Matt. 11:25 ff. = Luke 10:21 f. While the setting of this saying is different in Matthew and Luke, the theological context is the same. In Matthew, the setting is the visit of John's disciples to Jesus to ask if Jesus really was the Coming One. Jesus' reply involves the recognition that the Kingdom of God had been at work among men since the days of John the Baptist, yet in a manner which was not altogether self-evident (see pp. 199 ff., 203 ff.). These truths were hidden by God from the "wise and understanding," i.e., from those who were the religious leaders and authorities of the day, but revealed to babes—to those who were ordinarily recognized to be innocent of religious wisdom and perception, who stood outside the circle of scribes and Pharisees but who had responded to Jesus' message. This truth of the present Kingdom, which includes an intimate knowledge of the Father, is mediated through the person of Jesus. Yet while there is an exclusiveness about this Kingdom which is withheld from the "wise and understanding," it is not esoteric in character, for Jesus openly invites all men to take upon them his yoke.

We may conclude that the "mystery of the kingdom" is the key to the understanding of the unique element in Jesus' teaching about the Kingdom. He announced that the Kingdom of God had come near; in fact, he affirmed that it had actually come upon men (Matt. 12:28). It was present in his word and in his messianic works. It was present in his person; it was present as the messianic salvation. It constituted a fulfillment of the Old Testament expectation. Yet the

---

[24] Cf. J. Schniewind, Das Evangelium nach Markus (1952). p. 76. See also C. E. B. Cranfield, The Gospel according to Saint Mark (1959), pp. 157 f.

coming and presence of the Kingdom was not self-explanatory and altogether self-evident. There was something about it which could be understood only by revelation.[25]

This meant that while the presence of the Kingdom was a fulfillment of the Old Testament expectation, it was a fulfillment in different terms from those which one might expect from the prophets. Before the end of the age and the coming of the Kingdom in glorious power, it was God's purpose that the powers of that eschatological Kingdom should enter into human history to accomplish a defeat of Satan's kingdom and to set at work the dynamic power of God's redemptive reign among men. This new manifestation of God's King-

[25] Against this background, we can understand the difficult saying in Luke 17:20. The question of the Pharisees about the coming of the Kingdom reflects their rejection of the presence of the Kingdom in Jesus' person and mission. The only manifestation of the Kingdom they would acknowledge was its coming in power to crush evil and vindicate Israel as God's people. Jesus replied that the Kingdom was already in their midst, but in an unexpected form; it was not accompanied by the signs and outward display the Pharisees expected, and without which they would not be satisfied. The presence of the Kingdom in this saying is acknowledged, with differing emphases, by W. G. Kümmel, *Promise and Fulfilment* (1957), p. 33; R. Otto, *The Kingdom of God and the Son of Man* (1943), pp. 131–137; G. Bornkamm, *Jesus of Nazareth* (1960), p. 68; R. Schnackenburg, *Gottes Herrschaft und Reich* (1959), pp. 92–94; D. Bosch, *Die Heidenmission in der Zukunftsschau Jesu* (1959), p. 66; Bent Noack, *Das Gottesreich bei Lukas: Eine Studie zu Luk. 17*, 20–24 (1948), pp. 44 ff. (Noack includes a history of the interpretation of this logion.) There remains in the future a coming of the Kingdom with apocalyptic power (Luke 17:24); but before this, the Kingdom is present in one who must suffer and die (Luke 17:25). Other interpretations are: "The signs of the Kingdom are present, but not the Kingdom itself": M. Dibelius, *Jesus* (1949), pp. 74 ff.; R. H. Fuller, *Mission*, pp. 28 ff.; H. Conzelmann, *The Theology of St. Luke* (1960), pp. 120 ff. "The Kingdom of God is within you—in your hearts": Adolf von Harnack, *What is Christianity* (1901), p. 66; C. H. Dodd, *The Parables of the Kingdom* (1936), p. 84, n. 1; L. H. Marshall, *The Challenge of New Testament Ethics* (1947), pp. 26 ff. "The (apocalyptic) Kingdom will come suddenly, like a bolt of lightning": W. Michaelis, *Täufer, Jesus, Urgemeinde* (1928), p. 79; R. Bultmann, *Jesus and the Word* (1934), p. 40; E. Dinkler in *The Idea of History in the Ancient Near East* (R. C. Dentan, ed.; 1955), p. 176. "The (apocalyptic) Kingdom does not come in such a way that one can make a programme of its coming": T. W. Manson, *The Sayings of Jesus* (1949), p. 304. "When the (apocalyptic) Kingdom comes, it is in your midst and will fill the whole horizon": H. Ridderbos, *The Coming of the Kingdom* (1962), p. 475. "The Kingdom of God is within your reach": C. H. Roberts, *HTR*, XLI (1948), pp. 1–8; A. R. C. Leaney, *The Gospel according to St. Luke* (1948), p. 330.

dom was taking place on the level of human history and centered in one man—Jesus Christ. However, it was not a purely historical phenomenon for it was occurring also in the spiritual realm, involving the defeat of Satan and the impartation to men of the blessings of the Kingdom. Therefore this working of the Kingdom could be apprehended only by revelation. It required response to be intelligible. While the activity of the Kingdom is conceived of as an objective fact, its recognition by men requires their personal participation.

As we turn to the parables which illustrate the mystery of the Kingdom, we cannot discuss alternate views at length but must largely limit ourselves to a positive interpretation. We shall discuss the parables found in Matthew 13. While it is clear from internal evidence that the chapter as it stands is due to the author of the Gospel and contains secondary elements, we believe this group of parables illustrates the actual situation in Jesus' ministry and his message of the Kingdom.

The Four Soils

The parable of the soils[26] involves allegorical elements, but the authenticity of either the parable or the interpretation may not reasonably be rejected for this reason. There is no a priori ground for assuming that Jesus could not have employed allegorical parables.[27] However, this is not a true allegory, for the details are quite secondary to the central teaching of the parable. There are four kinds of soil, only one of which is fruitful. The message of the parable would not be affected in the least if there were only two kinds of soil, or if there were three, or six. Neither would the message be affected if the three unfruitful soils were unfruitful for entirely different reasons than those illustrated. Some seed might be washed away by an unseasonable cloudburst. Tender shoots of grain might be crushed under the feet of a careless passer-by. Some seeds might be devoured by rodents.

---

[26] For the parable of the self-growing seed in Mark 4, see above, pp. 188 ff.
[27] Cf. C. E. B. Cranfield, *SJTh*, IV (1951), pp. 405–412, for a detailed study of the authenticity of the parable.

Such details would not affect the central message: the Kingdom of God has come into the world to be received by some but rejected by others. The Kingdom is in the present to have only partial success, and this success is dependent upon a human response.

While the parable may have an application to the Gospel in the world during the church age as older interpreters thought,[28] this is not its historical meaning. The *Sitz im Leben* of the parable is Jesus' announcement that the Kingdom of God *had come* among men. The Jews thought that the coming of the Kingdom would mean the exercise of God's mighty power before which no man could stand. The Kingdom of God would shatter the godless nations (Dan. 2:44). The dominion of wicked rulers would be destroyed and the Kingdom be given to the saints of the Most High, that all nations should serve and obey them (Dan. 7:27). In apparent disagreement with the Old Testament promises, which were elaborated in great detail in the contemporary apocalyptic expectations, Jesus said that the Kingdom had indeed come upon men, but not for the purpose of shattering evil. It is now attended by no apocalyptic display of irresistible power. Rather, the Kingdom in its present working is like a farmer sowing seed. It does not sweep away the wicked. In fact, the word in which the Kingdom is proclaimed may lie like seed on the roadside and never take root; or it may be superficially received only to die; or it may be choked by the cares of the age which is hostile to the Kingdom of God.

The Kingdom is working quietly, secretly among men. It does not force itself upon them; it must be willingly received. But wherever it is received, the word of the Kingdom, which is practically identical with the Kingdom itself,[29] brings forth much fruit. There is no emphasis upon the harvest, either in the parable or in its interpretation. The single emphasis is upon the nature of the sowing—the present action of God's Kingdom.

[28] See the standard studies by Trench, A. B. Bruce, M. Dods. See also A. Plummer, *The Gospel according to St. Mark* (1914), p. 125; N. Geldenhuys, *Commentary on the Gospel of Luke* (1950), pp. 244 f.

[29] For the presence of the Kingdom in Jesus' words, see pp. 164 ff.

THE TARES

The parable of the tares further illustrates the mystery of the Kingdom, i.e., its hidden, unexpected presence in the world. At the outset we should note that there are details in the parable which do not bear any meaning in its interpretation. The identity of the servants is utterly irrelevant. The fact that the enemy goes away after sowing weeds is unimportant. The bundles into which the weeds are gathered is entirely local color. Similarly, the sleeping of the servants does not suggest negligence. This is only what workmen did after a hard day. In the same manner, nothing is to be made of the fact that the tares are gathered first before the gathering of the wheat.

The interpretation of the parable which dominated the older Protestant scholarship sees an identification of the Kingdom with the church. The parable describes the state of things which is to exist in the Kingdom-church. When the Son of Man comes, he will gather out of his Kingdom all causes of offense and all evildoers (Matt. 13:41). This shows that the church contains both good men and evil, and that the Kingdom exists in the world as the church before the final consummation.[30]

Other interpretations find a reference to the Kingdom-church in the interpretation of the parable but not in the parable itself. Since the interpretation allegedly reflects a condition which did not exist in the time of Jesus' ministry but does reflect the actual life of the early church, the authenticity of the interpretation of the parable is rejected and is attributed to the early Christian community when the Kingdom was identified with the church.[31] However, entirely apart

[30] Cf. N. B. Stonehouse, *The Witness of Matthew and Mark to Christ* (1944), p. 238. A similar view will be found in B. F. C. Atkinson in *The New Bible Commentary* (F. Davidson, et al., eds.; 1953), p. 790, T. Zahn, *Das Evangelium des Matthaus* (1922), pp. 493 ff., and in the studies on the parables by A. B. Bruce, R. C. Trench, S. Goebel, H. B. Swete.

[31] Cf. A. E. Barnett, *Understanding the Parables of our Lord* (1940), pp. 49, 61 f., S. E. Johnson, *IB*, VII, pp. 415, 418; E. Klostermann, *Das Matthäus-evangelium* (1927), p. 123; C. G. Montefiore, *The Synoptic Gospels* (1927),

from the question of whether Jesus could and did forecast the status
of things which followed his resurrection and ascension, this objection to the secondary character of the interpretation loses its force
when it is seen to refer to an "open secret" about the Kingdom of
God which had its immediate application to Jesus' disciples.

Another view, widely held, seems to be correct so far as it goes,
but in the form usually presented it is colorless and without relevance
to its historical situation. The main point of the parable teaches that
good men and evil must grow together in the world (not in the
church) until the end of the age when a separation will at last take
place. To attempt such a separation before the eschatological consummation will involve the uprooting of society itself.[32] This, however, is but to affirm the obvious. What Jew needed to be told that
the righteous and the wicked would exist together in the world until
God brought about a final separation at the day of judgment? To be
sure, both the Pharisees and the Qumran Community tried to create
an exclusive, holy, religious society on the basis of a principle of
separatism; but this did not involve the uprooting of the Am-ha-
arez, only aloofness from them. The Qumran Community achieved a
pure society by breaking off all intercourse with the "sons of darkness"
and withdrawing to the desert. Jesus did not try to create a separatist
fellowship. Precisely here is the point of the parable: the Kingdom
has come into the world without effecting a separation of men; this
awaits the eschatological consummation. This setting alone gives the
parable its real point.[33]

The coming of the Kingdom, as predicted in the Old Testament
and expected in Jewish apocalyptic literature, would bring about the
end of the age and inaugurate the age to come, disrupting human

---

II, p. 209. Cf. also C. H. Dodd, *The Parables of the Kingdom* (1936), pp.
183 f.; B. T. D. Smith, *The Parables of the Synoptic Gospels* (1937), pp. 199 f.

[32] See B. T. D. Smith, *The Parables of the Synoptic Gospels* (1937), pp.
196 ff.; A. H. McNeile, *The Gospel according to St. Matthew* (1915), p. 202;
W. C. Allen, *The Gospel according to S. Matthew* (1913), p. lxx; and especially the discussion of W. G. Kümmel, *Promise and Fulfilment* (1957), pp.
132–135. Kümmel recognizes the presence of the Kingdom but does not give
this fact its proper weight.

[33] Such an interpretation will be found in J. Schniewind, *Das Evangelium
nach Markus* (1952), p. 169; N. A. Dahl, *StTh*, V (1952), pp. 151 f.

society by the destruction of the unrighteous. Jesus affirms that in the midst of the present age, while society continues with its intermixture of the good and the bad, before the coming of the Son of Man and the glorious manifestation of the Kingdom of God, the powers of that future age have entered into the world to create "sons of the kingdom," men who enjoy its power and blessings. The Kingdom has come; but society is not uprooted. This is the mystery of the Kingdom.

The only real difficulty for this interpretation is the expression, "they [the angels] will gather out of this kingdom all causes of sin and all evil-doers" (Matt. 13:41). His language appears to distinguish between the Kingdom of the Son and the Kingdom of the Father. Does this not plainly indicate that the wicked are already in the Kingdom (perhaps in the church) before the eschatological consummation? Granted that at first sight such an interpretation suggests itself, it is by no means the only interpretation, nor is it the compelling one. There is no adequate warrant, from either the Gospels or the rest of the New Testament, to distinguish between the Kingdom of the Son of Man and the Kingdom of God.[34] Furthermore, there are no sayings of Jesus where the Kingdom is clearly identified with the church; and such an identification ought not to be made here unless it is unavoidable.

Neither the parable nor its interpretation requires this identification. The language of Matthew 13:41 cannot be pressed to mean that the evildoers who will be gathered "out of his kingdom" have actually been in the Kingdom. It means no more than that they will be separated from the righteous so that they do not enter the Kingdom. This is supported by Matthew 8:12 where strangers will come from afar to enter the Kingdom of heaven along with the patriarchs, while "the sons of the kingdom will be thrown into the outer darkness." The Greek word, "will be cast out," indicates that the Jews

[34] O. Cullmann in *Christ and Time* (1950), p. 151 and in *The Early Church* (A. J. B. Higgins, ed.; 1956), pp. 109 ff., attempts to distinguish between the Kingdom of Christ and the Kingdom of God. This may be a valid theological distinction, but it cannot be exegetically supported. See Eph. 5:5; Rev. 11:15; John 3:5; Col. 1:13.

who by history and covenant were "sons of the Kingdom" will be excluded from entering the Kingdom, not rejected after having once entered. So the statement that the evil are to be gathered "out of his kingdom" means no more than that they will be prevented from entering it.

The meaning of the parable is clear when interpreted in terms of the mystery of the Kingdom, its present but secret working in the world. The Kingdom has come into history but in such a way that society is not disrupted. The sons of the Kingdom have received God's reign and entered into its blessings. Yet they must continue to live in this age, intermingled with the wicked in a mixed society. Only at the eschatological coming of the Kingdom will the separation take place. Here is indeed the revelation of a new truth: that the Kingdom of God can actually come into the world, creating sons who enjoy its blessings without effecting the eschatological judgment. However, this separation is sure to come. The Kingdom which is present but hidden in the world will yet be manifested in glory. Then there will be an end of the mixed society. The wicked will be gathered out and the righteous will shine like the sun in the eschatological Kingdom.

THE MUSTARD SEED

The parable of the mustard seed illustrates the truth that the Kingdom, which one day will be a great tree, is already present in the world in a tiny, insignificant form. Many interpreters have seen in the parable a forecast of the growth of the church into a great institution.[35] This interpretation is based upon the identification of the Kingdom and the church,[36] a view which we hold to be untenable.

[35] Cf. Trench, Goebel, H. B. Swete on the parables; cf. also N. Geldenhuys, *Commentary on the Gospel of Luke* (1950), p. 377; and B. F. C. Atkinson, *The New Bible Commentary* (F. Davidson, *et al.*, eds.; 1953), p. 790; H. Balmforth, *The Gospel according to St. Luke* (1930), p. 227.

[36] Other interpreters who would deny that Jesus foresaw the church believe that this is in fact what the parable taught, and therefore the parable cannot be authentic. Cf. C. G. Montefiore, *The Synoptic Gospels* (1927), I, pp. 107–108.

Other interpreters, without applying the parable to the church, find its meaning in the growth of the circle of Jesus' disciples,[37] who may be considered to be the new community.[38] However, the quick-growing mustard plant is not an apt illustration of slow, gradual growth, if that is what was intended. An oak growing from an acorn would provide a much better illustration of this truth (Amos 2:9).

The majority of modern exegetes see the emphasis of the parable in the contrast between the tiny beginning and the large end,[39] and this certainly lies at the heart of the parable. The mustard seed, while not actually the smallest seed known, was a proverbial illustration of smallness.[40] The burning question faced by Jesus' disciples was how the Kingdom of God could actually be present in such an insignificant movement as that embodied in his ministry. The Jews expected the Kingdom to be like a great tree under which the nations would find shelter. They could not understand how one could talk about the Kingdom apart from such an all-encompassing manifestation of God's rule. How could the coming glorious Kingdom have anything to do with the poor little band of Jesus' disciples?[41] Rejected by the religious leaders, welcomed by tax collectors and sinners, Jesus looked more like a deluded dreamer than the bearer of the Kingdom of God.

Jesus' answer is, first the tiny seed, later the large tree. The smallness and relative insignificance of what is happening in his ministry does not exclude the secret presence of the very Kingdom of God.[42]

[37] Cf. C. J. Cadoux, The Historic Mission of Jesus (n.d.), pp. 113-114, 131; T. W. Manson, The Teaching of Jesus (1935), p. 113.

[38] R. N. Flew, Jesus and His Church (1943), pp. 27 f.

[39] Cf. W. G. Kümmel, Promise and Fulfilment (1957), p. 131; A. E. Barnett, Understanding the Parables of Our Lord (1940), pp. 55-57; B. T. D. Smith, The Parables of the Synoptic Gospels (1937), pp. 120-121; J. Schniewind, Das Evangelium nach Markus (1952), pp. 81-82; J. Creed, The Gospel according to St. Luke (1930), p. 182; A. E. J. Rawlinson, St. Mark (1925), p. 58; B. H. Branscomb, The Gospel of Mark (1937), pp. 85-86; M. Dibelius, Jesus (1949), p. 68; A. H. McNeile, The Gospel according to St. Matthew (1915), p. 198; J. Jeremias, Parables, p. 90.

[40] Cf. Matt. 17:20; Luke 17:6; Strack and Billerbeck, Kommentar, in loc.

[41] Jeremias, The Parables of Jesus (1954), p. 91.

[42] N. A. Dahl, StTh, V (1952), pp. 147-148; Jeremias, The Parables of

THE LEAVEN

The parable of the leaven[43] embodies the same basic truth as that
of the mustard: that the Kingdom of God, which one day will rule
over all the earth, has entered into the world in a form that is hardly
perceptible.

This parable is of particular interest because it has been used to
prove diametrically different things. Many interpreters have found the
central truth in the slow but persistent process of permeation and
penetration. The parable is thought to show how the Kingdom grows.
On the one hand are those who find the truth that the Kingdom of
God is destined to permeate all human society until all the world is
transformed by a process of slow gradual penetration and inner permeation.[44] Some of these interpreters contrast the leavening character of the Kingdom with the apocalyptic view, to the detriment of
the latter.

On the other hand is the interpretation of so-called Dispensational-
ism which interprets leaven as evil doctrine permeating an apostate
Christian church.[45] However, leaven in Hebrew and Jewish thought
was not always a symbol of evil;[46] and the concept of the Kingdom

---

Jesus (1954), p. 91; cf. also T. Zahn, *Das Evangelium nach Matthäus* (1922),
p. 496; W. O. E. Oesterley, *The Gospel Parables in the Light of their Jewish
Background* (1936), pp. 77–78; C. E. B. Cranfield, *The Gospel according to
Saint Mark* (1959), p. 170.

[43] This parable is missing in Mark, but it appears in Luke 13:20 alongside
the parable of the mustard seed.

[44] W. O. E. Oesterley, *The Gospel Parables in the Light of their Jewish
Background* (1936), p. 78; R. Otto, *The Kingdom of God and The Son of
Man* (1943), p. 125; W. Manson, *The Gospel of Luke* (1930), p. 166; T.
Zahn, *Das Evangelium nach Matthäus* (1922), pp. 497–498; H. Windisch,
TWNT, II, pp. 907–908; H. D. A. Major in *The Mission and Message of
Jesus* (1946), p. 72.

[45] *The Scofield Reference Bible* (1945), p. 1016; J. D. Pentecost, *Things
to Come* (1958), pp. 147 f.; L. S. Chafer, *Systematic Theology* (1917), V, p.
352.

[46] Unleavened bread was prepared at the time of the Exodus because it
symbolized haste (Exod. 12:11, 39; Deut. 16:3; cf. also Gen. 18:6; 19:3);
leavened bread was sacrificed at the Feast of Weeks (Lev. 23:17), elsewhere
called the Feast of Harvest, and First Fruits (Exod. 23:16) because it represented the ordinary daily food which God provided for human sustenance. See

as a transforming power by slow gradual penetration may be an at-
tractive idea in a world familiar with concepts of progress and evolution, but it is foreign both to Jesus' mind and to Jewish thought.

The interpretation which suits the historical setting of Jesus' ministry is that which sees the central truth to lie in the contrast between
the absurdly small bit of leaven and the great mass of more than a
bushel of meal.[47] It is true that emphasis is placed on the fact that
the entire mass of dough is leavened, not on the small size of the
leaven.[48] Here is the difference between this parable and the parable
of the mustard seed. The latter teaches that the manifestation of the
Kingdom, which will become like a great tree, is now like a tiny seed.
The leaven teaches that the Kingdom will one day prevail so that no
rival sovereignty exists. The entire mass of dough becomes leaven.

This parable gains its significance only when interpreted in the life
setting of Jesus' ministry. The mighty, irresistible character of the
eschatological Kingdom was understood by all Jews. The coming of
the Kingdom would mean a complete change in the order of things.
The present evil order of the world and of society would be utterly
displaced by the Kingdom of God. The problem was that Jesus'
ministry initiated no such transformation. He preached the presence
of the Kingdom of God, but the world went on as before. How then
could this be the Kingdom?

Jesus' reply is that when a bit of leaven is put in a mass of meal,
nothing seems to happen. In fact, the leaven seems quite engulfed
by the meal. Eventually something does happen, and the result is the
complete transformation of the dough.[49] No emphasis is to be placed
upon the way the transformation is accomplished. The idea of the
Kingdom of God conquering the world by a gradual permeation and

---

O. T. Allis, EQ, XIX (1947), pp. 269 ff. I. Abrahams (Studies in Pharisaism
and the Gospel [First Series; 1917], pp. 51-53), shows that leaven did not
always symbolize evil in rabbinic thought.
[47] J. Jeremias, The Parables of Jesus (1954), p. 90; W. G. Kümmel, Promise
and Fulfilment (1957), pp. 131 f.; A. H. McNeile, The Gospel according to
St. Matthew (1915), p. 199; A. E. Barnett, Understanding the Parables of our
Lord (1940), pp. 58-60.
[48] H. Windisch, TWNT, II, p. 907.
[49] Cf. N. A. Dahl, StTh, V (1952), pp. 148-149.

inner transformation was utterly foreign to Jewish thought. If this was Jesus' meaning, he certainly must have reiterated the truth again and again, even as he did the unheard-of truth that the Son of Man must die. The idea of gradualness is contradicted by the parables of the tares and the dragnet, where the Kingdom comes by apocalyptic judgment and separation of evil rather than by its gradual transformation of the world.

The emphasis of the parable lies in the contrast between the final, complete victory of the Kingdom when the new order comes, and the present, hidden form of that Kingdom as it has now come into the world. One would never guess Jesus and his small band of disciples had anything to do with the future glorious Kingdom of God. However, that which is now present in the world is indeed the Kingdom itself. This is the mystery, the new truth about the Kingdom. How or when the future Kingdom will come is no part of the parable.[50]

The Treasure and the Pearl

We need not tarry long over the parables of the treasure and the pearl. The identity of the man or of the field, as well as the contrast between the accidental discovery of the treasure and the purposeful search of the merchant, are not part of the message of the parables but only local color. We must admit that the conduct of the man who found the treasure involved a bit of sharp practice, but this belongs to the lifelike character of the parabolic form. People did things like this. Nor can any objection be made to the fact that in both parables the treasure and the pearl are acquired by purchase.[51]

The one thought in both parables is that the Kingdom of God is of inestimable value and is to be sought above all other possessions. If

[50] This interpretation is reinforced by the parables of the treasure and the pearl where the method of acquisition by purchase is no part of the message of the parables. So the method of the coming of the Kingdom is not here in question, only the fact that it will come, even though in a real sense it is already present.

[51] G. C. Morgan permitted this feature to determine his interpretation. This is a complete misunderstanding of the parabolic method (*The Parables of the Kingdom* [1907], p. 136).

it costs a man everything he has, that is a small price in return for gaining the Kingdom. Thus stated, however, it is a truism. If there is no "mystery" of the Kingdom, Jesus here said no more than devout Jews believed already. They longed for the Kingdom of God. What gives these parables their point is the fact that the Kingdom had come among men in an unexpected way, in a form which might easily be overlooked and despised. To accept the "yoke of the Kingdom" and join the circle of the Pharisees in their utter devotion to the law gave one great prestige in the eyes of the Jews.[52] The offer to lead an insurrection against Rome to establish the Kingdom could arouse an enthusiastic response.[53] But to follow Jesus meant association with tax collectors and sinners. How could such an association have anything to do with the Kingdom of God?

These parables gain their central point from the fact that, contrary to every superficial evaluation, discipleship of Jesus means participation in the Kingdom of God. Present in the person and work of Jesus without outward display or visible glory was the Kingdom of God itself. It is therefore a treasure worth more than all other possessions, a pearl exceeding all else in value. Man should seek to gain possession of it at any cost.

THE NET

In the final parable illustrating the mystery of the Kingdom, a net is dragged through the sea catching all kinds of fish. When the catch is sorted out, the good fish are kept and the bad discarded.

The older interpretation saw in this parable a prophecy of the church. The Kingdom-church is to consist of a mixture of good and bad people who must be separated in the day of judgment.[54] Other

[52] Cf. Josephus, Antiquities, XIII, 10.6.

[53] See Acts 5:36 37; 21:38; John 6:15; T. W. Manson, The Servant-Messiah (1953), p. 8.

[54] Cf. Trench, Gocbel, Swete on the parables. In more recent writers, a similar view appears in B. F. C. Atkinson, The New Bible Commentary (F. Davidson, et al., eds.; 1953), p. 790; N. B. Stonehouse, The Witness of Matthew and Mark to Christ (1944), p. 238; H. Martin, The Parables of the Gospels (1937), p. 79.

interpreters, while not insisting upon the church, see in the parable an identification of the Kingdom of God with a society of people which includes the good and the bad.[55] This view has the weakness of failing to give due recognition to the historical setting in Jesus' ministry of the parable, and it involves an identification of the Kingdom with the church, for which clear exegetical support cannot be found.

A second view limits the application to Jesus' immediate experience. Jesus and his disciples must offer the Kingdom to all kinds of men without discrimination.[56] This view sees the eschatological interpretation as a secondary element which does not fit the parable as a whole. Inconsistencies are found in the fact that the parable has to do with the catching, not the sorting, of fish; that the parable has the fishermen sorting the fish while the interpretation has angels carrying out this function; that fire is not the means of disposing of bad fish. These objections overlook the fact that the parable does speak of the sorting of the fish.[57] When the net is full, it is drawn to land and the good and bad fish are separated. The objections to the angels and to fire rest upon an insistence that parables must be allegorical in character, i.e., that the details in the parable must precisely match the details in the interpretation. Since the genius of a parable is its illustration of redemptive truth by common realistic experiences rather than by an artificially constructed story, details may require modification in the application. Therefore the problem of the angels and fire is artificial and really constitutes no problem.

Still other interpreters find the one truth in the final separation of men when the Kingdom comes. The day of judgment will separate

55 T. Zahn, Das Evangelium nach Matthäus (1922), p. 501; W. O. E. Osterley, The Gospel Parables in the Light of their Jewish Background (1936), p. 85; "Bad as well as good elements must exist in the kingdom during the period of its development." C. J. Cadoux, The Historic Mission of Jesus (n.d.), emphasizes that here the Kingdom is clearly likened to a society (p. 114).

56 Cf. B. T. D. Smith, The Parables of the Synoptic Gospels (1937), pp. 200 f.; Charles W. F. Smith, The Jesus of the Parables (1947), pp. 102–104; T. W. Manson, The Sayings of Jesus (1949), p. 197; S. E. Johnson, IB, VII, p. 421; C. H. Dodd, The Parables of the Kingdom (1936), pp. 187–189.

57 W. G. Kümmel, Promise and Fulfilment (1957), pp. 136 f.

the wicked from the righteous.[58] However, this by itself is a truism. Of course the Kingdom would mean a separation of the wicked and the righteous. "The sinners shall be destroyed before the face of the Lord of Spirits, and they shall be banished from off the face of His earth. And they shall perish forever and ever" (En. 53:2). This was the hope of devout Jews.

This parable is similar to that of the wheat and the weeds, but it adds another element. Both parables teach the future separation of men at the judgment. Both parables must be understood in terms of the life-setting of Jesus' ministry, that the Kingdom has now come into the world without effecting this eschatological separation and is to work in a mixed society. The parable of the net adds this fact: that even the community created by the working of the Kingdom in the world is not to be a pure community until the eschatological separation.

Historically, the parable answers the question of the strange character of Jesus' followers. He attracted tax collectors and sinners. In the popular expectation, the coming of the Kingdom would mean not only that Messiah would "destroy the godless nations with the word of his mouth; . . . and . . . reprove sinners for the thoughts of their hearts"; he would also "gather together a holy people whom he shall lead in righteousness," "and there shall be no unrighteousness in his days in their midst, for all shall be holy" (Ps. of Sol. 17:28, 36). Jesus did not gather together such a holy people. On the contrary, he said, "I came not to call the righteous, but sinners" (Mark 2:17).The invitation to the messianic feast was rejected by those who were invited and their places taken by loiterers in the streets (Matt. 22:1–10). How could the Kingdom of God have anything to do with such a strange fellowship? Is not the function of the Kingdom by definition to destroy all sinners and to create a sinless community?

[58] Cf. A. E. Barnett, Understanding the Parables of Our Lord (1940), p. 69; W. G. Kümmel, Promise and Fulfilment (1957), pp. 136 f.; A. H. McNeile, The Gospel according to St. Matthew (1915), p. 204; J. Schniewind, Das Evangelium nach Matthäus (1950), pp. 173 f.

Jesus answers that the Kingdom will indeed one day create such a perfect community. But before this event an unexpected manifestation of God's Kingdom has occurred which is like a net gathering both good and bad fish. The invitation goes out to all kinds of men, and all who respond are accepted into present discipleship of the Kingdom. The perfect, holy community must await the last day.[59] While the parable has an application to the church which, as a later development of Jesus' disciples, is indeed a mixed people, its primary application is to the actual situation in Jesus' ministry.

All of these parables illustrate the mystery of the Kingdom. All bear a central truth which has its *Sitz im Leben* in Jesus' historical ministry. The Kingdom of God has come into the world, but it comes with persuasion rather than power and must be accepted to be effective, even as the ground must receive the seed. The Kingdom has come, but it is not now effecting a separation among men. The sons of the Kingdom and the sons of evil are to be mixed together in the world until the eschatological separation. Nevertheless, it *is* the Kingdom of God which has come into the world, which, like the self-growing seed, has power within itself to accomplish its ends. It is God's superhuman rule and working. Therefore, even though its present manifestation is small and insignificant (the mustard seed), it will one day fill the whole world (the leaven) and, like a treasure and priceless pearl, is even now to be desired at all costs. It will one day create a holy society; but for the present, the invitation goes out to all kinds of men, and all who will respond are welcomed into its fellowship. Thus the Kingdom has come into history in the person and mission of Jesus; and in the same way, the Kingdom will continue to work in the world until the hour of its eschatological manifestation.

---

[59] See N. A. Dahl, *StTh*, V (1952), pp. 150–151; A. Schlatter, *Der Evangelist Matthäus* (1948), pp. 447 f.

10 Jesus, Israel, and His Disciples

One of the most difficult questions in the study of the Kingdom of God is its relationship to the church. Is the Kingdom of God in any sense of the word to be identified with the church? If not, what is the relationship? For Christians of the first three centuries, the Kingdom was altogether eschatological. An early second-century prayer says, "Remember, Lord, Thy church, to . . . gather it together in its holiness from the four winds to thy kingdom which thou has prepared for it."[1] Augustine identified the Kingdom of God with the church,[2] an identification which continues in Catholic doctrine,[3] although Schnackenburg claims that the new Catholic concept conceives of the Kingdom in *heilsgeschichtlichen* terms as the redemptive working of God through the church.[4] A measure of identification between

[1] Didache 10:5. See A. von Harnack, "Millennium," *Encyclopaedia Britannica*, 9th ed.; XVI, pp. 328–329; D. H. Kromminga, *The Millennium in the Church* (1945); R. Frick, *Die Geschichte des Reich-Gottes-Gedankens in der alten Kirche bis zu Origines und Augustine* (1928); K. L. Schmidt, *BKW: Basileia* (1957), pp. 56–59.

[2] *City of God*, XX, 6–10.

[3] D. M. Stanley in *Theological Studies*, X (1955), pp. 1–29.

[4] *Gottes Herrschaft und Reich* (1959), p. 78; see also D. Kuss in *Theologische Quartalschrift*, CXXXV (1955), pp. 28–55; F. M. Braun, *Neues Licht auf die Kirche* (1946).

the Kingdom and the church was perpetuated, though in a modified form, through the Reformed tradition[5] to recent times.[6] It is necessary to examine closely these two concepts to determine what relationship exists between them.

The Critical Problem

Back of the theological question lies a historical problem. Could Jesus have entertained the purpose of establishing a church? Supporters of Consistent Eschatology have denied it. Alfred Loisy has given this viewpoint classic expression: Jesus foretold the Kingdom of God, but it was the church which came.[7] To be sure, Mathew 16: 18–19 reports Jesus' words about building his church, but their authenticity has been widely rejected. One of the most important reasons for rejecting this saying[8] is the claim that Jesus' eschatological perspective leaves no room for the idea of a church. If his mission was to announce the imminent inbreaking of the eschatological Kingdom of God, there could be little place in his thought for a new people of God.[9] His one purpose must have been to summon Israel as the covenant people to repentance in preparation for the imminent coming of the eschatological Kingdom.

Therefore, the question of Jesus and the church is of vital importance in discussing the eschatological problem. If the expectation of an early end of the world dominated Jesus' thought, then it easily follows that Matthew 16:18–19 is a secondary product of the church

---

[5] See Calvin on Matt. 13:47–50.

[6] See J. Orr, Christian View of God and the World (1897), p. 358; H. B. Swete, The Parables of the Kingdom (1920), p. 31, 56; A. M. Fairbairn, The Place of Christ in Modern Theology (1893), p. 529; J. Denney, Studies in Theology (1906), p. 184. G. Vos, The Teaching of Jesus Concerning the Kingdom of God and the Church (1903), pp. 140–168; Ernst Sommerlath, ZSysTh, XVI (1939), pp. 562–575; O. Michel, Das Zeugnis des Neuen Testaments von der Gemeinde (1941), pp. 80–83.

[7] The Gospel and the Church (Eng. trans., 1908), p. 166.

[8] A survey of other reasons will be found in R. N. Flew, Jesus and His Church (1943), pp. 89–91, and in T. W. Manson, The Sayings of Jesus (1949), pp. 202–203.

[9] G. Bornkamm, Jesus of Nazareth (1960), p. 187.

and does not reflect his mind.[10] This approach decides the question in advance. A better approach is to let the question of Jesus' eschatological perspective be conditioned by his entire teaching, including that about the church. If Jesus regarded his disciples as a new people of God who are to take the place of Israel, and if he gave them a mission to the world, we must make allowance for this in his eschatological perspective. Therefore, back of the specific question of the authenticity and meaning of the church logion in Matthew is the larger question of the meaning of the discipleship and the relation of Jesus' disciples to his own mission and to the Kingdom of God.

Some scholars have felt that the authenticity of Matthew 16:18–19 is entirely compatible with thoroughgoing eschatological perspective. Kattenbusch discovered the source for the idea of the church[11] in Daniel 7 where the Son of Man represents the saints of the Most High. Jesus thought of himself as "Son of Man," the representative of a community which was the new people of God, embodied in his disciples. Kattenbusch was followed by K. L. Schmidt, one of the earliest form critics, first in a brief essay and then in this article in Kittel's *Wörterbuch*.[12] He traces the meaning of the word *ekklesia* to the Aramaic *kenishta* or synagogue. The synagogue of Jesus the Messiah constituted the holy remnant; the part represents the whole and embodies the true people of God.

Many scholars have acknowledged the genuineness of this saying.[13]

[10] "The time after his death was for Jesus limited by the nearness of the Parousia. Therefore Jesus founded no congregation nor church, appointed no officers, established no ecclesiastical rites or sacraments" (W. Michaelis, *Reich Gottes und Geist Gottes nach dem Neuen Testament* (n.d.), p. 20.

[11] "Der Quellort der Kirchenidee," *Festgabe für Harnack* (1921), pp. 143–172.

[12] "Die Kirche des Urchristentums," *Festgabe für Adolf Deissmann* (1926), pp. 259–319, published separately in 1932; *TWNT*, III, pp. 502–539; Eng. trans., *BKW: Church* (1951).

[13] See the survey of recent literature in O. Cullmann, *Peter: Disciple-Apostle-Martyr* (1953), pp. 164–170; (2nd ed., 1961), pp. 170–176. The authenticity of the saying is recognized also by A. Fridrichsen in *This Is the Church* (Anders Nygren, ed.; 1952), pp. 21 f.; H. E. W. Turner, *Jesus Master and Lord* (1953), pp. 270 ff.; H. Roberts, *Jesus and the Kingdom of God* (1955), pp. 93 f.; A. Richardson, *An Introduction to the Theology of the New Testament* (1958), pp. 307 ff.; D. Bosch, *Die Heidenmission in der Zukunftsschau Jesu* (1959), pp. 135–138; F. V. Filson, *The Gospel according to St. Matthew* (1960), p. 186;

Others echo the sentiment of Lindeskog, "Even if the statement was of later formulation, Jesus surely did speak and act in the way which this passage declares.[14]

If Jesus' mission was, as we contend, that of inaugurating a time of fulfillment in advance of an eschatological consummation, and if in a real sense, the Kingdom of God in his mission invaded history even though in an utterly unexpected form, then it follows that those who received the proclamation of the Kingdom were viewed not only as the people who would inherit the eschatological Kingdom, but as the people of the Kingdom in the present, and therefore in some sense of the word, a church. We must first examine Jesus' attitude toward Israel, the concept of discipleship, and the relation of Israel and Jesus' disciples to the Kingdom of God. Then against this background, we may discuss the meaning of the logion about founding the church.

JESUS AND ISRAEL

In this examination, several facts are crucial. First, Jesus did not undertake his ministry with the evident purpose of starting a new movement either within or without Israel. He came as a Jew to the Jewish people. He accepted the authority of the law, conformed to temple practices, engaged in synagogue worship, and throughout his life lived as a Jew. Although he occasionally journeyed outside Jewish territory, he insisted that his mission was directed to the "lost sheep of the house of Israel" (Matt. 15:24). He directed the mission of his disciples away from the Gentiles, commanding them to preach only to Israel (Matt. 10:5–6). The reason for this is not difficult. Jesus took his stand squarely against the background of the Old Testament

---

"Peter," *IDB*, III, pp. 751 f.; S. H. Hooke, *Alpha and Omega* (1961), pp. 148, 242; P. S. Minear, *Images of the Church in the New Testament* (1961), p. 51. K. Stendahl leaves the question open in "Kirche," *RGG* (3rd ed.), III, col. 1303.

[14] G. Lindeskog, "The Kingdom of God and the Church," in *This Is the Church* (A. Nygren, ed.; 1952), p. 141. See T. W. Manson, *Journal of Ecclesiastical History*, I (1950), p. 3, "Jesus did gather a community round himself during the course of his ministry; and we may well ask what it was, if it was not the Church." See also A. R. George, *ET*, LVIII (1946–47), p. 314.

covenant and the promises of the prophets, and recognized Israel, to whom the covenant and the promises had been given, as the natural "sons of the Kingdom" (Matt. 8:12). The saying about the lost sheep of the house of Israel does not mean that the Gentiles were not also lost but that only Israel was the people of God, and to them therefore belonged the promise of the Kingdom.[15] Therefore his mission was to proclaim to Israel that God was now acting to fulfill his promises and to bring Israel to its true destiny. Because Israel was the chosen people of God, the age of fulfillment was offered not to the world at large but to the sons of the covenant.

Jesus did not appeal to Israel in terms of national solidarity but in terms of a personal relationship. In this he followed John the Baptist whose call to baptism denied the efficacy of Abrahamic sonship to qualify for the Kingdom but demanded personal, individual repentance (Matt. 3:9–10). While Jesus' mission was directed to the people as a whole, his appeal cut through external national relationships and demanded an individual response to his own person. In fact, his mission was often disruptive to normal social ties. This is the meaning of his word that he came not to bring peace but a sword, to set members of a family against one another (Matt. 10:34–36). The one bond which brought his disciples together was personal relationship to his person. This set him apart from other Jewish leaders. The disciples of the rabbis found common ties in the rabbinic teachings, the Pharisees in their observances, the apocalyptists in their eschatological hopes, while Jews as a whole recognized a common bond in their Abrahamic descent and the covenant. The disciples of Jesus had no common bond other than the person of Jesus.[16] Jesus challenged Israel to find in personal relationship to himself her divinely ordained destiny.

The second fact is that Israel as a whole rejected both Jesus and his message about the Kingdom. It is true that Jesus appealed to Israel to the very end;[17] but it is most unlikely that he expected, to the end,

---

[15] See W. Gutbrod in *TWNT*, IV, p. 387.
[16] See N. A. Dahl, *Das Volk Gottes* (1941), p. 159.
[17] W. G. Kümmel, *StTh*, VII (1953), p. 9.

to be accepted by the nation and to establish a kingdom of morality and righteousness which would have led the Jewish people to a moral conquest over Rome.[18] The reality of Jesus' disappointment and grief over Israel's rejection (Matt. 23:37 ff.) and the prophecy of her destruction (Luke 19:42 ff.) does not demand the conclusion that Jesus failed to recognize at an early hour the reality and intransigence of her rejection.[19] While we may not be able to reconstruct the exact chronology of events or to trace all the stages in Jesus' rejection because of the character of our Gospels, we can conclude that rejection is one of the early motifs in his experience. Luke deliberately placed the rejection at Nazareth at the beginning of his Gospel (Luke 4:16–30; cf. Mark 6:1–6) to sound the notes of messianic fulfillment and rejection by Israel early in Jesus' ministry.[20] Mark pictures conflict and rejections from the beginning and records a saying which probably contains a veiled illusion to an expected violent end: "The days will come when the bridegroom is taken away from them" (Mark 2:20).[21] While the reasons for Jewish rejection of Jesus were complex, J. M. Robinson finds at the heart of the struggle between Jesus and the Jewish authorities their rejection of the Kingdom which Jesus proclaimed and of the repentance that proclamation demanded.[22] The proclamation of the Kingdom and the call to repentance characterized Jesus' mission from the start, and it is therefore both psychologically and historically sound that opposition was early incurred which grew in intensity until Jesus' death was accomplished.

The gravity of Israel's rejection of the messianic fulfillment can be

---

[18] This is the thesis of R. Dunkerley, *The Hope of Jesus* (1953). Bultmann also thinks that Jesus hoped to the very last to bring Israel to repentance. See *Das Verhältnis der urchristlichen Christusbotschaft zum historischen Jesus* (1961), p. 12.

[19] A. M. Hunter, *The Works and Words of Jesus* (1950), p. 94.

[20] N. B. Stonehouse, *The Witness of Luke to Christ* (1951), pp. 70–76; N. Geldenhuys, *Commentary on the Gospel of Luke* (1950), p. 170.

[21] W. G. Kümmel, *Promise and Fulfilment* (1957), pp. 75–77; V. Taylor, *Jesus and His Sacrifice* (1951), pp. 82–85; *The Gospel according to St. Mark* (1952), pp. 211 f.; C. E. B. Cranfield, *The Gospel according to Saint Mark* (1959), pp 110 f.

[22] *The Problem of History in Mark* (1957), p. 49. See also V. Taylor, *The Life and Ministry of Jesus* (1954), p. 89.

seen in the numerous sayings of judgment and rejection of Israel.[23] Israel is no longer the object of God's blessing but of his judgment. A fearful fate awaits the cities which refused to respond to the presence of the Kingdom in their streets (Matt. 11:20–24). Judgment will fall upon Jerusalem and its inhabitants because of their spiritual blindness (Luke 13:34 f. = Matt. 23:37–39; Luke 19:41–44; 23: 27–31; 21:20–24). The temple is to be destroyed and razed to the ground (Mark 13:1–2; cf. 14:58; 15:29). These sayings anticipate a historical event. Israel will cease to exist as the people of God. Other sayings of judgment are directed against the evil generation of Jesus' day (Matt. 11:16–19; Mark 8:11–13; 9:19; Matt. 12:34; Luke 13:1–5; 13:6–19). The last week in Jerusalem was one of constant conflict between Jesus and the scribes and the Pharisees, as well as the Sadducees, and is climaxed[24] with the saying that the Kingdom of God will be taken away from them and given to others (Mark 12:9; Matt. 21:43). Possibly the form of the language of this saying has been modified by tradition, but the central idea appears to be sound. The Jewish nation which has rejected the offer of the Kingdom of God has therefore been set aside as the people of God and is to be replaced by a new people.

A third fact is equally important. While Israel as a whole, including both leaders and people, refused to accept Jesus' offer of the Kingdom, a substantial group did respond in faith. Discipleship to Jesus was not like discipleship to a Jewish rabbi. The rabbis bound their disciples not to themselves but to the Torah; Jesus bound his disciples to himself. The rabbis offered something outside of themselves; Jesus offered himself alone. Jesus required his disciples to surrender without reservation to his authority. They thereby became not only disciples but also *douloi*, slaves (Matt. 10:24 f.; 24:45 ff.; Luke 12:35 ff., 42 ff.). This relationship had no parallel in Judaism.[25] Discipleship to Jesus involved far more than following in his retinue;

[23] See N. A. Dahl, *Das Volk Gottes* (1941), pp. 149 f.

[24] Logically, not necessarily temporally.

[25] K. H. Rengstorf, *TWNT*, IV, pp. 450 f.; G. Duncan, *Jesus, Son of Man* (1949), pp. 209 ff.

it meant nothing less than complete personal commitment to him and his message. The reason for this is the presence of the Kingdom of God in Jesus' person and message. In him, men were confronted by God himself.

It follows that if Jesus proclaimed the messianic salvation, if he offered to Israel the fulfillment of her true destiny, then this destiny was actually accomplished in those who received his message. The recipients of the messianic salvation became the true Israel, representatives of the nation as a whole. While it is true that the word "Israel" is never applied to Jesus' disciples,[26] the idea is present, if not the term. Jesus' disciples are the recipients of the messianic salvation, the people of the Kingdom, the true Israel.

THE BELIEVING REMNANT

This concept of Jesus' disciples as the true Israel can be understood against the background of the Old Testament concept of a faithful remnant (see pp. 72 ff.). The prophets saw Israel as a whole as rebellious and disobedient and therefore destined to suffer the divine judgment. Still there remained within the faithless nation a remnant of believers who were the object of God's care. Here in the believing remnant was the true people of God.

It is true that Jesus makes no explicit use of the remnant concept.[27] However, is not the designation of the disciples as a "little flock" (Luke 12:32) an express reference to the Old Testament concept of Israel as the sheep of God's pasture, now embodied in Jesus' disciples (Isa. 40:11)? Does this not suggest precisely the faithful remnant? This does not mean a separate fold.[28] Israel is still ideally God's flock (Matt. 10:6; 15:24); but it is a disobedient, willful

---

[26] W. Gutbrod in TWNT, III, p. 387.

[27] D. Bosch, Die Heidenmission in der Zukunftsschau Jesu (1959), p. 135.

[28] Jeremias is right in his insistence that Jesus refused to gather a separate remnant but extended the call to salvation to all Israel (ZNTW, XLII [1949], pp. 184–194). However, the prophets often think of a faithful remnant within the unfaithful nation, not separated from it. Campbell has pointed out that the remnant in the Old Testament is never identified with any special group or class, such as the Rechabites (J. C. Campbell, SJTh, III [1950], p. 79). See Jer. 5:1–5; Amos 5:14–15; Isa. 6:13.

flock, "lost sheep." Jesus has come as the shepherd (Mark 14:27; cf. John 10:11) to "seek and to save the lost" (Luke 19:10) in fulfillment of Ezekiel 34:15 f., to rescue the lost sheep of Israel, to bring them into the fold of the messianic salvation. Israel as a whole was deaf to the voice of her shepherd; but those who heard and followed the shepherd constitute his fold, the little flock, the true Israel. There are direct and explicit links between the image of the flock and the covenant community of Israel.[29]

While the saying in Luke 12:32 emphasizes the eschatological aspect of the Kingdom, Jesus' disciples will inherit the Kingdom because they are now his little flock. The shepherd has found them and brought them home (Luke 15:3–7). It is because they are already the true flock, God's people, that God will give them the eschatological Kingdom.

Jesus' call of twelve disciples to share his mission has been widely recognized as a symbolic act setting forth the continuity between his disciples and Israel. That the twelve represent Israel is shown by their eschatological role. They are to sit on twelve thrones, "judging the twelve tribes of Israel" (Matt. 19:28; Luke 22:30). Whether this saying means that the twelve are to determine the destiny of Israel by judgment[30] or are to rule over them,[31] the twelve are destined to be the head of the eschatological Israel.

Recognition that the twelve were meant to constitute the nucleus of the true Israel does not exclude the view that the number 12 also involved a claim upon the entire people as Jesus' qahal.[32] The

[29] P. S. Minear, *Images of the Church in the New Testament* (1961), p. 85.
[30] See G. Schrenk, *Die Weissagung über Israel im Neuen Testament* (1950), pp. 17 ff.; K. H. Rengstorf, *TWNT*, II, p. 327.
[31] See I Sam. 8:5; II Kings 15:5; Ps. 2:10; I Macc. 9:73; Ps. of Sol. 17:28; So W. G. Kümmel, *Promise and Fulfilment* (1957), p. 47; E. Stauffer, *New Testament Theology* (1955), p. 308; V. Taylor, *Jesus and His Sacrifice* (1951), p. 189.
[32] *Qahal* is the Hebrew word for Israel as the congregation of God; see below p. 259, n. 50. This significance of the twelve has been emphasized by W. G. Kümmel, *Kirchenbegriff und Geschichtsbewusstsein in der Urgemeinde und bei Jesus* (1943), p. 31, *Promise and Fulfilment* (1957), p. 47; K. H. Rengstorf, *TWNT*, II, p. 326; H. D. Wendland, *Eschatologie*, p. 159. Wendland also recognizes that the twelve embody the nucleus of the new Israel, as does Gloege. See *Reich Gottes und Kirche im Neuen Testament* (1929), p. 247.

twelve as a symbolical number looks both backward and forward: backward to the old Israel and forward to the eschatological Israel.[33]

The twelve are destined to be the rulers of the eschatological Israel; but they are already recipients of the blessings and powers of the eschatological Kingdom. They therefore represent not only the eschatological people of God but also those who accept the present offer of the messianic salvation. By the acted parable of choosing the twelve, Jesus taught that he was raising up a new congregation to displace the nation which was rejecting his message.[34]

THE MEANING OF DISCIPLESHIP

If Jesus saw in his disciples the true people of the Kingdom, the problem remains of the relationship between this new qahal and the Kingdom; and this requires an analysis of the meaning of discipleship. This ought to be a simple task, but it is notoriously difficult, for the terminology used in the Gospels for discipleship is neither technical nor precise. Three different circles of disciples can be detected.[35] The most distinctive group is the twelve, who are called both apostles (Mark 3:14; 6:30) and disciples.[36] However, Mark suggests that the twelve were selected from a prior band of disciples, who must therefore have included more than the twelve (Mark 2:15, 16, 18; 3:7, 9). This second group of disciples is in turn distinguished from a still larger company who enjoyed fellowship with Jesus and listened to his message (Mark 2:16) and who "followed" Jesus in the broadest sense of the term (Mark 3:7). Thus we have three circles: a large crowd who "followed" and listened to Jesus' preach-

[33] See D. Bosch, Die Heidenmission in der Zukunftsschau Jesu (1959), p. 82.
[34] See C. E. B. Cranfield, The Gospel according to Saint Mark (1959), p. 127; J. W. Bowman, The Intention of Jesus (1943), p. 214.
[35] See the articles by K. H. Rengstorf in TWNT, IV, pp. 447-460 and by G. Kittel in TWNT, I, pp. 213-215. See also E. Schweizer, Lordship and Discipleship (1960), pp. 11-21; W. G. Kümmel, Kirchenbegriff und Geschichtsbewusstsein in der Urgemeinde und bei Jesus (1943), pp. 28 ff.
[36] Cf. Mark 6:30 (apostles) with 6:35 and 6:45 (disciples); and Mark 14:12-16 (disciples) with 14:17 (the twelve). Matthew has the expression, "the twelve disciples" (Matt. 10:1; 11:1; 20:17; 26:20).

ing; an indeterminate circle of personal followers who are called disciples; and a smaller select group of disciples, the twelve.

That a group of personal disciples, larger than the twelve, followed Jesus is indicated by a number of sayings. Mark tells of one who wished to become a disciple but was refused this privilege and was told to go home and witness there to his healing (Mark 5:18–19). On other occasions, Jesus called men to personal discipleship who were not willing to make the sacrifice involved in leaving all to follow the master (Matt. 8:19–22 = Luke 9:57–60). This appears to have been the challenge extended to the young man who asked the way to eternal life (Mark 10:17–22). Jesus set before him the challenge of the Kingdom in terms of personal discipleship. Joseph of Arimathea is called a disciple (Matt. 27:57). One Cleopas (Luke 24:18) is in the circle of disciples to whom Jesus appeared after his resurrection. Luke records a mission of seventy disciples (Luke 10:1 ff.) who were sent out on a mission similar to that of the twelve (Mark 6:7 ff.) as representatives of Jesus to preach the good news of the Kingdom and to perform its signs. Mark (15:40–41), as well as Luke (8:2–3), indicates that certain women were in Jesus' retinue.

Beyond these two circles of personal disciples was a large undefined group consisting of those who responded to Jesus' proclamation of the Kingdom but were not called upon to forsake their homes and families to follow Jesus. The saying about giving a cup of water to a "little one" because he is a disciple of Jesus (Matt. 10:42) points to such a large undefined circle. Twice Luke refers to a large band of disciples (Luke 6:17; 19:37) who are probably not personal disciples. This provides the background to understand the difficult saying in Mark 9:40: "He that is not against us is for us." A man could be a believer and even exercise the powers of the Kingdom without being in the personal retinue of Jesus.[37] The five hundred to whom Jesus appeared after his resurrection are too large a number to have been personal disciples (I Cor. 15:6).

[37] Matt. 12:30, "He who is not with me is against me," means that there can be no neutrality in a man's reaction to the presence of the Kingdom in Jesus' person. A neutral reaction is in fact a negative decision.

The picture which emerges from this analysis is that of three widening circles of followers. To all Israel, as the natural "sons of the Kingdom" (Matt. 8:12), was addressed the proclamation of the Kingdom and the summons to repent. However, only those who received the message became the true sons of the Kingdom (Matt. 13:38). To all who are poor in spirit, i.e., who realize their utter dependence on God, belongs the Kingdom of heaven (Matt. 5:3). All who receive favorably and treat kindly the "brethren" of Jesus will inherit the Kingdom (Matt. 25:34–40; cf. also Matt. 10:40). All who acknowledge Jesus on earth will one day be acknowledged by him before the Father (Matt. 10:32). Thus the followers of Jesus in the largest sense constitute an eschatological community— those who will enter into the Kingdom in the day of eschatological consummation.[38]

But this is not all. Those who accept Jesus' message are also an eschatological fellowship in the sense that they have already experienced the Kingdom of God. They have received the forgiveness of their sins; they enjoy fellowship with Jesus and with those called into the Kingdom; they have come to know God who is the Father of Israel (Isa. 64:8; Mal. 2:10) as their own Father. They have received the Kingdom of God as little children and have entered into the enjoyment of its blessings. They are indeed the people of both the future and the present Kingdom of God, for they have submitted themselves to God's reign.

It is difficult therefore to avoid the conclusion that Jesus saw the realization of Israel's true destiny in the circle of his disciples. If the acceptance of the messianic salvation promised to Israel and fulfilled in the mission of Jesus would have brought Israel to her true destiny in the purpose of God,[39] then it follows unavoidably that in that portion of Israel which did receive the messianic salvation, the true mission and destiny of Israel as the people of God attained fulfillment. The disciples of Jesus did not constitute a sepa-

---

[38] See N. A. Dahl, Das Volk Gottes (1941), pp. 158 f.; H. D. Wendland, Eschatologie, pp. 146–163.

[39] N. A. Dahl, Das Volk Gottes (1941), p. 147, "In der Berufung zum Gottesreich durch Jesus wird die Erwählung Israel bestätigt und vollendet."

rate synagogue as Schmidt suggested (see pp. 259 ff.). They had no special place of meeting, nor did they appear to have engaged in regular worship after the fashion of a synagogue. They had no fixed teachings like the disciples of the rabbis. They had no new *halachah* or legislation like the Pharisees. They had no evident organization. As Dahl has forcefully put it, "The fellowship of Jesus' disciples was something strange within Judaism: a separate synagogue without a synagogue and without halachah! An apocalyptic circle without an apocalyptic teaching! A messianic movement without the ardor of the zealots."[40] The one thing which bound them together was their personal relationship to Jesus and his message about the Kingdom of God.[41]

The disciples constituted not a new Israel but the true Israel, not a new church but the true people of God (Jer. 7:23; 31:33; Ezek. 11:20); the righteous nation that keeps faith (Isa. 26:2); the true *qahal Jahweh* who have been summoned by Jesus into the blessings of the messianic fulfillment. This is true of the largest circle and not only of Jesus' personal followers, for Jesus promised salvation to many who heard his message but who did not enter into personal discipleship (Mark 10:15; 12:34; Matt. 7:21; Luke 6:20). Out of this large circle who accepted his gospel, Jesus called certain men to be personally associated with him in his proclamation of the Kingdom. This group, whom we may call disciples, probably varied in size from time to time. These are sons of the Kingdom who not only accepted the message of the Kingdom but were called to leave all to share Jesus' mission. Many of the rigorous ethical sayings are directed to these personal disciples. They were called upon to make sacrifices in preaching the Kingdom which were not demanded of disciples at large (Mark 10:17 ff.; 10:28–30). However, all disciples must be ready to forsake everything if called upon to do so (Matt. 8:19–22 = Luke 9:56–60).

There is one important fact experienced by the two inner circles

---

[40] *Das Volk Gottes* (1941), p. 161.
[41] This has been made strikingly clear in Rengstorf's article on Discipleship in *TWNT*, IV, pp. 448 ff.

—the twelve and the disciples—which was not true of the largest circle. To these disciples was granted the privilege of proclaiming the Kingdom and exercising its powers which were at work in Jesus himself.[42]

The twelve were selected to be closer to Jesus than his other disciples, to preach and to have authority to cast out demons (Mark 3:14-15). When he sent the twelve on a preaching mission, he gave them authority over unclean spirits (Mark 6:7), and the commission to preach repentance and perform the works of the Kingdom (Mark 6:12-13). Luke tells us that their mission was to preach the Kingdom of God (Luke 9:2); and Matthew adds other material which defines more precisely the nature of their mission. Their announcement that the Kingdom was at hand (Matt. 10:7) was not merely an announcement about the future. "The Kingdom is the future breaking into the present, and manifesting itself in the things which the disciples are to do in addition to their preaching."[43] Rejection of these emissaries will incur judgment (Matt. 10:15). This is a threatening saying. The reason for special judgment is seen in the fact that the Kingdom of God had actually visited these cities in the person of Jesus' representatives and displayed its presence in their mighty acts. "The whole of the dealings of the messengers with the people, to whom they come, are to be a manifestation of the Kingdom in its grace and saving power. . . . The messengers are, in a sense, the Kingdom of God itself."[44] Judgment is pronounced because rejection of the disciples means rejection of the Kingdom itself.

This working of the Kingdom through the disciples was not limited to the twelve, but was also experienced by a larger group who were sent out on a similar preaching mission. Their message and mission were the same as the earlier mission of the twelve: the presence of the Kingdom and the works of the Kingdom (Luke

---

[42] For an exception to this rule, see p. 268, n. 30.

[43] T. W. Manson, *The Sayings of Jesus* (1949), p. 180.

[44] *Ibid.*, pp. 75-78. "The deeds of the apostles, like his own, were an activity of the Kingdom of God" (C. K. Barrett, *The Holy Spirit and the Gospel Tradition* [1947], p. 65).

10:9).[45] When the emissaries of the Kingdom were rejected, they were to pronounce a veiled judgment. Men might reject these preachers with apparent impunity; "nevertheless know this, that the kingdom of God has come near" (Luke 10:11)—in the persons of the rejected preachers. There follows again a word of judgment; such towns will fare worse than Sodom in the day of judgment.

This interpretation of the presence of the Kingdom in the mission of the Seventy is confirmed by Jesus' words when they returned to him. When they expressed delighted surprise at the power they had exercised, he replied that their mission only illustrated the defeat of Satan—his fall from his place of power (Luke 10:17–18). This is the most important passage illustrating the fact that the Kingdom of God was present not only in Jesus but also in his disciples, both in the smaller circle of the twelve and in the larger circle of the Seventy. Kümmel avoids this conclusion by holding that Luke 10:18 is an independent logion having no connection with its present context. The saying makes no reference to exorcism and still less to the authority of the disciples in such action.[46] With this conclusion we cannot agree. On the contrary, the thought structure is similar to Matthew 12:28–29, which Kümmel accepts as one of the most important evidences for the present activity of the Kingdom of God. Jesus' exorcism of demons means the binding of Satan; and the mighty works of his disciples mean that Satan has been cast down from his place of power. There is no compelling reason to question the conclusion that this passage pictures the Kingdom working in and through Jesus' disciples. Kümmel admits they did indeed share the powers of the approaching Kingdom of God which had broken into this passing aeon in Jesus, and to this extent the coming Kingdom of God was already active in the circle of Jesus' disciples.[47]

[45] The Greek of this verse is stronger than the English: "The Kingdom of God has come upon you" (eph' humas).

[46] W. G. Kümmel, Promise and Fulfilment (1957), p. 113. However, H. Conzelmann recognizes that Luke 10:18 provides a natural basis for 10:17 and explains the bestowal of power in 10:19 (The Theology of St. Luke [1960], p. 107). For further discussion of this passage see above, pp. 154 ff.

[47] In one place Kümmel admits, "Vielmehr haben die Zwölf ebenso wie alle

Here again the question of definition is of primary importance. If the Kingdom is the future eschatological realm of salvation, it is difficult to think of it as actually present in Jesus' disciples; but if it is the redemptive reign of God, the admission that the powers of the Kingdom are active in them is equivalent to saying that the Kingdom of God itself is working in and through them.

It is now time to summarize the results of our study thus far and to deal more directly with the relationship between Jesus' disciples, the church, and the Kingdom. Jesus came to bring to Israel the promised messianic fulfillment. He offered the promised salvation to Israel not because Israel had a claim upon the Kingdom but because God had a claim on Israel.[48] Acceptance of the Kingdom of God would have meant the realization of the true destiny and the divine purpose in the call of Israel. This purpose was fulfilled only in those who responded to God's call. These constituted neither a new Israel nor a separate synagogue nor a closed fellowship nor an organized church, but the believing remnant within the unbelieving nation, the ecclesiola in ecclesia. They were in a twofold sense an eschatological community; they had received the present Kingdom proclaimed by Jesus and were therefore destined to inherit the Kingdom in its eschatological consummation. Their only common bond was their relationship to Jesus and their participation in the blessings of the Kingdom resident in him. A smaller group enjoyed a further privilege of sharing the mission of Jesus, of proclaiming with him the presence of the Kingdom and exercising its powers through exorcisms and healings.

MATTHEW 16:18–19

Against this background of discipleship and its relation to Israel and the Kingdom of God, the saying in Matthew 16:18 f. is consist-

anderen Jünger, denen Jesus den Auftrag zur Mithilfe an seiner eschatologischen Wirksamkeit gegeben hat, durch diessen Auftrag Anteil an den mit Jesus in diesen vergehenden Aeon eingebrochenen Kräften des nahenden Gottesreiches, und insofern ist auch im Kreise dieser Jünger Jesu die kommende Gottesherrschaft schon wirksam" (StTh, VII (1954), p. 7).
[48] N. A. Dahl, Das Volk Gottes (1941), p. 148.

ent with Jesus' total teaching. In fact, the saying expresses in explicit form a basic concept underlying Jesus' entire mission and Israel's response to it. The saying does not speak of the creation of an organization or institution, nor is it to be interpreted in terms of the distinctively Christian *ekklesia* as the body and the bride of Christ, but in terms of the Old Testament concept of Israel as the people of God. The idea of "building" a people is an Old Testament idea.[49] Furthermore, *ekklesia* is a biblical term designating Israel as the congregation or assembly of Yahweh, rendering the Hebrew word *qahal*.[50] It is not certain whether Jesus used the word *qahal* or *edhah*, each of which is used commonly in the Old Testament, of Israel as God's people.[51] K. L. Schmidt has argued for a later term, *kenishta*, on the ground that Jesus viewed his disciples as a special synagogue embodying the true Israel.[52] However, Kümmel is certainly correct in his insistence that Jesus showed no purpose of establishing a separate synagogue.[53] Jesus could have looked upon the fellowship of his disciples as the true Israel within the disobedient nation and not as a separatist or "closed" fellowship. He did not institute a new way of worship, a new cult, or a new organization.

---

[49] See Ruth 4:11; Jer. 1:10; 24:6; 31:4; 33:7; Ps. 28:5; 118:22; Amos 9:11.

[50] Acts 7:38 speaks of Israel as the "*ekklesia* in the wilderness," and does not refer to the church in the New Testament sense. See Deut. 5:22; Ezra 10:12; Ps. 22:22; 107:32; Joel 2:16; Mic. 2:5. (See aso G. Johnston, *The Doctrine of the Church in the New Testament* (1943), pp. 36 f.)

[51] *Edhah* is usually translated in the LXX by *synagoge*; it is not translated by *ekklesia*. In the first four books of Moses and in Jeremiah and Ezekiel, *qahal* is also rendered in the LXX by *synagoge*. Both *qahal* and *edhah* were displaced in the first century A.D. by *keneseth* (Aram. *kenishta*) which was also used of the local Jewish synagogue.

[52] BKW: *Church* (1951), pp. 48 f.; *Die Kirche des Urchristentums* (1932), pp. 286 ff.

[53] StTh, VII (1954), pp. 15 f. The early Christian community after Pentecost as pictured in Acts may be viewed as a new synagogue, but it was not a *separatist* synagogue. The believers in Jesus as Messiah continued to worship in the temple (Acts 2:46) as faithful Jews. The fact that they enjoyed the good will of the people (Acts 2:47; 5:13) and did not incur the hostility of the Pharisees shows that they formed no separatist party. Comparison with the Qumran Community is enlightening. Both the church and the Qumran Community considered themselves the true Israel. However, the church did not consider itself a sectarian Israel and break fellowship with the old Israel as did the Qumran Community.

His preaching and teaching remained within the total context of Israel's faith and practice. Jesus' announcement of his purpose to build his *ekklesia* suggests primarily what we have already discovered in our study of discipleship, viz., that the fellowship established by Jesus stands in direct continuity with the Old Testament Israel.[54] The distinctive element is that this *ekklesia* is in a peculiar way the *ekklesia* of Jesus: "My *ekklesia*." That is, the true Israel now finds its specific identity in its relationship to Jesus. Israel as a nation rejected the messianic salvation proclaimed by Jesus, but many accepted it. Jesus sees his disciples taking the place of Israel as the true people of God.

There is no need to discuss at length the meaning of the rock on which this new people is to be founded. In view of the Semitic usage lying behind the Greek text, we should see no play on the two Greek words, *petros* (Peter) and *petra* (rock). Jesus probably said, "You are *kepha* and on this *kepha* I will build my church." Many Protestant interpreters have reacted strongly against the Roman view of Peter as the rock in an official capacity, and have therefore interpreted the rock to be either Christ himself (Luther) or Peter's faith in Christ (Calvin).[55] However, Cullmann has argued persuasively that the rock is in fact Peter, not in an official capacity or by virtue of personal qualifications, but as representative of the twelve confessing Jesus as Messiah. The rock is Peter the confessor.[56] Jesus anticipates a new stage in the experience of his disciples in which Peter will exercise a significant leadership. There is no hint

---

[54] Cf. W. G. Kümmel, *Kirchenbegriff und Geschichtsbewusstsein in der Urgemeinde und bei Jesus* (1943), p. 24. Kümmel recognizes this to be the significance of the word even though he does not believe it is authentic.

[55] See B. Ramm, *Foundations*, V (1962), pp. 206–216. Knight contends that the rock is God himself (G. A. F. Knight in *ThTo*, XVII [1960], pp. 168–180).

[56] *Peter: Disciple-Apostle-Martyr* (1941), pp. 206–212; see also A. Oepke, *StTh*, II (1948), p. 157; O. Betz, *ZNTW*, XLVIII (1957), pp. 72 f.; D. H. Wallace and L. E. Keck, *Foundations*, V (1962), pp. 221, 230. That such an expression need carry no official authority is illustrated by an interesting analogy in a rabbinic midrash on Isa. 51:1. God was troubled because he could build nothing upon godless men. "When God looked upon Abraham, who was to appear, he said, 'See I have found a rock upon which I can found and build the world.' Therefore he called Abraham a rock." (Strack and Billerbeck, *Kommentar*, I, p. 733.)

in the context that this is an official leadership which Peter can pass on to his successors. Indeed, Peter the rock foundation can readily become the rock of stumbling, as the next verses show.[57]

We may conclude that the saying about founding the church fits the total teaching of Jesus and means that he saw in the circle of those who received his message the sons of the Kingdom, the true Israel, the people of God. There is no intimation as to the form the new people is to take. The saying about discipline in the "church" (Matt. 18:17) views the disciples as a distinct fellowship analogous to the Jewish synagogue, but it throws no light upon the form or organization the new fellowship is to take.[58] The church as a body separate from Judaism with its own organization and rites is a later historical development; but it is a historical manifestation of a new fellowship brought into being by Jesus as the true people of God who, having received the messianic salvation, were to take the place of the rebellious nation as the true Israel.

[57] See P. S. Minear, *Christian Hope and the Second Coming* (1954), p. 186.
[58] The authenticity of this passage is frequently rejected, but "nothing justifies the view that Jesus could not have spoken the words" (F. V. Filson, *The Gospel according to St. Matthew* (1960), p. 201).

11 The Kingdom and the Church

We must now examine the specific relationship between the Kingdom and the church, accepting the circle of Jesus' disciples as the incipient church if not yet the church itself.[1] The solution to this problem will depend upon one's basic definition of the Kingdom. If the dynamic concept of the Kingdom is correct, it is never to be identified with the church. The Kingdom is primarily the dynamic reign or kingly rule of God, and derivatively, the sphere in which the rule is experienced. In biblical idiom, the Kingdom is not identified with its subjects. They are the people of God's rule who enter it, live under it, and are governed by it. The church is the community of the Kingdom but never the Kingdom itself. Jesus' disciples belong to the Kingdom as the Kingdom belongs to them; but they are not the Kingdom. The Kingdom is the rule of God; the church is a society of men.[2]

[1] Via speaks of them as the "embryo church." Cf. D. O. Via, *SJTh*, XI (1958), p. 271.
[2] See R. N. Flew, *Jesus and His Church* (1943), p. 13; H. Roberts, *Jesus and the Kingdom of God* (1955), pp. 84, 107; H. D. Wendland, *Eschatologie*, p. 162; G. Gloege, *Reich Gottes und Kirche im Neuen Testament* (1929).

THE CHURCH IS NOT THE KINGDOM

This relationship can be expounded under five points. First, the New Testament does not equate believers with the Kingdom. The first missionaries preached the Kingdom of God, not the church (Acts 8:12; 19:8; 20:25; 28:23, 31). It is impossible to substitute "church" for "kingdom" in such sayings. The only references to the people as *basileia* are Revelation 1:6 and 5:10; but the people are so designated not because they are the subjects of God's reign but because they will share Christ's reign. "They shall reign on earth" (Rev. 5:10). In these sayings, "kingdom" is synonymous with "kings," not with the people over whom God rules.

None of the sayings in the Gospels equates Jesus' disciples with the Kingdom. Such an identification has often been seen in the parable of the tares; and indeed the statement that the Son of Man will gather all causes of sin "out of the kingdom" (Matt. 13:41) before the coming of the Kingdom of the Father (13:43) seems to suggest that the church is equated with the Kingdom of Christ.[3] However, the parable itself expressly identifies the field as the world, not as the church (Matt. 13:38). The message of the parable has nothing to do with the nature of the church but teaches that the Kingdom of God has invaded history without disrupting the present structure of society. Good and evil are to live mixed *in the world* until the eschatological consummation, even though the Kingdom of God has come. The language about gathering evil out of the Kingdom looks forward not backward.[4]

It is also erroneous to base an identification of the Kingdom and the church on Matthew 16:18–19. Vos presses metaphorical lan-

---

[3] This identification is found in the studies on the parables by Trench, A. B. Bruce, S. Goebel, S. B. Swete. See also T. Zahn, *Das Evangelium des Matthäus* (1922), pp. 493–496; N. B. Stonehouse, *The Witness of Matthew and Mark to Christ* (1944), p. 238; T. W. Manson, *The Teaching of Jesus* (1935), p. 222; S. E. Johnson, *IB*, VII, pp. 415, 418; A. E. Barnett, *Understanding the Parables of Our Lord* (1940), pp. 48–50; G. MacGregor, *Corpus Christi* (1958), p. 122.

[4] See above, pp. 231 ff. for the interpretation of this parable.

guage too far when he insists that this identification must be made
because the first part of the saying speaks of the founding of the
house and the second part sees the same house complete with doors
and keys. "It is plainly excluded that the house should mean one
thing in the first statement and another in the second." Therefore,
Vos confidently affirms that the church is the Kingdom.[5]

However, it is precisely the character of metaphorical language to
possess such fluidity. This passage sets forth the inseparable relationship between the church and the Kingdom, but not their identity.
The many sayings about entering into the Kingdom are not equivalent to entering the church. It is confusing to say that "the church
is the form of the Kingdom of God which it bears between the departure and the return of Jesus."[6] There is indeed a certain analogy
between the two concepts in that both the Kingdom as the sphere
of God's rule and the church are realms into which men may enter.
But the Kingdom as the present sphere of God's rule is invisible,
not a phenomenon of this world, whereas the church is an empirical
body of men (see Chap. 8, especially pp. 202 ff.). John Bright is
correct in saying that there is never the slightest hint that the visible
church can either be or produce the Kingdom of God.[7] The church
is the people of the Kingdom, never that Kingdom itself. Therefore
it is not helpful even to say that the church is a "part of the Kingdom," or that in the eschatological consummation, the church and
Kingdom become synonymous.[8]

THE KINGDOM CREATES THE CHURCH

Second, the Kingdom creates the church. The dynamic rule of

[5] *The Teaching of Jesus concerning the Kingdom of God and the Church*
(1903), p. 150.

[6] E. Sommerlath, ZSysTh, XVI (1939), p. 573. So Lindeskog, "Christ's
kingdom on earth is the church" (*This Is the Church* [A. Nygren, ed.; 1958],
p. 144); S. M. Gilmour, "The Church [not as the institution, but as the be-
loved community] has been the Kingdom of God within the historical process"
(*Int*, VII [1953], p. 33).

[7] *The Kingdom of God* (1953), p. 236.

[8] R. O. Zorn, *Church and Kingdom* (1962), pp. 9, 83, 85 ff. In spite of this
confusing language, Zorn for the most part adequately distinguishes between
the Kingdom and the church.

God, present in the mission of Jesus, challenged men to response, bringing them into a new fellowship. The presence of the Kingdom meant the fulfillment of the Old Testament messianic hope promised to Israel; but when the nation as a whole rejected the offer, those who accepted it were constituted the new people of God, the sons of the Kingdom, the true Israel, the incipient church. "The church is but the result of the coming of God's Kingdom into the world by the mission of Jesus Christ."[9]

The parable of the draw net is instructive as to the character of the church and its relation to the Kingdom. The Kingdom is the action which is likened to drawing a net through the sea. It catches in its movement not only good fish but also bad; and when the net is brought to shore, the fish must be sorted out. Such is the action of God's Kingdom among men. It is not now creating a pure fellowship; in Jesus' retinue could even be a traitor. While this parable must be interpreted in terms of Jesus' ministry, the principles deduced apply to the church. The action of God's Kingdom among men created a mixed fellowship, first in Jesus' disciples and then in the church. The eschatological coming of the Kingdom will mean judgment both for human society in general (tares) and for the church in particular (draw net). Until then, the fellowship created by the present acting of God's Kingdom will include men who are not true sons of the Kingdom. Thus the empirical church has a twofold character. It is the people of the Kingdom, and yet it is not the ideal people, for it includes some who are actually not sons of the Kingdom. Thus entrance into the Kingdom means participation in the church; but entrance into the church is not necessarily synonymous with entrance into the Kingdom.[10]

THE CHURCH WITNESSES TO THE KINGDOM

Third, it is the church's mission to witness to the Kingdom. The

[9] H. D. Wendland in *The Kingdom of God and History* (H. G. Wood, ed.; 1938), p. 188. "The community does not bring forth the Kingdom as a product, but the Kingdom creates the community" (*Eschatologie*, pp. 199). See also D. O. Via in *SJTh*, XI (1958), pp. 270–286.

[10] R. Schnackenburg, *Gottes Herrschaft und Reich* (1959), p. 160.

church cannot build the Kingdom or become the Kingdom, but the church witnesses to God's Kingdom—to God's redeeming acts in Christ both past and future. This is illustrated by the commission Jesus gave to the twelve and to the seventy; and it is reinforced by the proclamation of the apostles in the book of Acts.

The number of emissaries on the two preaching missions appears to have symbolic significance. Most scholars who deny that the choice of twelve disciples-apostles was intended to represent the nucleus of the true Israel recognize in the number the symbolic significance that Jesus intended his message for the whole of Israel (see p. 251). Therefore, we should also recognize that seventy had a symbolic meaning. Since it was a common Jewish tradition that there were seventy nations in the world and that the Torah was first given in seventy languages to all men, the sending of seventy emissaries is an implicit claim that Jesus' message must be heard not only by Israel but by all men.[11]

The inclusion of the Gentiles as recipients of the Kingdom is taught in other sayings. When Israel's rejection of the offer of the Kingdom had become irreversible, Jesus solemnly announced that Israel would no longer be the people of God's rule but that their place would be taken by others who would prove trustworthy (Mark 12:1-9). This saying Matthew interprets to mean, "The kingdom of God will be taken away from you and given to a nation producing the fruits of it" (Matt. 21:43). Jeremias thinks that the original meaning of this parable is the vindication of Jesus' preaching the gospel to the poor. Because the leaders of the people rejected the message, their place as recipients of the gospel must be taken by the poor who hear and respond.[12] However, in view of the fact that in Isaiah 5 the vineyard is Israel itself, it is more probable that Matthew's interpretation is correct and that the parable means that Israel will no longer be the people of God's vineyard but will be

[11] K. H. Rengstorf, *TWNT*, II, pp. 630 f.
[12] J. Jeremias, *The Parables of Jesus* (1954), p. 60. A. M. Hunter points out that this interpretation appears to be arbitrary (*Interpreting the Parables* [1960], p. 94).

replaced by another people who will receive the message of the Kingdom.[13]

A similar idea appears in an eschatological setting in the saying about the rejection of the sons of the Kingdom—Israel—and their replacement by many Gentiles who will come from the east and the west to sit down at the messianic banquet in the eschatological Kingdom of God (Matt. 8:11-12).

How this salvation of the Gentiles is to be accomplished is indicated by a saying in the Olivet Discourse. Before the end comes "the gospel must first be preached to all nations" (Mark 13:10); and Matthew's version, which Jeremias thinks is the older form, makes it clear that this is the good news about the Kingdom of God (Matt. 24:14) which Jesus himself had preached (Matt. 4:23; 9:35). Recent criticism has denied the authenticity of this saying[14] or has interpreted it as an eschatological proclamation by angels by which a salvation of the Gentiles will be accomplished at the end.[15] However Cranfield points out that the verb *keryssein* in Mark always refers to a human ministry and that it is therefore far more probable that the word in Mark 13:10 has its characteristic New Testament sense. It is part of God's eschatological purpose that before the end, all nations should have the opportunity to hear the gospel.[16]

Here we find an extension of the theology of discipleship, that it will be the mission of the church to witness to the gospel of the

---

[13] See F. V. Filson, *The Gospel according to St. Matthew* (1960), pp. 229 f. The rabbis taught that in the past the Kingdom had been taken away from Israel because of her sins and given to the nations of the world (Strack and Billerbeck, *Kommentar*, I, pp. 876 f.).

[14] W. G. Kümmel, *Promise and Fulfilment* (1957), pp. 85 f.

[15] J. Jeremias, *Jesus' Promise to the Nations* (1958), pp. 22 f.; E. Lohmeyer, *Das Evangelium des Markus* (1937), p. 272; see also Lohmeyer on Rev. 14:6 in *Die Offenbarung des Johannes* (1926), p. 121.

[16] C. E. B. Cranfield, *The Gospel according to Saint Mark* (1959), p. 399, "The preaching of the Gospel is an eschatological event." See also G. Friedrich, *TWNT*, II, p. 726; F. V. Filson, *The Gospel according to St. Matthew* (1960), p. 254; G. R. Beasley-Murray, *Jesus and the Future* (1954), pp. 194 ff.; D. Bosch, *Die Heidenmission in der Zukunftsschau Jesu* (1959). The last-mentioned book is a detailed study of whether the eschatological perspective of Jesus allowed for a mission to the Gentiles, and comes to an affirmative conclusion.

Kingdom in the world. Israel is no longer the witness to God's Kingdom; the church has taken her place. Therefore, as K. E. Skydsgaard has said, the history of the Kingdom of God has become the history of Christian missions.[17]

If Jesus' disciples are those who have received the life and fellowship of the Kingdom, and if this life is in fact an anticipation of the eschatological Kingdom, then it follows that one of the main tasks of the church is to display in this present evil age the life and fellowship of the age to come. The church has a dual character, belonging to two ages. It is the people of the age to come, but it still lives in this age, being constituted of sinful mortal men. This means that while the church in this age will never attain perfection, it must nevertheless display the life of the perfect order, the eschatological Kingdom of God.[18]

Implicit exegetical support for this view is to be found in the great emphasis which Jesus placed on forgiveness and humility among his disciples. Concern over greatness, while natural in this age, is a contradiction of the life of the Kingdom (Mark 10:35 ff.). Those who have experienced the Kingdom of God are to display its life by a humble willingness to serve rather than by self-seeking.

Another evidence of the life of the Kingdom is a fellowship undisturbed by ill-will and animosity. This is why Jesus had so much to say about forgiveness, for perfect forgiveness is an evidence of love. Jesus even taught that human forgiveness and divine forgiveness are inseparable (Matt. 6:12, 14). The parable on forgiveness makes it clear that human forgiveness is conditioned by the divine forgiveness (Matt. 18:23–35). The point of this parable is that when a man claims to have received the unconditioned and unmerited forgiveness of God, which is one of the gifts of the Kingdom, and then is unwilling to forgive relatively trivial offenses against himself, he denies the reality of his very profession of divine forgiveness and by his conduct contradicts the life and character of the Kingdom.

---

[17] In *SJTh*, IV (1951), p. 390.
[18] This theme has been splendidly worked out in the article by Skydsgaard cited in the preceding footnote.

Such a man has not really experienced the forgiveness of God. It is therefore the church's duty to display in an evil age of self-seeking, pride, and animosity the life and fellowship of the Kingdom of God and of the age to come. This display of Kingdom life is an essential element in the witness of the church to the Kingdom of God.

THE CHURCH IS THE INSTRUMENT OF THE KINGDOM

Fourth, the church is the instrument of the Kingdom. The disciples of Jesus not only proclaimed the good news about the presence of the Kingdom; they were also instruments of the Kingdom in that the works of the Kingdom were performed through them as through Jesus himself. As they went preaching the Kingdom, they too healed the sick and cast out demons (Matt. 10:8; Luke 10:17). Although theirs was a delegated power, the same power of the Kingdom worked through them that worked through Jesus. Their awareness that these miracles were wrought by no power resident in themselves accounts for the fact that they never performed miracles in a competitive or boastful spirit. The report of the seventy is given with complete disinterestedness and devotion, as of men who are instruments of God.[19]

This theology of the church as the instrument of the Kingdom was strongly emphasized by G. Gloege, but it has been denied by Sommerlath and Michel.[20] The deciding factor is the definition of the Kingdom. Both Sommerlath and Michel insist that the Kingdom is a realm into which one enters; and therefore to be in the church is to be in the Kingdom of God, for the church is the present form of the Kingdom. This definition amounts to a denial of the dynamic aspect of the Kingdom. If the Kingdom of God is primarily God's kingly rule, and secondarily the spiritual sphere of his rule, there can be no objection to the recognition that the church is the organ of the Kingdom as it works in the world. While it is true that

---

[19] K. H. Rengstorf, BKW: Apostleship (1952), p. 41.
[20] Reich Gottes und Kirche im Neuen Testament (1929), pp. 255 ff.; E. Sommerlath in ZSysTh, XVI (1939), pp. 562–575; O. Michel, Das Zeugnis des Neuen Testaments von der Gemeinde (1941), pp. 80–83.

"God's Rule can obviously be exercised by no one save Himself,"[21] God can exercise his rule through men if he chooses.

This truth is implicit in the statement that the gates of Hades shall not prevail against the church (Matt. 16:18). This image of the gates of the realm of the dead is a familiar Semitic concept.[22] The exact meaning of this saying is not clear. It may mean that the gates of Hades, which are conceived as closing behind all the dead, will now be able to hold its victims no longer but will be forced open before the powers of the Kingdom exercised through the church. The church will be stronger than death, and will rescue men from the domination of Hades to the realm of life.[23] However, in view of the verb used, it appears that the realm of death is the aggressor, attacking the church.[24] The meaning then would be that when men have been brought into the salvation of the Kingdom of God through the mission of the church, the gates of death will be unable to prevail in their effort to swallow them up. Before the power of the Kingdom of God, working through the church, death has lost its power over men and is unable to claim final victory. There is no need to relate this to the final eschatological conflict, as Jeremias does;[25] it may be understood as an extension of the same conflict between Jesus and Satan[26] in which, as a matter of fact, Jesus' disciples had already been engaged. As instruments of the Kingdom they had seen men delivered from bondage to sickness and death (Matt. 10:8). This messianic struggle with the powers of death, which had been raging in Jesus' ministry and shared by his disciples, will be continued in the future, and the church will be the instrument of God's Kingdom in this struggle.

A serious objection can be raised against this view that the King-

---

[21] G. Johnson, The Doctrine of the Church in the New Testament (1943), p. 52.

[22] Isa. 38:10; Ps. 9:13; 107:18; Job 38:17; Wisd. of Sol. 16:13; III Macc. 5:51; Ps. of Sol. 16:2. Cf. J. Jeremias, TWNT, VI, pp. 923 f.

[23] This is the view of Cullmann (Peter: Disciple-Apostle-Martyr [1953], p. 202).

[24] J. Jeremias, TWNT, VI, p. 927.

[25] Loc. cit.

[26] P. S. Minear, Images of the Church in the New Testament (1960), p. 50.

dom of God and its powers were present and active both in Jesus and in his disciples. If men were brought into the enjoyment of the blessings and life of the Kingdom through the ministry of Jesus, why was there any need for the cross, resurrection, and Pentecost? The Primitive Church proclaimed the presence of the eschatological blessings of the age to come. The resurrection of Jesus was the beginning of the eschatological resurrection (I Cor. 15:23). The Pentecostal gift of the Holy Spirit was in the Old Testament a promise for the eschatological Kingdom (Joel 2:28–32); and Paul speaks of the gift of the Spirit as a "down-payment" (II Cor. 1:22; 5:5; Eph. 1:14) and a "first fruit" (Rom. 8:23) of the eschatological inheritance.[27] Another way of describing this experience of redemptive blessings is the presence of God's Kingdom.[28] However, if the powers and blessings of the same Kingdom were present in Jesus and his disciples, was there any theological difference between the days of Jesus and the experience of the early church? Why did not Jesus simply leave his disciples with the message of the present inbreaking of the Kingdom of God, urging them to carry this proclamation with its attendant powers and blessings into all the world?[29]

To this difficulty there is a twofold answer. Before Easter and Pentecost, the Kingdom of God was limited to the person of Jesus and to those who had direct personal contact with him. Not everyone in Palestine could enjoy the blessings of the Kingdom, but only those who heard Jesus' message, beheld his works, and submitted to

[27] To this degree, C. H. Dodd is correct in his analysis of Realized Eschatology. See *The Apostolic Preaching and Its Developments* (1936). This should not require the elimination of all futuristic eschatology.

[28] Paul speaks of the Kingdom as a present blessing in Col. 1:13; Rom. 14: 17; see also Acts 8:12; 19:8; 20:25; 28:23, 31.

[29] W. G. Kümmel in *Kirchenbegriff und Geschichtsbewusstein in der Urgemeinde und bei Jesus* (1943) argued against the authenticity of Matthew 16: 16–18 on the ground that if Jesus foresaw the church, he must have had two different views of history: one which saw in his own person and mission the beginning of the future aeon before the end of the present aeon, and another which anticipated an entirely different historical situation after his resurrection in which the coming aeon is present in the church; and two such different views of history in one person are extremely unlikely. However, under the criticisms of A. Oepke and N. A. Dahl, Kümmel has withdrawn this objection. See *StTh*, VII (1954), p. 15. See also O. Cullmann in *TZ*, I (1945), pp. 146–147.

his claims. There is indeed a seeming contradiction to this: Jesus sent his twelve disciples and the seventy to proclaim the same message, bring the same blessings, and perform the same works of the Kingdom. But this very contradiction in reality proves the point; for in the case of these emissaries, the powers of the Kingdom of God were inseparably related to the person of Jesus. Only those whom he specifically commissioned could proclaim the Kingdom and exercise its powers.[30] Furthermore, the exercise of the powers of the Kingdom by Jesus' disciples could be carried out only at definite times, when Jesus specifically charged them to do so. These powers were not subject to the disciples' control; they were inseparable from the person and authority of Jesus. The enjoyment of the blessings of the age to come was limited both temporally and spatially in that they were bound to the person of Jesus.

Kümmel has made this essential relationship between the present Kingdom and the person of Jesus one of the central theses of his careful study (see pp. 29 ff.). We may recognize the basic validity of this position without accepting the unnecessary conclusion that since the Kingdom was present in Jesus' person and mission, we may not think of his disciples exercising its powers. It is possible to recognize this limitation of the powers and blessings of the new age to the person of Jesus and yet admit that Jesus had the authority to extend these blessings and powers to those in immediate personal fellowship with him. We have in fact noted that Kümmel admits that the powers of the Kingdom were in reality operative in Jesus' disciples (see p. 257, n. 47).

After Easter and Pentecost, this situation was changed. Both the blessings and powers of the Kingdom were no longer limited to a historical person or place. Jesus was now glorified and had returned in the Spirit (John 14:16–18) to indwell his people. The presence of Christ—and therefore the blessings of the new age—were now available to all believers, regardless of the limitations of time and space.

[30] An apparent exception is found in Mark 9:38. However, we do not know what contact these men may have had with Jesus.

Therefore Paul could write years later to the believers in distant Rome, "The kingdom of God . . . [is] righteousness and peace and joy in the Holy Spirit" (Rom. 14:17), and to the Colossians, who had never seen Jesus, that they had been "delivered from the dominion of darkness and transferred . . . into the kingdom" of Christ (Col. 1:13).

A second important fact follows the first: if the experience of the powers of the Kingdom of God—which are the blessings of the age to come—has been lifted above all spatial and temporal limitations because of Easter and Pentecost, it has also acquired a new dimension of depth of meaning by virtue of this fact. Before Pentecost the life and blessings of the Kingdom of God were experienced in fellowship with the person of the historical Jesus. After Pentecost, they were experienced by the indwelling of Christ through the Spirit. Both of these are blessings of the age to come. We have seen that among the blessings of the Kingdom in Jesus' ministry were forgiveness and fellowship, especially table fellowship with Jesus (see pp. 210 ff.). After Pentecost, this table fellowship was continued, but in a new form. Believers everywhere assembled at table with one another (Acts 2:46; I Cor. 11:20 ff.) invoking the presence of Christ in the Spirit. The Aramaic prayer marana tha in I Corinthians 16:22 is probably a prayer not only for the Parousia of Christ but also for his visitation of the church in Christian fellowship (Didache 10:6).

THE CHURCH: THE CUSTODIAN OF THE KINGDOM

Fifth, the church is the custodian of the Kingdom. The rabbinic concept of the Kingdom of God conceived of Israel as the custodian of the Kingdom (see p. 131). The Kingdom of God was the rule of God which began on earth in Abraham, and was committed to Israel through the law. Since the rule of God could be experienced only through the law, and since Israel was the custodian of the law, Israel was in effect the custodian of the Kingdom of God. When a Gentile became a Jewish proselyte and adopted the law, he thereby took upon himself the sovereignty of heaven, the Kingdom of God. God's rule was mediated to the Gentiles through Israel; they alone were the "sons of the Kingdom."

In Jesus, the reign of God manifested itself in a new redemptive event, displaying in an unexpected way within history the powers of the eschatological Kingdom. The nation as a whole rejected the proclamation of this divine event, but those who accepted it became the true sons of the Kingdom and entered into the enjoyment of its blessings and powers. These disciples of Jesus, his *ekklesia*, now become the custodians of the Kingdom rather than the nation Israel. The Kingdom is taken from Israel and given to others—Jesus' *ekklesia* (Mark 12:9). Jesus' disciples not only witness to the Kingdom and are the instrument of the Kingdom as it manifests its powers in this age; they are also its custodians.

This fact is expressed in the saying about the keys. Jesus will give to his *ekklesia* the keys of the Kingdom of heaven, and whatever they bind or loose on earth will be bound or loosed in heaven (Matt. 16:19). Since the idiom of binding and loosing in rabbinical usage often refers to prohibiting or permitting certain actions, this saying has frequently been interpreted to refer to administrative control over the church.[31] Background for this concept is found in Isaiah 22:22 where God entrusted to Eliakim the key to the house of David, an act which includes administration of the entire house. According to this interpretation, Jesus gave Peter the authority to make decisions for conduct in the church over which he is to exercise supervision. When Peter set aside Jewish ritual practices that there might be free fellowship with the Gentiles, he exercised this administrative authority (Acts 10–11).

While this is possible, another interpretation lies nearer at hand. Jesus condemned the scribes and the Pharisees because they had taken away the key of knowledge, refusing either to enter into the Kingdom of God themselves or to permit others to enter (Luke 11:52). The same thought appears in the first Gospel. "Woe to you,

---

[31] For literature, see O. Cullmann, *Peter: Disciple-Apostle-Martyr* (1953), p. 204.

scribes and Pharisees, hypocrites! Because you shut the kingdom of heaven against men; for you neither enter yourselves nor allow those who would enter to go in" (Matt. 23:13). In biblical idiom, knowledge is more than intellectual perception. It is "a spiritual possession due to revelation."[32] The authority entrusted to Peter is grounded upon revelation, that is, spiritual knowledge, which he shared with the twelve. The keys of the Kingdom are therefore "the spiritual insight which will enable Peter to lead others in through the door of revelation through which he has passed himself."[33] The authority to bind and loose involves the admission or exclusion of men from the realm of the Kingdom of God. Christ will build his *ekklesia* upon Peter and upon those who share the divine revelation of Jesus' messiahship. To them also is committed by virtue of this same revelation the means of permitting men to enter the realm of the blessings of the Kingdom or of excluding men from such participation.

This interpretation receives support from rabbinic usage, for binding or loosing can also refer to putting under ban or to acquitting.[34] This meaning is patent in Matthew 18:18 where a member of the congregation who is unrepentant of sin against his brother is to be excluded from the fellowship; for "whatever you bind on earth shall be bound in heaven, and whatever you loose on earth shall be loosed in heaven." The same truth is found in a Johannine saying where the resurrected Jesus performs the acted parable of breathing on his disciples, thus promising them the Holy Spirit as equipment for their future mission. Then Jesus said, "If you forgive the sins of any, they are forgiven; if you retain the sins of any, they are retained" (John 20:23). This cannot be understood as the exercise of an arbitrary authority; it is the inevitable issue of witnessing to the Kingdom of God. It is furthermore an authority exercised not by Peter alone but by all the disciples—the church.

As a matter of fact, the disciples had already exercised this authority of binding and loosing when they visited the cities of Israel pro-

---

[32] R. Bultmann, *BKW: Gnosis* (1952), p. 22.
[33] R. N. Flew, *Jesus and His Church* (1943), p. 95.
[34] Strack and Billerbeck, *Kommentar*, I, p. 738; A. Schlatter, *Der Evangelist Matthäus* (1948), pp. 510 f.

claiming the Kingdom of God. Wherever they and their message were accepted, peace rested upon that house; but wherever they and their message were rejected, the judgment of God was sealed to that house (Matt. 10:14, 15). They were indeed instruments of the Kingdom in effecting the forgiveness of sins; and by virtue of that very fact, they were also custodians of the Kingdom. Their ministry had the actual result either of opening the doors of the Kingdom to men or of shutting it to those who spurned their message.[35]

This truth is expressed in other sayings. "He who receives you receives me, and he who receives me receives him who sent me" (Matt. 10:40; see Mark 9:37). The dramatic picture of the judgment of the sheep and the goats tells the same story (Matt. 25:31–46). This is not to be taken as a program of the eschatological consummation but as a parabolic drama of the ultimate issues of life. Jesus is to send his disciples (his "brethren," cf. Matt. 12:48–50) into the world as custodians of the Kingdom. The character of their mission-preaching is that pictured in Matthew 10:9–14. The hospitality they receive at the hands of their hearers is a tangible evidence of men's reaction to their message. They will arrive in some towns worn out and ill, hungry and thirsty, and will at times be imprisoned for preaching the gospel. Some will welcome them, receive their message, and minister to their bodily needs; others will reject both the message and the missioners. "The deeds of the righteous are not just casual acts of benevolence. They are acts by which the Mission of Jesus and His followers was helped, and helped at some cost to the doers, even at some risk."[36] To interpret this parable as teaching that men who perform acts of kindness are "Christians unawares" without reference to the mission and message of Jesus lifts the parable altogether out of its historical context. The parable sets forth the solidarity between Jesus and his disciples as he sends them forth into the world with the good news of the Kingdom.[37] The final destiny of men will be determined by the way they react to these representatives of Jesus. To

[35] See the excellent discussion in O. Cullmann, Peter: Disciple-Apostle-Martyr (1953), p. 205.
[36] T. W. Manson, The Sayings of Jesus (1949), p. 251.
[37] Loc. cit.

receive them is to receive the Lord who sent them. While this is no official function, in a very real way the disciples of Jesus—his church—are custodians of the Kingdom. Through the proclamation of the gospel of the Kingdom in the world will be decided who will enter into the eschatological Kingdom and who will be excluded.[38]

In summary, while there is an inseparable relationship between the Kingdom and the church, they are not to be identified. The Kingdom takes its point of departure from God, the church from men. The Kingdom is God's reign and the realm in which the blessings of his reign are experienced; the church is the fellowship of those who have experienced God's reign and entered into the enjoyment of its blessings. The Kingdom creates the church, works through the church, and is proclaimed in the world by the church. There can be no Kingdom without a church—those who have acknowledged God's rule—and there can be no church without God's Kingdom; but they remain two distinguishable concepts: the rule of God and the fellowship of men.

---

[38] D. O. Via, *SJTh*, XI (1958), pp. 276 f.

12 The Ethics of the Kingdom

Much of Jesus' teaching was concerned with human conduct. The Beatitudes, the Golden Rule, the parable of the good Samaritan are among the choicest selections of the world's ethical literature. We must here attempt to understand the relationship between Jesus' ethical teaching and his preaching about the Kingdom of God. As background for our analysis, we may outline several of the more important interpretations.

SURVEY OF THE PROBLEM

Many scholars disapprove of Jesus' theology but laud his ethical teaching, finding in it an enduring significance. According to F. G. Peabody, Jesus' first demand was not for orthodox instruction or for ecstatic religious experience but for morality.[1] The Jewish scholar Klausner would like to omit the miracles and the mystical sayings

---

[1] *Jesus Christ and Christian Character* (1905), p. 103. F. C. Grant denies that Jesus taught a Kingdom ethic. Jesus was only a first-century Jewish teacher who set forth God's purposes for men in terms of the revealed character of God. (See *The Study of the Bible Today and Tomorrow* [H. R. Willoughby, ed.; 1947], pp. 310-313). Grant believes that it was only Jesus' ethics, i.e., his quality of life, which saved Christianity from the fate of other Jewish messianic movements (See *JR*, XXII [1942], p. 370).

which tend to deify the Son of Man and preserve only the moral precepts and parables, thus purifying one of the most wonderful collections of ethical teaching in the world. "If ever the day should come and this ethical code be stripped of its wrappings of miracles and mysticism, the Book of the Ethics of Jesus will be one of the choicest treasures of the literature of Israel for all time."[2]

The old liberal interpretation found the essential truth of the Kingdom of God in personal religious and ethical categories. Apocalyptic was the husk which encased this spiritual kernel of Jesus' religious and ethical teaching and could be cast aside without affecting the substance of his teaching. From this point of view, the ethic of Jesus was the ideal standard of conduct which is valid for all time in all situations and carries in itself its own authentication and sanction.

This basic viewpoint has been worked out in several studies on ethics. H. C. King was able to dispense altogether with eschatology because Jesus conceived of the Kingdom of God as the highest good in terms of the reign of love in the life of the individual and of society whereby men share the eternal, ongoing purposes of God. The parable of the mustard seed embodies a statement of the law of growth in the moral and spiritual realm designed to instruct men about the growth of the Kingdom in the world.[3]

Reference to this "old liberal" interpretation would have only archaic interest except for the fact that the same basic viewpoint is still with us. Marshall's recent analysis of Jesus' ethics gives eschatology little more place than did King. Marshall expresses skepticism about efforts to define and classify the conceptions of the Kingdom of God in the Gospels. However, the relationship between Jesus' idea of the Kingdom of God and ethics is as "clear as crystal." The locus classicus is Luke 17:20–21 which teaches that the Kingdom of God is God's rule in the individual soul. Marshall appeals to Harnack for this interpretation. While he admits that Jesus often spoke of an eschatological coming of the Kingdom, this plays no role in Marshall's study; for if the Kingdom comes to society only as it is realized in

---

[2] J. Klausner, *Jesus of Nazareth* (1925), p. 414; see also p. 381.
[3] H. C. King, *The Ethics of Jesus* (1912), p. 274.

the present, it follows that the consummation of the Kingdom will occur when all men have been won. "All the ethical teaching of Jesus is simply an exposition of the ethics of the Kingdom of God, of the way in which men inevitably behave when they actually come under the rule of God."[4]

T. W. Manson was able to discuss Jesus' ethics with practically no reference to eschatology. He insisted that ethics was an integral part of Jesus' conception of the Kingdom of God; but he conceived of the Kingdom as the community of the new Israel who have become subjects of the heavenly King and express obedience to his will.[5]

C. H. Dodd's widely influential Realized Eschatology, although using eschatological language, amounts to the same kind of interpretation. The teaching of Jesus is not an ethics for those who expect the end of the world but for those who have experienced the end of this world and the coming of the Kingdom of God. Jesus' ethics is a moral ideal given in absolute terms and grounded in fundamental, timeless, religious principles,[6] for the Kingdom of God is the coming of the eternal into the temporal. W. Schweitzer made no mistake in saying that it is difficult to see any difference between Dodd's view and an ethics based on the idea of the continuous creative activity of God or a belief in providence. The upshot would seem to be that ethics can in the last resort dispense with eschatology, and that all that is really needed is the Old Testament doctrine of the judgment and grace of God in history.[7]

---

[4] L. H. Marshall, *The Challenge of New Testament Ethics* (1947), p. 31. See also C. A. A. Scott, *New Testament Ethics* (1934), who interprets the Kingdom as "the world of spiritual realities and values realized in a social complex" (p. 63) and practically ignores eschatology.

[5] *The Teaching of Jesus* (1935), pp. 294 f. In *Ethics and the Gospel* (1960), the one differentia between Christian (including Jesus') and Jewish ethics is the Kingdom of God: i.e., the fact of Christ's reign in the world (pp. 64–68). Eschatology is also almost completely lacking in J. W. Bowman and R. W. Tapp, *The Gospel from the Mount* (1957).

[6] C. H. Dodd, *History and the Gospel* (1938), p. 125; *The Parables of the Kingdom* (1936), p. 109; "The Ethical Teaching of Jesus" in *A Companion to the Bible* (T. W. Manson, ed.; 1939), p. 378. Dodd's viewpoint is accepted by L. Dewar, *An Outline of New Testament Ethics* (1949), pp. 58 f., 121.

[7] W. Schweitzer, *Eschatology and Ethics* (1951), p. 11. This pamphlet in the

Diametrically opposed to these noneschatological interpretations is Albert Schweitzer's "interim ethics." Albert Schweitzer held that Jesus did not teach the ethics of the future Kingdom, for the Kingdom would be supra-ethical, lying beyond distinctions of good and evil. Jesus' ethics is emergency ethics, designed for the brief interval before the Kingdom comes, consisting primarily of repentance and moral renewal. However, this ethical movement would exert pressure on the Kingdom and compel its appearance. Since Jesus' ethics is the means of bringing the Kingdom, eschatological ethics can be transmuted into ethical eschatology and thus have permanent validity.[8]

Few scholars who have accepted the substance of Albert Schweitzer's eschatological interpretation have adopted his interim ethics. Hans Windisch[9] re-examined the Sermon on the Mount in the light of Schweitzer's view and discovered that it contained two kinds of ethical teaching standing side by side: eschatological ethics conditioned by the expectation of the coming Kingdom and wisdom ethics which were entirely noneschatological. Windisch insists that historical exegesis must recognize that these two types of ethics are really foreign to each other. Jesus' predominant ethics is eschatological and is essentially diverse from wisdom ethics. They are new legislation, i.e., rules of admittance to the eschatological Kingdom; therefore they are to be understood literally and fulfilled completely. Their radical character is not conditioned by the imminence of the Kingdom but by the absolute will of God. It is irrelevant to ask whether or not these ethical demands are practical, for the will of God is not governed by practical considerations. Jesus considered men capable of fulfilling his demands; and their salvation in the coming Kingdom depended on obedience. The religion of the Sermon on the Mount is predominantly a religion of works. However, this eschatological ethic

---

"Ecumenical Studies" is an excellent but brief survey of this problem in contemporary thought.

[8] A. Schweitzer, *The Mystery of the Kingdom of God* (1913), pp. 94–115. C. Guignebert, *Jesus* (1935), pp. 405–407; 369–388, also attributes to Jesus "interim ethics." See G. Lundström, *The Kingdom of God in the Teaching of Jesus* (1963), p. 75, for a critique of A. Schweitzer's interpretation of ethics.

[9] *The Meaning of the Sermon on the Mount* (1951).

is an extreme, heroic, abnormal ethic which Jesus himself was unable to fulfill.

Other scholars, such as Martin Dibelius, who believe Jesus proclaimed an eschatological Kingdom, interpret his ethics as the expression of the pure, unconditioned will of God, without compromise of any sort, which God lays upon men at all times and for all time. It is incapable of complete fulfillment in an evil world and will therefore attain full validity only in the eschatological Kingdom of God.[10]

E. F. Scott and Paul Ramsey both felt that Jesus' ethics was totally conditioned by eschatology, setting forth the will of God for life in the eschatological Kingdom. This very fact gives ethics its abiding relevance, for it is not conditioned by the frustrating limitations of the present world but expresses the moral law in its unconditioned form. "Apocalypticism served as a burning glass to bring biblical ethics to pin-point focus and intensity."[11]

A. N. Wilder's study on *Eschatology and Ethics in the Teaching of Jesus*[12] is one of the most important recent analyses of this problem. In our sketch of Wilder's interpretation, we noted that he appears to admit the importance of eschatology. Jesus cast his ethics in the form of entrance requirements into the coming eschatological Kingdom, and the sanctions of reward or punishment are patent. However, Wilder believes that apocalyptic by its very nature is mythical in character. It is an imaginative way of describing the ineffable. Jesus looked forward to a great historical crisis which he described in poetical apocalyptic language which is not intended to be taken literally. Therefore the eschatological sanction of Jesus' ethics is formal and secondary. In addition to the apocalyptic Kingdom with its eschatological sanction, Jesus taught that a new situation had arisen with the presence of John the Baptist and himself; and the ethics of this new situation was determined not by eschatology but by the nature

---

[10] M. Dibelius, *The Sermon on the Mount* (1940), pp. 51 f. See also *Jesus* (1949), p. 115.

[11] P. Ramsey, *Basic Christian Ethics* (1952), p. 44; see also E. F. Scott, *The Ethical Teaching of Jesus* (1924), pp. 44-47.

[12] See above, pp. 30 ff. for an analysis of Wilder's interpretation of eschatology.

and character of God. The relation between the future eschatological Kingdom and the present time of salvation is only a formal one.

The conception of that eschatological culmination so partook of the nature of myth or poetry that it did not other than formally determine the ethic. The conception of the Judgment and the supernatural rewards, including the Kingdom, stand to Jesus and to the community as *representations*, with full validity and credibility, indeed, of the unprophesiable, unimaginable but certain, God-determined future. This future and God's action in it lend immense weight and urgency to their present moral responsibility. Yet this temporal imminence of God is but a function of his spiritual imminence, and it is this latter which really determines conduct.[13]

Rudolf Bultmann accepts Consistent Eschatology but finds the meaning of Jesus' message not in the imminence of the Kingdom but in his overwhelming sense of the nearness of God. Bultmann views Jesus' ethics as setting forth the conditions for entering the coming Kingdom. These conditions are not, however, rules and regulations to be obeyed that one may merit entrance into the coming Kingdom. The content of Jesus' ethics is a simple demand. Because the Kingdom is at hand, because God is near, one thing is demanded: decision in the final eschatological hour.[14] In this way, Bultmann translates Jesus' ethics into the existential demand for decision. Jesus was not a teacher of ethics, either personal or social. He did not teach absolute principles or lay down rules of conduct. He demanded only one thing: decision.

This survey makes it obvious that Jesus' ethical teaching and his view of the Kingdom must be studied together. We would contend that Jesus' ethics can be best interpreted in terms of the dynamic concept of God's rule which has already manifested itself in his person but will come to consummation only in the eschatological hour.[15]

---

[13] A. N. Wilder, *Eschatology and Ethics in the Teaching of Jesus* (1950), p. 161. E. C. Gardner, *Biblical Faith and Social Ethics*, Chap. 3, follows Wilder's view of eschatology.

[14] R. Bultmann, *Jesus and the Word* (1934), pp. 72 ff; *Theology of the New Testament* (1951), I, pp. 11–22.

[15] See S. M. Gilmour in *JR*, XXI (1941), pp. 253–264, for a similar argument. See also A. M. Hunter, *A Pattern for Life* (1953), pp. 106–107.

JESUS AND THE LAW

Jesus stood in a relationship to the law of Moses which is somewhat analogous to his relationship to Israel as the people of God. He offered to Israel the fulfillment of the promised messianic salvation; but when they rejected it, he found in his own disciples the true people of God in whom was fulfilled the Old Testament hope. There are also elements of both continuity and discontinuity in Jesus' attitude toward the law of Moses. He regarded the Old Testament as the inspired word of God and the law as the divinely given rule of life. He himself obeyed the injunctions of the law (Matt. 17:27; 23:23; Mark 14:12) and never criticized the Old Testament per se as not being the word of God. In fact, his mission accomplishes the fulfillment of the true intent of the law (Matt. 5:17).[16] The Old Testament therefore is of permanent validity (Matt. 5:17–18).

This note of fulfillment means that a new era has been inaugurated which requires a new definition of the role of the law. The law and the prophets are until John; after John comes the time of the messianic salvation (Matt. 11:13 = Luke 16:16). In this new order, a new relationship has been established between man and God. No longer is this relationship to be mediated through the law but through the person of Jesus himself and the Kingdom of God breaking through in him.[17] Jesus viewed the entire Old Testament movement as divinely directed and as having arrived at its goal in himself. His messianic mission and the presence of the Kingdom is the fulfillment of the law and the prophets.

Therefore Jesus assumed an authority equal to that of the Old Testament. The character of his preaching stands in sharp contrast to

[16] The word translated "fulfill" can mean to "establish, confirm, cause to stand" and need mean only that Jesus asserted the permanence of the law and his obedience to it (see B. H. Branscomb, *Jesus and the Law of Moses* [1930], pp. 226–228). However, in terms of Jesus' total message, "fulfill" probably has the meaning of bringing to full intent and expression. "The coming of Jesus is just what is meant by the fulfillment of the law" (H. Kleinknecht and W. Gutbrod, *BKW: Law* [1962], p. 86. See also G. Delling in *TWNT*, VI, pp. 292–293; J. Murray, *Principles of Conduct* [1957], pp. 149 ff.).

[17] H. Kleinknecht and W. Gutbrod, *BKW: Law* (1962), p. 81.

the rabbinic method which relied upon the authority of earlier rabbis. His preaching does not even follow the prophetic formulation, "Thus saith the Lord." Rather his message is grounded in his own authority and is repeatedly introduced by the words, "I say unto you." His frequently repeated "Amen" by which he introduced so many sayings is to be understood in this light, for it has the force of the Old Testament expression, "As I live, saith the Lord."[18]

On the authority of his own word, Jesus rejected the scribal interpretations of the law which were considered part of the law itself. This includes the scribal teachings regarding the Sabbath (Mark 2:23-28; 3:1-6; Luke 13:10-21; 14:1-24), fasting (Mark 2:18-22), ceremonial purity and washings (Matt. 15:1-30; Mark 7:1-23; Luke 11:37-54), and distinctions between "righteous" and "sinners" (Mark 2:15-17; Luke 15:1-32). Furthermore, he reinterpreted the role of the law in the new era of the messianic salvation. When he declared that a man could not be defiled by food (Mark 7:15), he thereby declared all food clean, as Mark explains (7:19), and in principle annulled the entire tradition of ceremonial observance. On his own authority alone, Jesus set aside the principle of ceremonial purity embodied in much of the Mosaic legislation. This is a corollary of the fact that the righteousness of the Kingdom is to be no longer mediated by the law but by a new redemptive act of God, foreseen in the prophets, but now in process of being realized in the event of his own mission.[19]

THE ETHICS OF THE REIGN OF GOD

We must now consider the question of the positive relationship between Jesus' ethical teaching and his message about the Kingdom of God. Long ago, F. G. Peabody pointed out that we ought not to interpret Jesus' ethics in light of his eschatology but ought to try to

[18] See above, p. 163. See also G. Bornkamm, *Jesus of Nazareth* (1960), p. 99.

[19] See H. Kleinknecht and W. Gutbrod, *BKW: Law* (1962), pp. 89, 91. The sayings about a new garment and new wineskins indicate that the blessings of the messianic age, now present, cannot be contained in the old forms of Judaism (Mark 2:21-22).

understand his eschatology in light of his ethical teaching.[20] When this is done, one finds large blocks of ethical teaching which are not dominated by eschatology. Dibelius admits this, but insists that the eschatological orientation should be everywhere assumed.[21] Windisch recognizes two different types of ethical sayings: those which are eschatologically conditioned and those which are independent of eschatology, which he calls "wisdom" ethics.[22] The sanction of the wisdom ethics is not eschatological but religious, i.e., the will and nature of God. Windisch admits that some of Jesus' teachings, such as the parable of the prodigal son, the story of the Pharisee and the tax collector, and the Beatitudes, seem to point away from the legalistic righteousness of works, which he thinks dominates the eschatological ethics, toward a soteriology of grace.[23] However, historical exegesis must recognize that the eschatological ethics which dominate the Sermon on the Mount lack any promise of divine help to attain the righteousness which they demand. They are not gospel but law, and lead only to despair.[24] Elsewhere, Windisch says that the very imminence of the eschatological Kingdom kindles faith in the hearts of Jesus' disciples, thus providing the particular attitude that releases the willingness and the power to obey these new Kingdom commandments.[25] He further admits that Jesus' ethics demand a new heart which can be created by his teaching.[26] It is difficult to reconcile such statements with the main thrust of his work.

One of the most important contributions of Windisch's book is his distinction between historical and theological exegesis. Historical exegesis must interpret the Sermon on the Mount strictly in terms

[20] "New Testament Eschatology and New Testament Ethics," *Transactions of the Third International Congress for the History of Religions* (1908), II, pp. 307–308.

[21] *The Sermon on the Mount* (1940), p. 60.

[22] *The Meaning of the Sermon on the Mount* (1951), pp. 30 ff. See a convenient analysis in H. K. McArthur, *Understanding the Sermon on the Mount* (1960), pp. 90–91.

[23] H. Windisch, *The Meaning of the Sermon on the Mount* (1951), pp. 110–111.

[24] *Ibid.*, pp. 172–173.

[25] *Ibid.*, p. 113.

[26] *Ibid.*, pp. 102, 105, 111.

of Old Testament and Jewish categories and regard the Kingdom as the "holy habitation of the messianic salvation era," i.e., the age to come. This is Consistent Eschatology; and in this light, Jesus' ethics are rules to determine who will enter the eschatological Kingdom. This historical interpretation has little relevance for the modern man, for he is no longer looking for an apocalyptic Kingdom; and Jesus' eschatological ethics are really impractical and unfulfillable. Therefore, the modern man must resort to theological exegesis which "will make grateful use of the important discovery of historical exegesis that in the Talmud the word that Jesus must have used (*malkuth*) almost always means the Lordship of God, the rule that is established wherever men undertake to fulfill God's Law."[27]

Windisch's use of this distinction appears to the present writer arbitrary, obscuring the fundamental meaning of the Kingdom of God. If historical exegesis has discovered that *malkuth* in rabbinic thought means the Lordship of God, and if rabbinic thought is an important fact in the historical milieu of Jesus, is it not possible that this was historically the fundamental meaning of the term in Jesus' teaching?[28] Windisch admits that the imminence of the eschatological Kingdom is not the central sanction; it is the fact that God will rule.[29] In light of these facts, we would contend that Jesus' proclamation about the Kingdom of God historically considered meant the rule of God. Furthermore, the two types of ethics can be understood against this background, *for the so-called wisdom ethics are ethics of God's present rule.* Windisch admits that the Sermon on the Mount is for disciples, "for those already converted, for the children of God within the covenant of Israel. . . ."[30] Yet when Windisch adds, "or the Christian community," he has said far more than the text suggests. Granted that the Gospels are the product of the Christian community, the Sermon presupposes nothing about the new birth or the indwelling of the Holy Spirit or the new life in Christ, but only about the Kingdom of God, which may be understood as

[27] *Ibid.*, pp. 199 f.; 62, 28 f.
[28] See G. E. Ladd, *JBL*, LXXXI (1962), pp. 230–238.
[29] H. Windisch, *The Meaning of the Sermon on the Mount* (1951), p. 29.
[30] *Ibid.*, p. 111.

the reign of God, both future and present. It is true, as Jeremias has pointed out,[31] that the Sermon presupposes something: the proclamation of the Kingdom of God. The Sermon is not law but gospel. God's gift precedes his demand. It is God's reign present in the mission of Jesus which provides the inner motivation of which Windisch speaks.[32] When Windisch admits that the eschatological and wisdom ethics are both dominated by the same idea of God,[33] he has in our judgment pointed to the solution to the problem. The God whom Jesus proclaimed was not one who made rigorous demands upon men which, as Windisch thinks, they were unable to fulfill and so were only thrown into despair; he is the God who has visited men in the person and mission of Jesus to bring them the messianic salvation of forgiveness and fellowship. It is this fact which binds together the wisdom and eschatological ethics. It is those who have experienced the present rule of God who will enter into the eschatological consummation. The "different soteriology" which Windisch detects in the Beatitudes is not really different; it is in fact the most distinctive feature about Jesus' mission and message. "Understood apart from the fact that God is now establishing his realm here on earth, the Sermon on the Mount would be excessive idealism or pathological, self-destructive fanaticism."[34]

A second important recent study comes to very different conclusions from Windisch's. Wilder, like Windisch, finds both eschatologically sanctioned ethics and noneschatological ethics of the present time of salvation whose sanction is the pure will of God. Wilder differs from Windisch by insisting that the primary sanction is the will of God, while the eschatological sanction is merely formal and secondary. As we have seen,[35] this led some critics to conclude

[31] Die Bergpredigt (1961), pp. 21 ff., esp. p. 25.

[32] See p. 286, n. 25. Dibelius, like Windisch, denies that the Kingdom of God is a present power; but when he says that the message of the Kingdom "lays hold on [one's] entire being and changes him" (Jesus [1949], p. 115), he is in effect admitting the presence of the Kingdom as the transforming power of God.

[33] The Meaning of the Sermon on the Mount (1951), p. 40.

[34] O. Piper, "Kerygma and Discipleship," Princeton Seminary Bulletin, LVI (1962), p. 16.

[35] See above, pp. 30 ff. For a further discussion of Windisch and Wilder, see I. W. Batdorf, JBR, XXVII (1959), pp. 211–217.

that Wilder has attempted to eliminate the significance of the eschatological sanction altogether. We agree with Wilder that apocalyptic imagery is not meant to be taken with wooden literalness, but is employed to describe an ineffable future.[36] This is also true of nonapocalyptic statements about the future. Jesus said that in the resurrection redeemed existence will differ from the present order to such a degree that sex will no longer function as it now does, but that the "sons of that age" will be like the angels, having no need for procreation (Mark 12:25 = Luke 20:35). Who can imagine in terms of known human experience what life will be like without the sex motivation? Who can picture a society which is not built around the home and the husband-wife, parent-child relationships? Such an order is indeed ineffable.

The recognition of the symbolical character of eschatological language does not require the conclusion that the eschatological sanction is really secondary and only formal, for symbolical language can be used to designate a real, if ineffable, future. Perhaps one might say that the *form* of the eschatological sanction, such as the lake of fire, outer darkness, on the one hand, and the messianic banquet, on the other, is formal and secondary; but it does not follow that the eschatological sanction itself is secondary. The heart of the eschatological sanction is the fact that at the end, men will stand face to face with God and will experience either his judgment or his salvation; and this is no formal sanction but an essential one, standing at the heart of biblical religion. Wilder has not clearly established that Jesus used apocalyptic language only as symbolic imagery of a historical, this-worldly crisis which he saw lying in the future. Wilder admits that beyond the historical crisis, Jesus saw an eschatological event. We have concluded that those critics who feel that Wilder is attempting to eliminate the eschatological dimension altogether have not correctly interpreted him, for he expressly denies that he wishes to rule out entirely the place of the eschatological sanction. Therefore, although apocalyptic language is symbolic language used

[36] A. N. Wilder, *Eschatology and Ethics in The Teaching of Jesus* (1950), pp. 26, 60. See our discussion of apocalyptic language, above, pp. 45 ff., 58 ff.

to describe an ineffable future, it is nevertheless a real future which will be God's future. If then, as Wilder correctly says, the primary sanction of Jesus' ethics is the present will of God made dynamically relevant to men because of the new situation created by Jesus' mission, which may be characterized as the time of salvation,[37] the eschatological sanction is also to be taken as a primary sanction, because the eschatological consummation is nothing less than the ultimate complete manifestation of the reign and the will of God which has been disclosed in the present.

The ethics of Jesus, then, are Kingdom ethics, the ethics of the reign of God. It is impossible to detach them from the total context of Jesus' message and mission. They are relevant only for those who have experienced the reign of God. It is true that most of Jesus' ethical maxims can be paralleled from Jewish teachings; but no collection of Jewish ethics makes the impact upon the reader that Jesus' ethics do. To read a passage from the Mishnah is a different experience from reading the Sermon on the Mount. The unique element in Jesus' teaching is that in his person the Kingdom of God has invaded human history, and men are not only placed under the ethical demand of the reign of God, but by virtue of this very experience of God's reign are also enabled to realize a new measure of righteousness.

Absolute Ethics

If Jesus' ethics are in fact the ethics of the reign of God, it follows that they must be absolute ethics. Dibelius is right; Jesus taught the pure, unconditioned will of God without compromise of any sort, which God lays upon men at all times and for all time.[38] Such conduct is actually attainable only in the age to come when all evil has

[37] *Ibid.*, pp. 145 ff.
[38] See note 10. This intensity of the absolute ethical demand is one of the facts setting Jesus' teaching apart from Judaism. Not a little love and a little purity, not a lot of love and a lot of purity, but only perfect love and perfect purity satisfy the demand of God's rule. See G. Kittel in *ZSysTh*, II (1924), p. 581.

been banished; but it is quite clear from the Sermon on the Mount that Jesus expected his disciples to practice his teachings in this present age. Otherwise the sayings about the light of the world and the salt of the earth are meaningless (Matt. 5:13–14). Jesus' ethics embody the standard of righteousness which a holy God must demand of men in any age.

It is this fact which has raised the difficult question of the practicality of Jesus' ethics. Viewed from one point of view, they are impractical and quite unattainable. If the Sermon on the Mount is legislation to determine admission into the future Kingdom, then all men are excluded, as Windisch recognizes. We might add, even Jesus himself is excluded; for Windisch admits that Jesus did not fulfill his own heroic ethic. His castigation of the Pharisees does not sound like an expression of love (Matt. 23); and before Annas he did not turn the other cheek (John 18:22 f.).[39] Jesus taught that anger is sin and leads to condemnation. Lust is sin, and whoever looks upon a woman to lust is guilty of sin. Jesus required absolute honesty, an honesty so absolute that Yes and No are as good as an oath. Jesus required perfect love, a love as perfect as God's love for men. If Jesus demanded only legalistic obedience to his teaching, then he left men hanging over the precipice of despair with no word of salvation. However, the Sermon is not law. It portrays the ideal of the man in whose life the reign of God is absolutely realized. This righteousness, as Dibelius has said, can be perfectly experienced only in the eschatological Kingdom of God. It can nevertheless to a real degree be attained in the present age, insofar as the reign of God is actually experienced. An important question is whether the perfect experience of God's rule in this age is a necessary prerequisite to enter the eschatological Kingdom, and this question cannot be answered apart from Jesus' teaching about grace.

There is an analogy between the manifestation of the Kingdom of God itself and the attainment of the righteousness of the Kingdom. The Kingdom has come in Jesus in fulfillment of the mes-

[39] H. Windisch, *The Meaning of the Sermon on the Mount* (1951), pp. 103–104.

sianic salvation within the old age, but the consummation awaits the age to come. The Kingdom is actually present but in a new and unexpected way. It has entered history without transforming history. It has come into human society without purifying society. By analogy, the righteousness of the reign of God can be actually and substantially experienced even in the present age; but the perfect righteousness of the Kingdom, like the Kingdom itself, awaits the eschatological consummation. Even as the Kingdom has invaded the evil age to bring to men in advance a partial but real experience of the blessings of the eschatological Kingdom, so is the righteousness of the Kingdom attainable, in part if not in perfection, in the present order. Ethics, like the Kingdom itself, stand in the tension between present realization and future eschatological perfection.

Ethics of the Inner Life

The ethics of the Kingdom place a new emphasis upon the righteousness of the heart. A righteousness which exceeds that of the scribes and the Pharisees is necessary for admission into the Kingdom of heaven (Matt. 5:20). The illustrations of this principle contrast with the Old Testament as it was interpreted in current rabbinic teaching. The primary emphasis is upon the inner character which underlies outward conduct. The law condemned murder; Jesus condemned anger as sin (Matt. 5:21–26). It is difficult to understand how this can be interpreted legalistically. Legislation has to do with conduct which can be controlled; anger belongs not to the sphere of outward conduct but to that of inner attitude and character. The law condemned adultery; Jesus condemned lustful appetite. Lust cannot be controlled by laws. The regulations about retaliation are radical illustrations of an attitude of the will; for a person could actually turn the other cheek in legal obedience to an external standard and yet be raging with anger or inwardly poisoned with a longing for revenge. Love for one's enemies is deeper than mere kindliness in outward relationships. It involves one of the deepest mysteries of human personality and character that a man can deeply and earnestly desire the best welfare of one who would seek his hurt. This and this alone is love. It is character; it is inward righteousness; it is the gift of God's reign.

T. W. Manson has insisted that the difference between Jesus' ethics and those of the rabbis was not the difference between the inner springs of action and outward acts.[40] It is of course true that Judaism did not altogether neglect the inner motivation. The ethical teaching of the Testaments of the Twelve Patriarchs is a moving demand for an inner righteousness. "Love ye one another from the heart; and if a man sin against thee, speak peaceably to him, and in thy soul hold not guile; and if he repent and confess, forgive him. But if he deny it, do not get into a passion with him . . ." (Gad 6:3). "He that hath a pure mind in love looketh not after a woman with a view to fornication; for he hath no defilement in his heart, because the Spirit of God resteth upon him" (Benjamin 8:2).

However, this is not typical. The most casual reading of the Mishnah makes it clear that the focus of rabbinic ethics was upon outward obedience to the letter of the law. In contrast, Jesus demanded a perfect inner righteousness. In spite of Windisch's criticisms, it is difficult to reject Stange's conclusion that the ethic of the Sermon on the Mount is fundamentally an ethic of intention (Gesinnungsethik).[41] While Wilder agrees with Windisch that Jesus' ethics cannot be characterized as directed to disposition rather than action, to inwardness as against outward performance, he summarizes Jesus' teaching as demanding "no anger, no desire to retaliate, no hatred; that hearts must be wholly pure."[42] Anger, desire, hatred belong to the sphere of the inner man and the intention which motivates his deeds. The primary demand of Jesus is for righteous character.

This demand appears elsewhere in Jesus' teachings. A good man out of the good treasure of his heart produces good, and the evil man out of his evil treasure produces evil. Conduct is a manifesta-

[40] Ethics and the Gospel (1960), pp. 54, 63.
[41] C. Stange in ZSysTh, II (1924), pp. 41-44. See H. K. McArthur, Understanding the Sermon on the Mount (1960), pp. 142 f.
[42] A. N. Wilder, "The Sermon on the Mount," IB, VII, pp. 161, 163.

tion of character (Luke 6:45). Good or evil fruit is the manifestation of the inner character of the tree (Matt. 7:17). In the judgment, men will render account for every careless word they utter (Matt. 12:36); for by the careless word when one is not on guard, the true character of the heart and disposition is manifested. Final acquittal and condemnation will rest not upon one's formal conduct but upon conduct which evidences the true nature of one's inner being.

Thus the essential righteousness of the Kingdom, since it is a righteousness of the heart, is actually attainable, qualitatively if not quantitatively. In its fullness it awaits the coming of the eschatological Kingdom; but in its essence it can be realized here and now, in this age.

ETHICS OF AN ACTIVE RIGHTEOUSNESS

While the righteousness of the Kingdom is primarily of the heart and not a legalism more comprehensive than that of the rabbis, it does not follow that this righteousness is satisfied with mere good intentions that are never put into practice. Stange insisted that the ethics of intention must be manifested in conduct, that the right attitude is only the point of departure.[43] Jesus concluded the Sermon by contrasting the man who hears his word and does them with the man who hears but does nothing (Matt. 7:26). A righteous heart must manifest itself in righteous conduct. The priest and the Levite who passed by the wounded traveler did no wrong and broke no law. Their formal righteousness was not impaired; but they had failed to manifest in conduct the righteous character which motivated the Samaritan (Luke 10:31). The man with only one talent was condemned not because of sinful conduct but because he was negligent with a gift which had been entrusted to him; he simply did nothing (Matt. 25:25).

This principle of an active righteousness enables us to understand the parable of the judgment of the nations where salvation is de-

---

[43] C. Stange, ZSysTh, II (1924), p. 44. The antithesis—inwardness vs. outward performance—is artificial.

termined by what men have done toward Jesus' "brethren" (Matt. 25:41). To construe this as salvation on the basis of personal merit is to violate the basic character of God's Kingdom as a gift. The parable teaches in dramatic terms that one's response to the gospel of the Kingdom proclaimed by the representatives of Jesus will manifest itself in conduct. Those who are not ashamed to receive Jesus' brethren and minister openly to them reflect by their conduct their attitude toward the Lord himself (Mark 8:38).

In this connection, one must not ignore the fact that there is an obvious hyperbolic element in many of Jesus' sayings.[44] Surely the command to shut the door when one prays (Matt. 6:6) is not meant to be a prohibition of public prayer; it is a warning against religious ostentation. The command to give whatever is asked (Matt. 5:42) cannot mean that one is to give a sword to a madman or an affirmative response to the solicitations of a prostitute. Certainly Jesus did not mean that it is sinful to call a man a fool (Matt. 5:22) but an innocent thing to call him an idiot; any ejaculation which reflects an evil heart is sinful. The diaspora Jew who had journeyed from Ephesus or Rome to worship in the temple in Jerusalem would find it impossible to return home to be reconciled to his brother before offering his gift at the altar (Matt. 5:23). Such sayings do not embody a new legalism. They are radical illustrations of the kind of conduct which will characterize the life perfectly submitted to the reign of God.

If this is an active righteousness, it is also an ethic designed for this world. We have agreed with Dibelius that Jesus taught absolute ethics which were valid both for the age to come and for this age, because the will of God for men does not change. However, the form in which Jesus structured his ethical teaching is concerned with life in this world. In the eschatological Kingdom of God, there will be no evil. Men will not smite one another in the face. If the sexual relation is transcended in the resurrection, lust will no longer be a

---

[44] H. K. McArthur, *Understanding the Sermon on the Mount* (1960), p. 141; A. N. Wilder, *Eschatology and Ethics in the Teaching of Jesus* (1950), p. 161; M. Dibelius, *The Sermon on the Mount* (1940), p. 56.

temptation. Jesus' disciples will no longer be reviled and persecuted on his account. The setting of the Sermon on the Mount is this evil age (Matt. 5:13–16) where Jesus' followers are to display the character of their heavenly Father. "The followers of Jesus must be representatives of this new world within the old age."[45] Therefore while Jesus' ethics embody a righteousness which can be perfectly attained only in the Kingdom of God, there is truth in Wendland's contention that this ethic is an "interim ethic" in a sense altogether different from that of Albert Schweitzer. The "interim" is not a short period before an imminent end which demands an emergency ethic, but the interim between creation and the consummation, however long it lasts.[46] Wendland adds that the sanction for this ethic is not the brevity of the time, as Schweitzer thought, but the absolute will of God. There is an inescapable unity between eschatology and ethics. Ethics are eschatological, for life must be lived in this age with a view to the eschatological consummation. However, eschatology is ethical, for it will see the perfect accomplishment of the pure will of God.

THE ATTAINMENT OF RIGHTEOUSNESS

How is the righteousness of the Kingdom to be attained? While Windisch insists that Jesus' ethics are legalistic, i.e., a righteousness determined by obedience to commandments, he also admits that Jesus presupposed an inner renewal which would enable men to fulfill his teachings. This inner renewal is either assumed to have been already experienced by the covenant people of God, or Jesus believed that his own teaching would implant God's command in the hearts of his hearers. "The faith in the Kingdom that is thus kindled by Jesus' proclamation is therefore also the particular attitude that releases the willingness and the power to obey these new Kingdom commandments." "Power becomes available to the person who be-

---

[45] M. Dibelius, *The Sermon on the Mount* (1940), p. 59. We cannot agree with Dibelius when he says that the Sermon was meant to be the law for the coming Kingdom rather than a law governing life in this world (*Ibid.*, p. 94).
[46] H. D. Wendland, *Eschatologie*, pp. 104 f.

lieves in the Kingdom."[47] "Jesus, having demonstrated the interrelation of being a child of God and of having a loving disposition toward one's persecutors, is convinced that he has actually planted this disposition in the hearts of his pious hearers."[48] The problem is that Windisch does not explain how this new disposition and energizing of the will is accomplished. If, as Windisch seems to suggest, it is faith in the imminence of the eschatological Kingdom,[49] then we are compelled to conclude that the central motivation in Jesus' ethical teaching was faith in a fancy; for in point of fact, the Kingdom was not imminent. We are thrown back again upon Dibelius' bald statement that it still looks as though a monstrous illusion lies at the basis of the whole mission of Jesus.[50] And if, as Dibelius also says,[51] it is this message of the imminent Kingdom which lays hold of a man's entire being and changes him, it is difficult to avoid the conclusion that Jesus' entire ethical structure is cast under a cloud. Martin Rist, who holds a very different theological position from that of the present author, pointedly asks the question, if "Jesus was in error concerning not only the timing but also the concept of his apocalyptic hope, how may we be sure that he was not fallible in other areas including that of ethics? . . . If he was in error concerning the Kingdom, why should he be a valid judge of men with reference to their attitude concerning his program for the preparation of the Kingdom?"[52]

This problem is unavoidable for the adherents of Consistent Eschatology; but it is no problem if the Kingdom of God is not only the future eschatological realm of salvation, but also the present

[47] H. Windisch, *The Meaning of the Sermon on the Mount* (1951), pp. 113, 115; cf. also pp. 102, 73.

[48] *Ibid.*, p. 120.

[49] "This ability truly to obey is increased in their case by the fact that a new messenger appears before them with his new message: The Kingdom you have longed for stands at the door." (*Ibid.*, p. 113. Copyright 1951 by W. L. Jenkins. The Westminster Press. Used by permission.)

[50] *Jesus* (1949), p. 70. See *The Sermon on the Mount* (1940), pp. 70 f. where the radicalism of Jesus' teaching is determined not by the will of God but by the proximity of the Kingdom.

[51] *Jesus* (1949), p. 115.

[52] In *JBR*, XIX (1951), p. 161. Quoted by permission.

redeeming action of God. The future Kingdom has invaded the present order to bring to men the blessings of the age to come. Men need no longer wait for the eschatological consummation to experience the Kingdom of God; in the person and mission of Jesus it has become present reality.[53] The righteousness of the Kingdom therefore can be experienced only by the man who has submitted to the reign of God which has been manifested in Jesus, and who has therefore experienced the powers of God's Kingdom. When a man has been restored to fellowship with God, he becomes God's son and becomes the recipient of a new power, that of the Kingdom of God. It is by the power of God's reign that the righteousness of the Kingdom is to be attained. Gutbrod summarizes this new situation by saying that Jesus looked upon the law no longer as something to be fulfilled by man in an effort to win God's verdict of vindication. On the contrary, a new status as a child of God is presupposed, which comes into existence through companionship with Jesus and has its being in the forgiveness thus bestowed.[54]

The righteousness of the Kingdom is therefore both attainable and unattainable. It can be attained, but not in its full measure. S. M. Gilmour has expressed this idea vividly from the later Christian perspective: "In so far as the Christian is part of the church . . . the ethics of Jesus is a practicable ethic. In so far as he is part of the world, it is relevant but impracticable."[55]

This interpretation is supported by the fact that the most basic demand which Jesus laid upon men if they would be his disciples was for a radical, unqualified decision.[56] A man must make a decision so radical that it involves turning his back upon all other relationships. It may involve forsaking one's home (Luke 9:58). The demand

---

[53] This perspective is emphasized in the essays of C. Stange and G. Kittel (see p. 293, n. 41 and p. 290, n. 38), by Jeremias (see p. 288, n. 31), Wilder (see pp. 282 ff.), Gilmour and Hunter (see p. 283, n. 15). It is unfortunately neglected in McArthur's helpful study (see p. 286, n. 22).

[54] H. Kleinknecht and W. Gutbrod, BKW: Law (1962), p. 91.

[55] JR, XXI (1941), p. 263.

[56] To this extent Bultmann is right in saying that God is the Demander (der Fordernde) who requires absolute decision (see p. 283, n. 14).

of the Kingdom must take supremacy over the normal human obligations (Luke 9:60). It may even involve the rupture of the closest family relationships (Luke 9:61). In fact, when loyalty to the Kingdom conflicts with other loyalties, even though they involve life's most cherished relationships, the secondary loyalties must give way. Discipleship will mean sometimes that a man is set against his father, the daughter against her mother, the daughter-in-law against her mother-in-law; and a man's foes will be those of his own household. He who loves father or mother more than he loves Jesus is not worthy of the Kingdom (Matt. 10:34–39). The affection which one sustains for his loved ones compared to his love for the Kingdom of God is described as hate (Luke 14:26).

Any tie or human affection which stands in the way of one's decision for the Kingdom of God and for Jesus must be broken. This is why Jesus commanded the rich young ruler to dispose of his possessions and then to become a disciple. Jesus put his finger upon the particular object of this man's affection; it must be renounced before discipleship could be realized. A man must be ready to renounce every affection when he renders a decision for the Kingdom (Luke 14:33). The most radical form of this renunciation includes a man's very life; unless he hates his own life he cannot be a disciple (Luke 14:26). Obviously, this does not mean that every disciple must die; he must, however, be ready to do so. He no longer lives for himself but for the Kingdom of God. What happens to *him* is unimportant; for the fate of the Kingdom is all-important. This is the meaning of the words, "If any man would come after me, let him deny himself and take up his cross and follow me" (Matt. 16:24). This does not mean *self-denial*, that is, denying oneself some of life's enjoyments and pleasures. Self-denial can have a selfish end. By practicing self-denial men have sought their selfish advantage. *Denial of self* is the opposite; it means the renunciation of one's own will that the Kingdom of God may become the all-important concern of life. Taking up one's cross does not mean assuming burdens. The cross is not a burden but an instrument of death. The taking of the cross means the death of self, of personal ambition and self-centered purpose. In the place of selfish attainment, however altruistic and noble, one is to desire alone the rule of God.

Man's destiny rests upon this decision. When one has made this radical decision in the denial and death of self, when he has thereby forfeited his life, he has the promise of the Son of Man that in the day of the Parousia, he will be rewarded for what he has done. In the person of Jesus, men are confronted here and now by the Kingdom of God; and he who decides for Jesus and the Kingdom will enter into the future Kingdom; but whoever denies Jesus and his Kingdom will be rejected (Matt. 10:32, 33). Those who experience the Kingdom of God and its righteousness in this age will enter into the eschatological Kingdom in the age to come.

REWARDS AND GRACE

Many sayings in Jesus' teachings suggest that the blessings of the Kingdom are a reward. Contemporary Jewish thought made much of the doctrine of merit and reward, and at first sight this seems to be true also of Jesus' teachings. There will be a reward for persecution (Matt. 5:12), for practicing love toward one's enemies (Matt. 5:46), for the giving of alms when done in the right spirit (Matt. 6:4), for fasting (Matt. 6:18). The relation between God and man is that of employer or master to his laborers or slaves (Matt. 20:1–16: 24:45–51; 25:14–30). Reward seems sometimes to be posited as a strict equivalent for something done (Matt. 5:7; 10:32, 41 f.; 25: 29), or a compensation for loss or self-sacrifice (Matt. 10:39; Luke 14:8–11). Rewards are sometimes promised according to the measure of success with which a duty is performed (Matt. 5:19; 18:1–4; 19:30; Mark 9:41; Luke 19:17, 19); and sometimes punishment is similarly graduated (Matt. 10:15; 11:22, 24; Luke 12:47 f.). In such sayings Jesus' teachings seem close to the ordinary Jewish concept of merit in which reward was payment quantitatively conceived.

There are, however, other sayings which place the teaching about rewards in an entirely different light. While Jesus appeals to reward, he never uses the ethic of merit. Faithfulness must never be exercised with a view to reward; the reward itself is utterly of grace. Precisely those parables which speak of reward make it clear that all reward is after all a matter of grace.[57] When a man has exercised the largest possible measure of faithfulness, he still deserves nothing, for he has done no more than his duty (Luke 17:7–10).[58] The same reward is accorded to all who have been faithful regardless of the outcome of their labor (Matt. 25:21, 23). *The reward is the Kingdom of Heaven itself* (Matt. 5:3, 10) which is given to those for whom it has been prepared (Matt. 20:23; 25:34). Even the opportunities for service are themselves a divine gift (Matt. 25:14 f.). Reward therefore becomes free unmerited grace and is pictured as out of all proportion to the service rendered (Matt. 19:29; 24:47; 25:21, 23; Luke 7:48; 12:37). While men are to seek the kingdom, it is nevertheless God's gift (Luke 12:31, 32). It is God's free act of vindication which acquits a man, not the faithfulness of his religious conduct (Luke 18:9–14).

This free gift of grace is illustrated by the healing of the blind, the lame, the lepers, the deaf, the raising of the dead, and the preaching of the good news to the poor (Matt. 11:5). The parable of the laborers in the vineyard is designed to show that the divine standard of reward is utterly different from human standards of payment; it is a matter of sheer grace (Matt. 20:1–16). The laborers who put in the full day received a denarius, which was a usual day's wages; this was what they deserved. Others who were sent into the field at the eleventh hour and worked only one hour received the same wages as those who had borne the heat and burden of the day. This is God's way: to bestow upon those who do not deserve it on the basis of grace the gift of the blessings of the Kingdom of God. Man's reckoning is: a day's work, a day's pay; God's reckoning is: an hour's

[57] C. A. A. Scott, *New Testament Ethics* (1934), pp. 53, 54. See A. N. Wilder, *Eschatology and Ethics in The Teaching of Jesus* (1950), pp. 107–115.

[58] Windisch cites this passage to prove that the fundamental character of Jesus' ethics is an obedience which God's servant can actually give (*The Meaning of the Sermon on the Mount* [1951], p. 106). On the contrary, the passage teaches that when a servant has done all that he can do, he has not merited God's blessings. Obedience is never enough; there must be grace.

work, a day's pay. The former is merit and reward; the latter is grace.[59]

In view of these teachings, we can hardly conclude that the Kingdom in its eschatological form is a reward bestowed in return for obedience to Jesus' teachings. It is the gift of God's grace. But the Kingdom is not only a future gift; it is also a present gift to those who will renounce all else and throw themselves unreservedly upon the grace of God. To them both the Kingdom and its righteousness are included in God's gracious gift.

The Kingdom and Social Ethics

Does Jesus' teaching about the Kingdom of God provide any basis for social ethics? This question is of vital concern to the modern church. Before the eschatological interpretation of Albert Schweitzer, the social interpretation of the Kingdom of God exercised wide influence, especially in America. Walter Rauschenbusch interpreted the Kingdom of God as the ideal human society, and Jesus' ethics set forth the standard of social conduct which would create the true society.[60] C. C. McCown boldly attempted to translate apocalyptic concepts into social terms.[61] It is disappointing that recent studies on eschatology and social ethics have made little use of the concept of the Kingdom of God.[62] Recent biblical studies have sought for a scriptural basis for social ethics in the Kerygma rather than in the teachings of Jesus.[63]

---

[59] The fact that the one-hour workers had worked for one hour and therefore deserved something, if not a full day's pay, is one of the colorful details of the parabolic form and cannot be pressed.

[60] Rauschenbusch, Christianity and the Social Order (1908), p. 71; A Theology for the Social Gospel (1917), pp. 134-145. See G. Lundström, The Kingdom of God in the Teaching of Jesus (1963), Chap. 3, for a good survey.

[61] The Genesis of the Social Gospel (1929).

[62] See E. C. Gardner, Biblical Faith and Social Ethics (1960); see above, p. 283, n. 13. R. C. Petry's Christian Eschatology and Social Thought (1956) accepts neither the eschatological nor the dynamic concept of the Kingdom but defines it as a "community in which the divine will was to be realized on earth as it is already in heaven" (p. 59).

[63] A. N. Wilder in The Background of the New Testament and Its Eschatology (W. D. Davies and D. Daube, eds.; 1956), pp. 509-536.

It is of course true that there is little explicit teaching on social ethics in the Gospels. The reason for this need not be that Jesus had such a shortened view of the future that he was not concerned about such questions.[64] It may rather be due to the fact that social ethics must be an outworking of a properly grounded personal ethics. The dynamic concept of the Kingdom of God suggests several principles which can issue in a biblical social ethics.

First is a negative fact. If the Kingdom of God belongs to the age to come, we are never to expect that this age will see the full realization of God's rule. "Christian eschatology means the end of all social and political Utopias which expect to achieve a perfect pattern of peaceful society by human means and human strength."[65] The attainment of the ideal social order is not the work of man but the result of the eschatological coming of God's Kingdom.

This conclusion does not lead to apocalyptic pessimism. Jewish apocalyptic was pessimistic, feeling that God stood aloof from history. The present age was surrendered to evil; hope of God's Kingdom lay altogether in the future. In Jesus' teaching, however, the Kingdom of God has invaded this evil age. The powers of evil have been attacked and defeated. The Kingdom of God has entered into dynamic conflict with the realm of Satan, and God's reign is to manifest its powers in history through the church. The Kingdom of God working through Jesus' disciples is to make an impact upon the world. When Jesus said that they were to be the light of the world and the salt of the earth (Matt. 5:13-14), he meant that the world was to feel the influence of God's Kingdom.

Furthermore, the presence of God's Kingdom in Jesus was concerned not only with the spiritual welfare of men but also with their physical well being. The Kingdom of God in its eschatological consummation will mean the redemption of the complete man, thus requiring the resurrection of the body and a transformed natural and social order. We have seen that the miracles of healing were a pledge

---

[64] See E. C. Gardner, *Biblical Faith and Social Ethics* (1960), pp. 249 f.; G. Bornkamm, *Jesus of Nazareth* (1960), p. 121.

[65] H. D. Wendland in *Ecumenical Review*, V (1952), p. 365.

of this ultimate eschatological redemption. The Kingdom of God is
concerned with the evils that bring misery and suffering on the
physical level.

In these principles is implicit a "social gospel," for the reign of
God in the lives of his people must be concerned with the total
man and with the conquest of evil in whatever form it manifests
itself. The church is the people of God, the instruments of the
Kingdom of God in conflict with evil. Here is an incipient theology
which needs far more study and attention than it has thus far been
given.

PART IV

THE CONSUMMATION OF THE PROMISE

13 The Consummation
of the Kingdom

The thesis of this book is that, for Jesus, the Kingdom of God was the dynamic rule of God which had invaded history in his own person and mission to bring men in the present age the blessings of the messianic age, and which would manifest itself yet again at the end of the age to bring this same messianic salvation to its consummation. We must now consider the nature of the eschatological consummation.

We are faced with two distinct but inseparable questions: What did Jesus teach? and, What is the relevance and meaning of his teaching for modern theology? The first is the historical question, the second the theological. Modern biblical scholarship is realizing that history and theology cannot be severely separated. The era of pure disinterested "objective" scholarship has proved sterile and unproductive, and a new revival of interest in biblical theology is in progress.[1] This theological approach to the study of the Bible finds

[1] See Robert C. Dentan, *Preface to Old Testament Theology* (1950), pp. 34–40; A. N. Wilder, "New Testament Theology in Transition," in *The Study of the Bible Today and Tomorrow* (H. R. Willoughby, ed.; 1947), pp. 419–436; A. M. Hunter, *Interpreting the New Testament 1900–1950* (1951), pp. 124–140.

its most important focus in the question of the person and teachings of Jesus.

Admittedly, the portrait of Jesus in the Gospels is a theological picture painted by Christian faith. However, this does not mean that the tradition has been seriously distorted and the person and teachings of Jesus misrepresented. C. F. D. Moule has lately emphasized that it was the intention of the evangelists to record for admittedly evangelistic and apologetic purposes "the plain story of what happened in the ministry of Jesus."[2]

The so-called "objective" historian is likely to be dominated by presuppositions which will not allow him to accept the essential soundness of the Gospel portrait of Jesus and his mission. H. G. Wood has pointed out that this search for pure objectivity by the representatives of the *religionsgeschichtliche Schule* has resulted in a severe limitation of Jesus to categories of first-century Jewish thought. He is not allowed to go beyond his Jewish inheritance and environment but must be interpreted as a Jewish apocalyptist.[3] This pure "objective" method tries to reduce Jesus' teaching to a simple homogenous consistency; and the effort to understand apparently diverse emphases in terms of some deeper underlying unifying principle has often been dismissed as "harmonizing" exegesis in which no scientific methodology can engage.

However, the only sources we have for the teachings of Jesus are the Gospels; and while they are admittedly the product of Christian faith, there is good reason to think that this faith has not distorted the facts but has been able more truly to represent Jesus than unbelief could have done.[4] Therefore, it is the first task of exegesis and biblical theology to interpret the Gospels as they stand, including their report of Jesus' sayings about the future, to see if they make sense historically.

On the other hand, biblical theology cannot be satisfied with an uncritical biblicism which fails to take into consideration the his-

---

[2] "The Intention of the Evangelists," in *New Testament Essays* (A. J. B. Higgins, ed.; 1959), p. 176.

[3] *Jesus in the Twentieth Century* (1960), p. 172.

[4] See B. Reicke in *Int*, XVI (1962), pp. 156–168.

torical conditioning of Jesus' sayings and the character of his language. Nor can it be dominated by dogmatic presuppositions which insist that if there is theological validity in the Incarnation, Jesus must have given the church a program of the future which provides an infallible chart of the eschatological consummation. Our approach must be that of dealing with the texts of the Gospels and of interpreting Jesus' view of the future in terms of his total teaching and his own historical setting.

THE OLIVET DISCOURSE

Three essential factors enter into Jesus' view of the future as it is set forth in the Gospels: a historical perspective, an apocalyptic consummation, and an apparent emphasis on the imminence of the end. These elements may be most vividly seen in the Olivet Discourse.[5]

All three Gospels speak of an apocalyptic consummation when the Son of Man will come in glory to gather his elect. This visitation is pictured in the Old Testament language of a theophany which will shake the natural order (Mark 13:24–27) and issue in the judgment of men (Matt. 11:22 = Luke 10:14; Matt. 24:37–39 = Luke 17:26–27; Mark 8:38; Matt. 25:31 ff.) and the establishment of the perfected Kingdom of God. According to Mark and Matthew, this consummation will be preceded by the appearance of an evil per-

[5] The author is conscious of the difficulty involved in trying to solve a problem by dealing with it in its most acute form; and there is no passage in the Gospels more replete with critical and exegetical difficulties than the Olivet Discourse. Indeed, so difficult are these problems that since Colani, a century ago, many critics have felt that the discourse, or at least a substantial part of it, is not authentic but represents an intrusion of Jewish apocalyptic materials into the Gospel tradition (see the exhaustive survey and analysis by G. R. Beasley-Murray, *Jesus and the Future* [1954]). One of the main difficulties is the apparent discrepancy between this discourse with its alleged typical apocalyptic signs of the end (Mark 13:5–13) and Jesus' teaching elsewhere (Luke 17:20) that the end would come suddenly, quite without signs (T. W. Manson, *The Teaching of Jesus* (1935), pp. 260 ff.). This difficulty must be faced; but it does not require a rejection of the basic authenticity of the Olivet Discourse. For scholars who accept it, see G. R. Beasley-Murray, *op. cit.*, pp. 146–167. See also C. E. B. Cranfield in *SJTh*, VII (1954), pp. 299 ff.

sonage and a terrible time of tribulation (Mark 13:14–20 = Matt. 24:15–22). Modern criticism has usually understood these to refer to an eschatological antichrist and the messianic woes.[6] The parallel account in Luke 21:20–24 is quite different, describing a siege of Jerusalem and a historical judgment upon the Jewish people.

The simplest solution to this apparent contradiction is the theory that Luke has historicized an earlier eschatological account in Mark.[7] However, the solution to the problem may be found in the very nature of the problem itself; for according to Mark 13:1–4, the eschatological discourse was given in answer to a question about the historical destruction of the temple; and it is exegetically possible that "these things" of Mark 13:4 looks forward to the eschatological consummation rather than backward to the destruction of the temple.[8] In this case, Matthew's form of the question gives the sense of Mark correctly.[9] If, then, the disciples' question had a two-fold concern—the fall of the temple and the end of the age—we can understand the divergent forms of the Olivet Discourse. It is evident from a comparative study that the form the discourse has assumed in the three Gospels is due to tradition and to the authors.[10] The original form of the discourse is lost to us. The Gospels are concerned with both questions recorded in Matthew 24:3, but in different ways. Therefore, since even Mark's account is not exclusively eschatological,[11] we may conclude that in the original discourse, the historical event of the fall of Jerusalem and the eschatological consummation were blended in a form impossible for us to recover; and the traditions preserved in Mark-Matthew and in Luke have emphasized the two elements in different ways. "Neither

[6] See the references in E. Stauffer, New Testament Theology (1955), pp. 213–215; V. Taylor, The Gospel according to St. Mark (1952), p. 511.
[7] See T. Zahn, Introduction to the New Testament (1909), III, pp. 157–159.
[8] V. Taylor, The Gospel according to St. Mark (1952), p. 502.
[9] C. E. B. Cranfield, "St. Mark 13," SJTh, VI (1953), p. 196; see Cranfield's entire discussion in SJTh, VI (1953), pp. 189–196; 287–303; VII (1954), pp. 284–303.
[10] The most conspicuous evidence of this is the appearance of Matt. 24:26–28 outside of the Olivet Discourse in Luke 17:23–24.
[11] See G. R. Beasley-Murray, A Commentary on Mark Thirteen (1957), pp. 66–72.

an exclusively historical nor an exclusively eschatological interpretation is satisfactory, . . . we must allow for a double reference, for a mingling of historical and eschatological."[12]

Thus in the Olivet Discourse two elements stand in dynamic tension with each other: the anticipation of certain historical events and the eschatological consummation. A second tension is found between a historical perspective and a note of imminence. The discourse looks forward to the historical destruction of Jerusalem and gives to Jesus' disciples a mission of preaching the gospel in all the world (Mark 13:10; Matt. 24:14).[13] These two events involve an indeterminate continuation of history.[14]

On the other hand, there is a strong note of imminence and expectancy. The disciples are repeatedly cautioned to watchfulness because of the suddenness and unexpectedness of the end (Mark 13:33-37; Matt. 24:37-25:13).[15] There is in addition the statement, "This generation will not pass away before all these things take place" (Mark 13:30). This text has dominated modern criticism of Jesus' teachings about the future. Here, it is alleged, Jesus is reported as saying without qualification that the apocalyptic consummation will occur within the present generation.

In modern discussions of the problem, the two most difficult elements in the reports of Jesus' view of the future have been the

---

[12] C. E. B. Cranfield, The Gospel according to Saint Mark (1959), p. 402; SJTh, VI (1953), p. 298. See also H. H. Rowley, The Relevance of Apocalyptic (1947), p. 147, "I find no reason to deny that most of the material of this chapter consists of genuine utterances of Jesus, and if we had these utterances in their original setting, the transitions might be less baffling. Even the linking together of the fall of Jerusalem and the end of the age may be due to Him, who expressly disclaimed omniscience on the matter." Quoted by permission of Association Press.

[13] See above, p. 267 for Jeremias' view of this passsage, but see the criticism of Cranfield in SJTh, VI (1953), pp. 293 ff.

[14] See G. R. Beasley-Murray, Jesus and the Future (1954), pp 191-199, and W. G. Kümmel, Promise and Fulfilment (1957), pp. 64-82 on the question of Jesus' expectation of an interval between his death and Parousia. However, neither of these scholars views this interval as undetermined but accepts the interpretation that Jesus announced the coming of the end within a generation.

[15] Kümmel has pointed out that this problem of the two types of assertions about imminence and uncertainty has seldom been dealt with in the literature (Promise and Fulfilment ([1957], p. 151, n. 24).

apocalyptic character of the end and its imminence. Four solutions have been offered. The first admits the presence of both factors in Jesus' teaching but insists that he was wrong on both counts. This is the solution of Consistent Eschatology. Jesus believed in an imminent, apocalyptic event, but the modern man can believe neither. Albert Schweitzer frankly admits that the historical Jesus is an offense to modern religion, a stranger to our time. The religious value of Jesus is quite independent of historical knowledge of the Jesus who lived in Palestine.[16] Bultmann agrees with Schweitzer, insisting that all concepts of an apocalyptic consummation, whether early or late, are mythological. However, Bultmann "demythologizes" these ancient thought-patterns, finding their true meaning in the concept of God that they express.[17]

A second solution eliminates both the apocalyptic fulfillment and its imminence from Jesus' teaching. Some scholars believe that Jesus taught a pure spiritual "prophetic" religion, but that his teaching was misunderstood by the church and misinterpreted in terms of Jewish apocalyptic concepts. Therefore the modern critic must sift out the apocalyptic accretions and misinterpretations to recover the pure spiritual message of Jesus.[18] Others eliminate the eschatological element by interpreting apocalyptic language as symbolic expressions of spiritual realities or of God's acting in historical events.[19]

A third solution accepts the essential role of eschatology in Jesus' view but rejects the note of imminence. Some scholars feel that Jesus was mistaken about the time of the coming of the Kingdom but not about the Kingdom itself. He asserted that he did not know when the Kingdom would come (Mark 13:32), and his error at this

[16] A. Schweitzer, The Quest of the Historical Jesus (1911), p. 399.
[17] Jesus and the Word (1934), pp. 35-56; Theology of the New Testament (1951), I, pp. 22-23.
[18] See in Chap. 1, p. 14 ff., the views of F. C. Grant, H. B. Sharman, L. Waterman, and A. T. Olmstead. C. H. Dodd also thinks that Jesus was misunderstood by the early church. See also T. F. Glasson, The Second Advent (1945); J. A. T. Robinson, Jesus and His Coming (1957).
[19] See C. J. Cadoux, The Historical Mission of Jesus (n.d.); E. J. Goodspeed, A Life of Jesus (1950); C. H. Dodd, The Parables of the Kingdom (1936); W. Manson, Jesus, the Messiah (1946).

point reflects merely his humanness. However, this error does not affect the basic structure of his eschatological teaching and the genuine futurity of the Kingdom.[20] A modification of this view accepts that Jesus taught the end would come within a generation but interpreted the idea of imminence in a theological rather than a chronological way. The sayings about the nearness of the end are designed to describe the character of the present rather than the chronology of the future: the present is determined by the future. The mission of Jesus is the decisive stage in the coming of the Kingdom.[21] The motive for Jesus' statements about the end was not chronological but pastoral: to create in his disciples a spiritual response to watchfulness.[22]

Kümmel also reinterprets the meaning of imminence. He speaks strongly against such scholars as Dodd and Bultmann, who would remove the Kingdom altogether from its future coming in time. Jesus was, however, mistaken about the imminence of the Kingdom; but the true meaning of imminence is not to be found in apocalyptic speculations about time. Imminence is a time-conditioned thought-form by which Jesus expressed both the certainty of the presence of the Kingdom and also the certainty of its future consummation. Therefore the form of imminence can be discarded but the reality thus expressed retained. However, the form of futurity is indispensable, for there is no other way to express God's redemptive action in history.[23]

This interpretation of imminence raises problems. How does imminence express certainty? At one place, Kümmel admits that the disciples' certainty of the coming of the Kingdom did not depend on

[20] T. W. Manson, The Teaching of Jesus (1935), pp. 282-284; but see above p. 12 for the difficulty with Manson's view.

[21] O. Cullmann, "The Return of Christ," in The Early Church (A. J. B. Higgins ed.; 1956), pp. 150 ff.

[22] G. R. Beasley-Murray, Jesus and the Future (1954), pp. 183-191. This is the central theme of W. Michaelis' Der Herr verzieht nicht die Verheissung (1942). Although Michaelis sees only a future apocalyptic Kingdom in Jesus' teaching (see above, p. 5), he feels that Consistent Eschatology is in error in placing the emphasis upon temporal imminence.

[23] W. G. Kümmel, Promise and Fulfilment (1957), pp. 141-155.

Jesus' teaching of its imminence.[24] This suggests that certainty is not necessarily dependent upon imminence. What then is the relationship between imminence and certainty? Was it Jesus' sense of the imminence of the Kingdom which gave him the certainty that God was already bringing his Kingdom, that the end had begun? Or was it the certainty of its presence which expressed itself in the form of an imminent eschatological event?

It is not easy to decide how Kümmel conceives this relationship, for he does not explicitly discuss it. However, a repeated examination of Kümmel's language leads to the conclusion, which we trust is not erroneous, that in his view certainty is dependent upon imminence. We have already pointed out in our discussion of the basic definition of *basileia* that Kümmel's interpretation is open to the criticism that the Kingdom is not really present but only imminent (see pp. 128 ff.). Kümmel represents the coming of the Kingdom as a process, not as a simple event. John the Baptist ended the old aeon; with the mission of Jesus, the Kingdom began to appear. The period of Jesus and the short interval which would elapse between his resurrection and Parousia was a transition period during which "the eschatological consummation is already in the present bringing the old aeon to an end."[25] This is why the Kingdom is both imminent and present. The period of transition has actually begun and will be terminated with the appearance of the Kingdom in glory in the near future. If, then, as Kümmel says, imminence means the certainty of the presence of the Kingdom, we must conclude that it was because Jesus conceived of the Kingdom as imminent that he thought of it as present. It was so near that its powers could be felt; the transition from the old age to the new had actually begun. This, however, leads in turn to the inescapable conclusion that imminence is not an unessential thought-form which can be discarded. On the contrary, it is the very source of Jesus' message about the presence of the Kingdom. For if Jesus thought that the coming of the Kingdom was a short process which had already been inaugurated; i.e., if he thought that the King-

---

[24] *Ibid.*, p. 154.
[25] *Ibid.*, p. 124.

dom was so near that its coming had already begun, but if in reality the eschatological Kingdom was not near at all in a temporal sense, as history has proved, then the conviction that a process of transition to the Kingdom was already under way must itself have been illusory—an erroneous conviction in the mind of Jesus.

A fourth solution finds the answer in the nature of the prophetic outlook which can hold the present and the future in a dynamic but unresolved tension. "The tension between imminence and delay in the expectation of the end is characteristic of the entire biblical eschatology."[26]

This may not be the thought-pattern of the modern scientifically trained mind, and the dissection of this prophetic perspective by a severe analytical criticism may serve only to destroy it. A proper historical methodology must try to understand ancient thought-patterns in terms of themselves rather than forcing them into modern analytical categories. Perhaps the question, When? is the wrong question; and possibly the seemingly contradictory indications of time in the Gospels are designed specifically to leave this question unanswered. Since we have been concerned in earlier chapters of this book to analyze the difference between the prophetic and the apocalyptic perspectives, we may now interpret Jesus' view of the future against this background and attempt to answer the question to what extent he shared the prophetic and the apocalyptic outlooks. (See Chaps. 2 and 3.) In the course of the discussion we will seek an answer to the problems raised above.

THE FORM OF JESUS' ESCHATOLOGICAL TEACHING: PROPHETIC OR APOCALYPTIC?

In the form of his teaching as the Gospels record it, Jesus stands much closer to the prophets than to the apocalyptists. The prophets

---

[26] A. Oepke, StTh II (1949–50), p. 145. "Die Verknüpfung von Spannung und Dehnung der Enderwartung ist der gesamten biblischen Eschatologie eigen." See also M. Meinertz, Theologie des Neuen Testaments (1950), I, p. 58, "One word can sound as though the end was near, another as though it only beckoned from the distance."

spoke the word of the Lord which was often received through visions; the apocalyptists wrote the content of alleged revelations using an artificial literary form, often employing pseudonymity, and writing as pseudo-prophets. Jesus used none of these apocalyptic techniques. He spoke as a prophet, yet as "more than a prophet," for he proclaimed not merely the word of the Lord but spoke with sovereign personal authority, "Truly, truly, I say unto you."[27]

The Olivet Discourse is not apocalyptic in form. It makes no use of pseudonymity; it lays no claim to heavenly revelations or visions; nor does it rewrite history in the guise of prophecy. It pictures Jesus taking his stand among his contemporaries and speaking to them about the future as the prophets did. It is distinctly prophetic rather than apocalyptic in form.

In the use of symbolic language, Jesus stands closer to the prophets than to the apocalypses. He made no symbolic use of various beasts as in Daniel 7 and Revelation 13 to forecast the future. The prophets described the final theophany to establish the Kingdom in what we have called semipoetical language (see pp. 50 ff.), and this idiom appears in the eschatological sayings attributed to Jesus. The end will come with the appearance of the Son of Man on the clouds, with power and great glory, accompanied by his angels (Matt. 16:27; 24:30 f.). This theophany will be like a blaze of lightning across the sky (Matt. 24:27; Luke 17:24) and will be attended by a cosmic disturbance which will disrupt the existing natural order (Mark 13: 24). The ultimate purpose of this apocalyptic consummation is to gather the people of God (Mark 13:27) and to bring the redeemed into the eternal life of the eschatological Kingdom (Mark 10:30; Matt. 25:34, 46).

Jesus devoted little time to picturing eschatological conditions. He used a dramatic parable drawn from the common experience of the shepherd separating sheep and goats to teach the principle of final judgment (Matt. 25:31 ff.). Kümmel has made a telling point that

----

[27] See above, p. 167. It must not be overlooked that Jesus placed all the authority of "Amen" behind his saying about this generation in Mark 13:30.

Jesus was not interested in apocalyptic instruction.[28] The picture of judgment does not delineate eschatological conditions. Jesus' "brethren" must be his disciples whom he is sending out into the world with the Gospel of the Kingdom.[29] All this parable teaches is that the final destiny of all men will depend upon the way they respond to Jesus' representatives, for "he who receives you receives me, and he who receives me receives him who sent me" (Matt. 10:40 = Luke 10:16).

The final destiny of the righteous and wicked is often described in conventional terms of the messianic banquet or marriage feast and in terms of fire (Matt. 13:50; 25:41) or darkness (Matt. 8:12, 22:13; 25:30). That the fact of final doom can be described by such diverse terms as fire and darkness suggests that both represent an indescribable reality. We conclude that Jesus described the consummation in semipoetical language and parabolic pictures which are not meant to be taken literally, but which represent eschatological events and an order of existence that transcend present historical experience.

The Content of Jesus' Eschatological Teaching: Dualism

The content of Jesus' eschatological conceptions is closer to the prophets than to the apocalyptists. The question of the nature of prophetic and apocalyptic religion has been much debated, and the answers tend to confusion because the two terms have been variously defined. In earlier chapters we discovered that many Old Testament critics have distinguished between prophetic and apocalyptic eschatologies, viewing the former as historical with an earthly kingdom and a human Davidic king and the latter as suprahistorical with a transcendental kingdom and a heavenly Son of Man. The former is produced by God's working within history; the latter results from God's breaking into history and is essentially dualistic.

New Testament scholars have used the terms differently. Some

---

[28] *Promise and Fulfilment* (1957), pp. 91–95. Even Bultmann agrees with this. See *Jesus and the Word* (1934), p. 39.

[29] See Mark 3:34–35, "Whoever does the will of God is my brother. . . ." See T. W. Manson, *The Sayings of Jesus* (1949), pp. 249 ff.

have accepted this basic distinction of two kinds of eschatology, one earthly and historical, and the other transcendental and cosmic.[30] Waterman views prophetic and apocalyptic as two mutually exclusive types of thought; and since Jesus obviously shared the ethical religion of the prophets, he could not have shared apocalyptic concepts (see p. 15). Bowman, although shifting his emphasis from time to time, finally makes a complete contrast between apocalyptic and prophetic types of religion, including in the former all theologies which hold God at a distance because of an inability to conceive of his acting prophetically within history. Prophetic religion conceives of the Kingdom of God "on the plane of history" (see pp. 15–17).

A very different distinction is maintained by Goguel, who admits that Jesus taught an apocalyptic eschatology of an altogether futuristic kingdom which would be established only by a supernatural inbreaking of God inaugurating a new world; but he holds that Jesus was not an apocalyptist because he did not share the apocalyptic speculations about the time of the end and the character of the eschatological Kingdom (see pp. 6 f.). Kümmel is close to Goguel at this point, arguing that while Jesus accepted the conceptions of late Jewish apocalyptic about resurrection, world renewal, and world judgment, his Weltanschauung was completely different from that of apocalyptic. His teaching was not apocalyptic speculation about the time and nature of the Kingdom but eschatological promise designed to prepare men for the end (see pp. 29 f.).

In view of such diverse use of the terminology, we have attempted a fresh analysis of the entire problem and have argued that we ought not to see a complete contrast between prophetic and apocalyptic eschatology. Apocalyptic eschatology can be explained as a development of elements essential in the prophetic view of the future but with the loss of certain important prophetic features. Jesus shared the dualistic eschatology of the apocalypses; and at this point, both Jesus and the apocalypses go beyond the prophets. However, we have at-

[30] See T. W. Manson, *The Teaching of Jesus* (1935), pp. 253–256. See also Manson's discussion on apocalyptic in *Aux Sources de la Tradition Chretienne* (1950), pp. 132–145. See also M. Rist, "Apocalypticism," *IDB*, I, p. 158.

tempted to show that even the prophets do not conceive of the Kingdom as arising out of history or as being produced by history but only
by a direct intervention of God. Here is a fundamental feature of the
entire biblical eschatology: the Kingdom of God will be established
only by God breaking into history. This is the indispensable feature
of apocalyptic eschatology.

The popular hope in Amos' day was that of a nonapocalyptic kingdom which would be established by Israel's victory over all her
enemies.[31] It would be the Kingdom of Israel rather than the Kingdom of God. This popular hope was resisted by the prophets. The
prophetic hope involves an incipient dualism, for it can conceive of
the Kingdom only through the direct intervention of God. Furthermore, the Kingdom will see the redemption of the present order from
all evil and its transformation to provide a perfect setting for God's
redeemed people. While the degree of transformation is described in
different terms, the principle is basic to the prophets and is developed
into the dualism of the two ages in later apocalyptic. If this analysis is
sound, then Jesus' eschatology was essentially apocalyptic. But since
there are important differences between the eschatology of the prophets and of the apocalypses, it is more meaningful to speak of
prophetic and nonprophetic apocalyptic rather than to try to make a
sharp contrast between the prophetic and apocalyptic eschatologies.[32]

While Jesus shared with the apocalyptists the dualistic terminology
of the two ages, he could also describe the final state in earthly terms.
The meek shall inherit the earth (Matt. 5:5). There is no note of
world denial in Jesus' teaching. God remains the Creator who cares
for his creation (Matt. 6:26, 28 f.). Jesus taught his disciples to sub-
ordinate material and physical concerns to the life of the Kingdom,
not to despise them. In fact, God is concerned that material needs be
met (Matt. 6:33 = Luke 12:31). There is every reason to conclude

---

[31] See Frost's preprophetic "Better Age" and Vriezen's "pre-eschatological"
form of the hope, above, pp. 55 f. Another nonapocalyptic eschatology is that of
personal immortality without resurrection. See Jub. 23:32; Wisd. of Sol. 2:22–
3:4.

[32] See G. E. Ladd, "Why Not Prophetic-apocalyptic?" *JBL*, LXXVI (1957),
pp. 192–200.

that Jesus shared with the prophets the expectation of a redeemed earth. Matthew 19:28, if secondary in form,[33] expresses the idea of the resurrection of the dead and the renewal of the world.[34]

HISTORY AND ESCHATOLOGY

At several important points Jesus stands with the prophets against the apocalyptists. One of the most important of these is the prophetic tension between history and eschatology which the apocalyptists had lost. The prophets viewed the immediate historical future against the background of the final eschatological consummation, for the same God who was acting in history would finally establish his Kingdom. Therefore, the Day of the Lord was near because God was about to act; and the historical event was in a real sense an anticipation of the final eschatological deed, for it was the working of the same God for the same redemptive purpose. The historical imminence of the Day of the Lord did not include all that the Day of the Lord meant; history and eschatology were held in a dynamic tension, for both were the Day of the Lord. This bond was broken in the apocalypses. Eschatology stood in the future, unrelated to present historical events. The God of eschatology was no longer the God of history.

An all-important fact in Jesus' proclamation of the Kingdom was the recovery of the prophetic tension between history and eschatology in a new and even more dynamic form. In this person and mission, the Kingdom of God had come near in history in fulfillment of the prophetic hope; but it would yet come in eschatological consummation in the future at a time known only to God (Mark 13:32).

The saying that "all these things" will take place within the present generation (Mark 13:30) has been widely used as a proof text that Jesus erroneously taught that the eschatological Kingdom would come in the immediate future. This is, however, too simple a solution. If Jesus was sure that the end was to occur in the present generation, he was in effect setting a date for the time of the end; for in terms of

[33] There seems to be no Aramaic equivalent for the Greek word *palingenesia*. Luke 22:30 has "in my Kingdom" and Mark 10:30, "in the age to come."
[34] F. Büchsel, *TWNT*, I, p. 687.

the centuries of redemptive history, the identification of the particular generation when the end would occur amounts to rather precise knowledge of the time of the end. John Wick Bowman is correct in pointing out that in this case Jesus would have allied himself with the entire apocalyptic point of view.[35] However, Jesus had just asserted that he did not know when the end would occur; this knowledge the Father had reserved to himself. Furthermore, the exegesis of "these things" can hardly refer to the eschatological consummation, for Jesus has just used the same word (*tauta*) in a context which clearly excludes the end. To say, "when you see the Son of Man coming, know that he is at hand" (Mark 13:29) would be pointless.[36] "These things" in verse 29 must refer to the signs described in verses 5-23. These signs would not be confined to the remote future; the present generation would witness them.[37] However, no one knew when the end would occur, not even Jesus himself (Mark 13:32).

We have seen that the present activity of the Kingdom of God in Jesus' person and mission included both a positive and a negative aspect. It meant salvation for those who received his message and judgment for those who rejected it. This salvation and judgment were interpreted primarily in individual terms, but not exclusively so. Bultmann's conclusion that Jesus' message of the Kingdom was concerned solely with individual decision and not with the people as a whole[38] can be supported only by attributing to the primitive church sayings which oppose this conclusion. *The rejection of the Kingdom meant judgment for Israel as a nation in history* (see pp. 186 f.). The temple would be forsaken by God (Matt. 23:38 = Luke 13:35), razed to the ground (Mark 13:2), the city destroyed (Luke 21:20-24). Because Israel rejected the Kingdom, God has rejected the nation and will choose others to be the people of his vineyard (Mark 12:9). In view of the fact that Jesus saw his disciples as the true Israel, the

---

[35] *The Religion of Maturity* (1948), p. 247.
[36] C. E. B. Cranfield, *The Gospel according to Saint Mark* (1959), p. 407.
[37] C. E. B. Cranfield, *SJTh*, VII (1954), p. 291. Cranfield lists eight different interpretations of this saying.
[38] *Theology of the New Testament* (1951), I, p. 25.

secondary Matthean saying that God will take the Kingdom from Israel and give it to another people (Matt. 21:43) is a correct interpretation.

Both Dodd and Wilder have recognized that Jesus could regard the future in two different ways. "Jesus saw himself as part of a great redemption-transaction being carried through to its climax in his generation, a work of God in community terms, forecast by the prophecies of the age of the Spirit and of the New Covenant."[39] "The element of judgment in the present crisis is seen historically in the rejection of Israel that now is, and especially in the destruction of the Temple."[40] This historical perspective included a mission entrusted to the disciples to preach the good news of the Kingdom in all the world (Mark 13:10).[41]

Jesus could also speak in dualistic terms as though the eschatological consummation completely filled his perspective of the future. In terms of rigid logic, these two perspectives are contradictory; and many critics have felt compelled to choose one viewpoint as authentic and to reject the other. However, it is precisely this *tension between the imminent historical and the indeterminate eschatological event* which is the genius of the prophetic perspective. It is the loss of this tension in the apocalypses which sets them apart from the prophetic writings. The tension between history and eschatology in Jesus' perspective means that the same God who is now acting in historical events to bring about a fulfillment of the messianic salvation will act at the end of history to bring his Kingdom to its consummation. The present historical acts include the rejection and judgment of the nation Israel and the emergence of a new people, the true Israel, with a mission to the world. The important point is that these two redemptive acts—the historical and the eschatological—are in fact one redemptive event in two parts.

---

[39] A. N. Wilder, *Eschatology and Ethics in the Teaching of Jesus* (1950), p. 209.

[40] *Ibid.*, p. 56. See also C. H. Dodd, *The Parables of the Kingdom* (1936), pp. 52, 104.

[41] This is the thesis of David Bosch, *Die Heidenmission in der Zukunftsschau Jesu* (1959).

Among recent critics, C. E. B. Cranfield has seen this most clearly: "The clue to the meaning of the nearness of the End is the realization of the essential unity of God's Saving Acts in Christ—the realization that the Events of the Incarnation, Crucifixion, Resurrection, Ascension, and Parousia are in a real sense one Event. The foreshortening, by which the Old Testament sees as one divine intervention in the future that which from the viewpoint of the New Testament writers is both past and future, is not only a visual illusion; for the distance actually brings out an essential unity, which is not so apparent from a position in between the Ascension and the Parousia."[42]

It is from this perspective that we are to understand the saying in Mark 9:1, "Truly, I say to you, there are some standing here who will not taste death before they see the kingdom of God come with power."[43] This saying shares the same perspective as those statements by the prophets which announce a historical judgment in the immediate future but describe it in terms of the eschatological Day of the Lord (see pp. 64 ff.). It *was* the Day of the Lord, for God did act; and this action of God in history was an anticipation of the eschatological consummation. The Kingdom of God was near; it *did* manifest its power before Jesus' disciples had all died. But it did not come without remainder; the consummation still lay in the indeterminate future. The substance of Jesus' saying cannot be reduced to a simple calendric statement. "Jesus' paradoxes are far too lively to be successfully caught and confined in so simple and rectilinear a strait-jacket."[44]

This perspective explains the exegetical difficulties of the Olivet Discourse. Probably the discourse in its original form involved an interweaving of the historical and the eschatological which the Gospels have reported with differing emphases. As is true with Isaiah 13 and the prophecy of Joel, it is difficult to say where the historical leaves off and the eschatological begins (see pp. 67 ff.). In the Olivet Discourse, the historical is described in terms of the eschatological

---

[42] *SJTh*, VII (1954), p. 288. Quoted by permission.
[43] Matthew's version reads, "before they see the Son of man coming in his kingdom" (16:28).
[44] C. E. B. Cranfield, *SJTh*, VII (1954), p. 287.

and the eschatological in terms of the historical. This perspective indeed creates difficulties which are perhaps insoluble for the modern exegete; but it can be understood and appreciated even if the texts cannot be dissected into neat chronological patterns.

By virtue of the very fact that Jesus shared the prophetic tension between history and eschatology, he did not share the apocalyptic pessimism about history. Here indeed is the most striking single difference between Jesus' view of the Kingdom and the apocalyptists: it was the God who was active in his Kingdom in history who would bring it to eschatological consummation. Indeed, Jesus even transcends the prophets, introducing a factor which sounds what has become the distinctively Christian note. *The eschatological consummation of the Kingdom is inseparable from and dependent upon what God is doing in the historical person and mission of Jesus.*

The parables of Matthew 13 teach that there is an inseparable relationship between the mystery of the Kingdom and its manifestation in power and glory. The fate of men in the eschatological consummation depends upon their relationship to Jesus and his proclamation of the Kingdom (Matt. 10:32–33; Mark 8:38). Another important saying in some unexplained way relates the coming of the Kingdom to Jesus' death. Before the Son of Man comes in the eschatological consummation, "he must suffer many things and be rejected by this generation" (Luke 17:25).[45] The essential relationship between Jesus' death and the coming of the Kingdom is illustrated again by the fact that the sayings about his death refer to him as the Son of Man (Mark 8:31; 9:31; 10:33 f.). The Son of Man by definition was an apocalyptic figure who would come with the clouds as the messianic figure in the eschatological consummation.[46] However, before he fulfills this eschatological role, the Son of Man must appear on earth in a mission of humility and suffering "to give his life as a ransom for

---

[45] While this saying is found only in Luke, see T. W. Manson, *The Sayings of Jesus* (1949), pp. 142 f., for the question of authenticity.
[46] See Dan. 7:13 f.; En. 46; 48; 62:6–16; 69.26–29; Mark 13:26, 27; 14:62; Luke 17:24; Matt. 13:41; 19:28; 25:31. On the Son of Man, see G. Vos, *The Self-Disclosure of Jesus* (1926), Chap. 13; O. Cullmann, *The Christology of the New Testament* (1959), pp. 137–164; T. Preiss, *Life in Christ* (1952), Chap. 3.

many" (Mark 10:45). The eschatological consummation is linked together with what God is doing in history in Jesus, especially in his death.

This is again illustrated in the Last Supper. Jesus gave his disciples a cup which represented his "blood of the covenant, which is poured out for many" (Mark 14:24).[47] These words take us back to the founding of the old covenant in Exodus 24:8 and to the promise in Jeremiah of a new covenant which God will make with his people in the Kingdom of God, issuing in a perfected fellowship. Israel will be regenerated, their sins forgiven, and perfect knowledge of God effected (Jer. 31:31-34). The words of Jesus about the blood of the covenant implicitly claim that this promise of the new covenant is about to be fulfilled through his own death. However, this new covenant is now established *not in the eschatological Kingdom but in history*; but it nevertheless looks forward to the coming of the Kingdom. In the varied tradition[48] is to be found a central idea. Jesus looked forward beyond death to the perfect fellowship of the consummated Kingdom. "The drinking of the cup is a present participation in that fellowship so far as it can exist here and now."[49] The meal symbolized the messianic banquet in the Kingdom of God; but it also symbolized Jesus' death. Thus his death and the coming of the Kingdom are somehow inseparable.[50]

In the teaching of Jesus, not only are history and eschatology held together in a dynamic tension; *the very coming of the apocalyptic Kingdom is made dependent upon what God is doing in history through the mission and death of Jesus.* It therefore follows that Jesus stands with the prophets against the apocalyptists in his view of God's relationship to history. The thread which binds the Old Testa-

[47] I Cor. 11:25 calls it a "new covenant."

[48] Mark 14:25 reads, "I shall not drink again of the fruit of the vine until that day when I drink it new in the kingdom of God" (Matt. 26:29 follows Mark). Luke 22:16 reads, "I shall never eat it again until it is fulfilled in the kingdom of God." I Cor. 11:26, "For as often as you eat this bread and drink the cup, you proclaim the Lord's death until he comes."

[49] V. Taylor, *The Gospel according to St. Mark* (1952), p. 547.

[50] It is significant that this same prophetic theme appears in the New Testament Apocalypse. The Lion of the tribe of Judah who will reign in the eschatological Kingdom is also the Lamb who was sacrificed (Rev. 5:5-6).

ment books together giving them canonical character is the sense of participating in redemptive history. This sense of God's acting redemptively in history the apocalypses lost. God's redeeming activity is shut up to the future; the present age is dominated by evil, and the righteous can only wait with patience for an eschatological deliverance in the Kingdom of God.

The heart of Jesus' message is that God has once again become redemptively active in history. But this new divine activity takes on an added dimension in comparison with the prophetic view: the eschatological Kingdom has itself invaded history in advance, bringing to men in the old age of sin and death the blessings of God's rule. History has not been abandoned to evil; it has become the scene of the cosmic struggle between the Kingdom of God and the powers of evil.[51] In fact, the powers of evil which the apocalyptists felt dominated history have been defeated, and men, while still living in history, may be delivered from these powers by experiencing the life and blessings of God's Kingdom.

SIGNS OF THE END

Indeed, history will continue to be the scene of this conflict until the eschatological consummation. While the Olivet Discourse is similar to apocalyptic at numerous points, its fundamental motif is different. Both describe evils and troubles which will precede the end; but the Olivet Discourse predicts evil in terms of ordinary historical experiences and stands in striking contrast to the unnatural phenomena described in the apocalypses. The Olivet Discourse describes no signs by which the end can be calculated. In fact, they are not eschatological signs at all. The Discourse itself makes this clear. False messiahs will arise; wars will occur; "but the end is not yet" (Mark 13:7). These events are not signs of an imminent end; they will occur, but the end delays. Rather than being signs of the end, they are only "the beginning of woes" (Mark 13:8) which will mark

[51] J. M. Robinson, *The Problem of History in Mark* (1957). Robinson shows that this is Mark's view, but does not discuss at length whether it was Jesus' view. But see *JBR*, XXIII (1955), pp. 17–24.

the entire age. When this fact is noted, there is no conflict between the Olivet Discourse and Jesus' saying that the end will come without signs which can be calculated (see p. 309, n. 5).

The apocalypses predict troubled times but also describe unusual phenomena. "Concerning the signs about which you ask me, . . . the sun shall suddenly shine forth at night and the moon during the day. Blood shall drip from wood, and the stone shall utter its voice. . . . The sea of Sodom shall cast up fish . . . and fire shall often break out, and the wild beasts shall roam beyond their haunts, and menstruous women shall bring forth monsters, and salt waters shall be found in the sweet, and all friends shall conquer one another, then shall reason hide itself, and wisdom shall withdraw into its chamber" (IV Ezra 4:52 ff.; see also 6:18 ff.; 8:63 ff.; En. 80:2 ff.; 99:1 ff.; 100:1 ff.; Jub. 23:16 ff.; Sib. Or. 2:199 ff.; Apoc. Bar. 25:1 ff.; 48: 31 ff.; 70:2 ff.). The motif of the apocalypses is that the evil which has dominated the age will become so intense at the end that complete chaos will reign, both in human social relationships and in the natural order. The motif in the Olivet Discourse is an extension of the conflict motif which characterized both Jesus' mission and the mission of his disciples in this age. Jesus agreed with the apocalyptists that evil will mark the course of the age; the Kingdom of God will abolish evil only in the age to come. But into this evil age something new has come: the good news (Mark 13:10) about the Kingdom of God (Matt. 24:14). This message of God's redemptive acts in history must be proclaimed in all the world before the end comes. Therefore, history is not abandoned to evil. The word of the Kingdom in which the powers of the Kingdom were resident (see pp. 164 ff.) has been sent into the world to continue the struggle with evil.

THE ETHICAL PURPOSE OF ESCHATOLOGY

Finally, Jesus' eschatological teaching, like the prophets', is fundamentally ethical in its character and purpose. He is never interested in the future for its own sake, but speaks of the future because of its impact upon the present. This is why it is impossible to structure a neat eschatological scheme from Jesus' sayings. The prophets preached eschatology to rebuke Israel for her sins and to challenge God's people with the will of God in the present; the apocalyptists preached eschatology to explain why the righteous were suffering and to assure them that soon salvation would come. The Olivet Discourse has as its primary purpose an ethical objective: to exhort to watchfulness and readiness for the end. Matthew and Luke omit a block of Marcan material (13:33–37) which exhorts the readers to be awake, "for you do not know when the master of the house will come." Matthew substitutes blocks of Q material (Luke 17:26–27, 34–35; 12:39–46) which warn against lapsing into a false sense of security and carelessness. The entire twenty-fifth chapter of Matthew is ethical in its intent. No one can carelessly take for granted his place at the eschatological banquet. If one is not properly prepared, like the foolish maidens he will find the door closed (Matt. 25:1–13). If one is unfaithful, like the idle servant (Matt. 25:14–30) he too will be shut out. Participation in discipleship to Jesus is no guarantee to salvation. The foolish maidens were invited to the wedding; the idle servant was called a servant. Salvation cannot be taken for granted; it will be given only to those who are awake and spiritually prepared. To this degree Kümmel is right; Jesus was not interested in depicting eschatological conditions but in preparing men for the day of judgment (see pp. 29–30).

This ethical concern conditioned Jesus' proclamation of the time of the eschatological event. William Michaelis has pointed out that the seemingly contradictory emphasis on the imminence and the remoteness of the last day was designed precisely to make it impossible to know the time, but it demanded readiness for a sudden event.[52] This is where the Gospels leave us: anticipating an imminent event and yet unable to date its coming. Logically this may appear contradictory, but it is a tension with an ethical purpose—to make date-setting impossible and therefore to demand constant readiness.

[52] *Der Herr verzieht nicht die Verheissung* (1942), pp. 1–21.

PART V

CONCLUSION

14 The Abiding Values for Theology

In conclusion we must consider the permanent values of the biblical doctrine of the Kingdom of God for modern theology. Our study has been primarily historical, attempting to understand Jesus' message in terms of its own historical milieu. We believe there are certain abiding values which modern theology must preserve if it is to interpret to our generation the essential elements in the Gospel.

GOD ACTS IN HISTORY

The first is that God acts in history. The Kingdom of God cannot be reduced to the reign of God within the individual soul or modernized in terms of personal existential confrontation or dissipated to an extraworldly dream of blessed immortality. The Kingdom of God means that God is King and acts in history to bring history to a divinely directed goal. Bowman is right in insisting that any biblical view of the Kingdom of God must recognize that God acts on the plane of history. Any theology which is able only to "converse with God at long range" because God is so "Wholly Other" that he cannot act in the plane of history has lost something essential to the biblical faith.[1]

[1] J. W. Bowman, *Prophetic Realism and the Gospel* (1955), Chap. 3.

Admittedly, this raises a problem for the modern historian, for it brings into focus the entire question of the nature of history. This is one of the most debated subjects in contemporary theology. Since Lessing's classic dictum that eternal truth can be revealed in ideas but never in the contingent facts of history, the problem of how the absolute and final meaning of life can be embodied in the relativities of history has become acute. Bultmann has insisted that the very nature of God is such that he cannot be described in objective terms. God must always be subject, never object.[2] Therefore God's revelation can never be in history, for history is the stuff of the scholar's critical examination and reconstruction. However, "God's revelation is not at the beck and call of human criteria; it is not a phenomenon within the world, but is his act alone."[3] Since Bultmann's view of God requires him to interpret God's acting in existential terms,[4] he is pessimistic about history. "Today we cannot claim to know the end and the goal of history. Therefore the question of meaning in history has become meaningless."[5] This result of demythologizing the biblical teaching of a God who is the Creator and the Lord of history sacrifices an essential element in the gospel and grows out of a philosophical concept of God which is other than the biblical revelation. God is not an indifferent spectator of human affairs. He is not merely concerned that the individual be brought into "authentic existence"; he is also in control of history,[6] and has acted in history for man's salvation. The fundamental difficulty with Bultmann's theology is that he has an unbiblical doctrine of God.

If God has acted in history in this Kingdom, he will bring history to his Kingdom. Christian faith "announces the Kingdom of God as the

---

[2] R. Bultmann, "Welchen Sinn hat es, von Gott zu reden?" *Glauben und Verstehen*, I (1933), pp. 26 ff.; Eng. trans. in *The Christian Scholar*, XLIII (1960), pp. 213–222.

[3] R. Bultmann, *Essays Philosophical and Theological* (1955), p. 113.

[4] "If we must speak of God as acting *only* [italics added] in the sense that He acts with me here and now . . ." (R. Bultmann, *Jesus Christ and Mythology* [1958], p. 78). Bultmann has not satisfactorily solved the inner contradiction of how he can maintain this position and still speak in some unique (*eph' hapax*) sense of God's act in Jesus.

[5] R. Bultmann, *History and Eschatology* (1957), p. 120.

[6] H. H. Rowley, *The Relevance of Apocalyptic* (1947), p. 151.

goal of history and the only hope of man's redemption."[7] " 'The Kingdom of God' describes the state of things after the Judgment as seen from the divine point of view. It is God's sovereignty consummated by the annihilation of everything hostile to it." "If there is no final victory of good over evil, the Kingdom of God becomes an empty dream."[8] The Christian gospel is concerned about mankind as well as about individual men. Its God is the Lord of history who acts in history and who will surely establish his Kingdom at the end of history.

THE NATURE OF EVIL

A second basic element in this theology of the Kingdom of God is the radical nature of evil. God is the Lord of history; but there are hostile elements, opposing forces which seek to frustrate God's rule. It is not the biblical view that, as John Bright says, all history moves toward the Kingdom of God.[9] There are demonic forces manifest in history and in human experience which move against the Kingdom of God. Evil is not merely absence of the good, nor is it a stage in man's upward development; it is a terrible enemy of human well-being and will never be outgrown or abandoned until God has mightily intervened to purge evil from the earth.

Jesus did not expect men to overcome evil by their own power. Nor did he conceive of a gradual conquest of evil by processes immanent within historical and societal experience. It is significant that Jesus said nothing about building the Kingdom or of his disciples bringing in the Kingdom—both being expressions which have been popular in modern theology. Evil is so radical that it can be overcome only by the mighty intervention of God.

[7] J. Bright, *The Kingdom of God* (1953), p. 250. Günther Bornkamm has insisted that the element of real futurity cannot be reduced to purely existential terms. See *Kerygma and History* (Carl E. Braaten and Roy A. Harrisville, eds.; 1962), pp. 194 ff.

[8] T. W. Manson, *The Teaching of Jesus* (1935), pp. 276, 284.

[9] *The Kingdom of God* (1953), p. 250. The author confesses that possibly he has not understood what Professor Bright means to communicate in this statement.

Furthermore, evil is greater than man. Evil is not found alone within the spirit of man who has rebelled against God. Neither can it be identified with the material character of the physical world in contrast to the world of spiritual reality. Evil is implicitly recognized to have societal character. This age, as long as it lasts, will be characterized by wars, international conflict, even family strife. Organized society reflects an evil character. Even religion can be hostile to the Kingdom of God (Mark 13:9). History will witness a continuing conflict between God's Kingdom and the realm of evil; and in this conflict, men in general and the disciples of the Kingdom in particular will be called upon to suffer. In fact, they may expect opposition and suffering to be their normal experience.

This is the meaning of the demonic nature of evil. Jesus attributed many of the evils which plagued men to a superhuman personality, called Satan, Devil, and Beelzebub. This is not mere mythology, as Bultmann would interpret it, but expresses a profound theology. As H. H. Rowley has written, "Goodness and evil are personal terms. Abstractions have no independent existence. And goodness and evil are not impersonal entities, floating around somewhere in space. They inhere in persons and only in persons. Goodness alone is eternal, for God is good, and He alone exists from eternity. Its logical correlate, evil, came into existence in the first evil being who opposed the will of God, and it continues in evil persons so long as evil persons continue to be."[10] Even Bultmann recognizes that men today feel their helplessness at the hands of foreign powers which are hostile to man's well being and which rule over him as fate, working themselves out through his own will and plans.[11] This is a modern "demythologized" way of describing what Jesus expressed in speaking of Satan. The main point of difference is that while Bultmann attributes evil to some nameless abstraction, Jesus rooted evil in personality. Therefore, we cannot accept the abrupt dismissal of the possibility of the exist-

[10] *The Relevance of Apocalyptic* (1947, pp. 159 f. Quoted by permission of Association Press. Schniewind speaks of the demonic as the "transsubjective reality" of evil. See *Kerygma and Myth* (H. W. Bartsch, ed.; 1953), I, p. 92.
[11] In *Kerygma and Myth* (H. W. Bartsch, ed.; 1953), I, pp. 1–3.

ence of such a superhuman spirit as a "surd"—an irrational element without obvious function in the mind and teachings of our Lord.[12]

THE KINGDOM IS GOD'S ACT

A correlative that the nature of evil is such that man cannot of himself overcome it and achieve the Kingdom of God is the theology of the Kingdom as God's supernatural act. One of the main theses of this book has been that both the prophets and Jesus taught that the final perfect realization of God's rule would be accomplished only by a supernatural, world-transforming act of God. In Christian theology, this is spoken of as the "Second Coming of Christ."[13] The consummation as Jesus viewed it would not be a "historical" event like other events but would be the inbreaking of God into history. Rowley is right in recognizing that the belief in the Second Advent was not a delusion of primitive Christianity but something inherent in fundamental Christian belief to destroy evil. "The concept of the Second Coming is one which was born of the inner logic, or rather dynamic, of [Jesus'] consciousness of His vocation." Therefore if the Kingdom of God is ever to be realized, Christ must have the supreme place in it.[14]

This Christian hope is not merely the Christianizing of a piece of Jewish apocalyptic; for the New Testament, including the Gospels, views Jesus not as a mere prophet but as one in whom God has redemptively entered into history. Jesus taught that the Kingdom of God, even in its mysterious presence, was the supernatural acting of God (see pp. 188 ff.), and this supernatural power was resident in his own person. Modern historians have tried to find a "historical Jesus" —a first-century Jew who is completely explicable in terms of the presuppositions of modern secular historiography. This alleged "his-

---

12 J. W. Bowman, The Religion of Maturity (1948), p. 258.

13 It is frequently objected that the Bible knows nothing about a "second" coming of Christ but only of his coming or Parousia. However, Heb. 9:28 clearly justifies the usual terminology.

14 H. H. Rowley, The Relevance of Apocalyptic (1947), pp. 122, 148.

torical" Jesus, however he was portrayed, has by James M. Robinson's admission turned out to be the "historians' Jesus," the reflection of the modern scholar's face, and may not at all coincide with the actual person who lived in the first century.[15] Long ago Martin Kähler insisted that the search for a "historical" Jesus was futile and that the only Jesus who had any reality was the "biblical Christ" as he is portrayed in the Gospels.[16] The Jesus of the Gospels is portrayed as conscious of being a divine person in whom the powers of the supernatural Kingdom of God are present and active in history; and Vincent Taylor has correctly insisted that historical criticism must reckon with this sense of unique relationship to God[17] even though it cannot explain it or pass judgment upon it. "What is claimed by Jesus, and by his followers on his behalf, is that in his Ministry God has revealed himself in saving action."[18] This conviction is expressed in the Christian doctrine of the Incarnation.

This means that *history cannot save itself*. However, God has not abandoned history to self-destruction. God has entered into history in the person of his Son to redeem history. The eschatological redemption will be the glorious, public manifestation of what God has already done in veiled form in Jesus of Nazareth. In him, the Word became flesh. In his ministry, the Kingdom of God was like a seed, a handful of dough. However, God's redemptive acting in Jesus will yet be clearly displayed for what it is: the victory of God over evil.

This victory of God's Kingdom was a real victory, yet it was a victory not seen by the world. The presence of the Kingdom in Jesus was not a worldly phenomenon (see p. 227) but a hidden presence which must one day be made public. Therefore what God did in history in Jesus and what he will do at the end of history by the Parousia are two forms of the same redemptive rule of God; and the

[15] *A New Quest of the Historical Jesus* (1959), p. 31.
[16] *Der sogennante historische Jesus und der geschichtliche biblische Christus* (1898; new abridged ed., 1956). See English translation by Carl E. Braaten as part of a Harvard dissertation entitled "Christ, Faith and History" (1959).
[17] *The Person of Christ* (1958), p. 186.
[18] T. W. Manson, "Present Day Research in the Life of Jesus" in *The Background of the New Testament and its Eschatology* (W. D. Davies and D. Daube, eds.; 1956), p. 221.

former demands the latter. "The final act of the drama of the history of salvation cannot be neglected without disparaging the previous acts. If the death and resurrection of Christ are not to be consummated in the future, they cease to be the central event in the past, and the present is no longer located in the space between the starting-point and the consummation of christology."[19]

There is one important difference between these two acts of God's Kingdom. In Jesus, God acted in history. The consummation of the Kingdom, although breaking into history, will itself be beyond history, for it will introduce a redeemed order whose actual character transcends both historical experience and realistic imagination.[20] However, its coming is inseparable from what God has already done in history. Therefore, even though the goal of history is beyond history, it nevertheless means the redemption of history, when history is transformed into a new and glorious mode of existence.

The Present Situation

The final question is that of the role of the church and its present relationship to the Kingdom of God. One thing the church shares with first-century apocalyptic communities, like the sect at Qumran, is the conviction of being an eschatological community and a witness both by word and deed to the sure victory of God's Kingdom. However, at one all-important point the church stands in a unique situation which no first-century Jewish group knew. Its witness to God's victory in the future is based on a victory already achieved in history. It proclaims not merely hope, but a hope based on events in history and its own experience. Indeed, the church is an eschatological community not only because it witnesses to God's future victory but because its mission is to display the life of the eschatological Kingdom in the present evil age. The very existence of the church is

[19] O. Cullmann, "The Return of Christ" in The Early Church (A. J. B. Higgins, ed.; 1956), p. 160. Quoted by permission of The Westminster Press.

[20] Whether Jesus' expectation of the coming of the Kingdom included a temporary period, known in Judaism as the Days of the Messiah, need not concern us, for it did not seem to concern either Jesus or the evangelists. See F. J. Foakes Jackson and K. Lake, The Beginnings of Christianity (1920), I, pp. 280 f.

designed to be a witness to the world of the triumph of God's Kingdom accomplished in Jesus.[21]

The church, as has often been said, is a people who live "between the times." They are caught up in a tension between the Kingdom of God and a sinful world, between the age to come and the present evil age. The church has experienced the victory of the Kingdom of God; and yet the church is, like other men, at the mercy of the powers of this world.[22] The church is a symbol of hope—a proof that God has forsaken neither this age nor human history to the powers of evil. The Kingdom of God has created the church and continues to work in the world through the church. This very situation creates a severe tension—indeed, acute conflict; for the church is the focal point of the conflict between good and evil, God and Satan, until the end of the age. The church can never be at rest or take her ease but must always be the church in struggle and conflict, often persecuted, but sure of the ultimate victory.

However, the church is not only the instrument of the Kingdom; it ever stands under the judgment of the Kingdom. It was to the representatives of the incipient church that Jesus said, "Watch therefore, lest he come suddenly and find you asleep" (Mark 13:35–36).

This leads to a final tension in which the church finds itself: the tension between history and eschatology. This question ought not to be dismissed with the critical discussion. The tension found in Jesus' teaching between a sense of imminence and a sense of history is, we believe, the tension God purposes for his church. Since the prophetic note of imminence had an ethical orientation, it has an abiding significance. The church should always live with a sense of urgency, feeling the pressure of the end. "It is because the church has more or less banished from its belief the near expectation of the End that biblical eschatology has become remote and has completely lost ethical power."[23] A dynamic sense of imminence will help the church

[21] We cannot agree with Stendahl that the Qumran community believed it had anticipated the powers of the age to come. See K. Stendahl in The Scrolls and the New Testament (K. Stendahl, ed.; 1958), p. 10.

[22] J. Bright, The Kingdom of God (1953), p. 252.

[23] G. R. Beasley-Murray, Jesus and the Future (1954), p. 189.

to preserve its eschatological character and not become absorbed by the world. The church is in the world and has become a worldly phenomenon. It is today an institution with elaborate organization and vested interests. Sometimes the church forgets its character as an eschatological community that is essentially alien to this age. A sense of imminence will preserve its true character and prevent the church from becoming merely a worldly phenomenon. As long as the church lives with a vital sense of an eschatological character and destiny, it will continue to be the church and not a part of the world.

However, a sense of history is also necessary to guard against fanaticism, date-setting and short-sightedness. A consciousness of this tension between history and eschatology would give to every generation of believers a powerful motivation and dynamic. The realization that they may well be the last generation before the final victory of the Kingdom, and yet the necessity to plan and work with the sanity of a long perspective for the future is a biblical tension. A truly biblical church will build for future generations, and yet will ever be praying with fervency: *Thy Kingdom come, Thy will be done on earth, as it is in heaven. Even so, come quickly, Lord Jesus.*

Selected Bibliography

Aalen, Sverre. " 'Reign' and 'House' in the Kingdom of God in the Gospels," *New Testament Studies*, VIII (1962), pp. 215–240.

Albright, William Foxwell. *From the Stone Age to Christianity*. Baltimore: Johns Hopkins, 1946.

Allis, Oswald T. "The Parable of the Leaven," *Evangelical Quarterly*, XIX (1947), pp. 254–273.

Baab, Otto J. *The Theology of the Old Testament*. Nashville: Abingdon, 1949.

Barnett, Albert E. *Understanding the Parables of Our Lord*. Nashville: Abingdon, 1940.

Barrett, C. K. "New Testament Eschatology," *Scottish Journal of Theology*, VI (1953), pp. 136–155, 225–243.

———. *The Holy Spirit and the Gospel Tradition*. London: S.P.C.K., 1947.

Bartsch, Hans Werner, ed. *Kerygma and Myth*. Eng. trans. by Reginald H. Fuller. London: S.P.C.K., 1953. Reissued by Harper & Row, 1961.

Batdorf, Irvin W. *Interpreting the Beatitudes*. Philadelphia: Westminster, 1966.

Baumgarten, Otto, et al., eds. *Die Schriften des Neuen Testaments* (4th ed.). Göttingen: Vandenhoeck and Ruprecht, 1929.

Beasley-Murray, G. R. *A Commentary on Mark Thirteen*. London: Macmillan, 1957.

———. "A Century of Eschatological Discussion," *Expository Times*, LXIV (1952–53), pp. 312–316.

———. *Jesus and the Future*. London: Macmillan, 1954.

Berkey, R. P. "Realized Eschatology and the Post-Bultmannians," *Expository Times*, LXXXIV (1972–73), pp. 72–77.

Betz, Otto. "Felsenmann und Felsengemeinde," *Zeitschrift für die Neutestamentliche Wissenschaft*, XLVIII (1957), pp. 49–77.

————. *Offenbarung und Schriftforschung in der Qumransekte*. Tübingen: Mohr, 1960.

Black, Matthew. "The Kingdom of God Has Come," *Expository Times*, LXIII (1951–52), pp. 289–290.

————. "The Parables as Allegory," *Bulletin of the John Rylands Library*, XLII (1960), pp. 273–287.

————. *The Scrolls and Christian Origins*. London: Thomas Nelson, 1961.

Bloch, Joshua. *On the Apocalyptic in Judaism*. Philadelphia: Dropsie College, 1952.

Bornkamm, Günther. *Jesus von Nazaret*. Stuttgart: Kohlhammer, 1956. Eng. trans. by Irene and Fraser McLuskey with James M. Robinson, *Jesus of Nazareth*. New York: Harper & Row, 1960.

Bosch, David. *Die Heidenmission in der Zukunftsschau Jesu*. Zürich: Zwingli, 1959.

Bousset, Wilhelm. *Die Religion des Judentums im späthellenistischen Zeitalter* (3rd ed.). Tübingen: Mohr, 1926.

Bowman, John Wick. "From Schweitzer to Bultmann," *Theology Today*, XI (1954–55), pp. 160–178.

————. *Prophetic Realism and the Gospel*. Philadelphia: Westminster, 1955.

————. *The Intention of Jesus*. Philadelphia: Westminster, 1943.

————. *The Religion of Maturity*. Nashville: Abingdon, 1948.

———— and Roland W. Tapp. *The Gospel from the Mount*. Philadelphia: Westminster, 1957.

Branscomb, B. Harvie. *Jesus and the Law of Moses*. New York: R. R. Smith, 1930.

————. *The Gospel of Mark*. (The Moffatt New Testament Commentary) New York: Harper & Row, 1937.

Braun, F. M. *Neues Licht auf die Kirche*. Köln: Einsiedeln, 1946.

Bright, John. "Faith and Destiny," *Interpretation*, V (1951), pp. 3–26.

————. *The Kingdom of God*. Nashville: Abingdon, 1953.

Brown, R. E. "The Pre-Christian Semitic Concept of Mystery," *Catholic Biblical Quarterly*, XX (1958), pp. 417–443.

Bruce, F. F. *Biblical Exegesis in the Qumran Texts*. Grand Rapids: Eerdmans, 1959.

Büchsel, Friedrich. *Jesus: Verkündigung und Geschichte*. Gütersloh: Bertelsmann, 1947.

Bultmann, Rudolf. *Jesus and the Word*. Eng. trans. by Louise Pettibone Smith and Erminie Huntress. New York: Scribners, 1934.

————. *Primitive Christianity in its Contemporary Setting*. Eng. trans. by R. H. Fuller. London: Thames and Hudson, 1956.

————. *Theology of the New Testament*. Eng. trans. by Kendrick Grobel. New York: Scribners, 1951–55. 2 vols.

Burkitt, F. C. *Jewish and Christian Apocalypses*. London: Oxford, 1914.

Burrows, Millar. *More Light on the Dead Sea Scrolls.* New York: Viking, 1958.

———. *The Dead Sea Scrolls.* New York: Viking, 1955.

———. "Thy Kingdom Come," *Journal of Biblical Literature,* LXXIV (1955), pp. 1–8.

Cadoux, A. T. *The Theology of Jesus.* London: Nicholson and Watson, 1940.

Cadoux, C. J. *The Historic Mission of Jesus.* New York: Harper & Row, n.d.

Campbell, J. B. Y. "The Kingdom of God Has Come," *Expository Times,* XLVIII (1936–37), pp. 91–94.

Campbell, J. C. "God's People and the Remnant," *Scottish Journal of Theology,* III (1950), pp. 78–85.

Charles, R. H. *A Critical History of the Doctrine of a Future Life in Israel, in Judaism, and in Christianity* (2nd revised ed.). London: Black, 1913.

———. *The Apocalypse of Baruch.* London: Black, 1896.

———. *The Apocrypha and Pseudepigrapha of the Old Testament in English.* Oxford: Clarendon, 1913. 2 vols.

———. *The Book of Enoch.* Oxford: Clarendon, 1912.

Clark, Kenneth. "Realized Eschatology," *Journal of Biblical Literature,* LIX (1940), pp. 367–383.

Coates, J. R., et al. eds. *Bible Key Words from Gerhard Kittel's Theologisches Wörterbuch zum Neuen Testament.* 3 vols. New York: Harper & Row, 1951–61.

Conzelmann, Hans. *Die Mitte der Zeit.* Tübingen: Mohr, 1957. Eng. trans. by Geoffrey Buswell, *The Theology of St. Luke.* London: Faber and Faber, 1960.

———. "Gegenwart und Zukunft in der synoptischen Tradition," *Zeitschrift für Theologie und Kirche,* LIV (1957), pp. 277–296.

———. "Jesus Christus," *Religion in Geschichte und Gegenwart* (3rd ed.). V, col. 641–46.

———. "Reich Gottes," *Religion in Geschichte und Gegenwart* (3rd ed.). V, col. 912–18.

Craig, C. T. "Realized Eschatology," *Journal of Biblical Literature,* LVI (1937), pp. 17–26.

Cranfield, C. E. B. "St. Mark 4:1–34," *Scottish Journal of Theology,* IV (1951), pp. 398–414; V (1952), pp. 49–66.

———. "St. Mark 13," *Scottish Journal of Theology,* VI (1953), pp. 189–196; 287–303; VII (1954), pp. 284–303.

———. *The Gospel according to Saint Mark.* Cambridge: Cambridge University, 1959.

Cross, Frank Moore, Jr. *The Ancient Library of Qumran and Modern Biblical Studies.* Garden City, N. Y.: Doubleday, 1957.

Cullmann, Oscar. *Christus und die Zeit.* Zürich: Zollikon, 1946. Eng.

trans. by Floyd V. Filson, *Christ and Time*. Philadelphia: Westminster, 1950.

————. *Königsherrschaft Christi und Kirche im Neuen Testament*. Zürich: Zollikon, 1946. Eng. trans. by A. J. B. Higgins, "The Kingship of Christ and the Church in the New Testament," in *The Early Church*. Philadelphia: Westminster, 1956.

————. *Le retour du Christ*. Paris: Delachaux et Niestlé, 1945. Eng. trans. by A. J. B. Higgins in *The Early Church*. Philadelphia: Westminster, 1956.

————. "Parousieverzögerung und Urchristentum. Der gegenwärtige Stand der Diskussion," *Theologische Literaturzeitung*, LXXXIII (1958), col. 1–12.

————. *Peter: Disciple-Apostle-Martyr*. Eng. trans. by F. V. Filson. London: S.C.M., 1953. 2nd rev. ed., 1962.

————. *The Christology of the New Testament*. Eng. trans. by Shirley C. Guthrie and Charles A. M. Hall. Philadelphia: Westminster, 1959.

————. *The State in the New Testament*. New York: Scribners, 1956.

Dahl, N. A. *Das Volk Gottes; eine Untersuchung zum Kirchenbewusstsein des Urchristentums*. Oslo: J. Dybwad, 1941; Neudruck, Darmstadt: Wissenschaftliche Buchgesellschaft, 1963.

————. "The Parables of Growth," *Studia Theologica*, V (1951), pp. 132–166.

Dalman, Gustaf. *The Words of Jesus*. Eng. trans. by D. McKay. Edinburgh: Clark, 1909.

Davies, W. D. "Apocalyptic and Pharisaism," in *Christian Origins and Judaism*. Philadelphia: Westminster, 1962, pp. 19–30.

———— and D. Daube, eds. *The Background of the New Testament and Its Eschatology*. Cambridge: Cambridge University, 1956.

————. *The Setting of the Sermon on the Mount*. Cambridge: Cambridge University, 1964. (This book appeared too late to be used in the present study.)

Dewar, Lindsay. *An Outline of New Testament Ethics*. London: Hodder and Stoughton, 1949.

Dibelius, Martin. *Jesus*. Eng. trans. by C. B. Hedrick and F. C. Grant. Philadelphia: Westminster, 1949.

————. *The Sermon on the Mount*. New York: Scribners, 1940.

Dinkler, Erich. "Earliest Christianity," in *The Idea of History in the Ancient Near East* (R. C. Dentan, ed.). New Haven: Yale University, 1955, pp. 169–214.

Dobschütz, Ernst von. *The Eschatology of the Gospels*. London: Hodder and Stoughton, 1910.

————. "The Significance of Early Christian Eschatology," in *Transactions of the Third International Congress for the History of Religions*. Oxford: Clarendon, 1908, II, pp. 312–320.

Dodd, C. H. "Biblical Ethics," in *A Companion to the Bible* (T. W. Manson, ed.). Edinburgh: Clark, 1939, pp. 348–366.

—. *The Apostolic Preaching and Its Development.* London: Hodder and Stoughton, 1936.

—. *The Coming of Christ.* Cambridge: Cambridge University, 1951.

—. *The Parables of the Kingdom* (3rd revised ed.)`. London: Nisbet, 1936.

—. *The Founder of Christianity.* New York: Macmillan, 1970.

Duncan, George S. *Jesus, Son of Man.* New York: Macmillan, 1949.

Dunkerley, Roderic. *The Hope of Jesus.* London: Longmans, Green, 1953.

Dupont-Sommer, A. *The Essene Writings from Qumran.* Eng. trans. by G. Vermes. Oxford: Blackwell, 1961.

Easton, Burton Scott. *Christ in the Gospels.* New York: Scribners, 1930.

Eichrodt, Walther. *Theology of the Old Testament.* Eng. trans. by J. A. Baker. Philadelphia: Westminster, 1961.

Enslin, Morton Scott. *The Prophet from Nazareth.* New York: McGraw-Hill, 1961.

Evans, O. E. "Kingdom of God," *Interpreter's Dictionary of the Bible,* III, pp. 20–23.

Farmer, William Reuben. *Maccabees, Zealots and Josephus.* New York: Columbia University, 1956.

Filson, Floyd V. *The Gospel according to St. Matthew.* New York: Harper & Row, 1960.

Flew, R. Newton. *Jesus and His Church.* London: Epworth, 1938; 2nd ed., 1943.

—. "Jesus and the Kingdom of God," *Expository Times,* XLVI (1934–35), pp. 214–218.

Fohrer, Georg. "Die Struktur der alttestamentlichen Eschatologie," *Theologische Literaturzeitung,* LXXXV (1960), col. 401–420.

Frey, J. B. "Apocalyptique," *Dictionnaire de la Bible: Supplement* (Louis Pirot, ed.). Paris: Letouzey, 1926; I, col. 325–354.

Frick, Robert. *Die Geschichte des Reich-Gottes-Gedankens in der alten Kirche bis zu Origines und Augustin (Beihefte ZNTW, VI).* Giessen: Töpelmann, 1928.

Fridrichsen, Anton. "The Conflict of Jesus with Unclean Spirits," *Theology,* XXII (1931), pp. 122–135.

—. "Messiah and Church," in *This Is the Church* (Anders Nygren, ed.). Philadelphia: Muhlenberg, 1952, pp. 16–39.

Frost, Stanley Brice. *Old Testament Apocalyptic.* London: Epworth, 1952.

Fuller, Reginald H. *The Mission and Achievement of Jesus* (Studies in Biblical Theology, XII). Naperville: Allenson, 1954.

Gardner, E. Clinton. *Biblical Faith and Social Ethics.* New York: Harper & Row, 1960.

George, A. R. "The Doctrine of the Church," *Expository Times*, LVIII (1946–47), pp. 312–316.

Gilmour, S. MacLean. "How Relevant Is the Ethic of Jesus?" *Journal of Religion*, XXI (1941), pp. 253–264.

———. *The Gospel Jesus Preached*. Philadelphia: Westminster, 1957.

———. "The Kingdom and the Church," *Interpretation*, VII (1953), pp. 26–33.

Glasson, T. Francis. "Apocalyptic: Some Current Delusions," *London Quarterly and Holburn Review* (1952), pp. 104–110.

Gloege, Gerhard. *Das Reich Gottes im Neuen Testament*. Leipzig: Borna, 1928.

———. *Reich Gottes und Kirche im Neuen Testament*. Gütersloh: Bertelsmann, 1929.

Goguel, Maurice. "Eschatologie et apocalypse dans le christianisme primitif," *Revue d'Histoire des Religions*, CVI (1932), pp. 382–434, 489–524.

———. *The Life of Jesus*. Eng. trans. by Olive Wyon. New York: Macmillan, 1933.

Grant, Frederick C. *An Introduction to New Testament Thought*. Nashville: Abingdon, 1950.

———. "Ethics and Eschatology in the Teaching of Jesus," *Journal of Religion*, XXII (1942), pp. 359–370.

———. *The Gospel of the Kingdom*. New York: Macmillan, 1940.

———. "The Idea of the Kingdom of God in the New Testament," in *The Sacral Kingship* (*Studies in the History of Religion: Supplements to Numen, IV*). Leiden: Brill, 1959.

———. "The Teachings of Jesus and First-Century Jewish Ethics," in *The Study of the Bible Today and Tomorrow* (H. R. Willoughby, ed.). Chicago: Chicago University, 1947, pp. 298–313.

Grant, Robert, "The Coming of the Kingdom," *Journal of Biblical Literature*, LXVII (1948), pp. 297–303.

Grässer, Erich. *Das Problem der Parusieverzögerung in den synoptischen Evangelien und in der Apostelgeschichte*. Berlin: Töpelmann, 1957.

Guignebert, Charles. *Jesus* (*The History of Civilization*). New York: Knopf, 1935.

Hamilton, Neill Q. "The Last Things in the Last Decade," *Interpretation*, XIV (1960), pp. 131–141.

Harnack, Adolf von. *What is Christianity?* Eng. trans. by Thomas Bailey Saunders. New York: G. P. Putnam, 1901. New issue, New York: Harper & Row, 1957.

Héring, Jean. *Le Royaume de Dieu et sa Venue*. Paris: Alcan, 1937.

Hiers, Richard H. *The Kingdom of God in the Synoptic Tradition*. Gainesville: University of Florida, 1970.

Higgins, A. J. B. "Jesus as Prophet," *Expository Times*, LVII (1945–46), pp. 292–294.

———. ed. *New Testament Essays*. Manchester: Manchester University, 1959.

Hölscher, G. *Die Ursprünge der jüdischen Eschatologie*. Giessen: Töpelmann, 1925.

Hunter, A. M. *A Pattern for Life*. Philadelphia: Westminster, 1953.

———. *Interpreting the New Testament 1900–1950*. London: S.C.M., 1951.

———. *Interpreting the Parables*. London: S.C.M., 1960.

———. *Introducing New Testament Theology*. London: S.C.M., 1957.

Huppenbauer, Hans Walter. *Der Mensch zwischen zwei Welten*. Zürich: Zwingli, 1959.

Jacob, Edmond. *Theology of the Old Testament*. Eng. trans. by Arthur W. Heathcote and Philip J. Allcock. New York: Harper & Row, 1958.

Jeremias, Joachim. "Der Gedanke des 'Heiligen Restes' im Spätjudentum und in der Verkündigung Jesus," *Zeitschrift für die Neutestamentliche Wissenschaft*, XLII (1949), pp. 184–194.

———. *Die Bergpredigt*. Stuttgart: Calwer, 1961.

———. *Die Gleichnisse Jesu*. Zürich: Zwingli, 1947. Eng. trans. by S. H. Hooke, *The Parables of Jesus*. London: S.C.M., 1954. The Eng. trans. of the 6th German edition, published by Scribners, 1963, appeared too late to be used in the present study.

———. *Jesus als Weltvollender (Beitrage zur Forderung christlicher Theologie*, XXVII). Gütersloh: Bertelsmann, 1930.

———. *Jesus' Promise to the Nations (Studies in Biblical Theology*, XXIV). Eng. trans. by S. H. Hooke, Naperville: Allenson, 1958.

———. *The Eucharistic Words of Jesus*. Eng. trans. by Arnold Ehrhardt. Oxford: Blackwell, 1955.

———. *New Testament Theology*. New York: Scribner's Sons, 1971.

Johnson, Sherman E. *Jesus in His Own Times*. New York: Scribners, 1957.

———. *The Gospel according to St. Mark*. New York: Harper & Row, 1960.

Johnston, George. *The Doctrine of the Church in the New Testament*. Cambridge: Cambridge University, 1943.

Kattenbusch, F. "Der Quellort der Kirchenidee," in *Festgabe für Harnack*. Tübingen: Mohr, 1921, pp. 143–172.

Keck, Leander E. "An Exegesis of Matthew 16:13–20," *Foundations*, V (1962), pp. 226–237.

Kingsbury, Jack Dean. *The Parables of Jesus in Matthew 13*. Richmond: John Knox, 1969.

Kittel, G. "Die Bergpredigt und die Ethik des Judentums," *Zeitschrift für Systematische Theologie*, II (1924), pp. 555–594.

————, et al., eds. *Theologisches Wörterbuch zum Neuen Testament.* Stuttgart: Kohlhammer, 1933–. 6 vols. to date.

Klausner, Joseph. *Jesus of Nazareth.* New York: Macmillan, 1925.

————. *The Messianic Idea in Israel from Its Beginning to the Completion of the Mishnah.* New York: Macmillan, 1955.

Kleinknecht, Hermann and W. Gutbrod. *Law: Bible Key Words from Gerhard Kittel's Theologisches Wörterbuch zum Neuen Testament.* London: Black, 1962.

Klostermann, Erich. *Das Markusevangelium (Handbuch zum Neuen Testament, III).* Tübingen: Mohr, 1926.

————. *Das Matthäusevangelium (Handbuch zum Neuen Testament, IV).* Tübingen: Mohr, 1927.

Knight, G. A. F. "Thou Art Peter," *Theology Today*, XVII (1960), pp. 168–180.

Knox, John. *Christ the Lord.* New York: Harper & Row, 1945.

Knudson, Albert C. *The Religious Teaching of the Old Testament.* Nashville: Abingdon, 1918.

Koehler, Ludwig. *Old Testament Theology.* Eng. trans. by A. S. Todd. London: Lutterworth, 1957.

Kraeling, Carl H. *John the Baptist.* New York: Scribners, 1951.

Kümmel, Werner Georg. *Die Eschatologie der Evangelien.* Leipzig: Hinrichs, 1936.

————. "Die Gottesverkündigung Jesu und der Gottesgedanke des Spätjudentums," *Judaica*, I (1945), pp. 40–68.

————. "Futurische und Präsentische Eschatologie im Ältesten Urchristentum," *New Testament Studies*, V (1958–59), pp. 113–126. Eng. trans. by Peter Kjeseth, "Futuristic and Realized Eschatology in the Earliest Stages of Christianity," *Journal of Religion*, XLIII (1963), pp. 303–134.

————. "Jesus und die Anfänge der Kirche," *Studia Theologica*, VII (1953), pp. 1–27.

————. *Kirchenbegriff und Geschichtsbewusstsein in der Urgemeinde und bei Jesus.* Zürich and Uppsala, 1943.

————. *Verheissung und Erfüllung.* Zürich: Zwingli, 1953. Eng. trans. by Dorothea M. Barton, *Promise and Fulfilment* (Studies in Biblical Theology, XXIII). Naperville: Allenson, 1957.

Kuss, D. "Jesus und die Kirche im Neuen Testament," *Theologische Quartalschrift*, CXXXV (1955), pp. 28–55.

Ladd, George Eldon. *Crucial Questions about the Kingdom of God.* Grand Rapids: Eerdmans, 1952.

————. "The Kingdom of God: Reign or Realm?" *Journal of Biblical Literature*, LXXXI (1962), pp. 230–238.

——. "The Life-Setting of the Parables of the Kingdom," *Journal of Bible and Religion*, XXXI (1963), pp. 193–99.
——. "The Place of Apocalyptic in Biblical Religion," *Evangelical Quarterly*, XXX (1958), pp. 75–85.
——. "The Revelation and Jewish Apocalyptic," *Evangelical Quarterly*, XXIX (1957), pp. 94–100.
——. "Why Not Prophetic-Apocalyptic?" *Journal of Biblical Literature*, LXXVI (1957), pp. 192–200.
——. *The New Testament and Criticism*. Grand Rapids: Eerdmans, 1967.
——. *The Pattern of New Testament Truth*. Grand Rapids: Eerdmans, 1968.
——. "The Search for Perspective," *Interpretation*, XXV (1971), pp. 41-62.
Leivestad, Ragnar. *Christ the Conqueror*. London: S.P.C.K., 1954.
Licht, J. "The Doctrine of the Thanksgiving Scrolls," *Israel Exploration Journal*, VI (1956), pp. 1–13, 89–101.
Lindblom, J. *Die Jesaja-apokalypse*. Lund: Gleerup, 1938.
——. "Gibt es eine Eschatologie bei den alttestamentlichen Propheten?" *Studia Theologica*, VI (1952–53), pp. 79–114.
——. *Prophecy in Ancient Israel*. Philadelphia: Muhlenberg, 1962.
——. "The Idea of the Kingdom of God," *Expository Times*, LI (1939–40), pp. 91–96.
——. *The Servant Songs in Deutero-Isaiah*. Lund: Gleerup, 1951.
Lindeskog, Gösta. "The Kingdom of God and the Church in the New Testament," *This Is the Church* (Anders Nygren, ed.). Philadelphia: Muhlenberg, 1952, pp. 136–147.
Linnemann, Eta. *Jesus of the Parables*. New York: Harper and Row, 1966.
Lohmeyer, Ernst. "Apokalyptik: Jüdische," *Die Religion in Geschichte und Gegenwart* (2nd ed.). Tübingen: Mohr, 1927; I, col. 402–404.
Lundström, Gösta. *The Kingdom of God in the Teaching of Jesus*. Richmond: John Knox, 1963. (This book appeared too late to be of much use in the present study.)
Major, H. D. A., T. W. Manson, and C. J. Wright. *The Mission and Message of Jesus*. New York: Dutton, 1946.
Manson, T. W. *Ethics and the Gospel*. New York: Scribners, 1960.
——. "Jesus, Paul, and the Law," *Law and Religion* (*Judaism and Christianity*, III [E. I. J. Rosenthal, ed.]). London: Sheldon, 1938, pp. 125–144.
——. "Some Reflections on Apocalyptic," in *Aux Sources de la Tradition Chrétienne*." Paris: Delachaux et Niestlé, 1950, pp. 139–145.

──────. "The Life of Jesus: Some Tendencies in Present-day Research," in *The Background of the New Testament and Its Eschatology* (W. D. Davies and D. Daube, eds.). Cambridge: Cambridge University, 1956, pp. 211–221.

──────. "The New Testament Basis of the Doctrine of the Church," *Journal of Ecclesiastical History*, I (1950), pp. 1–11.

──────. *The Sayings of Jesus*. London: S.C.M., 1949.

──────. *The Servant-Messiah*. Cambridge: Cambridge University, 1953.

──────. *The Teaching of Jesus*. Cambridge: Cambridge University, 1931; 2nd ed., 1935.

Manson, William. *Christ's View of the Kingdom of God*. London: Clarke, 1918.

──────. "Eschatology in the New Testament," in *Eschatology* (*Scottish Journal of Theology Occasional Papers*, II. William Manson, et al., eds.). Edinburgh: Oliver & Boyd, n.d.

──────. *Jesus, The Messiah*. Philadelphia: Westminster, 1946.

──────. "Principalities and Powers," *Studiorum Novi Testamenti Societas. Bulletin*, III (1952), pp. 7–17.

Mansoor, Menahem. *The Thanksgiving Hymns* (*Studies on the Texts of the Desert of Judah*. Ed. by J. van der Ploeg, III). Grand Rapids: Eerdmans, 1961.

Marcus, Ralph. "The Qumran Scrolls and Early Judaism," *Biblical Research*, I (1957), pp. 9–47.

Marshall, I. H. *Eschatology and the Parables*. London: Tyndale, 1963.

Marshall, L. H. *The Challenge of New Testament Ethics*. New York: Macmillan, 1947.

Masson, Charles. *Les Paraboles de Marc IV*. Paris: Delachaux et Niestlé, 1945.

McArthur, Harvey K. *Understanding the Sermon on the Mount*. New York: Harper & Row, 1960.

McClain, Alva J. *The Greatness of the Kingdom*. Grand Rapids: Zondervan, 1969.

McCown, C. C. "In History or beyond History," *Harvard Theological Review*, XXXVIII (1945), pp. 151–175.

──────. "Jesus, Son of Man: A Survey of Recent Discussion," *Journal of Religion*, XXVIII (1948), pp. 1–12.

──────. "The Eschatology of Jesus Reconsidered," *Journal of Religion*, XVI (1936), pp. 30–46.

McNeile, Alan Hugh. *The Gospel according to St. Matthew*. London: Macmillan, 1915.

Michaelis, Wilhelm. *Der Herr verzieht nicht die Verheissung*. Bern: Beg, 1942.

──────. *Reich Gottes und Geist Gottes nach dem Neuen Testament*. Basel: Reinhardt, n.d.

————. *Täufer, Jesus, Urgemeinde.* Gütersloh: Bertelsmann, 1928.

Michel, Otto. *Das Zeugnis des Neuen Testaments von der Gemeinde.* Göttingen: Vandenhoeck und Ruprecht, 1941.

Milik, J. T. *Ten Years of Discovery in the Wilderness of Judaea* (Studies in Biblical Theology, XXVI). Naperville: Allenson, 1959.

Minear, Paul S. *Images of the Church in the New Testament.* Philadelphia: Westminster, 1960.

Montefiore, C. G. *The Synoptic Gospels* (2nd ed.). London: Macmillan, 1927. 2 vols.

Moore, George Foot. *Judaism in the First Centuries of the Christian Era.* Cambridge: Harvard University, 1927. 3 vols.

Mowinckel, Sigmund. *He That Cometh.* Eng. trans. by G. W. Anderson. Oxford: Blackwell, 1956.

Murray, John. *Principles of Conduct.* Grand Rapids: Eerdmans, 1957.

Nineham, D. E., ed. *Studies in the Gospels.* Oxford: Blackwell, 1955.

Noack, Bent. *Das Gottesreich bei Lukas. Eine Studie zu Luk. 17, 20–24* (*Symbolae Biblicae Upsalienses*, X). Lund: Gleerup, 1948.

North, Christopher R. *The Old Testament Interpretation of History.* London: Epworth, 1946.

Noth, Martin. "Das Geschichtsverständnis der alttestamentlichen Apokalyptik," *Gesammelte Studien zum Alten Testament.* München: Kaiser, 1957, pp. 248–273.

Nygren, Anders, et al., eds. *This Is the Church.* Philadelphia: Muhlenberg, 1952.

Oepke, Albrecht. *Das Neue Gottesvolk.* Gütersloh: Bertelsmann, 1950.

————. "Der Herrnspruch über die Kirche: Matt. 16:17–19 in der neuesten Forschung," *Studia Theologica*, II (1948), pp. 110–165.

Oesterley, W. O. E. *The Gospel Parables in the Light of their Jewish Background.* London: S.P.C.K., 1936.

———— and G. H. Box. *The Religion and Worship of the Synagogue.* London: Pitman, 1907.

Olmstead, A. T. *Jesus in the Light of History.* New York: Scribners, 1942.

Otto, Rudolf. *The Kingdom of God and the Son of Man.* London: Lutterworth, 1943.

Peake, A. S. "The Roots of Hebrew Prophecy and Jewish Apocalyptic," in *The Servant of Jahweh and Other Lectures.* Manchester: Manchester University, 1931, pp. 75–110.

Percy, Ernst. *Die Botschaft Jesu.* Lund: Gleerup, 1953.

Pentecost, J. Dwight. *Things to Come.* Findlay, Ohio: Dunham, 1958.

Perrin, Norman. *The Kingdom of God in the Teaching of Jesus.* Philadelphia: Westminster, 1963.

——. *Rediscovering the Teaching of Jesus.* New York: Harper and Row, 1967.

Petry, Ray C. *Christian Eschatology and Social Thought.* Nashville: Abingdon, 1956.

Pidoux, Georges. *Le Dieu qui vient.* Paris: Delachaux et Niestlé, 1947.

Piper, Otto A. "The Mystery of the Kingdom of God," *Interpretation,* I (1947), pp. 183–200.

Porter, F. C. *The Message of the Apocalyptic Writers.* New York: Scribners, 1905.

Ramm, B. "The Exegesis of Matt. 16:13–20 in the Patristic and Reformation Period," *Foundations,* V (1962), pp. 206–216.

Ramsey, Paul. *Basic Christian Ethics.* New York: Scribners, 1952.

Rawlinson, A. E. J. St. *Mark (Westminster Commentaries).* London: Methuen, 1925.

Reicke, Bo. "Incarnation and Exaltation," *Interpretation,* XVI (1962), pp. 156–168. Translated in expanded form from *Der historische Jesus und der kerygmatische Christus* (ed. by Helmut Ristow und Karl Matthiae). Berlin: Evangelische Verlagsanstalt, 1961, pp. 208–218.

Richardson, Alan, ed. *A Theological Word Book of the Bible.* London: S.C.M., 1950; New York: Macmillan, 1962.

——. *An Introduction to the Theology of the New Testament.* London: S.C.M., 1958.

Ridderbos, Herman. *De Komst van het Koninkrijk.* Kampen: Kok, 1950. Eng. trans. by H. de Jungste and R. O. Zorn, *The Coming of the Kingdom.* Philadelphia: Presbyterian and Reformed, 1962.

Ringgren, H. "Jüdische Apokalyptik," *Die Religion in Geschichte und Gegenwart* (3rd ed.). Tübingen: Mohr, 1957; I, col. 464–466.

——. *The Faith of Qumran.* Philadelphia: Fortress, 1963.

Roberts, Harold. *Jesus and the Kingdom of God.* London: Epworth, 1955.

Robinson, H. Wheeler. *Inspiration and Revelation in the Old Testament.* Oxford: Clarendon, 1946.

Robinson, James M. *A New Quest of the Historical Jesus (Studies in Biblical Theology,* XXV). London: S.C.M., 1959. Enlarged ed. in German, *Kerygma und historischer Jesus.* Zürich: Zwingli, 1960.

——. "Jesus' Understanding of History," *Journal of Bible and Religion,* XXIII (1955), pp. 17–24.

——. *The Problem of History in Mark (Studies in Biblical Theology,* XXI). Naperville: Allenson, 1957.

Rowley, H. H. "The Baptism of John and the Qumran Sect," in *New Testament Essays* (A. J. B. Higgins, ed.). Manchester: Manchester University, 1959, pp. 218–229.

————. *Jewish Apocalyptic and the Dead Sea Scrolls*. London: Athlone, 1957.

————. "Jewish Proselyte Baptism," *Hebrew Union College Annual*, XV (1940), pp. 313–334.

————. *The Faith of Israel*. London: S.C.M., 1956.

————. *The Relevance of Apocalyptic* (2nd ed.). London: Lutterworth, 1947.

————. *The Unity of the Bible*. London: Carey Kingsgate, 1953.

Sanday, William. "The Apocalyptic Element in the Gospels," *Hibbert Journal*, X (1911–12), pp. 83–109.

Schlatter, A. *Der Evangelist Matthäus*. Stuttgart: Calwer, 1948.

————. *Die Geschichte des Christus*. Stuttgart: Calwer, 1923.

Schmidt, K. L. "Die Kirche des Urchristentums," *Festgabe für Adolf Deissmann*. Tübingen: Mohr, 1927, pp. 259–319.

Schnackenburg, Rudolf. *Gottes Herrschaft und Reich*. Freiburg: Herder, 1959. Eng. trans. by John Murray, *God's Rule and Kingdom*. New York: Herder and Herder, 1963.

Schniewind, Julius. *Das Evangelium nach Markus (Das Neue Testament Deutsch*, I). Göttingen: Vandenhoeck & Ruprecht, 1952.

————. *Das Evangelium nach Matthäus (Das Neue Testament Deutsch*, II). Göttingen: Vandenhoeck & Ruprecht, 1950.

Schweitzer, Albert. *The Mystery of the Kingdom of God*. Eng. trans. by Walter Lowrie. London: Black, 1913.

————. *The Quest of the Historical Jesus*. Eng. trans. by W. Montgomery. London: Black, 1911.

Schweitzer, W. *Eschatology and Ethics*. Geneva: World Council of Churches, 1951.

Scott, Ernest F. *The Ethical Teaching of Jesus*. New York: Macmillan, 1924.

————. *The Kingdom and the Messiah*. Edinburgh: Clark, 1911.

————. *The Kingdom of God in the New Testament*. New York: Macmillan, 1931.

Sharman, H. B. *Son of Man and Kingdom of God*. New York: Harper & Row, 1943.

————. *The Teaching of Jesus about the Future*. Chicago: Chicago University, 1909.

Skydsgaard, K. E. "Kingdom of God and Church," *Scottish Journal of Theology*, IV (1951), pp. 383–397.

Smith, B. T. D. *The Parables of the Synoptic Gospels*. Cambridge: Cambridge University, 1937.

Snaith, Norman H. *The Distinctive Ideas of the Old Testament*. London: Epworth, 1944.

Sommerlath, Ernst. "Kirche und Reich Gottes," *Zeitschrift für Systematische Theologie*, XVI (1939), pp. 562–576.

Sparks, H. F. D. "The Doctrine of the Divine Fatherhood in the Gospels," in *Studies in the Gospels* (D. E. Nineham, ed.). Oxford: Blackwell, 1955, pp. 241–262.

Stange, Carl. "Zur Ethik der Bergpredigt," *Zeitschrift für Systematische Theologie*, II (1924), pp. 41–44.

Stanley, D. M., "Kingdom to Church," *Theological Studies*, X (1955), pp. 1–29.

Stendahl, Krister, ed. *The Scrolls and the New Testament*. London: S.C.M., 1958.

Steuernagel, C. "Die Strukturlinien der Entwicklung der jüdischen Eschatologie," *Festschrift Alfred Bertholet* (W. Baumgartner, et al., eds.). Tübingen: Mohr, 1950, pp. 479–487.

Stonehouse, N. B. *The Witness of Luke to Christ*. London: Tyndale, 1951.

————. *The Witness of Matthew and Mark to Christ*. Philadelphia: Guardian, 1944.

Strack, Herman and Paul Billerbeck. *Kommentar zum Neuen Testament aus Talmud und Midrasch*. München: Beck, 1922–28. 5 vols.

Taylor, Vincent. *Jesus and His Sacrifice*. London: Macmillan, 1951.

————. *The Gospel according to St. Mark*. London: Macmillan, 1952.

Torrance, T. F. "The Foundation of the Church," *SJTh*, XVI (1963), pp. 113–131.

Turner, H. E. W. *Jesus: Master and Lord*. London: Mowbray, 1953.

Via, Dan O., Jr. "The Church as the Body of Christ in the Gospel of Matthew," *Scottish Journal of Theology*, XI (1958), pp. 270–286.

Vogt, E. "Mysteria in Textibus Qumran," *Biblica*, XXXVII (1956), pp. 247–257.

Volz, Paul. "Der eschatologische Glaube im Alten Testament," *Festschrift für Georg Beer* (A. Weiser, ed.). Stuttgart: Kohlhammer, 1935.

————. *Die Eschatologie der jüdischen Gemeinde im neutestamentlichen Zeitalter* (2nd ed.). Tübingen: Mohr, 1934.

Vos, Geerhardus. *The Teaching of Jesus concerning the Kingdom of God and the Church*. New York: American Tract Society, 1903.

Vriezen, T. C. *An Outline of Old Testament Theology*. Oxford: Blackwell, 1958.

————. "Prophecy and Eschatology," *Supplements to Vetus Testamentum*, I (1953), pp. 199–229.

Wallace, D. H. "An Exegesis of Matthew 16:13–20," *Foundations*, V (1962), pp. 217–225.

Walvoord, John F. *The Millennial Kingdom*. Findlay, Ohio: Dunham, 1959.

Waterman, Leroy. *The Religion of Jesus.* New York: Harper & Row, 1952.

Weiss, Johannes. *Die Predigt Jesu vom Reiche Gottes.* Göttingen: Vandenhoeck and Ruprecht, 1892; 2nd enlarged ed., 1900. Eng. trans. of first ed., *Jesus' Proclamation of the Kingdom of God.* Philadelphia: Fortress, 1971.

Wendland, Hans Dietrich. *Die Eschatologie des Reiches Gottes bei Jesus.* Gütersloh: Bertelsmann, 1931.

————. "The Relevance of Eschatology for Social Ethics," *Ecumenical Review,* V (1952–53), pp. 364–368.

Wilder, Amos N. "Eschatological Imagery and Earthly Circumstances," *New Testament Studies,* V (1959), pp. 229–245.

————. *Eschatology and Ethics in the Teaching of Jesus.* New York: Harper & Row, 1939; rev. ed., 1950.

————. "Kerygma, Eschatology and Social Ethics," *The Background of the New Testament and Its Eschatology* (W. D. Davies and D. Daube, eds.). Cambridge: Cambridge University, 1956, pp. 509–536.

————. *New Testament Faith for Today.* New York: Harper & Row, 1955.

————. "The Eschatology of Jesus in Recent Criticism and Interpretation," *Journal of Religion,* XXVIII (1948), pp. 177–187.

————. "The Sermon on the Mount," *Interpreter's Bible,* VII, pp. 155–164.

Willoughby, Harold R., ed. *The Study of the Bible Today and Tomorrow.* Chicago: Chicago University, 1947.

Windisch, Hans. *Der Sinn der Bergpredigt.* Leipzig: Hinrichs, 1929. Eng. trans. by S. M. Gilmour, *The Meaning of the Sermon on the Mount.* Philadelphia: Westminster, 1951.

————. "Die Sprüche von Eingehen in das Reich Gottes," *Zeitschrift für die Neutestamentliche Wissenschaft,* XXVII (1928), pp. 163–192.

Wolfzorn, E. E. "Realized Eschatology," *Ephemerides Theologicae Lovaniensis,* XXXVIII (1962), pp. 44–70.

Wood, H. G. *Jesus in the Twentieth Century.* London: Lutterworth, 1960.

———— et al. *The Kingdom of God and History.* New York: Harper & Row, 1938.

Wright, G. Ernest. *God Who Acts (Studies in Biblical Theology, VIII).* Naperville: Allenson, 1952.

Zahn, Theodor. *Das Evangelium des Matthäus* (4th ed.). Leipzig: Deichert, 1922.

Zorn, Raymond O. *Church and Kingdom.* Philadelphia: Presbyterian and Reformed, 1962.

SELECTED INDEX OF SOURCES

THE OLD TESTAMENT

JEWISH WRITINGS

THE NEW TESTAMENT

INDEX OF AUTHORS

INDEX OF SUBJECTS